THE CLASSROOM
AND THE CROWD

THE CLASSROOM AND THE CROWD

Poetry and the Promise of Digital Community

AL FILREIS

Columbia University Press

New York

Columbia University Press

Publishers Since 1893

New York   Chichester, West Sussex

Library of Congress Cataloging-in-Publication Data

Names: Filreis, Alan, 1956– author

Title: The classroom and the crowd : poetry and the promise of
digital community / Al Filreis.

Description: New York : Columbia University Press, [2026] |
Includes bibliographical references and index.

Identifiers: LCCN 2025021644 | ISBN 9780231221580 hardback |
ISBN 9780231221597 trade paperback | ISBN 9780231563819 ebook

Subjects: LCSH: Open learning—United States | MOOCs (Web-based instruction)—
United States | Poetry, Modern—Study and teaching—United States |
Poetry and the Internet—United States

Classification: LCC LC5805 .F55 2026

Cover design: Elliott S. Cairns

GPSR Authorized Representative: Easy Access System Europe,
Mustamäe tee 50, 10621 Tallinn, Estonia, gpsr.requests@easproject.com

In memoriam:
Jerome Rothenberg (1931–2024)
Lyn Hejinian (1941–2024)
Tyrone Williams (1954–2024)
& Marjorie Perloff (1931–2024)

Who is the other? Someone who has knowledge. And moreover, someone who knows what I do not. The other ceases to be the terrifying, threatening figure.

—Pierre Lévy, *Collective Intelligence*

Reader, you were meant to be legible
even in the failure to communicate. . . .
What will I miss if you blink?

—Erica Hunt, "Reader We Were Meant to Meet"

They feel their crowds and read crowd moods.

—Carl Sandburg, *The People, Yes*

CONTENTS

THE CLASSROOM
AND THE CROWD

INTRODUCTION

Disrupting the Failure to Disrupt

HERE COMES EVERYBODY TO THE POEM

I teach poetry at a university, and I'm happiest when the poems I discuss are difficult, even obscure. So how and why did I find myself being featured in a nationally televised segment of *The Today Show*? The flashy *Today* spot ran partly this way:

> TV JOURNALIST VOICEOVER: Want to discover your inner passion for Emily Dickinson?
>
> FILREIS TALKING, SHOWN IN VIDEO: Our work is done in the house of possibility.
>
> CHYRON READS: THE MILLION-USER CLASSROOM[1]

In December 2012, *Today* was reporting on "ModPo," the open online course about experimental poetry we had opened just three months earlier and that, by the time of this writing, has been joined by (all told) some 435,000 people from 179 countries.

This book, in one sense, is about how in the world my work as a poetry teacher came to be featured by such an outlet. It is partly a pedagogical autobiography. It is the story of evolving ideas about learner-centered learning—once it's rid of the lecture—that I and many collaborators have learned from modern ideas about education and from democratic practices of collective intelligence. It's partly, too, an account of projects created out of the Kelly Writers House as an open, program-generating writers' space at the end of its first thirty years and in particular, the surprisingly capacious extent and wide effect of its reach outward from an old cottage in Philadelphia through several interanimating, public-facing,

FIGURE 0.1 "The Million-User Classroom," Al Filreis and Anna Strong Safford.

Source: Screen grab from the *Today Show*, NBC, December 10, 2012. WBAL-TV recording available at the Internet Archive.

nonpaywalled ventures: PennSound, *PoemTalk*, *Jacket2* magazine; predecessor projects like PennMOO and English 88; spin-off series such as PhillyTalks, Speakeasy, Edit, M^<H1N3 ("Machine"), Cosmic Writers ("Word Camp" for kids); and especially ModPo.

Today caught a glimpse of ModPo at a passing moment of widespread elation about teaching and learning. Such elation waned. Yet what's consistently happened with ModPo in more than a dozen years presents, I believe, a strong case for poetry as a socially relevant and useful instance of massive, interpretive, humane (non-AI) crowdsourcing. Poetry matters for all sorts of reasons, but here was yet another. For me, the tale of its mattering goes back a long way. Writing this book entailed remembering all that.

As an aid to memory, I've taken the opportunity this project presented me to reconnect with some remarkable people with whom I've worked over the years and who, in a series of interviews, have clarified for me some notions about how learners and poetic ventures advance ideas of citizenship through the arts mostly without the use or need of anthemic claims, manifestos, or culture warring. The experience of ModPo people during the crisis time of the pandemic, also reported here—a time otherwise of bitter new distrust of online learning—is the hopeful exception that I think might remake the rule. Any account of digital learning in the first quarter of the twenty-first century must attempt to understand the effects of the COVID-19 pandemic on the cultural politics of online education as not precipitated but anticipated and even predictable. I'm asking questions related to such an idea of that period. Why are there no trolls among the many thousands of participants? Why might ModPo and projects like it offer constructive responses to old and new screeds about screens and moral panics over mediated inattention? And perhaps even to some of the historical failures of education? How and why did a free, noncredit, massive online course about poetry persist during an initial general backlash against such networked forms of education and then continue to develop and expand for years while many attempts at this sort of teaching ran into difficulties? And again, what's poetry got to do with it? What is it about these poems that might have led to the realization of this mode of learning?

The Classroom and the Crowd is a book about poetry, that's true. But I'm imagining engaged readers who aren't here for the poetry primarily or even at all. Readers will encounter close readings or listenings of a dozen or so poems—including several whose phrases become a kind of chorus echoing through the chapters—and I trust that these poems will give pleasure *as* poetry. But one needn't be a partisan of the form or at all knowledgeable about it to have full access to the meanings made by the large and diverse groups of people as they commit to meaning making together. I'm saying that a poem will have a noteworthy social point of view when it is set in such a vast, open, public discussion space, available to anyone. To adapt the title of a Clay Shirky book I admire: here comes everybody to the poem.[2] My work is also about our uses and misuses of the technologies that make such collaboration possible at a large scale. I have two topics at once and also alternately: poetry and collective intelligence. I'll be using another term for that combination: citizen poetics.

So when pages here are devoted to cooperative education in general, this book is also about the opaque verse that I have felt a strong inclination to share and that I have presented in college classes in person and online, in open public forums, in K–12 schools, at summer camps, in community libraries, with nonscholars in Prague and Paterson and Palo Alto and Providence and Péage-de-Roussillon and Pawcatuck (Connecticut) and Poland (Ohio) for forty years by the time I am writing this. In Kathleen Fitzpatrick's book *Generous Thinking: A Radical Approach to Saving the University* (2019), when she posed a question about audience—"Do we understand the people who are not on campus to be an audience?"—she was not thinking about a far-flung digital audience or about applications of technologies at all. She was querying the university's physically adjacent community. But I take such questions to be relevant to literary communities flung open as far and wide as imaginable. Fitzpatrick's idea of audience and her sense of adjacency are relevant to the most extensive contexts. "Do we understand them [people not at or admitted into the university] to be a public, a self-activated and actualized group capable not only of participating in multi-directional exchanges both with the university and among its members, but also acting on its own behalf?" When readers and teachers of poetry see the term *audience*, even in books such as Fitzpatrick's that are about the colossal structures of higher learning, they cannot help but think of the situation of a poem's speaker: the matter of poetic *address* and of readers as *addressees*. Here, the analogy I'm projecting onto Fitzpatrick's big idea about generosity guides me as I try to comprehend my own answer to her question about the way a university behaves with respect to its off-campus neighbors and partners. Is that audience "a passive group," she asks, "that merely takes in information that the university provides?"[3]

I am keen to explore concepts of learner-centered learning that form the sort of communitarian crowdsourcing that is, to my mind, the most exciting approach to poems—exciting not just in a public interpretive context but in *any* context. To the extent that *The Classroom and the Crowd* is, indeed, a record of a teacher's evolving approaches to learning with and without typical school structures, I confess first to having long held to the naïve dream of spending my poetry-reading time in a borderless utopia of rational collectivist poetic actors. Although the massive course I launched in 2012 was hardly new to me as a unit of curriculum—I had been offering it in classrooms since 1983 and had even taught it partly online, and then entirely online, starting in 1994—this time, the platform was robust and very trendy. Indeed, it was all the media rage. I sensed that the launch was likely to get a lot of attention, and it did. So much attention given over to heterodox poetry! Not just at *Today*: ModPo was also featured in the *Washington Post*; on NPR's *All Tech Considered*, and in an eighteen-minute segment of *All Things Considered*; in a *Chicago Tonight* interview with the senior senator from Illinois, Dick Durbin (a ModPo student who correctly answered quiz questions posed by the reporter about Emily Dickinson's "I dwell in Possibility"); in *Washington Monthly*; and elsewhere.[4] The platform was relatively new, and some of its basic elements were not fully developed and were actually still unfinished (the discussion forums, in particular).[5] None of it was quite ready for prime time despite the prime-time commotion. Yet within weeks of ModPo's launch, 2012 was dubbed by the *New York Times* among other outlets, "The Year of the MOOC."[6]

My team and I pressed ahead despite many unknowns. It was a heady moment for massive open online courses (MOOCs). An open-enrollment introduction to artificial intelligence had registered 140,000 people. Anant Agarwal created a new platform, MITx (he would later lead edX), and offered his Circuits and Electronics seminar as an open course, and 150,000 people signed up. Soon, there were some four- and five-week short courses built around their series of "short, snappy videos" on topics such as Time Management, How to Build a Blog, Power Searching with Google, Writing Professional Emails, and A Life of Happiness and Fulfillment that enrolled 225,000 and more.[7] "MOOCs: Usefully Middle-brow," read one *Chronicle of Higher Education* headline.[8] How would supposedly hard-to-read modern and contemporary poetry be received in the context of all this reductive hullabaloo?

Interpreting difficult poems together with all those people in a time when loud voices were advocating a frictionless new system of education that would "sweep away all the inefficiencies of a legacy system"?[9] Initially, I had no idea how the poetry would be received in an environment of curricular streamlining and abridgment, but my team and I were game. I held to my esoteric convictions about the demanding art I admired and had taught for years. Many warned that it would not go over. Despite the expectations of most people who might want to enroll in a course on modern and contemporary U.S. verse, there would be just one momentary nod toward Robert Frost in the syllabus—a complicated poet, to be sure, but thanks to Hallmark representations of the road "less traveled by," one who signals to many beginners a canonical middlebrow, "*usefully* middlebrow" to a fault. And there was not a trace of popular confessional poets—no Robert Lowell, no Sylvia Plath, no John Berryman.[10] Yet there *would* be a confounding, seemingly illegible New York Dadaist, the troubled and disruptive Baroness Elsa von Freytag Loringhoven; a forgotten Depression-era communist, Ruth Lechlitner, who wrote a frank churchly ballad about abortion; a little-known Harlem Renaissance gardener poet, Anne Spencer, whose verse about the productive soil had something innovative to say about writing race; and a so-called Flarfist, Mike Magee, whose poem was a homophonic translation of the "Pledge of Allegiance," what that customary pledge sounds like rather than what it says.

The raging tech-world mode, this strange new context for my optimism as a teacher, was indeed the so-called MOOC, an awful acronym given to the massive open online course. It was "stuck," someone rightly said, "with an absurdly unserious name."[11] It was easy to mock its supposed power and exaggerate its menacing strangeness—such as in the faux horror/sci-fi flick poster, styled after *The Blob*, making the rounds via Flickr and blogs starting on September 26, 2012: "INDESCRIBABLE . . . / INDESTRUCTIBLE! / NOTHING CAN STOP IT! /

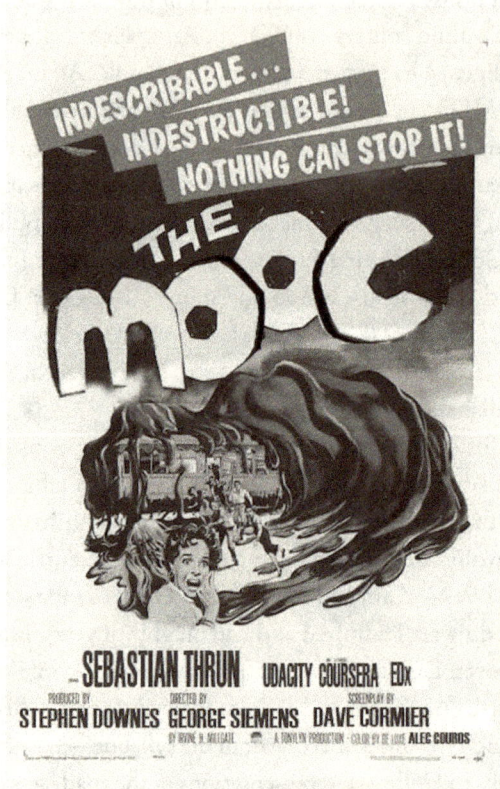

FIGURE 0.2 "What, if anything, can stop the MOOC?"

Source: Creative Commons-licensed picture via Giulia Forsythe on Flickr, based on *The Blob* movie poster. Posted September 27, 2012. See https://gforsythe.ca/nothing-can-stop-it.

THE MOOC." Nonetheless, "Higher Education's Napster moment" had serious potential[12]—the courses were free and open to anyone anywhere with a connection sufficient to read text and stream low-bandwidth videos. The MOOC created by me and my team would mostly entail reading poems on a screen of any size (including smartphones, of course) and then tapping out responses to what many others were saying about the poems.

We opened on September 4, 2012. For that inaugural season, 42,500 people worldwide enrolled. The platform, provided by Coursera, was built on the assumption that the video-recorded lecture would be the main teaching mode. But ModPo has never used lecturing. As its founding teacher/convener, I have felt that neither lecture nor quiz would offer much edification for an online course about poetry.[13] I had been harboring and for years already had been writing about a deep antagonism to such pedagogy. Since the early 1990s, I had been standing behind podiums here and there across the campus of the University of Pennsylvania to give a satirical one-minute antilecture titled "The End of the Lecture."

GUIDANCE DOES SCALE

Following such antagonism toward the lecture, ModPo was designed from the start to be a course with active, substantive discussion at its center. Here's how it works. Read a poem. Then watch a short video in which a handheld camera, directed at a table set up in an old parlor, has recorded my unrehearsed convening of a collaborative close reading of that poem with seven colleagues (soon after the first round of filming, these people began their work and became known as the ModPo TAs). My role in these conversations was to ask a few improvised questions and enthusiastically moderate so that all seven interlocutors could take unscripted turns responding to a phrase, line, or word in the poem and to one another's previous comments. Next, perhaps encouraged by the experience of seeing and hearing a fifteen- to twenty-minute close reading offered informally by a gathering of minds and voices, you click over to the forums to post a response to others' responses—to make an effort at discerning, in the company of others, what you and they think the poem is doing and saying. Do that 118 times across ten weeks in response to each poem on the main syllabus, and you have an interactive, often surprisingly intimate learning experience, almost entirely asynchronous, across time zones, generations, sensibilities, social status, and educational attainment.

Intimate? Really? Well, it is a term that has been used often by participants across the years. Interviewed about her ModPo experience, participant Tracy Sonafelt described the boisterous, chaotic discussion forums: "Sure, the forums can become unwieldy and [can] intimidate some because they are so huge ... but eventually study groups and webs of connection with others of a similar mind make that vastness feel small and intimate and personal. If a student wants to be noticed, she will be; if she wants to hide, she can do that too. We are responsible for our own learning, and we are partners in shaping the 'curriculum' that is ModPo." "You remember how much joy there can be in learning," said Alice Allan from Australia. "You'll see everyday things in a new light. . . . You'll form new bonds with your classmates and become part of a community that feels both intimate and global." "It's an intimate format," observed Laura Lee, "which allows the students to feel as if we are almost in the room with [Al and the TAs]. This feeling is even more enhanced during the once-a-week live webcasts where students can call in by phone, or submit questions via the website or Twitter, or even attend in person at the Kelly Writers House where the action takes place."[14] Karren Alenier, a poet and avid proponent of the art of Gertrude Stein, notes: "Numerous live web broadcasts for the purpose of answering questions all help to make ModPo intimate, as if a student was sitting at the table with Professor Al and his TAs whose preferences and personalities the students come to enjoy in their own educational reality show. Recently when TA Ali Castleman wasn't at the table for a couple of videos and a live webcast, the discussion forums were buzzing about where she was and would she be coming back."[15]

Dorian Rolston, who had joined in the first season, wrote an article about her experience for the *Paris Review*. She described the MOOC in relation to its home inside the fourteen-room 1851 post-Gothic hideaway in Philadelphia called the Kelly Writers House. "ModPo was designed to be the cottage's online extension," Rolston wrote, "and it is, in some ways, just as welcoming. . . . [The] intimate pedagogy shapes the course site's very infrastructure."[16] Disintermediation (the bypassing of traditional institutions) was never determinative in creating positive disruption, rather enabling emotional association, and multilateral personal guidance, or "welcoming," to use Rolston's word, was going to be the key factor. In "Who's Afraid of the Big Bad Disruption?" a professor of politics reviewed several early MOOCs and concluded that a helpful motto for "the brick and mortar college" strategizing for survival in this sudden new world should be, defensively: "Guidance does not scale." He noted that a MOOC on healthcare law he was auditing "offered almost no guidance."[17] Yet in ModPo, guidance *does* scale. But first, one must reframe the assumption that educational assistance can only come from one credentialed source and moves in one direction only. The screen goes both ways, *all* ways—or can be made to do so. "I feel it even through my phone screen," a retiree told us at the end of the 2024 ModPo season. "It" for her is the "encouraging beautiful and lovely energy" of responses, touchable on smart glass, from course conveners and learners moving around posts offering help and individualized concern in all directions at once.[18]

So the pedagogy is congenial, and even the infrastructure can feel intimate despite the supposed inherent alienation of screen time. These qualities would seem to align well with accessible subject matter. Online learning is said to increase accessibility, but is that the case when the poem being discussed is reasonably deemed, at least at first, to be intimidating, even forbidding? The ModPo poems do challenge easy access to what they mean. But actually, the challenge is rarely in the choice of wording. Many of the poems are relatively straightforward, even plain, at the level of the phrase or of the line.

No, if they are complex, it's because they are *metapoetic*. The poems learners encounter in ModPo can always somehow be understood to refer to themselves, to their own making, and inasmuch as that is the case, they befit a site of maximalist public convening and learning. Participants by the thousands come to know these poems as bearing a knowledge of themselves as objects of art requiring other minds, many other minds, to respond as cocreators of what they mean. The massive convening, ModPo participant Brian E. once suggested, is what "opens up these works." Brian adds: "The crazy thing is that even the 'difficult' poems are not difficult at all." For Brian, complexity is not in the poems but in the work of diminishing the typical claim of signifying sovereignty we have often given over to a poem. "I think the problem is one of authority," he writes. "The dynamic, I think, has shifted more into the reader making meaning. Once I understood so many authors' intents dealt somehow with democracy and not author(itarianism), it seemed crazy to me that anyone ever called some of these poets pretentious. It is exactly the opposite."[19] At moments of such broad convening, the back-and-forth situation I just described as a definition of metapoetic is also always about how most productively to learn and to be affected by what is being said. For that situation, we will be using the term *metapedagogical*. So a metapoem is the one open to participatory reading, a poem in some way about the poem. A metapedagogical poem further anticipates its role in readers' learning with it and with others about its relevance to the worlds of its readers—to what one ModPo participant called the "openness of the worldwide voice."[20]

The interanimations between writer and reader that the poems call for are an ideal model for the affiliation and convergence, an accord and affinity, of teachers and learners. And when people in those two typically distinct roles see themselves together as equal members of an audience—we're back to Kathleen Fitzpatrick's positive notion of audience—it is a form of citizenship. A poem is an *act* toward knowledge, and "any characteristic act is an act of *reciprocal invocation*"; so the poet Lyn Hejinian writes in her essay "Who Is Speaking?" "It activates a world," Hejinian explains, "in which the act makes sense. It invents."[21]

By the time ModPo was created as an attempt to put such reciprocal invocations into a MOOC, I had been teaching these inventive poems for a long while—even in all-online courses. Because I had long been advocating at my university for what in the 1990s was quaintly called "teaching with technology," I was familiar with a simple, persistent, skeptical assumption that made even me wary. Attempts to create a true learning community remotely, outside of the classroom with its traditions of spatial intimacy, would inevitably fail without the human connection that is a prerequisite to learning in general and (so people consistently reminded me) the hallmark of poetry in particular. As the teacher of poetry known for "doing tech," I was brought in to be part of some memorable conversations about prospective partnerships. Leaders of Columbia University's audacious for-profit digital courseware project, Fathom, came calling at my university with hopes for a prestigious commercial partnership. From my involvement in discussions of these and other intra- and intercampus initiatives—several of them during the techno-utopian moment of 1995–2001, for example, All-Learn, MIT's Open CourseWare (OCW), Open Yale Courses (OYC), among others—I had come to know the concerns of those who doubted the efficacy of such speculative focus, sudden administrative energy, and new investments. I was well versed in this distrust. Indeed, in part because of the precipitous solution-focused attention by some university administrators, I had begun to share some of the doubts. How terribly superficial would the touted revolution be? Still, in 2012, I was not entirely surprised by the elated response of thousands of ModPo participants who were discovering one another as intellects and admirers of poetry as a form of art despite the separations of distance and the many social, economic, and linguistic factors of difference and dislocation.

Nor was I surprised by the affirmative responses of a few journalists who decided in earnest to cover ModPo as part of the "Year of the MOOC" beat. Some of these reporters made an effort to venture deeply inside the ModPo community, interviewing vociferous far-flung participants. The key was not that a massive open online course could make college-level learning real for people anywhere. I still doubted *that* about the vast majority of MOOCs, in which learners passively watched a prescribed or notes-based lecture and took some multiple-choice quizzes and where the discussion forums were designed mainly for posting brief questions seeking clarification on points made in the lecture or, perhaps, searching for routine information about deadlines or requirements or requesting guidance in the use of the buggy, lecturer-friendly but otherwise recalcitrant, user-unfriendly platform. The focus on the (video-recorded, anytime-playback) lecture was the signature feature of what can be called the Disrupting Class moment, summarized and advocated by Harvard Business School's Clayton Christensen and colleagues and promoted as revolutionary by Salman Kahn, the Khan Academy founder (in 2008); his 2011 TED talk was titled "Let's Use Video to Reinvent Education."[22] *Wired* made Kahn its cover story, with this accompanying headline: "One Man, One Computer, 10 Million Students."[23]

Let's use video to reinvent education? Well, let's not.

Khan's vision of a "global one-world classroom" was, in practice, that of a one-*way* classroom.[24] Already in September 2012, I sensed that an open online course need not be impersonal if it could somehow invite learners to turn the platform toward the advantage of open discussion and unplanned interactive responsiveness. My experience immediately indicated to me that perhaps Khan and Christensen, first focused on mathematics and management, respectively, were missing special cues to be taken from a particular off-field content/form fit. I came to see that it was poetry as the choice of subject matter—moreover, a certain kind of poetry and a kind of approach to the technology of archiving recordings of performed poetry—that was creating not only a primary motive but also the modal power for repudiating the loneliness that seemed inherent in the impersonality of technology-based systems.

COLLEGE IS DEAD. LONG LIVE COLLEGE!

In 2012, I thought I knew enough to predict some transvaluations along these lines. I had obsessed over David Riesman's *The Lonely Crowd* (1950), and my concerns about its centrist reckoning of the educational culture of the booming postwar period led me to write a book of literary history called *Counter-Revolution of the Word: The Conservative Attack on Modern Poetry, 1945–60* (2008). What I did not expect four years later, as ModPo began to engage thousands of people worldwide in a chaotic, often directionless round-the-clock conversation about poetry, was the particular political valence the MOOC would take on almost immediately in the 2010s, not at all a matter of discernible lefts and rights. Some colleagues in the humanities felt that the quality of instruction in MOOCs was embarrassingly low, and I wondered how much of this stance owed to plain academic condescension. As noted, the format of most MOOCs left little to no opportunity for students to interact with the lecturer. While courses in several science, technology, engineering, and math (STEM) fields and on vocational topics might succeed in teaching concepts and especially skills in this mode, the arts and humanities, where iterative rounds of interpretation are the key to learning, would be disadvantaged. In contemplating this charge against MOOCs, by the way, we would also have to ponder whether in large- or even middle-sized in-person courses, those professing the humanities have been successfully practicing the sort of student-centered social interactivity said to be lacking in online instruction. How many lonely crowds were being formed unintentionally in our built classrooms?

Other skeptics observed that "Sage on Stage" academic superstars were being carelessly made by the MOOC revolution. Opportunists might emerge without much regard for real scholarly achievement in the fields they now far too readily represented to global publics forming their first impressions of academia. There might be a revival of the Segal syndrome, named in honor of Erich Segal, the Yale classics professor who wrote and hugely sold *Love Story*: "A professor's esteem on the faculty is in inverse proportion to his or her public popularity."[25] One hyperbolic cofounder of a MOOC platform told the *New York Times* in November 2012 that he "saw a day when MOOCs will disrupt how faculty are attracted . . . with the most popular 'compensated like a TV actor or a movie star.' "[26] Some faculty whose teaching was being subjected to MOOC versions of their own courses felt that they, on the other hand, would "suddenly be second-class citizens." When a dean at a public university in California suggested that the philosophy department adopt Michael Sandel's MOOC survey beamed transcontinentally from Harvard, the faculty refused and sent an open letter of protest to Sandel. "It's great to have Professor Sandel's lectures available free online, to use if we want," a faculty member said. "But if we buy them from edX as the basis for our classes, we would . . . basically be a teaching assistant."[27] Still other instructors resented the euphoric attentions of presidents and provosts while long-standing structural problems inside the college, directly affecting their own residential students, went unaddressed. Wild predictions were offered by columnists and national politicians about how MOOCs could radically reduce the cost of tuition and about how much more "efficient" this sort of teaching was or would soon become. The MOOC "explosion," offered a *Chronicle of Higher Education* commentary, will "accelerate the breakup of the college credit monopoly."[28] The phrase "elite education for the masses"—a headline plastered above the *Washington Post* article featuring ModPo and other courses—seemed wrongheaded in several respects. What, ultimately, was "elite" about it if it was to be so widely distributed? And the term *masses* bears its often negative historical connotations. These claims, implicit and explicit, tended to alienate faculty further and draw public attention to every new phase or turn in a way otherwise big changes in academia were ignored. Dave Cormier, who created the term *MOOC* in 2008, saw in December 2011 that MIT was accrediting a MOOC for the first time and named it "Black Swan 1" among his 2012 prognostications.[29] The terms *tsunami* and *avalanche* were summoned to describe the anticipated effects.[30] A *Bloomberg* headline screamed: "Google's Boss and a Princeton Professor Agree: College Is a Dinosaur."[31]

Thomas Friedman declared that a "Revolution Hits the Universities" and that they would never be the same. This widely shared *New York Times* column quoted a profoundly autistic seventeen-year-old who has played a role in the making of this book. Readers will encounter this remarkable person again here and there and once more in the final pages. Daniel Bergmann had enrolled in and completed ModPo and had composed his first-ever sustained piece of writing, the initial course assignment on Emily Dickinson's poem "I Taste a Liquor Never Brewed." He posted his essay on September 15, 2012. I happened to read it among the thousands submitted and posted a positive response. "I can't yet sit still in a classroom," Dan wrote soon after that first season, "so [ModPo] was my first real course ever. During the course, I had to keep pace with the class, which is unheard-of in special ed." Friedman was "incredibly hopeful," and he indulged in the sort of overstatement that was raising expectations impossibly high. "Nothing has more potential to unlock a billion more brains to solve the world's biggest problems."[32] He came to the University of Pennsylvania and repeated the hyperbole.[33] Surely, this was promising too much. Then again, Dan Bergmann has never hesitated to argue that this first experience with university-level education helped to unlock his brain.

Dan's academically successful presence in ModPo brought another matter into sharp focus: *Which* learners had first or primary rights to all this knowledge and instruction now being given away, for free, to anyone? On this point, I realized two academic leftisms were converging or, perhaps, were being partly contradicted. Some celebrated the liberation of paywalled academic knowledge, teaching, and resources. It was the partial fulfillment of the hopes of many scholars who had long criticized ivy-towered barriers to entry, the sequestering of knowledge created at the universities, and the dominant institutional ownership of intellectual property, to which, ideally, all people should have access, including people like Dan for whom available educational settings were unconducive.

Another faction featured what scholars of management education Ulrich Hommel and Kai Peters in "Shared Learning in Higher Education" call "a closed shop approach.[34]" These critics worried that the guild of hardworking and especially of underpaid non-tenure-track faculty, already leading precarious scholarly lives, were being further undermined as their employers were (at least initially) giving academic resources away for free. Making matters worse for these underappreciated members of the university community, administrators, trustees, and state legislators seemed to be seeking to score easy public and media points, betting that they could enter wide "new markets" of learners. In this view, the whole MOOC scheme entailed pseudo-populist teaching as an intellectual loss leader. Colleges and universities could be deemed knowledge cartels. "Monopolies are valuable things to control, and monopolists tend not to relinquish them voluntarily. But the MOOC explosion will accelerate the breakup of the college credit monopoly."[35] A survey released in 2014 showed already that MOOCs were "caus[ing] confusion about higher-education degrees."[36]

This critique reflected a measure of affective solidarity with students whose families struggled to pay rising tuitions so as to gain hard-won access to resources and instruction now being freely appropriated and uncontrollably scattered, such that the precious costly degree might soon accrue less value. Kristen Gallagher, a professor of English at LaGuardia Community College in the CUNY system, strongly felt this solidarity, but it took her in another direction. In response to the MOOC phenomenon that had swept up other universities the previous year, the LaGuardia provost announced in early 2013 that he "was looking for ways to incorporate technology in any way into teaching." Gallagher is an expert at gaming the system to lower a high teacher-student ratio, and she was seeking real ways to decouple the equation of the university and the relentless preprofessionalization of young people.[37]

Gallagher saw the *Washington Post* article about ModPo (with its mention of ModPo's *off-line* spin-off small communities of learners) and pitched a counterintuitive proposal: convene a small group of LaGuardia students, award them special internships, and have them join ModPo in the fall of 2013, follow the syllabus of poems, and thus affirm the LaGuardia student experience through the development of this special "social cohort." The counterintuition, of course, was the idea of using a *massive* open online course for the purpose of creating *small-group* intellectual cohesion. Years earlier, Gallagher had been a student in ModPo's predecessor in-person course, known as English 88, just when it was beginning to feature the use of internet tools (such as a frenzied all-class listserv), and she had been one of the founders of the Writers House in the mid- to late-1990s. But she hadn't heard about the MOOC before seeing the *Post*. She contacted her provost and department chair and shared that article, with its mentions of cozy meet-ups in cafés and living rooms. She was taking advantage of the moment's fervor for MOOCs to advocate on behalf of a tiny pedagogical experiment.[38]

I've tried here to summarize briefly, perhaps superficially, the complex first backlash against MOOCs and to hint at momentary strategies managed by advocates of democratic distributed learning. "If 2012 was the 'Year of the MOOC,'" George Siemens told a reporter at *Times Higher Education*, "2013 is shaping up as the 'Year of the anti-MOOC.'"[39] By November 2013, the *Chronicle of Higher Education* ran the headline: "MOOCs Are Over. . . . MOOCs Are a Sideshow."[40] James O'Donnell, a professor of classics who back in *1994* had taught a groundbreaking global five-hundred-person internet seminar on Augustine of Hippo, noted in 2012 that "the revolution [MOOCs] supposedly represent is already here, and has been happening," and offered this quip about the new sage-on-virtual-stage stars: "Charisma routinizes faster than ever these days, and—eventually—the magic fades."[41] Ann Kirschner, who during the first courseware bubble had energetically led Fathom.com and believed in its profitability (a mirage, it turns out), now enrolled in Ezekiel Emanuel's MOOC on healthcare reform; she enjoyed Dr. Emanuel's charisma but found it motivationally insufficient for keeping up with readings and assignments—and wanted someone with whom to register her frustration, but "in a MOOC, nobody can hear you scream." (As it happens, Kirschner did praise ModPo in the same piece, and its success prompted her to assert with hope that "something important is happening." *Poetry?*, she mused.[42]) One observer tracked the "cultural cycle of hype, saturation, backlash, and backlash-to-the-backlash," and this was only September 2012![43] In October of that first big season, a *Time* headline read: "College Is Dead. Long Live College!"[44] (Helpful overviews of these chaotic months can be found in Justin Reich's *Failure to Disrupt: Why Technology Alone Can't Transform Education* and Jeremy Knox's *Posthumanism and the Massive Open Online Course*; and there are other reliable accounts.[45]) Elated as I was by the successful new supercirculation through ModPo of the relatively little-known poetry I admired, I felt bitterly toward some of the promulgators of the rejoinders against MOOCs via Twitter disputes, dismissive commentaries in higher-ed journals, and a few quite contentious conversations on campus. Then I saw the counterreaction dissipate as the headlines shifted from hyperventilating reports of radical utopian transformation to dour accounts of so-called drop-out rates in MOOCS, and the struggles experienced by faculty seeking in the second wave to create their own MOOCs despite lessening incentives and rewards and diminishing institutional focus.[46]

ModPo, however, persisted and has continued to be noncredit and available to all participants for free, a stubborn insistence continuing more than a dozen years later. Our essay "assignments" are optional, ungraded, and peer reviewed. Each essay receives at least four responses, typically many more. A small percentage even of otherwise very active participants submit essays when they are "due." Some people share their essays during a second or third or still later season of the course. Indeed, many people have continued to be part of the ModPo scene, year after year, rereading poems and getting involved with the less structured aspects of the course outside its annual ten-week "symposium mode." This forty-two-week period has been given the name "SloPo" by the regulars, appreciating its more leisurely movement through poems that learners together decide will reward extra discussion. Some people committed to multiple seasons join the group of eighty or so Community TAs (CTAs), offering support to first-timers learning to navigate the chaotic platform. Many participate in the live interactive webcasts held on Wednesdays during the symposium mode from early September through November. During one busy weekly webcast, we took phone calls from ModPo regulars in Siberia, Oregon, Manila, Prague, and Atlantic City. People who are able to visit a webcast in person can meet Erica Hunt, Bernadette Mayer, Charles Bernstein, the photographer-poet Erica Baum, Tracie Morris, Jerome Rothenberg, Rae Armantrout, Douglas Kearney, Bob Holman, and others who have rotated as special guests of the program. Some learners travel to be part of in-person meet-ups at coffee shops, bookstores, taverns, public libraries, and living rooms around the world. In later seasons, various participants set up weekly or monthly Zoom-, Teams-, or Webex-enabled reading groups and workshops. Returners, in particular, read and discuss the hundreds of new poems and videos to accompany each that are added to "ModPoPLUS," a vast augmentation of the original main syllabus.

In all, there are at least fourteen ways to interact with the people and the poems. Participate in any or all of the poem-specific discussion subforums (create a thread or post a reply to an existing one). Join a study group or meet-up, virtually or in person. Chat with ModPo colleagues in the lively YouTube comment feed during any livestreamed activity. Seek guidance from a CTA in the weekly "hopelessly lost" thread. Attend a synchronous office hour convened weekly by each of the ten or so TAs. Leave a voicemail on the dedicated ModPo phone line or call in during a live webcast to offer a comment. Join one of the annual winter/spring SloPo minicourses. Post to any of the social media groups or threads established by ModPo participants. Consult the Teacher Resource Center (TRC), a parallel syllabus aligned with the ten weeks of the course, with its collection of videos recording discussions with teachers about how they teach the poems, and talk with other teachers in the TRC forum. Gather some friends or fellow ModPo learners and film your own improvised collaborative close reading of a ModPo poem, then post it along with the collection of other such recordings in yet another supplemental syllabus, Community Collaborative Close Readings; we will return to this learner-founded crowdsourcing project, "CCCR," in the final chapter. Travel within your city or to a city near you to meet the ModPo team during its annual visits (Montreal, San Francisco, Seattle, Edinburgh, Los Angeles, New York, Prague, Washington, Vancouver, Chicago, London, Boston); while you're there, join as new on-location ModPoPLUS videos are made with local poets, and you won't want to miss the on-the-road live webcast. Or visit the Kelly Writers House in Philadelphia and, if the timing is right, join a webcast, sit in on a session of the for-credit ModPo undergraduate seminar, or attend a live poetry reading with its spirited Q&A and plentiful free food.

I take much of the initial backlash against MOOCs to have been, ultimately, an expression of strategic antiutopianism. I understand why many critics gave little credence to chiliastic claims being made by or on behalf of deans and presidents and wildly expanding for-profit entities such as Coursera, Udacity, and Canvas Network. But in taking such a view, many of the critics missed how some of the already well-formed radical ideals of the "cMOOC" (connectivist MOOC) could be carried over into the colossal, bulky "xMOOC" mode (sometimes called "instructionist MOOC").[47] ModPo is an xMOOC but from the description of its multiple commitments to interaction just offered and its efforts to minimize instructionism, you can tell that we have learned a great deal from connectivism. These are key definitions and distinctions.

The intrepid, chaotic, productive connectivist open seminars or "cMOOCs": their fundamental reformism (through experimental groups and projects hosted primarily in Canada by George Siemens, Dave Cormier, Rita Kop, Alec Couros, and many others circa 2005–2011) preceded the star turn of the MOOC in 2011–2012. The cMOOC continued to contribute important ideas about collaborative and hybrid pedagogies that influenced a few xMOOCs. "xMOOC" was the label used by advocates of connectivism to identify the outsized, hyperenrolled, presumably impersonal, lecture-based open-enrollment courses with their typical top-down, instructor-determined approach to learning. It was possible to envision a future of xMOOCs, even those backed by tech start-up investors and through hastily arranged university/for-profit partnerships, that might benefit at least somewhat from the connectivist vision of students themselves learning contemporaneously how to alter the structures of learning (with its confidence that the "ability to see connections between fields, ideas, and concepts is a core skill"[48]); from participant-created, workshop-style modal innovations; from "multi-access learning" as described by Valerie Irvine and her colleagues;[49] and from process-oriented rather than content-dependent collective instructorships.

To the extent that an xMOOC can function like a cMOOC, it might be discovered that there is particular idealism and wisdom in the so-called crowd. How the crowd makes and alters meaning is the subject of my final two chapters, but for now, I emphasize that the resistance in 2012–2013 against that idealism was more skeptical, even dismissive, than counteridealistic. Ultimately, this account will be less focused on that initial counterargument, with its overblown and almost predetermined internecine journalistic and academic politics. More indicative, I believe, of the real challenges facing advocates of digital learning were the new waves of criticism that crashed back hard in 2020–2021. The ubiquity of the COVID-19 contagion forced nearly all educators to teach online, of course. That moment, not the ruckus a decade earlier, was when the politics of online teaching became a truly pervasive concern. Three moments in a long career—all three are told in the course of this book—have had practical ramifications: the founding of the Kelly Writers House in 1995; the invention of ModPo in 2012; and the ways that online community, supported by the resources inside the organization of the old house, was of service in 2020. I'm interested in the particular effects a major crisis of digitality had on people's collective understandings of difficult-to-discuss art.

DIGITAL AGENTS BORNE UPON THE WINGS OF VIRUS

The later turn against online teaching derived from a long-standing mistrust of centrist hopes and claims. Such doubts were now being pitched against those who saw the moment as a chance to explore another "silver lining" inside the social and intellectual restrictions imposed by the pandemic. This time, the resistance came variously from both progressives and conservatives. There were people who acknowledged the significant health dangers caused by the contagious airborne pathogen and thus tolerated most mitigation strategies *and* people who could not abide any sort of top-down dicta, with their already ideologically specific rhetoric of safety, care, and protectiveness, especially pertaining to education in schools. MOOCs already existed, of course, and while they were a special target here and there of the new anger, it was generally directed at modes of remote instruction being hastily assembled at middle and upper schools and at colleges and universities. Few leaders in education at any level had sufficient resources already set aside to make so rapid a shift. And surprisingly few teachers had experience leading productive discussions using remote technologies. Nor, before March 2020, had they felt the inclination or real encouragement to do so. Those who had actively disliked the various emerging options for online education, including people merely sufficiently fearful to prefer avoiding it, had assumed they could just continue to confine their teaching to classrooms.

ModPo had existed for eight years by then and had gathered around it a cacophonous community of current and former participants who, here and there, were now telling skeptical parents, teachers, colleagues, school boards, family members, neighbors, children, and grandchildren about a massive online educational community that had succeeded at maintaining itself and somehow encouraged intimacy and informality as prerequisite social traits for learning among others.[50] Enrollments soared through the spring and summer of 2020 (to the level of 71,000), even though it was ModPo's annual SloPo or off-season, and in spite of our making no special effort to reannounce the year-round availability of the course. Many new enrollees told us they were there not for poetry but to witness how such a remote community constructed itself. The retrospective testimonies we gathered in 2023 of participants who were encouraged by the digital experience during the pandemic follow roughly along these lines: *I came for a community at a time of depressing isolation; I finished realizing how much the poetry turned out to matter right at this moment.*

The discussion forums began to fill with metacommentaries about aspects of ModPo's collaborative approach that could serve as models or at least prompts in response to the apparent dysfunction of so much online instruction (and workplace interaction) that nearly every family was experiencing. The poet erica kaufman—director of the Institute for Writing and Thinking at Bard College (IWT) and a long-time ModPo TA—opened a thread in the ModPo forums titled "Pandemic Pedagogy." The discussion attracted a number of ModPo learners who were also, at the same time, teaching their own students online during lockdown. Gavin Adair reported that his university required synchronous meetings even though he was having greater success with asynchronous forms, such as the very post-when-you-can thread-based forum inside ModPo, where he contributed his comments and received guidance from erica kaufman and others. Asynchronicity did not thwart and arguably augmented the coming together of pedagogy and the problem of personal space as major topics. "The biggest issue is my partner and I are in a smaller temporary space for the foreseeable future," Adair told his ModPo colleagues, "and in my [synchronous] meetings I can get loud. I do the videos outdoors on the grounds of where we are staying, so it's only the morning birds that I annoy." Asynchronous teaching was practically easier as well as pedagogically sounder. Much can be said about this erratic phase and about the crucial differences between the backlashes of 2012–2013 and 2020–2021. And about why, again, the sort of poetry presented in ModPo—"open" (that is, open-ended) and unresolved, supposedly difficult, requiring slow, collaborative close reading—was especially pertinent to the crisis and why it helped Gavin and other teachers who sought each other in the "Pandemic Pedagogy" thread hosted inside the kind of gathering crowd otherwise infamous for its anonymity.

Crisis. Certainly, but of course, we are talking about a time of convergent plural crises since people across the spectrum of cultural positions in 2020–2021 tried to account for three issues at once: the risky future of education, the resurgent effects of racism, as well as of course the coronavirus. Until I happened upon a timely speculative essay by M. Gessen published in the *New Yorker*—given the title "What Do College Students Think of Their Schools' Reopening Plans?"— I hadn't sufficiently appreciated how things had changed nor how much the several concurrent emergencies might be synthesized. Gessen's piece offers a striking synthesis, although I hasten to point out that it was hardly the only analysis of its sort to appear in that period;[51] its convergence upon new arrangements for learning was particularly suggestive and, in something of a surprise to me, shed light on the special social significance of the *prepandemic* MOOC.

What could commentaries on the problem of reopening schools in 2020 have to do with ModPo overall? Here, at the end of this introductory chapter and near the start of the next, we'll be considering this provocative turn of logic about learning, but before doing so, we'll need to gather together some more details about scenes of the academy in the early spring of 2020. A good deal of panic had set in. NPR ran a story in which Anya Kamenetz (and her colleagues) coined the term *panicgogy* to describe the hurried and glitchy implementation of the move online, and the date of the piece is March 19.[52] Jonathan Zimmerman had already published a March 10 column summoning skeptical responses from students in the 1950s to an earlier experiment in distance learning—courses via television. "Social distancing is necessary to preserve good health," Zimmerman wrote, "but it's not good for education."[53] "Online School Demands More of Teachers. Unions Are Pushing Back" is a *New York Times* headline of that moment.[54] In the "Recode" section of *Vox*: "Paranoia about cheating is making online education terrible for everyone."[55]

It was all a far cry from Friedman's euphoria in 2012 over the coming new golden age of learning. Frank Bruni opined on June 4, 2020, in a column titled "The End of College as We Knew It?" perceiving the industries of airlines and restaurants to be tipping over the existential edge toward which higher education now also veered. "Shakespeare gets kicked when he's down," mused Bruni. The damage will come disproportionately to the humanities, he speculated. "Homer could be in particular peril, dismissed along with the rest of the humanities as a fusty luxury."[56] Jonathan Kramnick of Yale's English department already pondered "The Humanities After Covid-19," expecting, "at the extreme," that "we should contemplate the end of intellectual continuity." That's because, in part, of new hiring practices for professorial appointments: "Required online experience. . . . Remote pedagogy is here to stay. The people doing the hiring will demand that candidates are much better than they are themselves at using and exploiting the technology."[57] The *Chronicle of Higher Education* chose to use a photograph of the Damien Hirst sculpture, *For the Love of God*, a memento mori said to "proclaim . . . victory over decay." The artwork was presented with these words superimposed: "The Humanities After Covid-19 / What Happens When Hiring Dies?" Was this intended by *Chronicle* editors to illustrate Kramnick's concerns at a time of mass pandemic-related deaths and the predicted eerie, otherworldly death of the humanities at the hands of digital agents borne upon the

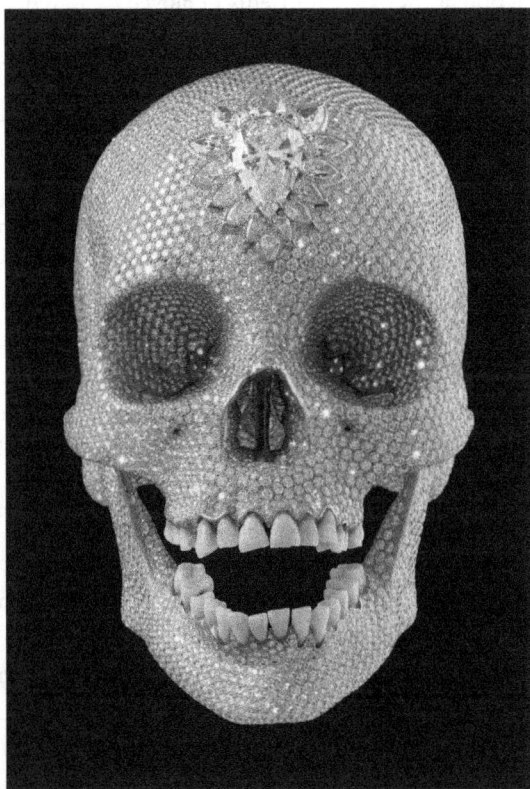

FIGURE 0.3 Photograph of Damien Hirst, *For the Love of God*, 2007.

Source: Courtesy White Cube. © Damien Hirst and Science Ltd. All rights reserved / DACS, London / ARS, NY 2025.

wings of virus? The ominous bling of AI? Projecting Hirst not just onto infection fatalities but also the menacing contagion of online teaching seems to bear out art historian Rudi Fuchs's understanding of the sculpture as sci-fi-like, "represent[ing] death as something infinitely more relentless."[58] As one ModPo participant commented when I crowdsourced interpretations of the *Chronicle*'s 2020 use of Hirst: "The mortality of humanities following upon the mortality of humans."[59]

Rebecca Barrett-Fox outlined a new supposedly practical form of resistance to administrators in a much-discussed blog post titled "Please Do a Bad Job of Putting Your Courses Online."[60] (Her opening sentence: "I'm absolutely serious.") Then, for many Humanities faculty, frustrations directed against modes of remote instruction as they were hurriedly deployed in March, April, and May of 2020 gave way in the summer and early autumn to anger directed against administrators who by that point seemed to some observers much too eager to send everyone back into classrooms for the new school year. The latter argument depended not on teachers' comfort or satisfaction with online teaching nor upon the arguments in favor of the exploration of these astonishingly accessible pedagogies that could and perhaps should have been made by these same people back in 2012–2013. Which was now more to be disliked: remote teaching or educational leaders demanding that we quit remote teaching as soon as the exigent reason for it had begun to abate? *Reopening* had become a loaded institutional term. Its connotation was quickly inflected by conservative pandemic economics.

Back to Gessen. After a sampling of various "defense[s] of campus life in the pandemic" then being put forward by the administrations of colleges and universities, we encounter an attempt at a holistic integration of the social responses to dysfunction that I and my colleagues had been seeing in the MOOC for years but had not yet formulated explicitly. A wide range of ModPo learners had all along been describing just such malfunctions in their educational experiences. The breakdown wasn't a pandemic-specific problem. ModPo people had become practiced in reporting on the myriad situations of displacement that were motivating learners toward idiosyncratic spaces of open education. (Understanding what such spaces entail is the first work of the next chapter.)

Gessen's essay surveyed the surprisingly COVID-safe activities associated with crowd gatherings that had been taking place in late spring and all summer in response to the new wave of bitter social hostilities and the cognizance of the effects of climate change. A veteran reporter on anti-authoritarian protests in Putinist Russia, Gessen confessed that they had never seen "this level of detailed, organized, and consistent mutual care" and quoted a popular call-and-response chant about safety and social distancing and self-responsibility from the outdoor gatherings—"Who keeps us safe? *We* keep us safe!"—in such a way as to cause the renewal of public engagement, fears of the pandemic's lasting effects, outrage at racist violence, frustration over disappointing trends in twentieth-century education, and a variational public use of the first-person plural, to seem essentially convergent. Then, pivoting back to the urgent situation of education, the *New Yorker* piece began to outline an idealistic pedagogy focused on learning rather than teaching. The speculations took cues from the very people who were making an effort to own responsibility for the new situational politics: a form of learning that could begin with the "community [that] students seek when they attend college in person," pandemic or not. "Trying to extend a sense of care to our students," noted Robin DeRosa at Plymouth State University, can't depend upon coursework conversion—digitalization. "Care," rather, requires fundamental forms of participation and basic changes in format. "The idea here," DeRosa said, "is really to help our students feel included in the process of rethinking education for a challenging time."[61] DeRosa, Gessen, Cait Kirby,[62] Erín Moure,[63] Yosefa Gilon and colleagues,[64] and others urged those in authority at schools to comprehend the experience of learners and, indeed, to confer with them—people who after all were subject to the old and suddenly rather outmoded (and, despite the shift to online, largely unchanged) methods of presenting knowledge, to create, as it were, a syllabus that itself included rather than sidelined the topic of "rethink[ing of] how colleges are interacting with students who are staying home."[65]

RETHINKING EDUCATION, AN OUTLINE

The dilemma of learning while staying home: one point of this book is that it was hardly a new thing in the spring of 2020. In the chapters that follow, I describe situations driving learners toward experimental forms of learning far more commonplace than perhaps many realize. A majority of the people who had been gathering in and around the ModPo course community have all along been staying home for a variety of reasons. The special empathy toward the variety of contexts for learning that commentators observed during 2020–2021 is relevant generally. Just one reason for teaching ourselves to care about those who must stay home during and beyond 2020 was obviously a perilous infection that especially inhibits people with prior chronic illness. But there have been many other important causes, and for the purpose of organizing a citizen poetics, each can not only be explored distinctly but also as often interrelated. No proximate access to a college or university. Lifelong learning differences that make traditional classroom learning irrelevant or impossible, or at any rate, disheartening and unproductive (witness the testimony of Dan Bergmann). Poverty in general, including massive student debt in particular, and often, as a result, a dread of burdensome real-life effects of schools. An inability to work synchronously. A loss of direction upon occupational retirement. Restrictions compelled by overwhelming domestic responsibilities. Various forms and causes of immobility. Still another cause has to do with the connectivist disposition that comes rather naturally to many people. Like the self-creative version of the cMOOC, then still somewhat wandering in the Edu-Tech wilderness at the start of the pandemic[66]—and pushed further to the edges by the immense scramble of panicgogy—networked connectivism and practices of multiaccess learning present an analog for what critics of education observed in 2020 of learners as they became conscious of their personal justifications for hoping that the teaching environments they enter, and indeed help to create, could be built upon detailed, organized, consistent mutual care.[67]

Digitality in response to crisis becomes a metonym here for the survival of personhood, for "non-market relations of care" (Fitzpatrick's phrase in *Generous Thinking*[68]), at a time of ubiquitous technologized media. In connectivism, it's said that learning is no longer strictly just personal but also inherently collective—and yet, it *does* remain personal, even as categories and modes of learning mix and connect. The experience of poems people read in ModPo and these still-then emerging open technologies could be aligned with—led by, not following—such a personal rationale. Another form of expressing this: *a learner-centered learning is akin to reader-centered reading*. That contention is a way of saying in one sentence what the first three chapters here argue. Both sides of the equivalence, the poetics and the pedagogy, were made to converge through a user-identified use of the new robust massive online platform in ways certainly not anticipated and, in some sense, not even desired by the platform's technical makers.

The alignment of the two apparently distinct categories—poems and digital teaching—is the convergence *The Classroom and the Crowd* traces and describes. At times, we will take them one at a time. Mostly, though, they are presented as one. Chapter 1 is an exploration of a digital poetics and a tour of the kinds of spaces upon which collaboration as an aspect of democracy can be founded. Chapter 2, where we return to virtual life in panicgogy, describes fraught culture warring over online learning during crisis—conflicts that served to sharpen a sense of rights and obligations already felt by members of an online community. Chapter 3 finds that the daring it takes to teach the disjunctive art of Gertrude Stein puts us in the middle of the battle in schools over whether skill has much to do with content and whether digital minimalism will make you a more healthful learner. (My view: it won't.) Looked at in one way, the chapters in my book's first part, "The Subject Village," are making a case against digital decluttering and in favor of rejections of closure.

Where did that rejection come from? To answer that question, it will be important to look back at the preceding eras in which the idea of a post-lecture intersubjective pedagogy first emerged. This retrospective, partly historical and partly memoiristic, is the work of the three chapters in part 2, "The Sound of the End of the Lecture." Those chapters progress their way toward a chronicle of the spatial event as a site—a teachable place in itself, a schooling of sorts—that gets created by the recorded and digitally reproduced and distributed public poetry reading, an assembling that has become crucial to the community ModPo establishes. The chapters of part 2, venturing back to the 1930s and accounting for certain legacies of the 1960s and 1990s, press pause on the discussion of ModPo and make a case for the general importance of sound—noise, audio, recording, close listening, aurality—to progressive education. These chapters look at the long history of the relationship between open learner-centered pedagogy and digitality and draw upon my personal experiences "teaching with technology" as part of a lineage dating back to preinternet educational reformism. In chapter 5, for instance, we'll meet Bob Brown, a "bibliomaniac" who believed long before computers that text-generating machines would improve reading. And John Dewey, a key figure whose ideas about teaching through sound are summarized; he urged learners to try to "stop thinking" because "the flow of suggestions goes on in spite of our will, quite as surely as our bodies feel"[69]—an optimistic concept of information overload that is fundamental, we have found, to the cascading of thoughts in the multiaccess online forum.

In the last part of the book, "The Crowd, Yes," we return to the people who have populated ModPo and further explore a conception of antiminimalist (in this book, we'll sometimes use the term *maximalist*) digital poetics put into practice by their interpretive collaboration. The book's final pages proceed from "the sound of the end of the lecture" having been heard across the three clamorous chapters of part 2, following which comes the culmination of a hopeful case for a citizen poetics. In part 3, chapters 7 and 8 present an argument based on a survey and analysis of human-powered crowdsourcing in an effort to reverse damaging twentieth-century connotations of the crowd, especially of the supposed lonely crowd. Some crowds, it turns out, are not lonely at all.

PART I

The Subject Village

CHAPTER 1

OPEN DOOR, OPEN TEXT, OPEN LEARNING

Learning to listen, that is taught not to talk. Can one take captive the roar of the city. Simon says sounds from the schoolyard. I'm standing here then I must be positive.

—Lyn Hejinian, *My Life*, in the section of the poem consisting of thirty-seven unchronological sentences about her thirteenth year

THE MADE PLACE

Without using the phrase, in "What Do College Students Think of Their Schools' Reopening Plans?" M. Gessen described what political geographer and spatial theorist Edward Soja identified as "third space learning"—a merging of real and imagined places into something potentially transformative. It is "a purposefully tentative and flexible term," Soja added, "that attempts to capture what is actually a constantly shifting and changing milieu of ideas, events, appearances and meanings."[1] Elaborating on Soja's earlier work and that of others, a group of critic-educators, including Elizabeth Birr Moje and Katheryn McIntosh Ciechanowski, described a place where the "integration of knowledges and discourses" is drawn from otherwise separate situations.

There's a first space of homes or familial community and/or adult-led networks. At its best, such a situation consists of "learning to listen," as Lyn Hejinian recalled in her experimental prose-poem memoir *My Life*. At worst, it's a matter of being "taught not to talk."[2]

Then there is a second space saturated with the socializing discourses of formal institutions such as schools. There, to stay with Hejinian's terms, one learns by replicating "sounds from the schoolyard" as social curricula.[3]

Thirdly, there can sometimes be a place that is neither home nor classroom but broadens people's motivation to continue improvising formats for learning, even to the extent of "tak[ing] captive the roar of the city" and venturing outward from the bewilderment of being stuck in classrooms or at home. This third option for learners, partly to be realized in fact and partly never more than an idealization of human uses of places, inspired Gessen to submit a report on a pivotal moment in the history of education.

The notion of a new kind of space caused this critic, among a few others, to feel a sense of counterintuitive hope for learners learning in the midst of the 2020–2021 crises, if not so much optimism for the schools. "What might students," notwithstanding such displacement from classrooms, "try to *apply* to college life?" That was the key question, and here was a tentative proposal: intent on exploring format-agnostic teaching, learners could create "affinity groups." They could study social issues independent of the faculty or administration of the university and discuss the very way in which the university's curriculum seemed estranged from the main concerns. Learners inside such pods would not only create their own safety protocols for the rapidly spreading virus but also, relatedly, an entirely "new approach to the academic schedule" aligned with Soja's theorizing toward a lived experience of space and duration. In fact, these self-created, self-enrolled workshops or ongoing forums could "plan a curriculum for a year together" and invent intensive course-like studies, the length and depth of which would befit the time it took to cover the topic rather than the venerable predetermined semester or quarter. "Colleges ought to be asking young people how to bring that knowledge"—the know-how of building curriculum—"and that sense of . . . responsibility, to campus." Canonical knowledge not only preceded the experiences of the learner, but it could also be shaped by circumstantial awareness of new motivation for wanting to know. "Let's reframe the question, by asking not whether colleges should get their tuition dollars by putting their students, faculty, and staff at risk, but how to insure that the current generation of students will be able to learn in a meaningful way."[4]

As Suzanne Choo worked to apply the idea of third spaces to *literary* education, she observed how the socialization of the first space (home, family; characterized by parental or elder-generation prerogative) selected what to know and thus generally taught through exclusions. At the same time, Choo noticed, discourse learning in the second space (classrooms where found texts are required by teachers and other curricular authorities, typically conforming to local political sensibilities) created a desire among some learners to join a different situation, one that would not be characterized much like either home or school. This is the site where what Kris Gutiérrez calls "a sociocritical literacy" can happen. "The assumption [in the classroom, a second space] that students can simply immerse themselves in the world of the text and enjoy the experience of reading," writes Choo, "naively ignores the fact that a particular world of home [a first space] has typically already been chosen for them to vicariously experience and the fact of selection means that other worlds have been excluded."[5] Such a theory of learning suggests that the meaning of culture, for Choo and Gutiérrez a specifically *literary* culture, is best found and learned elsewhere. And elsewhere can be built anywhere.

When learners occupy third spaces of some sort—in 2020–2021 this became the interstitial scene of civic engagement, start-up cocreative happenings, occurring while school continued otherwise remotely and (despite circumstances) rather routinely to be in session—they understand that spatial transpositioning is a form of constructive educational exchange that can be collaborative and *creative*. If this aspect of education is indeed cocreative in an actual way, then its inventive effects in the realms of culture, literature, and art would seem to suggest possible models. That's obviously because art, as fundamental to democratic culture, entails creative acts. In *The Location of Culture*, Homi Bhabha wrote that the third space "is the 'inter'—the cutting edge of translation and negotiation, the *inbetween* space—that carries the burden of the meaning of culture."[6] Noting the "multiple social spaces with distinctive participation structures" that her students needed to translate, Gutiérrez, like Bhabha, wants teachers to explore the borderlines of those activities, "what we later referred to as the 'underlife' of the classroom . . . and the remarkable sense-making character of those seemingly unrelated processes, what we called the 'script' and 'counterscript' from which Third Spaces emerge."[7]

For Choo, who studies "citizenship education,"[8] these scripts can be a poem or other unresolved piece of literary writing that, in communities of formally innovative poets, is typically called an "open text." The open poem in the open space can become a point of mutual translation (writer ↔ reader) and negotiation (instructor ↔ learner). An alternative form has appeared when some sense of equalizing of roles characterizes what a teacher is doing in the illocutionary speech act of presenting nothing but the *sound* of a supposedly difficult poem for learning. The four capacities (teacher, student, poet, reader) converge to make a noisy, even intensely clamorous, place. In stressing "cultural difference" as quite distinct from conventional liberal policies of "cultural diversity" in an interview about "The Third Space" (1990), Bhabha emphasized the importance of finding a hybrid "position of liminality" in "that productive space of the construction of culture as difference."[9]

Learning, my own experience suggests, can become a matter of translational convening just as reckoning with language is. It has been, for me, an agreed-upon differential "intersecting," to use Gutiérrez's term, a converging upon the place where "we were meant to meet." The phrase is Erica Hunt's, from "Reader we were meant to meet," a poem she wrote about the sense of the "room" that an intersubjective poem creates. The meeting is "where teacher and student scripts—the formal and informal, the official and unofficial spaces of the learning environment—intersect," in the phrasing of Gutiérrez. It "creat[es] the potential for authentic interaction and a shift in the social organization of learning and what counts as knowledge."[10] When Hunt directly addresses the reader of her poem, saying "Reader step into my room"—after all, *stanza* means *room*—she is flipping the typical writer-reader/teacher-learner script. Who's reading whom? Who's understanding whose difficulty? "Reader, you were meant to be legible," Hunt writes, "even in the failure to communicate." Poems for Hunt and Choo make places for respectful, dynamic, mutual convergence. Here's Hunt:

> Touch, reader, we were meant to touch
> to exchange definitions and feel the pulse of
> language. I promise if you step in
> it will propel you, me, it:
> topple distinctions,
> ease doubt and belief.[11]

And: "I promise if you step in / it will propel you."

Erica Hunt's second-person pronoun is that of third-space pedagogy. It's the *you* that is essential to any sort of civil meeting of minds, and that meeting makes the plural first-person *we*. "*We* were meant to / . . . exchange definitions." Such a get-together is hardly only theoretical, for, after all, "this page faces you" as a matter of simple experiential fact. Paper page or screen page regardless, it faces you and you face it. That's reading. Pause reading my book now, if you please, and type this address into your nearest browser, and you'll see it facing you:

modpo.org/reader-we-were-meant

That a poem now presents itself to you is a fundamentally practical aspect of all reading. What counts for Hunt as teacher-poet (and, not coincidentally, a long-time nonprofit organizer and executive) are *your* "back stories hostile to the wobbled word," whatever is *your* narrative that "resists being pinned to the truth." And what about the room the poem has made? Third spaces can be textual, and texts are made to be coaxial. The space reverses the situation in which the writer is the only one who has something to say and to show. Thus the key question is: "What will *I* miss if *you* blink."

Texts and spaces. Poetic texts *are* spaces, but they can also thrive or be thwarted by the built environment, physical or virtual. The intersubjective organization of learning can, of course, be a built environment—what people in the poetry world, following Robert Duncan's reputed opening of the field, sometimes call "a made place."[12] In poetry and the arts, the *made place* has come to refer to a space constructed or crafted with intention despite its mystery. It is distinct from the natural world yet signifies an imagined landscape that the writer, appealing to the reader's desire for mutual intellection, has the power to shape and bring to life through language and creativity. ModPo was designed, despite the flattening enormity of the platform housing it, to function at least modestly as a made place. The inclusion of many coaxial poems like Hunt's "Reader we were meant to meet" in the ModPo syllabus is meant to signal the concept and the intention. Obviously, then, a made place is not just naturally occurring. It is created or shaped by human will, imagination, invention, programming. Ideas about openness have resonated with various critics and poets—in the fields of ecological poetry (ecopoetics) and disability studies, for example—who explore themes related to human agency and its limits, creativity, and the otherwise unanticipated effects of the interplay between imagination and reality, including, to be sure, in spaces that are virtual or immaterial.

Not everyone agrees on the value of openness. Allan Bloom offered a sustained (and publicly consequential) case against the imaginative interplay just described. At its worst, "openness" ruins every intellectual and educational thing we should cherish, "leaving only [a] speechless, meaningless country."[13] This view gained prominence just as Hejinian's and her poet-theorist "Language poet" colleagues' rejections of closure were ascendent. Both views, both influential although in quite different ways, were in the air as the ideas that founded the Kelly Writers House in 1995 were being discussed. There's already been so much discussion here of openness that such a timely critique must be recognized. When considering the open poem, open education (the open-enrollment course), an open door to art spaces, the open forum for discussion, and open-ended interpretation all as a refusal of closure, many critics and poets provide a compelling response to Bloom's concerns. Erica Hunt, for example, is open to what a reader will have to say of her poem and, in a sense, *in* it. Kris Gutiérrez wants the educational script to be flipped, a situation that requires liminality and suspects any predeterminacy. Connectivists want learners to acquire the "ability to see connections between fields, ideas, and concepts [a]s a core *skill*" and distrust top-down originalism in all its forms.[14] The poet Larry Eigner, whose ellipsis (caesura, punctuation, spacing, pacing) has been important to the development of disability poetics, had been influenced by Charles Olson's distinction between "closed" verse and "'open' or 'projective' poetry," the latter (Olson claimed) being shaped by "physiology." (Eigner's poem titled "O p e n" invites open-ended interpretation: in that astonishing piece of concise writing, "I have been on all sides" is a phrase referring both to the writer's verse and body—as well as a heretical expression of antipartisanship that resists the typical ease with which poems, or people, take sides.[15]) Readings of open poems are meant to proliferate rather than narrow down to a few supposedly civilized options. Through ModPo, I and others seek, or at least gladly tolerate, the very qualities Bloom denounced in "the information explosion," even as we accept the risk of compromising tradition. And one of those traditions in jeopardy is the teacher who knows everything—or seems to. "Organizing instruction around open-ended tasks . . . risks exposing what teachers do not know," Jal Mehta and Sarah Fine conclude from their extensive survey of U.S. schools for *In Search of Deeper Learning* (2019), "because, as one loosens controls, students are increasingly likely to venture into unfamiliar territory."[16]

Bloom saw rendering "tradition . . . superfluous" in a time of "constant newness" as destructive. His case against the "closing of the American mind" in a best-selling eponymous book was made long ago—1987; it was a blast out of and against that final preinternet moment—and his concerns about technology were deep, significant, and, given what was about to happen, timely. But they turn out to be an effect rather than a foundation of his book-length argument against openness. "Openness," he wrote, "means accepting everything and denying reason's power." "If openness means to 'go with the flow,'" for him a hateful laziness, "it is necessarily an accommodation to the present" that tends to cancel the need to read, study, and discuss past verities. Thus, to Bloom, "the purpose of education is [unfortunately, he believes] not to make scholars but to provide [learners] with a moral virtue—openness." Openness can sometimes invite us to search for knowledge and certitude, he notes, but much more often it is "the openness of indifference," which is "promote[d] with the twin purposes of humbling our intellectual pride and letting us be whatever we want to be, just as long as we don't want to be knowers." Opening up means closing down.

ALT-POETRY, ALT-PEDAGOGY

Why does openness leave us with a "speechless, meaningless country"? The question seems political, and ultimately it is, but Allan Bloom was first and foremost worried about language in itself. There was a theory of language in his critical assessment. Citizenship is made first in a family, or anyway at home, before schooling occurs and apart from it: a child's elders are the ones *"providing names for all things."* That overwhelming and confident act of world denotation "transmits an interpretation of the order of the whole of things." Bloom celebrates a "sacred unity" of that first space, and he doesn't only refer to the traditional family teaching the meaning and value of things to its young members. He means the *unity* between words and things that words authoritatively identify. It's a kind of confident teaching that is about "believing in the permanence of what it teaches."[17]

This is not what Lyn Hejinian (1941–2024) experienced when she came of age in the 1940s and 1950s, as we learn from *My Life*. Through a language and style of impermanence, disjunction, newness, and openness, *My Life* tells a disordered American coming-of-age story of a person developing the desire to go with the flow and wishing to be a "knower." All while, disconcertingly, "learning to listen" to her confident idiom-spewing cultural elders—"that is[,] taught not to talk." Hejinian's being silenced in first spaces (see especially the opening sections of *My Life*) was the opposite of Bloom's "sacred unity," and she eventually translated this experience into an open poem. There, providing names for all things, at the level of the in-the-correct-order memoiristic unidiomatic sentence, would be completely wrong as a means of representing the truth of an American reality. In ModPo we read, study, and discuss Hejinian's *My Life*, Hunt's "Reader we were meant to meet," Harryette Mullen's "Sleeping with the Dictionary" (in which she brings her *American Heritage* tome to bed with her), Rosmarie Waldrop's chance-made "Shorter American Memory of the Declaration of Independence," Ron Silliman's "BART" (recording his every movement during a free all-day transit ride on U.S. Labor Day), Mike Magee's differently allegiant versified rewriting of the "Pledge" to the flag of the United States, and many other experiments in American representations, and that perhaps signals no more than a self-reinforcing, self-approving circularity through which openness as a moral value is uncritically accepted. The relationship among open poem, open course, open forum, and open interpretation should not be assumed. If the connections are productive, they need to be shown. For now I observe that in his lament over open interpretation Bloom stressed the essential truth of "an interpretation of the order of the whole of things" and that his book is indeed an *interpretation* of culture meant to be debated against other interpretations. This is where his fundamental technophobia—his critique of interconnecting technologies, somewhat before the fact of networking—became more than a minor strain in his argument. Bloom didn't mind insulting young people who have chosen to get educated as technologists. In a description of computer science engineering as a schooling, he complained of "the technical smorgasbord of the current school system, with its utter inability to distinguish between important and unimportant in any way other than by demands of the market." Technology is only an option in school, he claimed, because it beckons a segment of learners toward big salaries and profits. And so "a highly trained computer specialist need not have had any learning about morals, politics or religion than the most ignorant of persons."[18] If the massive open online course has taught me anything as an educator, it is that (to quote the connectivists again) "connections between fields, ideas, and concepts [constitute] a core skill" and that *ignorance*—I'll accept the pejorative term to refer merely a lack of subject-matter knowledge—characterizes *me* for all my formal moral, political, and religious learning as much as it does the young engineers at Coursera in its earliest days, who suddenly found themselves in a position to comprehend what poetry needed from the new mediatic system they were building with a surprising degree of improvisation. Pang Wei Koh, the third-ever employee at Coursera, then an engineering student from Stanford with scant curricular humanities education, "was considered [among the staff] the most reasonable choice to interact with a poetry course" (as he put it to me recently[19]) because his training in new-fangled open education had cultivated in him an openness sufficient to be a good translator of my team's commitment to opacity into the platform's necessarily precise language. Pang Wei and I were an unlikely but effective pair. He returns in the final part of this book, but for now I'll say that it's no exaggeration to recall my feelings of elation as I was being partially released from a disciplinary silo. Our first conversations, me a proper elder poetry guy and him, a with-it young technologist, had a generative cultural valence. We hoped that what we were making would be a contradiction of ignorance, the opposite of the "speechless, meaningless country" some feared would result from disruptive networking—concerns felt by skeptics from Bloom to digital minimalists of later years as they decry inattention and advocate unplugging.

In seeking to identify the "a socio-technical third space in higher education" as a made place, Steven White, Su White, and Kate Borthwick studied the work of the people who occupied an alternative zone of teaching and learning *themselves* and made the technological sites that enabled "third space roles and structures."[20] When the making of a third space is applied to MOOCs, the unusual sociality of learning designers themselves discloses "fluid institutional structures" and establishes not just a "new professional" category among people who work in education, but also a greater sense—applicable to places beyond the school or university—of role opacity.[21] If, as connectivists contend, "chaos is the new reality for knowledge workers,"[22] it should not come as a surprise that role opacity can be extended to both teachers and learners in the course being programmed and encoded within such a milieu. In a basic common-sense way, the idea of an interstitial space was here being applied to the collaborative albeit still *institutional* effort of making MOOCs by site designers who comprehended its special relevance as a made place. That effort potentially lessens the alienation of this sort of back-of-the-house educational labor. It entailed collaboratively building something that could be used to collaboratively build something. "Socio-technical" is nonetheless social. Hardly ignorant in Bloom's sense, such people are learning to choose to draw on "dimensions of 'spaces, knowledges, relationships, and legitimacies' characteristic of the work of blended professionals whose roles span conventional domains in higher education."[23]

Summarizing two points: First, the MOOC is itself a created/creative thing—understood to be a made place or, as Duncan also frames it, "a scene made-up by the mind, / that is not mine"[24]—built by curious people sharing and trading roles and implementing new applications of sudden robust technologies. Second, if this was going to be used by *participants* in a way anticipated by conceptions of third spaces, we can observe that the *prior* work of learning design had to be a particular "co-creation"[25]—poetic in the widest sense—which is "core" to the design and programming as well as to the global learners who would soon be using the program and would learn how to inhabit the result interestingly.

Connectivism has of course stressed these ideas about the new networked technologies all along. Here again is the key to the pairing of this book: the special poesis described above closely relates to the rationale supporting the work of teaching the experimental poets we present in ModPo. This is particularly the case for the generation of writers, among them Hejinian and Hunt, who came of age politically and poetically in the late 1960s and 1970s and who have engaged in metapoetry and the resistance to self-expressive closure. Closure is conventionally the point at which the author (as authority) is done, and there's nothing more to say on the subject. But in practice, a poem "begins and ends arbitrarily and not because there is a necessary point of origin and terminus," as Hejinian wrote. "Words and the ideas" of an open text "continue beyond the work. One has simply stopped because one has run out of units or minutes, and not because a conclusion has been reached nor 'everything' said."[26] Technoprogressive and participatory-democrat connectivists, allies of that generation of poets and many to follow, feel empowered within the cMOOC (connectivist MOOC) to alter the structures of the system to meet the needs of the discussion. And this makes for a defiance against the sadly typical situation in which the tail of learning management system (LMS) design wags the dog of the innovative forms of learning it was designed to enable. White, White, and Borthwick, and some people who were building the new networked sites, began to discover a profound cocreative activity in the actual work performed by the initial design teams. They rediscovered the joys of breaking from categories of knowledge and of diverging from departmentalization in secondary and higher education, and more generally from official knowledge-making culture.

The move away from prescribed roles and methods helped inspire an extended conference-retreat called Poetry & Pedagogy hosted by poets Joan Retallack and Juliana Spahr at Bard College in June 1999. I was there along with Kelly Writers House director Kerry Sherin Wright, and we were accompanied by a team of Writers House staff and affiliated poets. Back at the old cottage at 3805 Locust Walk in Philadelphia, we had begun, in 1998, to host live give-and-take audiocasts and webcasts that mixed discussion among in-room and remote participants. We somewhat knew what we were doing, as a technological matter—and, proudly, we were one of the first organizations in the poetry world at that time to put on such interactive live networked programming. But Kerry, our colleagues, and I went to Bard with questions about our aims. What did our unscripted networked colloquies, open to everyone everywhere, have to do with our aim to teach formally innovative poems, "alt-poetries"? How did the choice of presenting *such* poetry inspire—indeed necessitate—"alt-pedagogies"? Did alt-pedagogy correlate with the particularities of the new technologies we were beginning to refine as hosted by and from a writers' freespace?

These questions were meant to be asked by conference participants at Bard as "blended professionals" along the lines of investigations into digital-era hybridization of roles and categories. At every session, I wondered what to call my role as it was evolving. Educator? Convener? Poetry scholar? Arts administrator? Venturer in nonprofit tech education? The blending of identities was a major topic in a book to come out of the conference, edited by Retallack and Spahr, titled *Poetry and Pedagogy: The Challenge of the Contemporary* (2006). Another outcome was a gathering, joined by Retallack, curated and hosted by Kerry Sherin Wright at the Kelly Writers House in February 2001, titled "Is It Productive to Teach Experimental Poetry in an Experimental Way? If So, Why?" The event was designed to continue the conversation held at Bard. It was live-streamed, recorded, preserved, and then segmented by discussion topic as video and audio files (originally RealVideo and RealAudio) at the Writers House and archived in PennSound.[27]

In one segment of the recording of this symposium, poet Bob Perelman, conversing from the audience, can be heard describing "experimental poetics *as a pedagogy.*" In another segment, titled "On the interaction of contemporary poetry with the contemporary world," the concept of "the contemporary" is meant to connect to Gertrude Stein's understanding that composition is ipso facto contemporary. Composition is a form of the present. It lives.[28] This then was what Retallack and Spahr meant by "the challenge of the contemporary." Composing a poem is composing a place and time in which the composer is living contemporaneously. "Poethics" is the term Retallack has used to describe the ethical approach to life and writing that embraces complexity and openness rather than seeking to simplify or even to make coherent. Experimentation is ethical. The poethical place is a site where dialogue leading to learning can be creatively composed as a contemporariness. The Kelly Writers House came of age as a space in this period, from the late 1990s through the first half of the 2000s. Retallack's *The Poethical Wager* (2003), which I think must be seen as part of this turn-of-century metapedagogical moment, and Spahr's *Everybody's Autonomy: Connective Reading and Collective Identity* (2001), are both important influences upon what came next.

In *The Poethical Wager* Stein's "Composition as Explanation," always a central text in Retallack's advocacy of "living courageously,"[29] becomes a guide to pedagogy. John Dewey's famous progressive argument about learning held that it "is a process of living and not a preparation for the future,"[30] and further supports the poetry/pedagogy analogy along poethical lines. The Spahr/Retallack idea was fundamental: readers have the major role to play in the way a text lives. The notion was meant, in part, as an alternative to the traditionalist's anxiety—during the preceding years of culture wars as expressed by Bloom, E. D. Hirsch, Irving Kristol, Roger Kimball, Gertrude Himmelfarb, William Bennett, and others—over whether there was still a text to be found in the class. If the meaning-making activity of a text could shift to a reader, then teaching could be reoriented to the situation of the learner's reception of what is taught. Poethics sought to move beyond the defensive posturing that seemed required to counter doubts about learner-centered learning as a step forward from reader-centered reading. The question to be asked, rather, is: Is there a class in this text?[31]

The answer is yes. There is a class in the text. But when Stanley Fish provocatively posed the question decades ago, the word *class*, as in *classroom* or *course*, did not entail the crowd. If in the classic formulation of what became known as reader-response criticism "the reader was now given joint responsibility for the production of a meaning" and "the text was not the self-sufficient repository of meaning," this could be pushed *much* further when we began to think of the reading experience as a massive ongoing writerly or writer-like activity or event in "the process of living" in Stein's sense (and to use Dewey's phrasing). Fish, an early proponent of the shift in theory from writer to reader, had already moved far away from postliterary expressions of this reader-focused theorizing by the time his various essays on "the authority of interpretive communities" had been collected into a book; nonetheless, its most radical formulations and subsequent reassertions by others (including Hejinian in "The Rejection of Closure"[32]) had an impact two decades later upon Retallack and especially Spahr as they wrote about connective reading and collective identity. These ideas also shaped the social development, in turn, of the Kelly Writers House and eventually—in the fully networked era of crowd reading—the founding ideas of ModPo. "The reader's response is not *to* the meaning; it *is* the meaning." In ModPo, the notion has been that the making of the meanings of a poem was to be "itself redefined as an *event*" put on by a vast multiplicity of readers, on a big stage. One question—*What does this mean?*—was being replaced "by another—*What does this do?*—with 'do' equivocating between a reference to the action of the text" happening upon a readerly crowd and the actions performed *by* the crowd as they "negotiate[. . .] (and, in some sense, actualize[. . .]) the text."[33] All this is much more active and social than is implied by the concept of an implied reader inside a text.

EXPERIMENTAL IS THE OPERATIVE WORD

Gertrude Stein and John Dewey? It's a pairing that makes good sense when one thinks about it, especially in the context of the responses of readers. In the Deweyan classroom, the making of meaning is an event, an activity, and forms community property. Learners *do things* altogether with words. Students are active sense-makers. These ideas are said to be in the "family of pedagogies" sometimes known as social constructivism, deriving from two main convictions: first that "individuals construct new understandings from prior understandings [when] in the context of learning communities" and, second, that meanings "produced by an interpretive community are not subjective because they proceed . . . from a public point of view."[34] Instead, there is a kind of public objectivity or realism. Stein says, "The composition is the thing seen *by every one* living in the living they are doing, they are the composing of the composition that at the time they are living is the composition of the time in which they are living" (emphasis added).[35]

In Stein's formulation, we reach the point where "alt-poetry / alt-pedagogy" is most optimistic and verges on utopian. Utopianism, for that matter, has at times also been the philosophical disposition of Retallack herself, whose work as a teacher-poet-theorist is influenced by Stein and John Cage. "The poethics of [a] poem," Retallack says, "invites a practice of reading that enacts a tolerance for ambiguity and a delight in complex possibility. *Imagine what happens if such a practice were to become widespread.*"[36] The "complex realism" she means is recursively operative. It is a disposition meant to integrate modes of thinking into an ethical practice. The pragmatic, worldly act she describes is the serious/playful conversation about a difficult poem with others, including novice learners, in such a way as to align with—and, further, to be an instance of—the "contemporary" itself as Stein means the term. *The Poethical Wager* is Retallack's *Democracy and Education.*

So that's the argument here in sum: complex realism is recursively operative. "Recursively operative" might seem too vague a locution. While it is an apt phrase for understanding the complex plan underlying the essays of *The Poethical Wager*, it is not, in fact, Joan Retallack's phrase. It was coined by the Americanist scholar, essayist, and editor Wai Chee Dimock in an essay she wrote as editor of the journal *PMLA* about the nexus of projects highlighted in this book. "Experimental: this is the operative word . . . recursively operative, it seems, at every level of the Kelly Writers House's infrastructures: physical, digital, and philosophical." What she observes are projects interacting in a way that repeatedly apply operations to its outputs, which then become its new inputs. Dimock continues: "Having itself ventured into unchartered territory, the house looks for the same risk-taking spirit of the poets it showcases." Her 2017 synthesis—an issue-framing essay in a literary professional publication showing how the kind of poetry featured can be supported by and learned in *the kind of place that features it*—had of course been previously anticipated and modeled advantageously in other settings. There was Kristen Gallagher's synthesis, for instance. Gallagher's sense of the recursive qualities shared between and among English 88 (in which she had once been a student); the Writers House as a noncurricular freespace (she was among its founders); *Jacket2* magazine (where she has published a multipart series on "the scene(s) I occupy," focusing on poetry community events); *PoemTalk* as an unrehearsed four-person close reading that then, as a widely subscribed podcast, serves as a teaching tool in secondary school poetry units (she has joined six episodes)—and finally ModPo as a version of English 88 synthesizing the collaborative practices of *PoemTalk* and the welcoming of nonacademics at *Jacket2* and the public-facing social ethos of the Writers House—has helped guide Gallagher, she explains, toward the possibilities of a career as poet, teacher, and advocate of public university education. It's a career that has entailed a series of efforts at "anti-hierarchical organizing" and developing "processes of community building" that, despite the constrained resources of her institution, a college within the public CUNY system, enable "the dialogues that happen casually and off-the-cuff on your own time and are where the real learning happens." Their recursive operationalities open up any one of those linked projects—we will add PennSound in this conjunction of ventures—to the innovative elements of any one of them. For Gallagher, this kind of intellectual and pedagogical crossover is also a practical matter in dealing with the odds stacked against individualized education. We saw in the introduction how and why she leveraged funding to "incorporate technology *in any way* into teaching" for the sake of an intensely personal ten-person cohort operating inside a behemoth 45,000-person xMOOC beamed from a 28,000-student campus to a university system of 275,000.[37]

In her description of ModPo, Wai Chee Dimock notes that it is "the most controversial among Kelly Writers House's experiments," yet it "offers a reconciliation of sorts, bracketing . . . seemingly antithetical positions"—conscious curation of poems on the one hand, inconceivably wide-open enrollment on the other—"by putting poetry itself on the line, hard-pressed by the economics of a tech-driven media ecology."[38] Dimock's assessment of ModPo reflects Joan Retallack's optimism based on the assumption, one that needs testing, that made-place curation and anarchic openness are compatible, and are generative and attractive to learners and to conveners of learning projects in a variety of sites and situations.

THE OPEN DOOR

Andrew Zitcer, one of the founders of the Kelly Writers House and now a tenured professor of architecture, design, and urbanism and director of an urban strategy program, has gone on to think and write regularly about curation, sites of openness, and art as a model for place-based civic action. He has been influenced by Dewey's call for "creative democracy" as relevant to collaborative aesthetics.[39] Looking back three decades later, Zitcer remembers the design process in detail. "It was never a free-for-all," he notes. "There were thoughtful and dedicated teachers and mentors to frame inquiry and encourage experimentation, but W[riters] H[ouse] still had a politics, a standpoint, and a pedagogy. It was not an empty vessel, but a prism through which we could all look and form our own perceptions." Zitcer outlines four founding concepts: (1) curated content, facilitated and encouraged by "curious and caring" guides; (2) "the democratic belief that everyone has a right to poetry" ("or theory or philosophy or what have you"), a stance that encourages a reluctance to "patroniz[e] students as readers and participants by dumbing it down"; (3) the fundamental idea that writing is not just for writers; that "the House" was for "everyone possessing curiosity and open to experiencing its space"; and (4) the building and maintaining of "a home, a third place, in which to express these ideas . . . rooted in a physical context but open to the world." Elaborating on this last point: it must have "open doors and online portals."[40]

As it turned out, the sturdy old front door that Zitcer and the other founders conceptualized as being "open," featured a nonfunctioning lock. The door simply would not close. It no longer fit the frame. The portal was too historically significant to be quickly replaced, I recall, and despite the university's wealth, the nascent project had no earmarked capital budget, so we lacked the funds to repair it—*and* perhaps it's just as accurate to say that we chose not to tell our colleagues in facilities or security that anyone could walk into the house at any time. While the architects who coordinated the renovation of the house in 1996–1997, Harris Steinberg and Jane Stevens Steinberg, were of course able to plan the suitable replacement of that main door, they helped us celebrate the metaphor of a broken but open entry. They helped us suppress the tendency in research university design standards toward interior partitions and passages that might tend to isolate or shut off some of the discourse spaces, especially those rooms designed for learning and collaborative creation. Somewhere between the stated intentions of the original mid-nineteenth-century architect, Samuel Sloan, and the many hours in which the Steinbergs just listened to the spatial experiences of the writers and artists and other intellectual allies who were already habitués of the cottage, the renovation's complete upgrades (including technological ones) were both visible and invisible, so that "open doors and online portals" became key converged features of design, use, literary value, digitality, and populist impulse.

The house at 3805 Locust Street had been designed by the prominent architect Samuel Sloan (1815–1884). It was completed in 1851, just before the publication of his influential book *The Model Architect* (1852). The book and the house (and several others like it, though they no longer exist) expressed what amounts to an immodest anti-Victorianism: more than a touch of Gothic, with throw-back elements of Tudor style (later a fad in eastern U.S. residential design), a spirit of retreat from burly positivist commerce minus the usual reactionary aspects those counterstyles often convey. The hint also of affordable, not grand, proto-suburban Italianate villa, an idea that spread across middle-class West

FIGURE 1.1 "English Gothic Style" (sketch).

Source: In Samuel Sloan, *The Model Architect*, vol. 1 (E. S. Jones & Co., 1852), opp. p. 20.

Philadelphia—with its elements of low-pitched roofs, round-head windows, and overhanging eaves—suggested accessible intimacy and admitted plentiful light while providing exterior shade.[41] Sloan held the view that pure Gothic, while "admirably fitted for ecclesiastical purposes," was not good for much else. The home at 3805 Locust was part of Sloan's post-Gothic intervention, shorn of some of the style's long vertical lines, a flattening of the arc of its doorway arches (making entry a gesture less grand), supplemented by the overall irregularity of its outline. He wrote of "the flexibility of its principles"; an openness to lived mixes of urban, ex-urban, and "rural character";[42] and ideas of domestic life that were not to be predicted or foreclosed by top-down planning.

From the start, the house itself provided a metaphor for our new intentions, especially insofar as they sought to recollect outmoded educational intimacies and nonmonumentalities on a campus of glass-and-steel high-rises and global ambitions to match at a time of gargantuan new academic ventures as long-range planning headed toward the millennium. The late Robert Lucid, leader of a venture called The 21st-Century Project headquartered in the provost's office, was a prominent full professor with a wide anarchist streak. Exactly a decade earlier,

FIGURE 1.2 Photograph of 3805 Locust Street, Philadelphia, c. 1907.

Source: University of Pennsylvania Archives. Photographer unknown.

he had recruited me to the university, and he now led the founding group toward the then-vacant house (and eventually handed the keys to me)—he knew everything about hacking inexorable university space-planning processes and was thrilled to teach the semisecret skill. On Sunday, October 15, 1995, Lucid joined the first meeting, a day-long affair that had to be augmented by lit candles as dusk fell since the electric service had been shut off. He looked around the space, listened to our ecstatic programmatic blueprinting, and offered this succinct advice, a classic among his many expressions of academic Zen: "Architecture is destiny." Living up to his name, Lucid meant it to convey wisdom about collegiate planning particularly, but Zitcer, among others, has learned in the decades since to generalize from the experience far beyond tertiary education. It's his entire intellectual project in sum. Learning much later of Gallagher's project to engage ModPo and the Writers House as a supplement to her own students' experiences, Zitcer was prompted to remember the following about the original planning efforts prior to the opening of a house for writers in Sloan's cozy urban villa, now situated among and well below three sun-blocking, unvariegated, twenty-four-story student residences: "Intimacy, vulnerability, connection, and time/space for inquiry are under threat across society and in universities," Zitcer recalls. "These are the qualities we most need to foster human development and they are a collective practice of freedom and democratic citizenship." In the introduction to *Democracy as Creative Practice* (2025), Zitcer stresses the productive association with aesthetic culture—the connection between "artists as practitioners (and teachers) of democracy" and the useful common understanding of democracy "in *procedural* terms."[43] Studying art and democracy together, he describes "an ongoing relational process" between the two.[44] As democracy is a method, so is the interpretation of creative expression.

Harris Steinberg's architectural career in Philadelphia has been devoted to the interactive processes of inclusive civic planning. He has worked on the project to "pedestrianize" the Benjamin Franklin Parkway, taking actions to support the actual practices of actual pedestrians. He founded an institute (with which Zitcer became affiliated) "to forge innovative strategies to equitably advance cities," and he has taught Philadelphia architects and planners how to listen during site and space planning sessions. He believes in the principle of "planning to stay," and this attitude befit the idealistic literary synthesists who dreamed of integrating the sights and sounds of poetry into plans for the open house. "We must learn," the urban planners who wrote *Planning to Stay* recommend, "the 'visual rhythm' of open spaces, houses, churches, public buildings."[45] A few years before Steinberg started work on the Writers House, he had envisioned a row of urban homes, each serving a use without which the others could not remain as livable entities. Sketched by hand in this early ideational vision, ours turned out to be the "House of the Book." The drawing is framed and hangs prominently in the Writers House to this day. It reminds us that if just one house in the row is the house for writers and their works, the entire row might be opened up: the visual rhythm of built proximity becomes generative intimacy. Zitcer puts it this way:

> It is long established in the field I have come to occupy (arts-based community development) that arts and artists build community across difference. Some topics are just too hard to tackle through direct means—we have our guard up; we are fearful and angry; we don't have the civic muscle. But that scaffolding of arts and culture . . . can make us open up. When we eat together and share foodways; when we dance together, however awkwardly; when we feel the pulse of music even when the genre is unfamiliar to us; and in the case of WH, when we engage in a democratic, collaborative, egalitarian, close reading of a poem—judgment and the need to be "right" fall away and a real civics is born.

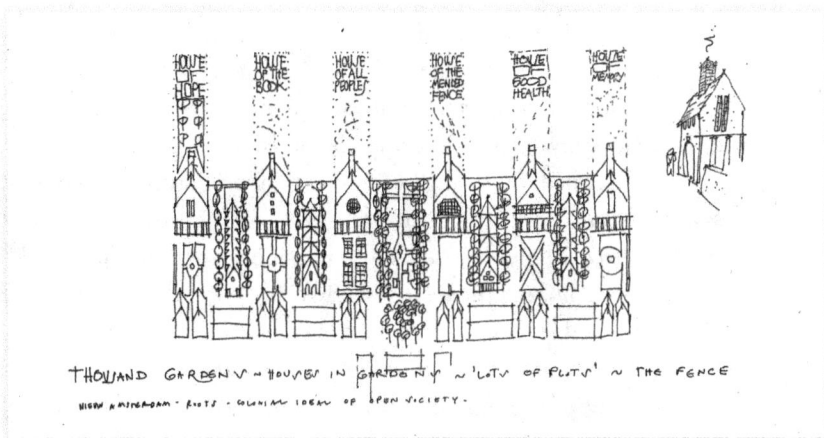

FIGURE 1.3 "Thousand Gardens | Houses in Gardens . . . | Colonial Ideal of Open Society," sketch by Harris Steinberg and Jane Stevens Steinberg, 1993.

Source: Reprinted with permission of Harris Steinberg.

"Having itself ventured into unchartered territory," to quote Dimock again, "the house looks for the same risk-taking spirit of the poets it showcases"—a sentiment Zitcer, Lucid, and the Steinbergs echo for the spirit of people who plan to inhabit the space. Zitcer argues that the open wired portal through which ModPo crossed years after the founding efforts of planning had occurred was inherent in the initial conception. So even if it's true that "the space is everything"—if "there is a poetics of space and place [and] WH embodied that from its first moments. The green couch. The clawfoot tub. The nooks and hiding places. The kitchen! The garden"—then the question becomes how does its spatiality get extended and sustained beyond it?[46]

This is Dimock's main question in her *PMLA* essay, "Education Populism." She discerns an aspirational democratic motive. "Starting out at an elite university but not bound by it, this . . . populism proceeds not by building walls and banning out-groups," she writes, "but by insisting that no walls are necessary, that everyone is 'in.'" Here and there, to be sure, that openness must be challenged. "To my mind," Dimock writes, "the populism of the Kelly Writers House is tested by one of its own programs: PennSound."[47] Technically, PennSound—the archive of poetry recordings designed and codirected by poet Charles Bernstein, Michael Hennessey, Chris Mustazza (a sound studies scholar and professional technologist), and me—is "broadly accessible," but poetically its selections are "decidedly nonneutral." For "nonneutral" read: aesthetically partisan. If these qualities, open and partisan, can coexist, then it's true once again that the very structure of the space hosting these populist projects, a throw-back house with "a politics, a standpoint, and a pedagogy," must convey the "risk-taking spirit" of its poets. That is to say, a *certain* sort of poetics rebuilds the built environment rather than the other way around. Poetic destiny is an architecture. It was ModPo's partisan curation that Dimock also described, following her summary of criticisms of selectivity. That is to say, it is *ModPo* as well as PennSound that is "a meticulously planned and nonneutral way to teach poetry, 'with an emphasis on experimental verse.' "[48]

ModPo, PennSound, *Jacket2*, the roster of writers presenting in the Arts Café at the Writers House, and let's now add the over two hundred monthly episodes of the *PoemTalk* podcast (most episodes become integrated into the ModPo syllabus) are all curatorially nonneutral. But in the realms of access and distribution, they are operationally indiscriminate. Can that distinction hold? What happens when these qualities are reconciled? Michael Nardone, a poet and scholar of sound archives, argues that the tenets and strictures of poetic ideology assert themselves less profoundly in the structure and home of the digital archive than does the idea of widely disseminating the sound files. "One of the site's core credos is, after all, 'Make it free,' " writes Nardone, "adapting Ezra Pound's modernist dictum to 'Make it new' so as to apply to poetry and poetics in an era of digital networks." And "free" does not only refer to wide, easy, low-barrier diffusion. It also signals an open agnosticism about the ways and spaces in which inclusion and even production can happen. An "important aspect of [PennSound's] impact is its commitment to exploring and expanding the many spaces of production and use that inform the site's interface."[49]

Nardone argues that PennSound as a digital site enables both local and remote "interface" and augments the Writers House as a public space and its noncurricular methods of teaching, learning, conversing, planning, performing, and project-making. "Here," he continues, "interface defines both a technical object and shared boundary between electronic media and human users, as well as a zone of activity, of processes that transform the material states of media. In [Charles] Bernstein and Filreis's attention to these components of PennSound's interface—as a technical object and its effects—they have developed a unique model of pedagogical exchange concerning poetry and poetics, one that Filreis describes as 'our format.' "

REJECTIONS OF CLOSURE

Michael Nardone was researching protocols for archiving analog and digital sound files. This work led him to report in detail on his visit to the Writers

House in Philadelphia. He traveled from an extremely isolated location, some hours distant from the remote town of Yellow Knife in Canada's Northwest Territories. Having arrived at the Writers House, he found himself obliged to depict the live interactive webcast he witnessed in person after previously participating from Montreal and the Canadian wilderness. He could see and hear people dialing in by telephone—a "POTS" line, also known as Plain Old Telephone Service!—to offer comments vocally and pose questions to discussion leaders, others in the in-person audience, and those also joining remotely. Nardone's essay explains the convivial social life of the kitchen in the back of the first floor of the old house. He conveys the ardent focus of the young literary learners who are denizens of the space and involve themselves in "the *making things public* aspect of publication." The recording studio, still farther back on the first floor, presumably his visit's main objective, seems in the end to have been the least of it. Nardone decided that the eccentric space, all told, was a "subject village." He had been taught the term by poet-programmer Loss Pequeño Glazier, who used it to describe web-based interactivity achieved through the "peer-to-peer or many-to-many model."[50] "Our format" is generally—not just digitally—interlocutory. Nardone meant, in particular, the give and take between myself, Bernstein, Mustazza, and others as we were creating PennSound.

The ambiguous phrase "our format" is in the title of the essay Nardone wrote about digital archiving, but it's not just a reference to PennSound's proud choice of MP3 over RealAudio, .au, .aiff, or professional archivists' preferred .wav as file type. Nor even is format a matter of filename conventions or standards for our wide array of recording devices. "Our format," rather, is a contingent theory of the digital archive as an incremental, connectivistic, self-learning set of activities. In an interview, Bernstein told Nardone that a key planning "conception of PennSound is . . . that [we] will learn how to archive the materials better through the production of materials for it." Or again: "By making new audio materials, we will better understand how to do *everything else*."[51] What constitutes this "everything else"? At its heart, this method borrows from experiments in tertiary education of the 1960s and early 1970s. In the gathering of materials for the book *Five Experimental Colleges* (1973), for instance, one finds a description of the ethos as identified for one of those schools: "This is a program-in-emergence at any moment."[52] An emergent program built upon building, a curatorial plane being built while it is flown, PennSound continues to be a cumulative digital space, making available by the time of this writing more than seventy-five thousand once-rare and/or once-inaccessible poetry recordings not just for streaming but also for downloading and redistributing. So it turned out that Bernstein's "everything else" was Nardone's topic. The subject village has its important "technical protocols," to be sure, but it is fundamentally defined by, in Nardone's terms, the "social protocols." At the end of his article, he describes a digital archive qua connectivist third space:

> PennSound sets an important precedent for humanities computing projects in an era of media laboratories, online education, unprecedented funding for digital innovation [alas, PennSound has received none of those dollars], and the uncertain viability of past platforms into the future. The social protocols that combine collaborative production with online and off-line participation support the cultivation of the technical interface among various communities of practice; the technical protocols geared toward access, dissemination, and use support the possibility of that social interface to expand beyond a main hub of production to new spaces of engagement.[53]

Earlier I quoted connectivist co-originator George Siemens ("Chaos is the new reality for knowledge workers") and suggested that it cannot be a surprise—but I wonder if it is a welcome surprise—when role opacity is extended to both teachers and learners in the act of creating a networked education. Returning to that conjecture, let's again replace "teachers and learners" with "poets and readers" and observe what happens as we extend the PennSound experience outward to other public-facing modes. If the poet does indeed welcome role opacity, and if in an open text writes or records toward the social life of its reception by readers as citizens of an interpretive community, then topically "everything else" I am writing about in this first group of chapters pertains to cultural matters well beyond the realm of techno-progressives and advocates of collective intelligence and the digital commons. Certainly, Siemens sought such wide relevance for his manifesto-like statement, "Connectivism: A Learning Theory for the Digital Age" (2005), as did Pierre Lévy in *Collective Intelligence* (1994, translated into English in 1997). Written to encourage institutional and social change, these ideas map well onto the poetics of many of the people gathered together for ModPo, their poems represented in syllabi or, in some cases, presence in live streamed and filmed discussions. Ron Silliman is a typical example: his writing can be found as text and audio in the syllabus so that his poems can be widely discussed; he's also in videos that document his various visits (some impromptu) to live webcasts and his ventures into the Kelly Writers House studio for unrehearsed interactions with teachers and learners about the poems of other poets. He can be variously seen and heard making his persistent, contentious claim that human contact happens in poetry *only* because of the writer-reader connection. "In poetry," he argues, "the self is a relation between writer and reader that is triggered by what [linguist Roman] Jakobson called contact, the power of presence.

There is no subject that is not, strictly speaking, intersubjective."[54] Framing it differently via theories of speech acts, Tracie Morris, a ModPo and PennSound poet who has taught at the Writers House, makes essentially the same case for performer/witness axiality; Morris appears variously, to date, in twenty-nine videos, her work discussed in an additional thirty-one. (We will return later to Morris in the context of the live poetry reading.)

Or, to take another example, that of Silliman's Bay Area Language colleague Hejinian, once a Kelly Writers House Fellow whose ideas presented in her prein-ternet essay "The Rejection of Closure" (1985) are fundamental to the open-text poetics of ModPo. For our purposes, Lévy's digital theorizing and Hejinian's Lan-guage writing make for a fortunate pairing. Here is Lévy in *Collective Intelligence*:

> The emerging techno-cultural environment, however, will encourage the devel-opment of new kinds of art, ignoring the separation between transmission and reception, composition and interpretation. . . . Our primary goal should be to prevent closure from occurring too quickly, before the possible has an opportu-nity to deploy the variety of its richness. . . .
>
> Rather than distribute a message to recipients who are outside the process of creation and invited to give meaning to a work of art belatedly, the artist now attempts to construct an environment, a system of communication and produc-tion, a collective event that implies its recipients, transforms interpreters into actors.[55]

And here is Hejinian in "The Rejection of Closure":

> The "open text," by definition, is open to the world and particularly to the reader. It invites participation, rejects the authority of the writer over the reader and thus, by analogy, the authority implicit in other (social, economic, cultural) hierarchies. It speaks for writing that is generative rather than directive. The writer relinquishes total control and challenges authority as a principle and con-trol as a motive. The "open text" often emphasizes or foregrounds process, either the process of the original composition or of subsequent compositions by read-ers, and thus resists the cultural tendencies that seek to identify and fix material and turn it into a product. . . .
>
> Whether the form is dictated by temporal constraints or by other exoskeletal formal elements . . . the work gives the impression that it begins and ends arbi-trarily and not because there is a necessary point of origin or terminus, a first or last moment. The implication (correct) is that the words and ideas (thoughts, perceptions, etc.—the materials) continue beyond the work.[56]

The idea of meaning developed in "The Rejection of Closure" is not only soft-wired across the content but also in the very structure of ModPo: "Writing develops subjects that mean the words we have for them."[57] "The Rejection of Closure" imagines and theorizes coconstitutive meaning-making. *My Life* is an instance of it, an experiment in writing constraint-based nonnarrative (nonsequential and unchronological) antimemoir. We discuss the poem in week 8 (of 10) in the course. Participants variously appreciate its refusal of the authority of writer over reader, its "generative rather than directive" writing. They take up the challenge by reading it as a metatext for the progressions of their *own* discussions—their very right to openly discuss what it means. In it, they begin to see themselves as part of a "collective autobiography." For long-time ModPo participant Thea Terpstra, the poem "delivers both a private/singular and public/communal 'commentary,'" and she comprehends her own written response, in a thread she titled "What's Mine Is Yours"—and the reactions of her ModPo colleagues as they respond in the same subforum to a writer democratically "relinquish[ing] total control"—as belonging to "the murky intersubjective space they cohabit." This then leads Thea to comment on "the social/political/historical" significance of *My Life* and the challenge to authority.[58]

Fellow learner Edward Kranz, making a similar point, quotes a central idea of reader-response theory and in doing so makes certain to insert that the ModPo people are themselves, right there in an extended forum discussion, the interpretive community that Hejinian's writing argues is needed for the text to make any sense. "It is the act of interpretation," Edward writes, "by an interpretive community {*that's us*} that creates any text."[59] He reads "us" as presence in the poetic text and the accompanying asynchronous forum: *that's us*. That *is* us indeed, a continuous present tense that you can feel even when coming upon his comment years after the fact. Elaine Eppler finds her encounter with *My Life* in ModPo to be an encouragement of "trust" extended from writer to reader as from teachers to learners. "We can piece the parts together and create meaning. To think of a poet inviting the reader to do this is so moving. It requires trust. I'll humbly say 'yes' to this project," whereupon Elaine's subsequent comments, in the forums for weeks 8, 9, and 10, aspire to a new level of energy and insistence.[60] ModPo people have tended to read the collaborative experience of encountering *My Life* as, in Lévy's words, "a collective event that implies its recipients, transforms interpreters into actors." For Kristen Gallagher, this was exactly the value of inviting her students into the course community. They became aware of themselves as actors in a drama of crowd interpreting. "They watched the videos but the videos weren't the main drag," she recalled for me. "They really liked the forums, engaging with people beyond their world. I think that for them it really felt like an actual nonhierarchical situation."[61]

Some ModPo participants are explicit about the democratic implications of the convergence of the open format and the writing. "I too have had my challenges with the Language poets," writes Linda Ireland, "and continue to do so, but I do love how they ask work of me, invite me to be a democratic participant and open me up to new ways of thinking (at the core of why I keep coming back to ModPo)."[62] Elaine Eppler likens the democratic text to a symphony, the variations of which she was able to hear in the forums. Responding to another's affirmation of an earlier comment she had made, she wrote: "Yes, if we think of this poem as a symphony and actively, closely, with open ears and mind, listen for the musical themes and movements, we can piece the parts together." Lévy anticipated this quality in *Collective Intelligence*: "Cyberspace could harbor mechanisms of speech capable of producing living political symphonies, which would enable human communities to continuously invent and express complex utterances, open up the range of singularity and divergence without the need for pre-constrained forms of participation. Real-time democracy tries to construct the richest collective voice possible."[63] When the cohort of LaGuardia Community College students led by Gallagher and two of her colleagues visited the Writers House in person at the end of their ModPo semester, they gathered with the ModPo team for an in-the-round discussion of the whole experience. Reviewing a recording of it years later, I understood that they were much less interested in the prerecorded video close readings than in the democratic feel of the forums. A decade later, Gallagher too remembered the forums as welcoming the students with its agnosticism about the relative value of high and low talk: "We're all capable of talking to each other. Everyone has something to lend to the conversation and we're weaving in . . . high-minded stuff and pop-cultural stuff and telling personal stories. It all just weaves together, so for my students being in the ModPo forums, just talking to people in that way, is a flattening out of the power dynamics. You're just learning through conversing. It was really confidence-building. You're just another person having experiences and sharing them. You're being heard and responded to."[64]

WE SAY THIS, WE SAY THAT

What sort of a relation is there then between a work like *My Life* that defies conventional in-order explanations of our lives and the opening up of "the range of singularity and divergence" in the disordered online conversing? The democratic action some ModPo participants explicitly seek is the making and sustaining of Thea Terpstra's "intersubjective space," notwithstanding its chatty chaos and eccentric dimensions. Mary Hannahan, who described herself as a "57-year old pharmacist and mother of 3 sons and 1 daughter," living in Ashland, Kentucky, a product of "12 years of Catholic education," observed: "It . . . feels like we, the class, are helping to define MOOC[s] for the humanities. . . . Distance learning, global learning, whatever the future brings, I want to do my small part in shaping it. . . . Th[is] experience formed my idea that learning poetry in particular is democratic."[65] Kimberly McGee was "disappointed" by "the lack of self-control and topic control in the forums," although "torn on the issue of [who should] control it." Still, "everyone should have access to this level of interaction," she urged. "What they take away is their responsibility. That is the underlying truth of democracy. Perhaps also why the open discussions work and don't work at the same time."[66]

The subject village simultaneously works and doesn't work, but it's not self-canceling. Participants constructively reckon with their right of access to a conversation moving widely and sometimes rapidly across styles, tones, rhetorics, attitudes, and political points of view. Everything freely shared always means at least *something* and assumes responsibility for what's said, even by others. Is this why so many participants mention citizenship and democracy? It rarely strikes me as loose talk, and I have observed that references such as to an "underlying truth of democracy" have spiked in 2012, 2016, 2020, and 2024. Perhaps this is merely because such talk is ambient in those years. Then again, perhaps iterative collaborative interpretation seems more important to these citizens when those who interpret untruthfully in public, if challenged, say they just didn't mean what we took them to mean. Learners often describe the work of emerging together with agreed-upon dissensus that by its special social form resists the "I didn't mean anything" defense. They suggest that active interpretation in a continuous present tends to counteract the situation Claudia Rankine describes as "the fiction of the facts." "The fiction of the facts assumes innocence, ignorance, lack of attention, misdirection," writes Rankine in her poem *Citizen: An American Lyric*. These are "the necessary conditions of a certain time and place."[67] Here is how Laura Lippman, an award-winning writer of detective novels and a long-time ModPo regular, describes in an interview the modest efforts made by people to reverse this misdirection: "ModPo is that rare space where everyone can be 'correct' if they're willing to make the argument for their reading/interpretation. Where one person's rightness doesn't vanquish another person's rightness. What if we could all be right together? . . . In so many aspects of life, people do not lack for certainty. It's kind of amazing how fixed opinions are about very subjective things, and how the subsequent 'debate' tends to be about doubling, tripling down—increasing volume and rhetoric, but seldom offering a true argument."[68] Democracy, for Laura, is a creative practice. As we will see in the next chapter, this sensibility was a prominent aspect of the discussions during 2020 in particular.

An interpretive ethics—where one person's rightness doesn't vanquish another person's rightness—appeals to José Reyes, a poet, teacher, and secondary school administrator who has strived with his colleagues to create democratic learning in public school classrooms. When interviewed by Amaris Cuchanski (one of the founding TAs) in 2013, he was asked how he first came to ModPo. He recalled reading some of the MOOC hype, probably David Brooks's 2012 column "The Campus Tsunami."[69] In response he "decided to enroll because I wanted to . . . carve out a space for poetry in my life. This may seem odd, since I'm a high school English teacher, but for various reasons, poetry is marginalized in high school—at least poetry as language."

José Edmundo Ocampo Reyes was born and came of age in the Philippines, where he graduated with a B.S. in management engineering from Ateneo de Manila University, then spent five years working in finance in Manila and Hong Kong, and eventually moved to the United States. Since 2002, he has taught secondary-school English, and more recently, as department chair and administrator, has led a team of forty-five to fifty teachers. His poems have appeared in various Philippine and U.S. journals and have been anthologized in *The Powow River Anthology, No Tender Fences: An Anthology of Immigrant and First-Generation American Poetry*, and elsewhere. His book of verse, *Present Values* (2018), won the Jean Pedrick Chapbook Award. He has been involved with ModPo since 2012 and, as of this writing, continues to be affiliated each year as a Community TA. I have interacted with him asynchronously many times, spoken with him by phone during weekly live webcasts, and met him in person once, in 2019, at a ModPo meet-up in Brookline, Massachusetts, where he joined a group of twenty-three people, none of whom had met each other in person previously. That evening, we filmed an unrehearsed collaborative close reading of two poems by Larry Eigner.[70] One of the poems particularly intrigued Reyes. It seems to be about how we are to interpret what we see in a poem that is about seeing outward from the place where it has been composed. You can get all that sometimes from a short poem by Eigner. He wrote just this:

```
a structured field is
    the mind
     light
    and the view
        with whatever eyes.[71]
```

As I facilitated the close reading, I saw from his expression that Reyes was intrigued. So I suddenly turned to him and asked if he would describe the language of the last line for the group. I had assumed that "eyes" would be read here as a noun, leaving "whatever" thus to serve as some sort of modifier, maybe suggesting a tone of indifferent or unfocused vision. *Whatever!* But Reyes was struck by the importance of the ambiguity of the speaker's point of view. He offered his reading of "whatever" as a *pronoun* and of "eyes" as a *verb*. I was surprised. He was emphasizing that the poem is seen with eyes "depending on your view" of the grammar of vision—"your" in his phrase indicating Reyes's and readers' views as we reckon together what structures Eigner is and is not able to make as a poet who often refers indirectly during composition to his restricted physical mobility.

During his years working in the finance sector, José Reyes recalls, "I was pretty much on my own, reading and writing whenever I could." Then came teaching. Then ModPo. "The course has shattered my expectations," he told Amaris Cuchanski after the second season. "I simply expected Al to lecture us onscreen,

FIGURE 1.4 Still from ModPoPLUS video, filmed by Zach Carduner and Chris Martin, October 12, 2019, Brookline, MA.

Source: Kelly Writers House video archive.

assign us a few poems to read, a paper here and there that I would bang out just to get it done, and that would be that. . . . What I did not expect was the level of interaction, both in the videos and on the forums." He especially appreciated the lively asynchronous conversations taking place in the poem-specific subforums. By then already a believer in "a student-centered environment . . . something I've tried to create in my own teaching," he encountered anti-MOOC moral panic—as explained (though only partly endorsed) by David Brooks—and it led the teacher-poet toward explorations of "real-time democracy" online. "Many of us view the coming change with trepidation," Brooks wrote in the *New York Times* of the impending MOOC tsunami. "Will online learning diminish the face-to-face community that is the heart of the college experience? Will it elevate functional courses in business and marginalize subjects that are harder to digest in an online format, like philosophy? Will fast online browsing replace deep reading?"[72] "Online courses make the transmission of information a commodity," Brooks complained in another column, "The Big University."[73] MOOCs could well be related to the general phenomenon of "captology" that Brooks has denounced as an effect of the amplification through social media of rampant fears of missing out. Phone addiction, he argued, for instance, in a commentary titled "Intimacy for the Avoidant," was leading to a paucity of deep friendships.[74] Yet José Reyes came to ModPo for deep reading and was then surprised by a bonus: the critical importance of the goal of "social relations"—of friendship. "I believe that the democratic, open-ended, we-say-this-we-say-that, crowdsourced form of the course," he wrote, "has made me excited about poetry again and allowed me to learn more with others than I thought was possible."[75]

By "social relations," José Reyes means something much like what Michael Nardone discerns as "social protocols." And it's the opposite of Brooks's sense of detrimental "social multitasking"[76]—inscribed in Brooks's anxieties about the too-rapid dispersal of personal energy. Both Nardone's and Reyes's usages refer to those *loose ties* which, in Nardone's words, "support the cultivation of the technical interface among various communities of practice." The teacher learns to view a democracy of learning through poetics as "we-say-this-we-say-that" asynchronicity. "Computer-mediated pedagogy," writes Mara Holt in her book *Collaborative Learning as Democratic Practice* "clearly favors social relations, amplifying their importance."[77] If Kimberly McGee found herself somewhat disheartened by "the lack of self-control and topic control in the forums," it turned out that that very feeling, the feeling of being "torn on the issue of [who should] control it," was what reinforced her sense that she was witnessing participatory democratic action—that "everyone should have access to this level of interaction" and that nothing less than "social responsibility" would derive from it. This was, in fact, what David Brooks has been advocating in columns and books. In the rush of 2012, Brooks could perhaps be forgiven for having missed this sense of responsible popular participation in the MOOC. But I cannot get out of my mind the conclusion drawn about the busy forums by Mary, our Kentucky pharmacist: "That is the underlying truth of democracy." And what is "that"? It is the absence, or at least the lessening, of a final authority. In open online discussions, Mara Holt observes, "teacher authority is easy to lose, difficult to maintain—clearly the opposite of the situation in previous collaborative pedagogies." Authority "is a reciprocal relationship among, not between, students and teacher." Finally then, for Holt, there's a special role opacity: *teacher* and *student* "begin . . . to seem like unhelpful categories."[78] A doctoral student, conducting research inside ModPo to learn how to teach poetry, wrote up a detailed report on a ninety-minute live-streamed webcast and surprised herself by observing the following: "The participants have, in a sense, become their own favorite teacher."[79]

Certainly, Reyes's response to entering the amorphous, unmappable ModPo chat space was that, after all his experience teaching in face-to-face (F2F) classrooms, he was now learning how to be teacher and student at once. Holt's book chronicles experiments in collaborative learning—its subtitle is "A History"— and the key story there is the development of preinternet feminist pedagogy out of the modern epoch of learner-centered learning. As Holt progresses from a chapter on feminist teaching to another on computer-mediated collaboration, she summarizes the research of Carol Winkelmann, who studied what happened when collaborative online composition was defined as the collective "product and process" of an entire class of students together, all at once, learning to write. One result, Winkelmann observed, was "that electronic literacy is rooted in collaborative work that is anarchic, nonhierarchical, and transformative," following from and extending (Holt contends) experiments in reformist techniques applied to the in-person classroom.[80] "The interplay of human and technological factors in the classroom leads to a reaffirmation of literacy as a social process," Winkelmann argues. "The radical democratization and multivocality of the . . . collaboratively written text demands a critical problematizing of our roles and actions as teacher-readers."[81]

Another result from Winkelmann's research aligns with what many ModPo people say they experience, as learners learning together, during their encounter with Hejinian's and other poets' rejections of closure: a sense "that the resulting text will break the conventions of linear, academic texts."[82] This "break" is productive at the level of the paragraph and even of the sentence or of the verse line. The antisequential, paratactic "New Sentence" of *My Life* and other texts of its sort,[83] when presented by what might be called a New Sentence-informed pedagogy, causes something of a hallucination of rightness beyond the justification of the group's prior preparation or expected level of knowledge. In drawing this analogy here, I've warily used the term *hallucination* as akin to the disconcertingly confident "not correct," unjustified, or erring responses sometimes offered by large-language models (LLMs) that seem not to be warranted by their training.[84] Is ModPo a human poetic LLM? Hardly. Yet that something might feel *wrong* perhaps inheres in the structure. At least in learner David Blaine's experience, participating in the ModPo forum "was like taking a class where you were allowed to talk to the other students while the teacher lectured. It actually felt wrong at first."[85] Kimberly McGee, like David and others, felt it apt to worry, as noted earlier, about "the lack of self-control and topic control" while at the same time sensing that the asynchronous phantasmagoria of all these threads—made hybrid through modal mixes of live webcasts, in-person and remote meet-ups, and ecstatic unpredictable social-intellectual concatenations—might lead to new knowledge that is cumulative, shareable, and even scalable through mass amateurization, with every one of the pluses and minuses of immersive "reply all"-style discussion: perhaps interpretively wrong-headed in any given conversationally chaotic moment dealing with any given poem, but on the whole, ultimately, neither misleading nor unearned or unfair. "It is as fatal to good thinking," writes Dewey in *How We Think*, "to fail to make conscious the standing source of some error or failure as it is to pry needlessly into what works smoothly. . . . To exclude the novel for the sake of prompt skill, to avoid obstacles for the sake of averting errors, is as detrimental as to try to get [learners] to formulate everything they know."[86]

CONCLUSION: AGAINST DIGITAL MINIMALISM

Cal Newport has written *Digital Minimalism: Choosing a Focused Life in a Noisy World* (2019). Newport's title alone might already indicate that I take an opposing view. More about that opposition is ahead. In the second part of this book, "The Sound of the End of the Lecture," I turn to the choices people make in favor of that "noisy world" as a means of encouraging humane attentiveness, caring, close listening, and active learning.

There are many books of Newport's sort, advocating various practices of "digital decluttering."[87] He is hardly alone in claiming that our digital lives inherently lead to "ceding more and more of their autonomy."[88] He and others calling for full or partial unplugging, replacing smartphones with dumb phones, for instance, are not wrong about some aspects of information overload. Nor are they misguided, of course, about the pernicious effects of social media. But by advocating disconnection as healthful, let's not exclude the notion that something like the platform technologies enabling ModPo is, indeed, to be reckoned as part of a social media landscape. The participants we have encountered in the first two chapters are right to think of ModPo as a social medium. And they are correct in assessing what happens to a poem there as something akin to virality. They don't mind rescuing the concept of a medium for online sociality from its ubiquitous derogatory connotations. Conversations that would ideally take place in a room, in person, but cannot, between and among people who cannot otherwise connect and cannot elsewhere work playfully together on ideas, are nonetheless a crucial part of living a focused life. I'm a digital maximalist. I'm wary of digital decluttering. To declutter ModPo—or PennSound—would mean losing the surfeit, the subjective cascade, the digression-encouraging overabundance that is not only vital to a community's full functioning but, as a bonus, is the quality of the art that gives the site its rationale for being.

I'm probably overstating a case against a well-intentioned correction. Yet consider the following summaries of the various arguments implicitly against digital minimalism I've made in this chapter.

Rejections of closure open out to a spreading maximum of methods, disordered, scattered, untried, and agnostic as to discipline or category. Roles and positions in the world of contemporary learning—student, reader, author, speaker, learner, listener, programmer, convener—become more opaque, less simply legible.

The act of reading writing like Larry Eigner's, by becoming "open . . . on all sides," like the poem itself, can transport you everywhere. That kind of reading accommodates broad and even contradictory viewpoints, making a social insight out of supposedly lonely and limited repetitive gestures.

John Dewey, an Eigner for education, is against any exclusions in schools made for the sake of avoiding wrong-headed digressions. Learning, like ideal reading, is trying everything, even at the risk of our seeming to become (in Newport's fearful phrase) "manic information addicts."[89] Some of the ModPo people you've already met—and there are many more to meet—might seem manic, I suppose, in their vast and fast asynchronous assemblies, but one person's frenzy is another's deep focus. A synonym for Emily Dickinson's sense of *dwelling* (in "I dwell in Possibility") is obsession—not so bad when expanded possibility is at issue. Third spaces proliferate definitions of focused human gatherings.

Architectural destiny opens built places to possibilities rather than shutting the door on them, and since there is truly such a thing as a digital architecture—it's vital not just to programming but to open planning—it invents what it creates with permutations of 1s and 0s boundless because of unplanned uses of the machine. Recursive operations blend F2F and digital projects rather than sort them into discrete successes and failures, into preferred versus disfavored spaces.

When a reader's response *is* the meaning of what is being read, it becomes not just impossible but irresponsible to declutter what a text does for that person. Shutting it off doesn't simplify things. Nor even does finishing with it.

So far, I've been asking you to imagine dozens, hundreds, thousands of readers, some careful and persistent, others just passing through, doing all this all at once and over time. Readers who are "meant to meet" what (and whom and with whom) they read: these people make every variation of connection legitimate and real.

CHAPTER 2

POETICS OF PANICGOGY

In memory of Paul Kelly (1939–2020)

History is who *did* what *to* whom,
expressed in nominal *and* verbal groups.
The clause *conveys the meanings we assume.*

—José Edmundo Ocampo Reyes, "Systemic Functional Linguistics"

DESIGNING FOR FATIGUE

José Reyes's poem arose from his efforts to teach teachers how language works as history.[1] It contemplates what David Tyack and Larry Cuban, in their history of a century of school reform, call "the grammar of schooling."[2] The phrase underscores how much alike—how closely connected, not just analogous—discussions of learning and of language are. The grammar of traditional education is elemental and idiomatic and contains invisible structure you have to know. The choices made by "bureaucrats who built at the end of the nineteenth century the American school systems that persists to this day" are deeply ingrained in the way we talk and write about learning.[3] The speaker of Reyes's poem seems to be an educator, a bit on the didactic side—someone who ponders what history does. The teacher conveys, Reyes has explained, "how we learn about such events *through* language and how they will eventually be recounted in history books *using* language."[4] As we are about to delve into the dizzying, volatile politics of asynchronicity, it is apt to first consider that underlying the problem of teaching and the problem of poetry, equally, is the commonly held assumption (to quote this teacher's poem again) that "purpose shapes the grammar" rather than the other way around.

The heterodoxy of this notion, running deeply against typical ideas about the framing rules governing our use of language, cannot be understated. That grammar does not or should not set the protocols constraining what our words mean is an assumption of poetry. It is one of the few things that defines the genre. Most people tolerate such an idea for a *poem* in a way they would likely refuse to do so for a newspaper article or essay. Reyes's poem is a rewriting of the language problem in a way that is similar to the productive writing predicament presented by the poet Eigner as he lived and wrote within "a structured field" of view, using a syntax of history prospectively seen by every one of us "with whatever eyes." Have an aim to make meaning, no matter how idiosyncratic, then find the language rules, even the syntax, for conveying it, and then the aim can change in the act of the writing. The most effective way to teach is to "figur[e] out how to teach content *and* language," as Reyes puts it (with his emphasis).[5]

His poem appeared in the magazine *Rattle* on January 12, 2020. Starting exactly two months later, the teacher-administrator would have no time at all for writing new verse; it was the first day of institutional suspensions and cancellations. Once the pandemic took hold, his days became an extended emergency. During the first fatiguing weeks of remote instruction, one of the teachers in the group he supervised had to take a medical leave, so Reyes stepped in and experienced pandemic classroom teaching first-hand. He guided his team as best he could, using his already significant experience with online learning in ModPo to encourage "adaptive" practices. He noticed that many teachers in the cohort, using platform-specific techniques to support asynchronicity, defaulted to the traditional teacher-gives/students-receive approach. "To use your Freirean terminology," Reyes recalled for me in 2023, "the default mindset in education is the 'I know-you don't' mentality. Using tools like discussion boards and Google Docs but maintaining the banking mindset will not lead to students' engagement. The adaptive piece is the hardest piece to tackle."[6]

And yet, let us just say that the first pandemic semester, spring 2020, was— and, fair warning, this might seem counterintuitive—relatively straightforward. Scramble and go online somehow. The bar was low. Take a "'tools-based' approach." Solace and sympathy abounded, as most people involved with schools had to be just where they were, more or less frenetically, yet situated. Panicgogy was a panic, to be sure, but many major complexities, political and pedagogical, would not fully intrude themselves upon the situation until the fall of 2020 and on into the 2020–2021 winter, as the most challenging forms of "reopening" variously held sway.[7] We'll stay for now with Reyes's Massachusetts, politically mapped with the color blue on most national issues yet red and blue at once on the vexed matter of local community control. Guided by standards hurriedly set by the state-wide Department of Elementary & Secondary Education (DESE), in September 2020 students went back into classrooms but in reduced numbers to ensure physical distancing. Now "teachers had to navigate the hybrid world," Reyes recalled for me, "by having to teach alternating cohorts of face-to-face and asynchronous groups, then teaching face-to-face and at-home students synchronously." Half the students would report to school masked and half would learn asynchronously at home for one week, then the two cohorts would swap the following week. Discussion-based asynchronous learning counted for teachers as proper teaching time since it entailed real pedagogical work. In synchronous Zoom sessions, assumed popularly to be the closer equivalent to the in-school F2F classroom, teachers observed many students muted and with cameras off, whereas asynchronous (email or other DM, chat, text, voicemail, small What'sApp workshop-sized groups, and threaded forum discussion and project-making) could creatively enable individualized attention and support. Teachers could hold lively, productive drop-by "office hours" for individuals in the asynchronous group.

Then, in December 2020, DESE dramatically reversed course and announced a new policy, issuing "Student Learning Time Regulations" and then "Guidance on Amendments to Student Learning Time Regulations." The regulations would go into effect at the restart of school on January 19, 2021. "Districts and schools operating a remote learning model must provide students with access to synchronous instruction each school day," the guidance emphasized. The kind of education being enforced was defined as "learning that is directed by a teacher and that happens in real time with other students, such as during live, whole-class instruction." In response to concerns raised after the initial roll-out of the new policy, the supplemental "Guidance on Amendments" recommended strategies for making the change. Here is one such strategy: "Assign teachers or other staff to facilitate instruction during periods that are currently designated by independent (asynchronous) learning."[8]

"DESE said that asynchronous learning was not learning at all," Reyes summarized for me, "and would not count toward [a teacher's] 'time on learning' metric." Teachers now felt forced to abandon all manner of asynchronous forms of student support, including open-ended office hours, flexible time-to-finish activities, and personal "messaging (asynchronously) with individual care-givers (parents and others)."[9] They now had to teach students in person en masse in the classroom *and* those in that week's at-home group using their laptops' webcams or glitchy Polycom Studios that the school district had hastily purchased and installed. Another suggested strategy for complying with the rules was this: "re-group [students] into *larger* remote classes, creating opportunities to add *more* synchronous class periods."[10]

I asked Reyes about this bias against asynchronous pedagogy. He told me of a video recording of the DESE hearing held to discuss the new rules. I have watched it three times—all three hours and fifty-five minutes of it. It happened on December 15, 2020. I can't quite tell whether it took place during the day or evening. The windows seemed to be covered. Seating was distanced, so camerawork is only spottily edifying; several participants were located remotely. It makes for eerily compelling COVID theater, both bureaucratic and tense. Although the political pressures that caused the state's educational administrators to impose this change were not disclosed during the four hours, the cultural and political subtexts were just below the surface throughout. "If the goal of the new mandates is to improve the intellectual and social well-being of the students," a teacher from the Revere district testified, "this is not achieved by eliminating all those ways in which teachers interact with students and their families." A survey done in Revere found that 80 percent of students and their parents said they received the right amount of asynchronous time; only 7 percent said it was too much. Asynchronous learning is "in part how we serve the social-emotional needs of our students." This assessment conformed with predictions made by respondents to a Pew Research Center survey back in 2012 on the impact of the internet in education—that online teaching "will allow for *more individualized, passion-based learning* by the student" and more rather than fewer social "opportunities to connect to others." The Pew respondents, who had been asked to predict what teaching would be like in the year 2020, offered such views without being able to anticipate pandemic and panicgogy. Nor could they predict the virulent politics of asynchronicity.[11]

Timothy Piwowar, superintendent of the Billerica Public Schools, who had spent his entire celebrated teaching career in that local system—he won the Massachusetts Superintendent of the Year award—stood up at the December 15 meeting and made his case against the new DESE plan in a way that reminded me of what I already knew from eight years working in the world of an interactive online course: "These regulations rely on the faulty assumption that synchronous learning is synonymous with engagement and that the quality of the synchronous learning is the measure of engagement. Nothing could be further from the truth. I have seen talented teachers create exciting activities that are done asynchronously, lessons *that engage the spaces in which the students actually live.* These activities are consistent with our goal of being student-centered and not teacher-centered."[12] The new rules valued poor-quality Zoom and GoogleMeet sessions, Piwowar argued, where many students inevitably turn cameras off and were inattentive, over asynchronous activities where learners complete the work as best they can in their own way at a time that is conducive given their spatial and temporal situations.

Throughout the articles gathered by Melissa Castillo Planas and Deborah Castillo under the title *Scholars in Covid Times* (2023), the contributing writers realize the need to confront cultural aspects of the prejudice against asynchronicity. They considered a range of venues and institutional contexts. One essay, "Pandemic Community Engagement," investigating what happened when a non-curricular nonschool community project for teens quickly moved online, summarized a survey of opinions of participants and their families quite plainly: "A mix of synchronous and asynchronous learning was preferred for virtual implementation." Yet everywhere these researchers turned, they discovered strenuous efforts to delegitimize asynchronous forms as both students and teachers were becoming "cogs in a pandemic-inspired productivity agenda." The scholars described ways that education had become an intense "machine we built," pushing forward motion despite the circumstances.[13]

The machine demanded a traditional sense of learning time and educational productivity. The editors and contributors to *Hybrid Pedagogy* were especially sensitive to this hard push. Since 2011, as MOOCs arose, this journal published critiques of top-down online education, and its editors were among the early advocates of "connected courses," digital accessibility, and learner-centered learning. Its editors issued "Designing for Fatigue," a three-part response to panicgogy urging "slowing down teaching" by adapting for asynchronicity Alison Kafer's and colleagues' concept of "crip time," with its advocacy of a "flexible standard for punctuality," "a flexible approach to normative time frames,"[14] respect for students' and teachers' irregular sense of work and life schedules, "increased time-to-completion of activities," and "bending the clock" rather than trying to bend oneself to meet it.[15]

MISTAKING FASTER FOR DEEPER

Aiden Hunt has long been subjected to the strains caused by that ticking clock. Editor of an online review of poetry chapbooks who came to ModPo after seeking literary colleagues in Goodreads chat boards, he has never fared well in "in-person or live" educational settings. His circumstances—as he identifies them: Tourette's syndrome, chronic headaches, panic attacks—mean "I often miss things because of attention issues or get busy with something else" and thus, "the pressure of a daily schedule just ruins [a class] for me." He adds: "Assignments tend to overwhelm me."[16] His memories of traditional education are more about loss than gain. Ignoring the usual attractions of correcting students' written assignments during 2020–2021 was for some teachers akin to bending the clock. Cecile Sam of Rowan University discovered that one version of pandemic "learning loss" was the idea of learning about—or rather *through*—loss in its several profound senses. "Someone accidentally typed 'remorse-learning' instead of 'remote-learning,'" Sam wrote in the middle of it all, "and I'm tempted not to fix the typo since I find it still works, and in fact may be an improvement."[17] How effective was online learning going to be, Professor Sam wondered by way of her student's meaningful error, if it was disconnected from the lessons of personal regret and sorrow?

Cait Kirby described in "Designing for Fatigue" how she "allowed participants flexibility in choice of the amount of their participation." She found that, far from depressing the quality of the learning overall, it "normalize[d] the idea that work is always in progress" and enabled learners to prioritize their investment so they "always came to class having done *some* reading and with *some* answers in hand."[18] Rather than straying further from the virtues of the traditional F2F seminar, Kirby and her collaborators found that online asynchronous activities *came closer* than "real"-time Zoom or GoogleMeet sessions to replicating those achievements.

And, of course, asynchronicity can stretch time. It offers a wide redefinition of the concept of "class in session" that moves beyond the traditional semester or quarter. The person we know as WareforCoin, who works days as the cashier in a smoke shop and did one poetry lesson per evening when possible, matriculated into ModPo in 2020. In a "victory post" after slowing down the ModPo curriculum in the extreme, they observed that it had been "worth the long struggle against my own brain" and that they would "miss my days of squinting critically at a weird bunch of words on a page." They told me of experiencing "untreated ADHD" and of maintaining a "deep interest in phrases."[19] ModPo for WareforCoin was "my white whale, my friend, my foil, and my on and off again interest. I didn't let the class defeat me." (Now, they add, "I find myself going to thrift stores looking for poetry books," and thus, the learning extends further offline.) All told, it took WareforCoin "4 years to finish this course."[20]

I want to put together what Aiden Hunt and WareforCoin have observed about their rather typical (not eccentric) belatedness of learning and what Cait

Kirby has written about teaching. We begin to consider a rough functional cor-relation: slow teaching + deep reading = deep learning. We mean deep reading as distinct from wide or voluminous. Notwithstanding the positive connections between slowness and depth for many learners, there's the dominant "pedagog-ical fiction," as Jacques Rancière in *The Ignorant Schoolmaster* (1987) noticed it, that "works by representing inequality [among students' performances] in terms of velocity." That fiction enables an ableist "homology of delay," writes Kristin Ross when discussing Rancière's argument: tardiness, backwardness, and delay are punitive judgments made to reassert the truth that "never will the student catch up with the teacher" and thus reinforce the interests of traditional hierar-chical pedagogies.[21] When Jal Mehta and Sarah Fine toured and studied thirty high schools across the United States for their book *In Search of Deeper Learning*, they noticed a prevalent pattern among teachers—"mistaking faster for deeper."[22]

Nicole Braun, a devoted teacher of online courses in sociology across two decades, long ago embraced super-slow teaching and a concept of crip time and crip poetics similar to that identified by Kafer, Ellen Samuels, Tara Woods, Petra Kuppers, Travis Chi Wing Lau ("The Crip Poetics of Pain"[23]), and others who advocate nonlinear progress, interdependence, and asynchronous learning. "I have examined my love and preference for online learning over the years as I also worried that something was 'wrong with me' for preferring to teach online," Nicole shared in an asynchronous ModPo thread. "I prefer typing to talking, too, which might explain a lot of it. I also tend towards extreme introversion and I get very exhausted in F2F situations, which impacts my health." During the pandemic, Nicole continued to teach her own asynchronous classes, joined an online group of adjunct faculty trying to cope with the sudden pivot ("most of them do not like it at all"), and participated heavily in ModPo's discussion forums, including the "Pandemic Pedagogy" thread (mentioned earlier) created by poet-educator erica kaufman. "I have wondered, too, about the power of 'deep learning' online," she offered to the other teachers in the ModPo group, feel-ing that "students might be more inclined to reveal more honest 'truths' about themselves as they do not have to negotiate F2F group dynamics such as judg-mental facial expressions." Active any-time discussion "gives students who are less inclined to have a voice speak out with more of a voice."[24]

Now let's recall David Brooks back in 2012, worrying at the start of the MOOC phenomenon: "Will fast online browsing replace deep reading?" To be sure, it's a toss-off line made for a weekly newspaper commentary, written in broad-brush style during a precipitous moment (*the end of the university as we know it*, and so forth). But it's fair to ask a hard question of it. Exactly what sort of ratio of opposition is this?

fast	replaces	deep
	[as]	
browsing	replaces	reading

Many have argued against such binaries. For example, Cait Kirby's ideas about flexible active learning, permitting students to exist in a broadened sense of time, defined, in part, as permitting repetition as they need it—and the ideas of her *Hybrid Pedagogy* colleagues; teacher Reyes and superintendent Piwowar along with other proasynchronicity partisans in the Massachusetts public schools; and of the essayists in *Scholars in COVID Times*. Browsing can of course be slow and inspire depth, although probably not the sort of deep reading (presumably of a "great book"—novels by Tolstoy, Stendhal, Trollope, Philip Roth, et alia) that Brooks idealizes variously across his commentaries.[25] Johann Hari is not wrong in summarizing the research of Anne Mangen and others who find that reading books "trains us" productively to read in a certain way—"in a linear fashion, focused on one thing for a sustained period" yet moving forward. The problem with arguments that closely associate linear reading with beneficial socialization and thus with cures for the social ill of "why you can't pay attention" and why our kids can't "think deeply" is that they too veer into standard jeremiads against screens and, at the same time implicitly, against the kind of texts—such as poetry!—that are never well understood when read in the way Hari's book *Stolen Focus* recommends. For Allan Bloom, there was a close connection between his claim, on the one hand, that "the notion of books as companions is foreign to" his disappointing Generation X students and, on the other hand, that the way in which the modern pattern of "ceaseless moving from place to place," reinforced by the "constant newness of . . . first radio, then television," has "assaulted and overturned" the private time for quiet, undisordered reading.[26] "Reading from screens," Hari writes after lauding the verities of traditional book-reading, "trains us to read in a different way—in a manic skip and jump from one thing to another." Hari joins Brooks, Bloom, and the authors of a spate of books of the 2010s and 2020s in expressing concern about that "different way," and, although not as openly as they, he commends a moral panic that seems necessary for his popular thesis about our attention crisis. After all, alarm seems warranted. The focus of learners is being *stolen*. To be more panicked about it, per the ominous titular metaphor, there are thieves lurking out there. (I suppose I'm one of them.)[27]

Hari's hook (as a writer of books himself, after all) is not only thievery and loss—but also mania. Literarily, he's harking back to a golden age of good leisurely readers, presumably a premodern epoch. He discerns a sad retrogression into the modern with its distractedness. But his golden age is a mirage. Recent research into histories of reading, such as Cristina Lupton's *Reading and the Making of Time in the Eighteenth Century* (2018), demonstrates that reading has long "involve[d] irregular, stolen, and anticipated moments as often as it does routine or synchronized or profitable ones." Books have been seen by readers to be the technologies they are. "Reading books," Lupton observes, "has been, and continues to be, a juncture where technical and human agents collaborate freely in creating much-desired and nonlinear experiences of time." Hari focuses on a sense of loss that Lupton demonstrates was always itself lost in time and disrupted and zeroed, as "books pile up, get given, preserved, recycled . . . deferred, and absorbed at special rates because they are not punctual."[28] Yet Hari insists that people are "los[ing] some of the capacity for the deeper reading that comes from books," and his technophobic thesis necessitates his worries (1) that the book is the gold standard among formats, natural and not itself technological, and although it is *one* form of textual distribution, it is presumed to be a sufficient stand-in for *all* good reading; (2) that "cognitive patience" declines rather than increases when readers shift from books to other kinds of text, as, for example, from orderly unhindered advancing to repetitive dwelling; and (3) that the experience of "deep reading" inherently derives from a supposed linearity.[29]

WHEN REALITY IS NONLINEAR

Nonlinearity is where poetry comes back into the discussion. Poetry is our major nonlinear writing genre. Readers don't fuss when sequencing in a poem goes awry. We mostly expect it. There are many reasons why the field of critical disability studies has connected productively with teachers of experimental poetry. One reason is that poems tend to make for what Sara Hendren in *What Can a Body Do? How We Meet the Built World* (2020) describes as "frictionful" rather than smooth or straight linear experiences, and, whether positively or negatively, they model a " 'misfit' relationship with the world." The story of people with disabilities being told is "not the melodrama of a tragedy to overcome" but a complicated representation of lived misfitting, "a disharmony that runs both ways" even when, as is only *sometimes* the case with a poem, harmony is commended in the end. A poem can be understood, in effect, as itself an "assistive technology," and the "tools for assistance" themselves, as Hendren puts it, should be as "visible and unifying" as possible.[30]

A second reason for the convergence of these fields is that the experience of time in poetry can simultaneously be slowed down and sped up. Dozens upon dozens of poems painstakingly typewritten by Larry Eigner, to take a dramatic but not in this sense singular example, explore the matter of pace, mixing delay with prompt, deferral with intensity. "Ten words per minute," he puckishly listed among his typewriting skills in a Guggenheim grant application—using "the most ambulatory part of his right hand: his thumb and index finger."[31] "I have the manyana spirit, all right," Eigner slowly pecked on his keyboard one day in a letter to poet-editor Cid Corman, "by now, or mostly, or I kp subsiding to it quickly, pretty much."[32] It's never really a paradox for Eigner but a way of aiming at independent living and always of independent writing.[33]

A third reason for this alliance of fields, per writers such as Petra Kuppers, Michael Davidson, and Patrick Durgin, is that the presentation of disability through form-constrained writing aligns with core qualities overall in furtherances of twentieth- and twenty-first-century poetic modes: "instability of language," as Kuppers enumerates, "the ability of words to clasp both generic and specific meaning," self-reflexivity, nonnarrative nonlinearity, and "the gaps that surround the performances of self."[34] Durgin would add to that list the matter of what happens when "words are apart" and when morphemes drift the way clouds do and how they, clouds and words, clouds *of* words, move away from conventional ideas of identity, temporality, and cognitive progression. Durgin quotes Gertrude Stein thus: "It carefully comes about that there is no identity and no time and therefore no human nature when words are apart." Durgin turns toward the efforts of some contemporary poets to emphasize the " 'psycho-social' as a disability category." "The formal self-reflexivity of the [poems] engages the psycho-social per se" in the case of poets like Laura Moriarty whose work is thus for Durgin "post-ableist."[35] Stein can be counted as another such poet. Robert Duncan, when he was forming his ideas about the open field as a made place, viewed in Stein's words "a falling apartness in itself." "Clouds drifting" is Duncan's approximation. It was for him the right analogous "figure" of "dispersal" to explain Stein's writing generally, "in which are all the pleasures and pains of reading with *none* of the rewards and values."[36]

Aiden Hunt sometimes reads books in Hari's sense. He's been a major Goodreads activist, after all, reporting on his many good book-length reads. But Aiden's attraction to—I think he would say his *need* for—the ModPo poems and discussions, and with clouds of words, begins as a recognition that "multi-tasking is a compulsion for me" and that that might be why ModPo's focus on repetition in Stein psychosocially speaks to him. He is aligned with Hejinian's rejection of closure and contends that "repetition . . . challenges our inclination to isolate, identify, and limit the burden of meaning."[37] "Stein notes that people's preferences for repetition change as they enter new stages in life," Aiden has written in the ModPo forums. "This made writing analogous to life in my mind. . . . You show your love for the things that you love by repeatedly *choosing* them daily . . . by composing your day and your very quotidian existence out of those things that you repeat." Nonlinearity is natural. "What is a life but a series of repetitions?"[38] In a nod to Camus, Aiden created a thread about repetition in a Stein subforum titled "Loving Repetition as Anti-Sisyphean Boulder Rolling."[39]

Aiden identifies disability in Stein. He sees a recurring nonsequential "skip and jump from one thing to another." That is, of course, what worries Johann Hari as he raises a big social problem—"how to think deeply again." But is Aiden not thinking deeply? He and others think deeply in this manner across the ModPo syllabus. There is hardly a poem there that doesn't require *and itself evince* multitasking as a way of reading and responding, but this effort is not the least bit shallow. On the contrary, these poems, to use Hunt's phrasing, "challenge [. . .] our inclination to . . . limit the burden of meaning." The limitations he sometimes feels free him to extend meaning acutely.

Nicole Braun's experience with what she names "deep learning" had been real for her for a long while, although only belatedly affirmed and made to seem "normal" during lockdown in 2020. She and Aiden Hunt believe in what Hendren defines as "a social model of disability," which "invites you to widen the scenario from the body itself to include . . . interaction . . . [with] larger structures of institutions and . . . the tools for assistance."[40] The ModPo site, centrally featuring the open forums, is just such a tool for them and others. For both, poems and discussions of them, made accessible via the larger structure of ModPo, can be understood as assistive technologies. During the pandemic, Nicole found her people both "alone and together" in ModPo as she very slowly encountered the poems—a crucial pairing (i.e., slowness ↔ sociality)—the personal health benefits of which she is explicit. If a citizen of the ModPo community wished truly "to find [themselves] in the poetry, and not somebody else," Brisbane-based poet Laura De Bernardi has observed, then learning in ModPo, notwithstanding its great distance from literary authority and its location on what in the forums Laura designates "Struggle Street," actually aligns quite well with Brooks's moderate *hopes* for American education overall, where self-discovery, reflection, and frankly facing difficulties are or should be fundamental.

From inside the university, Stephen L. Carter shares exactly these hopes. An eminent professor of law at Yale University and a novelist, Carter published a commentary in the *New York Times* in response to the free speech crises on U.S. campuses that reemerged during the fall of 2023, continued through and well beyond the 2023–2024 academic year, and has inspired new rounds of culture warring that continue as I write this.[41] There is little mistaking Carter's general alignment with progressive theories of education. The classroom, for him, is not simply a place "to impart information." Rather, it is a place for inspiring in learners "a yearning for knowledge" and a recognition that there is, for each person, a "gap" based on "a desire to know more than we do." Content is less important than this individual process-oriented "desire to know more." Carter's defense against antagonists, most of whom are situated outside the sphere of education and who decry the views of some students and the methods of some of their teachers, is to argue—right out of Jean-Jacques Rousseau's *Emile* or Dewey's *School and Society*—that "college is all about curiosity" and that exploratory inquiry "requires free speech."

Carter's article was a brief but substantive intervention into the crisis of the universities, and it stimulated just the sort of open conversation he was advocating for the classroom. What's telling, however, is how he sets up blame for the current situation:

> The classroom is said to be an outdated technology: A teacher stands up front explaining a subject as students take notes. Future-minded critics insist that the model is near its inevitable end. The Covid-19 shutdowns accelerated the drive to develop better tools for asynchronous learning. The rise of generative A.I., together with the mutually parasitic relationship between young people and their screens, suggests that the old way is nearly done. . . . If the purpose of the university classroom is simply to impart information, digital agents will soon perform the task better than experienced teachers, and colleges will find themselves unnecessary, merely duplicative of what students can get at home, cheaply and efficiently.

We might call this the conservative progressive case against information technology (IT) in education. It offers a passing satire of arguments against the lecture, and the strategic offering by futuristic digital agents is meant to seem nefarious, menacing. That these cyber-operatives will help make colleges unnecessary recalls the logic of the moral panic against MOOCs in 2012–2013. But this time, we can blame the pandemic. Carter's opening gambit associates asynchronicity as fundamentally a "drive" propelled by panicgogy. Maybe, after all, *that's* the reason we're in this crisis of higher education. Again, the traditionalism of this argument—and its vocabulary of lament ("the old way is nearly done")—derives from liberal theories of learning. Carter says he is "moved to argue for the defense," at once, of the traditional classroom in which students are encouraged to think aloud and test their ideas in person, no matter how heretical or wrong-headed, *and* of education imperiled by adherents of more rather than less screen time, thus abetting a "mutually parasitic relationship"—meant to be horrifying—between young humans and their devices.

This argument elides asynchronous learning with a coup staged by AI. It more than just simplistically implies that asynchronicity leads inexorably to the further shut-down of open discussion and educational free speech. It assumes a correspondence between screen time and problems facing college campuses—arguable, but let's at least argue it out. Carter and others who defend the classroom against forces beyond the schools that would compromise the unfettered humanistic exploration of ideas believe that effective teaching discerns "gaps" and seeks through interactivity to fill those gaps when possible but to value not knowing as the most basic aspect of establishing the individual point of view. The idea, Deweyan, for sure, helps us discern the experimentalist pedagogy behind poet Rosmarie Waldrop's oft-quoted observation: "Dialogue cultivates gaps by definition, by the constant shift of perspective."[42] Perhaps in this statement Waldrop was thinking particularly about the teaching practice of the "duo-logue," a mainstay writing practice and alt-pedagogical mode employed at experimental colleges of the 1960s and which probably continues today in some curricular workshops. For the duo-logue, you would write entries in a log for yourself, but the heart of the assignment was sharing the log (or logue) with a teacher-advisor as mutual addressee (the writerly rule of thumb, or audience prompt, was: "Not to be seen by anyone but *So & So*").[43] These kinds of bridging "gaps" are exactly those Carter means when in his piece about open expression he borrows from the ideas of behavioral economist George Lowenstein who defines curiosity as "a result of an 'information gap,' " a space between the learner writing a learning log and advisor-mentor that is bridged by an intentional pedagogy. Carter's argument depends on the modern liberal idea that students should be helped to "realize that the gap always exists" between wanting to know and knowing. Yet, as we have seen, such "constant shift[ing] of perspective," in Waldrop's poetic sense, can happen in structured yet *unmediated* online discussion reminiscent surprisingly in many of its qualities of the old experimental colleges, perhaps, I dare say, more productively than in Carter's beloved traditional classroom. Nonetheless, his idealistic rejoinder to universities' external detractors, and that of advocates of digital modes about which he remains skeptical, have this persistent ideal in common: open discussion.

STOP AND THINK AND DREAM TOGETHER

"Open discussion!"—exclaimed Laura De Bernardi when recalling her first experiences in the ModPo forums in 2015. "How I enjoyed the opportunity! I was like a child let loose in a sandpit." Soon she joined the ongoing "Global Studies Group" (known by ModPo people as GSG) which actively "eschews creative expression as arising from a singular meaning-making voice," functions like a digital inheritor of the duo-logue, and has a founding consensus group goal of maintaining "highly individuated responses even as it crowdsources understanding." In regular GSG gatherings—synchronous by Zoom and asynchronous in the forums—a "poem is not known through one view." And this all happens "without a teacher in sight."[44] In a forum thread titled "Detaining You in ModPo" (2022), Matt Lutwen quotes Waldrop's wisdom on gaps when reflecting upon his own life in higher education: "I was fortunate as a college student to receive the message that 'knowledge is (co-)created, not imparted.' I've taken that with me everywhere. Nowadays I'm also thinking about this i[n] connection with dialogue." Here is the moment and context for Matt's reference to Waldrop's comment, quoted above: " 'Dialogue cultivates gaps by definition, by the constant shift of perspective.' In a way," Matt adds, "we are 'gap gardening,' to use her phrase." Responding directly to Matt, and delighted by the notion that "gaps are a positive," Miranda Jubb describes the thread-based discussion as itself an opportunity for gap gardening. "I also am frequently pleasantly surprised," Miranda writes, "by the kinds of things people come up with. I see a post and think, huh I have no idea what to say to that! and then there are people there saying all sorts of thoughtful and generous things. I do also enjoy being able to scroll through all sorts of posts from such a wide variety of perspectives and approaches that I might not be lucky enough to come across in a smaller (or possibly more homogenous) group."[45]

Miranda is of course referring ("small" and "more homogenous") to the typical in-person college classroom. The ModPo citizenry is far more heterogeneous than any learning space she had experienced prior to joining. Raymond M., enlisting in ModPo immediately upon retirement after decades in the U.S. Army and State Department, bringing with him a special interest in exploring formal poetic representations (for example, the English sonnet tradition) in Harlem Renaissance poetry, expected "cognitive diversity" to be an effect of "diversity across genders, races, ages, professions, religions" and that " 'social' diversity" would be crucial to "the learning process." On the topic of classical poetic form used by Black poets in the United States, which has been his major concern, Raymond immediately found a greater range of viewpoints in the forum threads than in the presentations given by leaders of the course. "Subforums have always been . . . safe spaces for exploring ideas, for testing different directions of thought and alternative paths, and, to use Army terminology, for 'socializing' concepts between and across learners."[46]

Laura De Bernardi takes the importance of cognitive and other aspects of heterogeneity and of socializing concepts a step further—including the idea of the asynchronous forum as a safe space *away* from the authority of the teacher. Her first instinct, in fact, was to go directly and exclusively to the asynchronous discussion forums as a way of participating in the world of wide-open colloquy and of averting the influence of the authorized teacher. "I yearned . . . to throw off the 'anxiety of influence'—the specialist, professorial voice telling me how to think and what to think about. . . . I decided to limit myself to the threads. . . . I was so inspired by others' readings that my mind was as if imbued by new resonances. I think it's safe to say that human beings yearn for intimacy because it is transformational, and that at ModPo I was gripped by conversations about poetry that were *precisely* that."[47] Such precision is meant to be a kind of people's realism. It is a practical facing of factional disagreement. It is the clarification of difference—all of it the opposite of illusion. In this populist view, "instruction *alone* leads to illusions." Thus pronounced the creator of the Modern School Movement, Francisco Ferrer, in a key heretical statement about education that has informed aspects of ModPo. Illusion, perhaps surprisingly, derives from instruction when left to its own devices. Somewhere *beyond* instruction, Ferrer contended, is where you'll find transformational intimacy,[48] the crowd in the act of socializing concepts—the very process of it—as a form of clarity.

My influence is not entirely absent from Laura De Bernardi's liberatory account.[49] She quotes a comment I made in the forums in response to her and others' interpretation of a poem by Cid Corman that, I had said, made the poem new and different for me even after years of reading and teaching it. "Again and again our experience with a poem," she quoted me as having posted, "is that it is much more interesting and accessible when there's a conversation being had about it!"[50] Indeed, I do converse more or less constantly *about* conversation—about socializing speculations between and among learners. But since the first two seasons, it has not generally been my aim to be a significant part *of* the conversations in ModPo. After the ten-week "symposium mode" session of 2013, I wanted to know if my involvement in discussion forum threads increased others' contributions—if my participation tended to stimulate more responses on the part of learners. The computational linguist Mark Liberman, with assistance from Ritika Khandeparkar, crunched and plotted the corpus of ModPo forum data for the period from September 7 through November 7, and discovered, as I might "either be relieved or disturbed to learn," that my interventions *made no difference* in the overall length of threads (either number or length of posts and replies).[51] I have continued to add comments right up to the time of this writing, usually very briefly in praise of the poster, but no longer with the goal of expanding the content of the discussion beyond what the crowd collectively decides should be its expanse or depth. Moreover, it is hardly my aim, when posting, to go gap gardening, to shovel in holes of participants' individual knowledge—that void Bloom lamented as "ignorance" in his preinternet study of closed minds. Regardless of my interventions or lack thereof, some poem-specific discussions do go on and on, filling up page screen after page screen. For instance, since September 2016 there have been 323 individual discussion threads created in which participants are offering readings of Cid Corman's tiny poem "It isnt for want." (Tiny indeed: it is all of thirty-seven words.) Raymond M., our veteran diplomat, believes this proliferation is both safe *and* "open" to all "alternative paths" and at the heart of his idea of a citizenship that has little or nothing to do with regular notions of cognitive leadership. Raymond, among others, loves nothing more than a busy thread. Raymond's colleague Hilary B. describes how the busyness and multivocality of a ModPo thread can "generate" an "appreciation where there was none, recognition of our own biases and blind spots, creative turns, quirky associations, an outfolding of meanings."[52]

Hilary B. and Meredith Lederer are among ModPo participants contending that the teeming fullness of the forums brings the participants closer to rather than further from a coherent reading of a poem. A former Reuters journalist, human rights worker, and translator living for two decades in Buenos Aires, Hilary plans to teach ModPo poems to high school students and, as such, has been attempting to understand how the state of "get[ting] dizzy in the chat" correlates to—perhaps even causes—"somehow beget[ting] astonishingly profound exchanges." "Dizzy" as a quality of chaotic human interchange enables learners to "stop and think and dream together." It creates a collectively gathered-together "thing" that is "beautiful" and begins to rival the beauty of the poems, thus being both aesthetic and "educational in the deepest way."[53] "I find," Meredith Lederer writes, "that each response is critical to the ongoing discovery of meaning, and feel that it expands the hearts and minds of those involved. If something is left out or un-said, the understanding of the poem is limited to a more narrow and subjective interpretation. So, though it feels counter-intuitive, the multiplicity of responses and the expansion of the discussion leads to a *contraction* of meaning—we get *closer* to a sense of definition and precision."[54]

Meredith provides an example of "problem reduction" as an advantage over "problem solving," a distinction researchers on expertise recommend.[55] When considering the matter of mass amateurization in the final pages of this book, we will return to difficult poems as problems, the settled "solutions" to which are successfully resisted when experts are absent or when specialists are, in some way, put in the unfamiliar position of disorientation.

I have found the latter option intriguing and instructive. Since 2007, I have hosted an unscripted monthly podcast, which in its first years served as an important trial run of the unrehearsed collaborative close readings that became the main method of ModPo. In producing the podcast episodes, I crave situations where specialists are thrown off their disciplinary game as a means of suppressing typical expert behavior. Sometimes the disarrangement fails as the three people I bring together end up only reinforcing their professional stances—making for some good podcast shows, I should add, but not providing a lot of what Meredith Lederer and other citizen-learners value in the open discussion. At other times, however, modest de-specialization through field nonadjacency succeeds because I've managed to convene a heterodox mix. Among favorite instances of this podcast admixture: experimental theater director Brooke O'Harra joined episode #184 to discuss a John Giorno audiotape, though she had scant knowledge of Giorno; Susan Schultz arrived from Hawaii for episode #129 to discuss Sylvia Plath positively, even though Schultz has openly disliked Plathian confession; Nada Gordon discussed Wallace Stevens for #14, an unexpected convergence that, in the end, generated Gordon's mesmerizing unserious "Flarfist" rewrite of a slow, dignified late Stevens lyric; Alan Loney, a visiting New Zealand poet for whom U.S. Black Arts poetics was an unaccustomed topic, talking Amiri Baraka on Wolfgang Mozart and Jomo Kenyatta in #20; Whitney Trettien, who studies "weird old technologies" and old histories of the book as far back as clay tablets, was invited to #182 so she could help us think through Douglas Kearney's new sound poems; Dan Bergmann, who only rarely vocalizes what he wants to say, improvisationally riffed during #168 via his spelling board on Jayne Cortez's jazzy, performative "She Got, He Got."

Describing the overwhelming forums as a method of reducing the problem of incomprehension rather than amplifying it, Meredith Leaderer is well onto the aspect of discussion I have been exploring as I curate *PoemTalk*—it might be called confounding expertise—and which I too found especially handy and productive during lockdown. I consider *PoemTalk* primarily a teaching tool. Its several hundred episodes certainly form a syllabus of sorts. I have corresponded with many teachers who use it in classrooms. They read the poem with their students, listen together to the episode, then discuss not just the poem but also the way the experts dealt with unanticipated questions and the topical cascade of conversation. Based on what ModPo participants have said about the close-reading videos there, the same disorientation of expertise becomes a primary motive for learners to enter. The goal is, in Ferrer's terms, to lessen the illusion instruction creates.

Matt Seybold deems *PoemTalk* to constitute public instruction because it lessens the illusion of medium. In his essay on close reading and its potential as a practice to break out beyond the academy, he turns to an episode of *PoemTalk* about Stein (#90).[56] Seybold writes that the recorded improvised talk among four scholars "manages to capture, store, reproduce, and freely distribute partial access to the interpretative community that informs close reading." In his conclusion, he imagines a fresh agnosticism about medium that can free scholars from preferential locations for creating and sharing "new knowledge":

> This is not to say that [*PoemTalk*] is necessarily preferable to the close readings produced in writing or those that take shape in the cloister of a classroom, reading group, or symposium and are only ever accessible via the memories of the participants. It is to say that our methods are not intrinsic to a medium, and any effort to make them so capitulates to the reactionary efforts to turn literary studies into a finished product, a dead discipline, a collection of myths and symbols that can safely be packaged and automated, because it will never need to integrate new knowledge.[57]

PoemTalk continued to record and distribute monthly episodes when we were shut out of the Wexler Studio, a tiny acoustically controlled room of finite ventilation that was added to the back of the first floor of the Writers House. For one of these episodes in exile, I decided to convene a pandemic-themed conversation about William Carlos Williams's famous poem from *Spring and All*, "By the road to the contagious hospital." I suggested a constraint as I invited the participants: experience the poem as an aspect of the fate of rereading. My intuition was that this episode should bring together ModPo regulars. They were Imaad Majeed, connecting from Colombo, Sri Lanka; the Madrid-based poet Irene Torra Mohedano, joining us from Paris (where she was living and was then confined); and Gabriel Ojeda-Sagué, the poet-scholar who has long been a ModPo TA, getting on the call from his confinement in a small apartment in Chicago. My goal was to decenter senses of poetic expertise as a way of respecting the dislocations of the pandemic and the ethos of disorienting rethinking. So I asked these colloquists to freshly reinterpret that old modernist standard about contagion. For Williams, the compositional situation had been the so-called Spanish flu of 1918–1920, which necessitated for him as a medical doctor many more than the usual number of emergency trips to the hospital and dangerous home visits. As he drove past the barren landscape during that transitional season, a typical prompt for jottings (sometimes on prescription pads set near the driver's seat) that became his jagged kinetic poems, the modernist made close observations of spring's unpretty, pulpy return to life to coincide with his poet-doctor's routine commute to foul wards of infection. The typical reading of the poem stresses that in early spring, life comes back, its modern shards poking up. But the three ModPo poets were being challenged to forget or neglect that automatic vernal revival, to abandon for the moment what they had been separately taught about modernism's Make It New, and to reread together what it signifies to "enter the new world naked, / cold, *uncertain of all.*"[58] Uncertain poem, uncertain time: an interpretive conversation featured a frank edifying tone of unconfidence and a collaborative international inquiry into the state of "feeling myself here," as Cid Corman puts it, despite fears of isolation.

Where was "here"? Once the episode was released to thousands of regular *PoemTalk* subscribers, and an unknown number of other people found it at the *PoemTalk* tab in *Jacket2* and clicked the link, where did we stand? What was next? A journal, school, or website might have sponsored this sort of gathering and hosted commentaries in response. Even if not widely seen, those sorts of follow-up comments might have had an ongoing community aspect. But I want to suggest that ModPo carries on in ways that are a constituent of the structure, recursively operating. There is an unsaid expectation that materials added— poems, webcast recordings, whole videos, video clips, new threads—should receive responses from *someone* even if in disagreement. The discussion of *Spring and All* was instantly added to the ModPoPLUS syllabus; those who watched or listened and then commented in forum threads knew several or all three of their ModPo confrères and seemed to feel at home, as it were, discussing with these familiars the delicate and messy Williamsesque topics—contagion, birth, "that breath-held period before life begins" (as one ModPo learner, Ken X., put it) and also when life ends. As moderator during the podcast, I quoted my former teacher, Terrence Des Pres. "*All things human take time,* which the damned never have," wrote Des Pres wrote about surviving the Nazi death camps in his book *The Survivor*, "time for life to repair at least the worst of its wounds."[59] The Poem-Talkers did not pick up on this, for whatever reason. But Ken X. did, writing in from Canada to a ModPo thread late one night. He decided that what I meant was a correctly analogous contemporary will to survive, a thought updated from Des Pres's sense of outlasting the Holocaust and thus a much-revised sense of Williams's Spanish flu: that we, in 2020, were all already survivors if we merely lived and digitally *responded*. I don't know if bearing witness is what I meant. But I was heartened by reading Ken's post just as it appeared in the thread on a lonely lockdown night, the end of the day that I had released the episode to the world. Des Pres via Ken X. caused me to reread the poem once more, right then. Where were we in the ModPo cycle? It was SloPo season. Ken thought he was alone in the forums (he wasn't—I was there that evening, among others): "Anyway," he added, "quiet night, no-one seems to be posting. Very strange. I hope my system is not malfunctioning." The system functioned quite well: a learner understood a teacher. "Yes, spring had come again." Ken added. "Now we are headed to a strange pandemic-driven autumn, winter and spring again. Not the same as before."[60]

Laura Lippman, the ModPo citizen and writer of detective fiction we met in the previous chapter, associates community-enhancing dissensus with matters of life and death. The point occurred to her on another night when sadness and loss were the topics. In an interview, Laura told me the story:

> The night my mom went into the ER, certain to die within a day or two, I decided to go to erica [kaufman]'s office hours to distract myself. And we read a difficult Dickinson poem and I came roaring in with a very personal life/death reading. But then [another ModPo learner] Suzanne Miller offered a more meta reading, one that was about writing itself, and I found her interpretation so much more charming, beguiling. Sure, the life/death stuff might be there. Life/death stuff is pretty much always there, everywhere. My reading and Suzanne's reading could live in the same space. . . . In ModPo, the readings aren't in opposition, they're just . . . different. What I'm saying is that when the stakes *seem* small, our brains open up, we can hear others, and even be persuaded.[61]

THE COURSE MEMORY

When I was composing this section, I asked Miranda Jubb and Matt Lutwen if they would be willing to read 849 post-2016 comments and replies across many subforum threads that constitute the current collaborative close reading of Corman's "It isnt for want." I did the math after the fact and only then realized I had asked them to read the equivalent of 156 double-spaced twelve-point pages.

Miranda's conclusions affirmed Meredith Lederer's observation that discursive expansion leads paradoxically to interpretive focus. She noticed that the thread "bears a strong resemblance to reading the poem itself." Here is the entire poem:

It isnt for want
of something to say—
something to tell you—

something you should know—
but to detain you—
keep you from going—

feeling myself here
as long as *you* are—
as long as you *are*.[62]

Because Miranda was overwhelmed by the threads, as she reread them, she became aware of the other people who had posted there previously and those asynchronously present at the time of her new visit. There was a good deal of data but after extracting or "scraping" it, she was not able to discern a larger, distant meaning. But way inside the threads, a comment at a time, they constitute a personal "there" that closely follows from Corman's usage of "here." "That of course," Miranda Jubb told me she realized, "leads to feeling myself *here*." She meant herself. Reading, not scraping, she was closer to the space of the poem, the words-made site from which Corman's readers either depart (when done reading) or remain (when "detain[ed]"). Her term for the experience is "incompletable." The endless—and to the moment of this writing, ongoing—discussion offers her an education in the feeling the poem gives over to the solitudinous speaker-poet. To sum it up: "It isnt for want of posts to read," Miranda added, only half-jokingly.[63] She discovered, by consulting the interpretive community to which she belongs, that the poem is about how its readers came to be the way they are.

Miranda encountered what George Landow in *Hypertext* (1992) described as "a course memory." Preserved forum asynchronicity is ipso facto networked hypertext as Landow first defined it. The ModPo crowd functions together as an unanticipated interconnected memory. The longitudinal reach of the site affords a thick fraction of recollection at any time. Just now, as I write, I search for instances when learners mention metapoetry. The result gives me 183 screens to scroll, connecting to 2,681 different discussions, some memorably of interest to me as quasi-randomly sequenced in my search result, but all told constituting the course memory. "The contributions of individual student (and faculty) reader-authors, which automatically turn Intermedia into a fully collaborative learning environment," wrote Landow, "remain . . . for future students to read, quote, and argue against."[64] Miranda told me she rediscovered *herself* in the old forum threads. She is part of an interpretive archeology. She was there but also "here," in Corman's sense. She existed as a past and present student at once.

Matt Lutwen had a similar encounter as he traversed time-stamped strata of expressive asynchronicity. He noticed that seven years prior to his own reread-ing of now-old readings of the poem, one Albert E. was already wondering what is left of Corman's poem when he's gone, a presence then in the forums antici-pating *his*, like the poet's, absence. "The content of conversation [in the poem] is unimportant because the conversation is an affirmation of life. When one is gone the other ceases to be complete because part of the essence of that person was made whole by the presence of the other. Or is my age showing?"[65] Albert's age might have been showing—but no one knew his age, notwithstanding his meditations on mortality. Still, he used the poem as a means of marking time differently, and it remains, for Matt Lutwen and anyone venturing behind, a matter of continuous caring. Matt summarizes the sense of the forum's conver-gence across years with the poem as a point along the spectrum of a common curricular core: "We care for the poetry community in part because of how it has cared for us. Corman cares for his reader, and it appears that among his most pressing concerns involved the sustaining of poetry. I don't believe that that concern was limited to his own poetry, but rather of that site, anywhere, where readers open poetry books."[66] This is Matt's definition of the subject vil-lage. Corman did not use the language of caring, but he frequently wrote about the figures of others in his poems. Among the fifty archival boxes of his manu-scripts, I found this typical remark: "We are born as fragments of other lives. . . . to occupy a space."[67]

One of the richest threads about that Corman poem is a conversation Miranda Jubb started, as noted earlier, titled "Detaining You in ModPo." There we are reminded that the poem can be read straightforwardly as a love poem. "You" in that interpretation is another person, a lover or intimate, who is urgently being asked to defer absence. The metapoetic reading, the one affirmed by Miranda's experience rereading *all* the commentary, has it that the speaker is addressing the reader or readers, a second-person singular or plural. As Albert E. noticed sometime in the ModPo past, so long as readers are reading the poem, the speaker continues to exist. The *content* of what the speaker or poet has to say is not at all what's important. To return to Corman's terms: It's not even an important tell-ing, a delivery of relevant information. Nor is it a gap in knowledge that "should" be filled. All conventional responses to a poem's speaker are set aside. Content is deemed merely an excuse for the convening of poet and reader. Reader, we were meant to meet. The longer the speaker can keep you reading, can "detain you— / keep you from going," the longer the presence of the poetry abides.

In this way, Miranda's "Detaining You" thread invites a general discussion of the metapedagogical nature of a poem and reflects Harry Boyte's view of public work as "an approach to citizenship in which citizens are co-creators" and "artisans of possibility."[68] The conversation among learners teaches us about the ModPo place as a public site of creativity and the potential of the massive open situation. Thus:

$$\begin{matrix} \text{poet} & \text{is to} & \text{reader} \\ & \text{as} & \\ \text{teacher} & \text{is to} & \text{learner} \end{matrix}$$

What kind of pedagogy is this? Miranda offers an answer: "I think it's a really interesting way of thinking about the relationship between the teacher and the learner, as analogous to that of the poet in 'It isnt for want' and the poem's reader. . . . Just as the real essence of that poem is not in its content but is in the connection you feel with Cid Corman when you read it, the real essence of learning is about the connection between the teacher and the learner. The poem is ultimately a co-creation of the poet and reader, and so is learning."

We have here a (please forgive the impersonal phrase) *user-generated* assessment of the space opened up by the MOOC as "a learning experience that is . . . co-creative and communitarian—that wants to know what *you* think—that seeks to detain you."[69] Just as it requires both browsing and slow reading to make one's way through all the years of asynchronous commentary around this tiny poem—no one coming upon it feels obliged or prepared to read it all—so too can one discover in that process an idea of socially responsible reading in general, or, in Boyte's phrase, "public work."

WORKING HARD

When I think of the concept of educational responsibility, and when I feel most prepared to chastise critics worrying over "incompletion" and "dropout rates" in open online learning, I think of Maureen Bailey and Anne Jongleux. Anne made her "first ModPo attempt in 2014 and lasted two weeks" ("for reasons I no longer remember," she told us later). Then came a decade of caregiving for aging relatives and supporting an ill spouse, hurricanes and other disasters, and feeling overwhelmed by the obligation to read only deeply when she had free moments. She returned in 2024, refusing to get caught up in "treat[ing] it like a regular academic course," where she "was always already behind with little hope of completing it all." She adjusted to here-and-there learning. She listened to the poems and recorded discussions while walking the dogs. She was finally "prepared to do it in whatever way worked for me." She joined the "Ongoing Poetry Game" started by a fellow learner. She volunteered to help with the "Postcard Poetry Fest." During week 2, she did *not* submit an assigned essay on Emily Dickinson, yet she posted comments on others'. Then, during week 4, Anne was forced to flee her home ahead of Hurricane Helene and was forcibly gone for a month. She had difficulty connecting with the discussion forums but found a way to join TA Dave Poplar's weekly Zoom office hours. She cherished the DMs coming in from her ModPo friends, the Poplar regulars, who sweetly inquired about her health and the state of her home.[70] As they discussed the disjunctive poems, she "pointed out where the rat-infested, smoldering FEMA dump for the debris of shattered lives had over-taken a nearby park." From one perspective, Anne Jongleux was one among the many MOOC drop-outs. From another, her humane presence in 2024, a decade tardy—marked incorrectly in the system as a "new" enrollee—was persistent and rightly timed to and for her needs.

Maureen Bailey describes herself as having been detained all along, years before discovering the MOOC. "A 60-something office clerk living in a small town in the middle of the Canadian prairies," she attempted university after high school, but it was not for her and she dropped out, and has had "no formal edu-cation." Maureen joined ModPo in 2016, engaging with it very slowly and quietly. In 2018, she "got up enough nerve to submit a post about a poem" in the forums.[71] In 2020, she finally challenged herself to write and post an essay. In 2021, she began to be seen by coworkers and neighbors passing by in their cars along her walking commute from home to work "with a poetry book in hand, reading aloud as I stroll."[72] Others happening upon Maureen Bailey's singular, hard-won appearances in the chaotic forums—painstaking significant steps forward in her much-belated education—might mistake the level and the in-and-out quantity of her involvement as part of the constantly sidetracking manic skip and jump decried by Hari, Brooks, Sanders, Dana Gioia (the neoformalist poet and former chair of the National Endowment for the Arts); in the later cautionary work of Sherry Turkle in *Reclaiming Conversation* (2016); and in the calls to action of books riding the simplification wave, such as *How to Break Up with Your Phone* (2018), *How to Do Nothing: Resisting the Attention Economy* (2019), *24/6* (2020), *Untethered: Overcome Distraction, Build Healthy Digital Habits . . .* (2021), *Digital Detox* (2022), and so on.[73] But such judgments and assumptions entirely miss Maureen's already unhurried particular sense of temporality and life choices and motivation for joining an MOOC.[74] Thank goodness she didn't break up with her phone. I suppose she was considered a "dropout" at one point in her life, but the seven-year engagement just described is not remotely that. Academic studies of MOOCs' so-called dropout rates—a mainstay of critiques—do not come close to accounting for a person's participation across even just two seasons of a course, as in Anne Jongleux's case, let alone seven. Nor will they find or assess the one excellent essay Maureen Bailey wrote in just one of the years she has learned with us in the site as "partial fulfillment" of the "course requirements." *Education Week* covered these sorts of studies, including one done at my university, and informed us of the commonly used term *persistence*. If you continue in an open course in a single six- or eight-week session through to the end, no matter what the quality of your work, you are satisfactorily persistent. One *Education Week* article summarized findings that showed "Student Persistence Low in MOOCs with Higher Workloads." The workload in ModPo is high. And no decent account of Maureen Bailey or Anne Jongleux would fail to describe them as persistent, although somewhere in those studies they are data points that misleadingly demonstrate a typical lack of completion among the crowd.[75]

Working hard is a major topic discussed in the world of citizen poetics. Welsh poet Jeremy Dixon also decided to do a close reading of the subforum threads. He chose those responding to Lorine Niedecker's programmatic poem of radical condensation, "Poet's Work." The poem is about—and is also itself an example of—the work the poet does in response to her elder's pointed advice to "learn a trade." He offers career counseling about her options, and in response, she writes out her choice to be a writer. The poem we read *is* that choice, *is* the making of it:

> Grandfather
>   advised me:
>   Learn a trade
>
> I learned
>   to sit at desk
>   and condense
>
> No layoff
>   from this
>   condensery[76]

Jeremy Dixon decided to focus not on the words of the poem but on the words and work of the forum posts about it. He asked, "Does the poem itself influence the behaviour and language of the Sub-Forum?" His answer is yes, and he noticed that forum conversations here more than elsewhere become terse discussions between two people, just as in the poem. The Walt Whitman subforum is full of enthused, extended "I" statements. In the intense Amiri Baraka threads, one finds a proliferation of pronoun confusions, mixed meanings of *he*, just as we find in Baraka's poem in the main syllabus, "Incident." Posts about Hejinian's *My Life* are both personal and disordered. The commentaries on Niedecker's "Poet's Work" are very simple, in honor of, and at times, I suppose, in imitation of, the poem.[77] In short, the subforum becomes an aspect or even is itself an instance of "this / condensery," and the poet's work is learner's work. ModPo citizens, to *be* citizens, "sit at desk / and condense" by way of understanding the poem deeply—intently yet modestly—from inside, and within the people's mass commentaries upon the poem.

Dixon is a formally and procedurally experimental poet (I recommend his 2019 book *In Retail*—it is about his experience as a worker at a superstore), and I take his close reading of the close readings of Niedecker's poem to be essentially poetic. By *doing* something with Niedecker's poem and by paying attention to and writing about others writing about her, Dixon as a *poet* was learning a good deal about the way Niedecker writes.

We can all learn how the poet deploys words and phrases not just through the typical practice of reading her words but also through reading the words of fellow reader-learners writing through their interactive experiences in the role of readers, as we witness her response to the grandfather's world-weary expectation that she should do something more practical with her time. The elder's default assumption is that writing is inaction. Learning from the life choice of writing, defined as a shift in thinking from inaction to action, is itself a classic instance of active learning, as Dewey described intellectual vocation in *Democracy and Education*. Following in the practical Deweyan tradition, Stephen Kosslyn's *Active Learning Online*—a timely publication, as it appeared in early 2021—organizes suggestions for activities perhaps not quite as self-reflexive as what Dixon was doing just then with Niedecker's idea of work but that align well with the concepts presented here in my paean to the readerly crowd: metacognition; "selectively paying attention" to what others tell you you should know; mixing synchronous and asynchronous settings; and "interleaving." The ModPo forums provide many examples of interleaving, which is defined as something a course can do to mix up different types of cases from general categories (e.g., in our case, poetry and learning), rather than presenting groups of cases together as a coherent curricular "block" already decided.[78]

THE DECENTRALIZATION OF THERE

Laura De Bernardi, Pamela Joyce Shapiro, Sanjeev Naik, and several other ModPo regulars inaugurated and sustained an active learning project years before the pandemic. Over time, it went under various titles: ModPo Renga, Japanese Renga ModPo Style, etc. Before the 2020–2021 edition, there had been fourteen previous thread-based editions. The original guidelines made clear the metapedagogical aspects of the term "ModPo Style" when it was being engaged: "renga is a traditional form of Japanese poetry that was written in groups. Renga writing sessions, referred to as 'renga or poem parties,' could last for hours with the resulting poems comprising as many as a hundred verses. At ModPo we have experimented with writing haiku-like, short-form sequential poetry based on this revered traditional form."[79] The guidelines were structured in the spirit of this kind of precise writing yet remained open as to form and wide open as to duration. Time, of course, is a key element in the tiny poems linked up in the renga—now even more so when asynchronously the collaborative creative party "could last for hours," which everyone in the threads knew well could mean days, weeks, months, and, as happens to be the case, *years*. The learner-hosts also set up a long-running thread called "Haiku Corner," where participants can discuss the poems they and others have posted to the episodic thread.

When Sanjeev Naik reintroduced the renga party for the fall 2021 "symposium mode" session of the course, he offered the usual guidelines but made no explicit mention of the pandemic. But it's pervasive. In rereading all the editions of this activity, archived in the forums,[80] I noticed how often the contributions of these micropoems refer to the paradoxical constraints and improvisational freedoms of the project. In ModPo, the renga turns out to be a call for minimalist maximalism and relates not only to pandemic rereadings of poems like Williams's imagist springtime but also to Instagram "poetry bombing" that was happening just then—tiny regular doses of epigrammatic verse.[81] In 2021, among the ModPo renga partiers, there emerged a special new emphasis on the strange vicissitudes of time, which included three main obsessive elements: first, the traditionally intense feeling of seasonal currency (typically these sequences begin in the season of the time of composition and follow the natural calendar sequence); second, the out-of-time aspects of ongoing asynchronous collaborative writing, or "course memory"; and third, the sheer durationality, by this point, of COVID time—remoteness and isolation, spatial disorientation, and lockdown disarrangements of calendar days. The relaunch of the collaborative project itself provided an intervention against the disrupted seasonality. For instance:

syllables needed
spring has turned to autumn
time for a reunion?

Indeed, these remote colleagues felt that gathering once again in a forum thread was a compositional reunion, a seasonal *there* for a group connected by loose ties from both hemispheres (late summer, late winter), all time zones, and various weather and climate situations. Virtual proximity offered closeness now that seasonality had become more cosmic and less locally informative:

what season is this
hundred million years halfway
round the milky way

The ModPo pandemic renga party enacted the "slowing down teaching" advocated by the *Hybrid Pedagogy* authors of "Designing for Fatigue," with its expanded sense of interval or epoch paradoxically marking off segments of time-insensitive exhaustion. The poems in the series inscribed as texts a "flexible standard for punctuality" and "increased time-to-completion of activities."[82]

Is there a site better suited for the inclusion of compositional speed and accommodation to temporal inaction than a poem? Poems tend to be lost in time. Posting to the thread titled "ModPo in the Age of Pandemic," a new pandemic-era participant, Margaret X., felt missing in action, more than ever, among the proliferating forums, yet still celebrated having "more space to breathe" (aware of the irony with respect to the airborne pathogen). She noted that she was "getting lost (and sometimes staying that way)" and was "slowly realizing that 'getting lost is how you learn' [she was quoting an African proverb]. Indeed, that being lost *is* the learning. And because of that frequent lostness, that sometimes stumbling around in the dark, I'm seeing also that THAT's what opens up new pathways, new views."[83] Prior to each week of the course, a fresh thread entitled "Hopelessly Lost" is created by the most CTA, the sleepless, self-taught Floridian chapbook poet Anthony Watkins. The weekly thread welcoming others who are "lost" creates a place where participants can find peer support as they encounter difficult poems in the rush of the syllabus sections and the one-week tours through poetic movements (imagism, cubism, Harlem Renaissance poetry, conceptualism, etc.). But during 2020–2021 the ModPo populace, flocking to this reliable thread, understood it to be a just-in-time space for confronting dislocation. The "lost" place Anthony made each week became a home base or shelter where Margaret X. and numerous others found a bearing before heading off to unknown poems

and forums. "Hopelessly Lost" is for adjusting speeds, switching gears. In the
2021 renga group, Terry Talty offered this:

> our world
> even while moving fast
> still standing still[84]

Terry and the other renga party people took extended time to experiment
with ideas about duration. Writing in a tradition of verse that has always been
about replicating the state of being stuck in time, they were encountering what
Courtney Naum Scuro has called "timesoup." Timesoup is defined as a function
of "missed meaning," a concept developed to help explain the feeling that time
was standing still during the pandemic. The content-form alignment that is a
hallmark of the ModPo syllabus, poems structured not only to mean but also to
do what they mean, starting with the very first poem in the course, Emily Dickinson's "I dwell in Possibility," like Williams's "Spring and all" later, invited readers during lockdown and quarantine to freely reinterpret the poem's language
for staying home, for seeing out but not being seen—"dwelling," "occupation,"
"chambers," "visitors" (only the "fairest"), "doors," "impregnable of eye," even
"house" (a dwelling fairer than prose, the poet contends)—as relevant to the situation of the reader's body confined to a space, feeling ill-at-ease but strangely
liberated by the constraints. It begins this way:

> I dwell in Possibility—
> A fairer House than Prose—
> More numerous of Windows—
> Superior—for Doors—
>
> Of Chambers as the Cedars—
> Impregnable of eye—

"I believe," Scuro has written in *Scholars in Covid Times*, "the radically disorienting nature of the last several years demands equally disorienting intellectual exploration in response."[85] Ultimately I think such exploration can be
found in, and its pleasures specially derived from, a moment of pandemic-era
and postpandemic experimentalism: in new unsettled readings of old poems
searching for human possibility being discovered in Dickinson, Niedecker,
Williams, and Corman, and in new poems composed by writers—some of the
very same people contemporaneously reinterpreting Dickinson, Niedecker,

Corman, Whitman, and Baraka. They discerned methods by which to expand the understanding of what constitutes both a social and personal *there*, not despite but because of uncertainties created by crowd asynchronicity in a time of crisis. Sophia Naz, a ModPo regular since 2013, has written a number of poems about the social *there* of concise writing, some published in her book *Bark Archipelago* (2023). José Reyes has written and published such poems as well. His metapoem "Type," composed in the midst of struggles with DESE-mandated ideas about what sort of screen time can be said to be sanctioned as educational, plays with the resilience of art, the depth discovered beyond screen surface, hybrid writing as ontology, and the digital bookshelf. Here's the poem:

TYPE

To see *these* characters
only as sculptures
arranged on shelves
of the thinnest glass.[86]

Reyes does not quite recall if his response to panicgogy as an educator resulted from a negative reaction to Jonathan Zimmerman's much-discussed criticism of online learning issued in the first days of the pandemic, but I like to think of "Type" (published September 14 as his students first ventured into the hybrid classroom arrangements) as at least in part a response to Zimmerman's skepticism. There, in a *Chronicle of Higher Education* commentary, he quoted a 1993 Louisiana State University student newspaper editorial issuing a "stark warning" about the digital future of learning: "A university is a place where the knowledge of one generation is passed on to the next, and this cannot be done by machine. Information can be found in a computer, but only by the human touch is the knowledge of generations transmitted."[87]

Reyes's "Type" addresses such a worry about devices. The poem is about touching the thin screen, a digital fourth wall, a techno-text machine, entering and beholding not only whole libraries of poetry books but also the "characters" resiliently made by persistent humans typing verses of *this* and *there*. Reader and writer, not dissociated by distances of epoch and eminence but joined through the gentle finger-touch of reader to screen. "I think that ModPo has decentralized the idea of 'there,'" Sophia Naz tapped out for her Twitter (now X) followers on May 13, 2020, "and the pandemic has doubled down on that, creating a new equality of space. #modpolive."

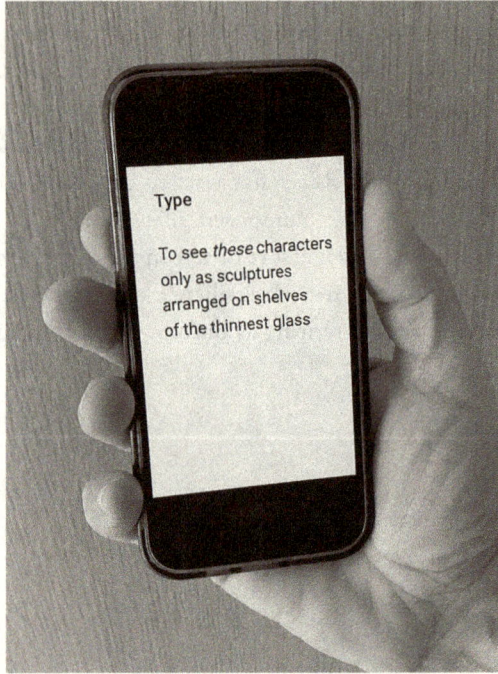

FIGURE 2.1 "Type," by José Edmundo Ocampo Reyes, as viewed on an iPhone 13.

————

Source: Photo by Hannan Judd, used with permission. Poem reproduced by permission of José Reyes.

The hashtag "#modpolive" was a special signal called out from lockdown. For those who knew to seek it, the tag, named by a crowd in a bottom-up process, precisely encoded loose ties and permitted perfect sorting inside the sprawling, ill-defined social medium. At the first instance of this hashtag back in 2013, the ModPo populace, searchable, began life as a coherent cohort. In 2020, coming in handy, it was a way to find your people amid the mess. That intentional located-ness among folks already seasoned in digitality forms the "new equality" Sophia Naz desires.

Rhian Morgan and Lisa Moody consider what Naz refers to as "the decen-tralization of *there*."[88] To stress this urgent priority, Morgan and Moody employ theories of technology that help us understand how human and nonhuman actors interact in constantly shifting relationship networks—how, for exam-ple, an LMS—such as the somewhat unrelenting platform in which the ModPo forums are embedded—itself becomes "a technological actor" that need not ipso facto dehumanize the knowledge and intellectual responsiveness of the thought beneath or behind "the thinnest glass" of on-screen typing, be it the pixelated video viscera of living teachers teaching (such as myself appearing, increasingly into the past, in more than a thousand clips) or copies of poems by dead poets as digital apparitions.

The poetics of "Type" suggests that sociological and technological factors hold equal weight in shaping what we mean. Morgan and Moody's descriptions of "the messy interrelatedness of technologies, experiences, humans, and social contexts that constitute the teaching and learning process" befit a new positive sense of "dwelling" in Possibility.[89] This, despite the sudden severe narrowing of what was possible in real life. For Naz and other ModPo poets, the indexical terms *this, that, there,* and *here*—appearing as that which José Reyes calls "*these* characters," pointer-words composed of letters—are writing's (as always) but also (now) *being's* pandemic immateriality. Per Morgan and Moody's deployment of network theorizing in service of forming something from "messy interrelatedness," *typing* is a form of persistence and resilience. Reyes's typing in "Type" is neat and messy at once. Similarly, in Naz's poem "One Thing Happens," there is a multiplicity of persistent happenings, but not one of them is narrative. This is Naz:

> One thing happens, then another
> dust accumulates in a corner
> addendum, footnote, detritus, junk
> mail from fluffy pillow makers
> All the virus in the world
> weighs about a gram
> This and that is overdue
> An extinct season.[90]

The season has gone awry. The thing that is the actual cause is unreal. We retreat to dwelling, and poems emerge from dwelling in its connotation as obsession. Poems about that unreality are good at noticing when a thing happens.

THE STRUCTURED GAP YEAR

Inside a ModPo thread titled "Possibility in the time of Covid 19," Joseph Aversano rereads Dickinson's response to spatial limitation, her status as a recluse in "a solitude of space" as she composes through her "sequestered Afternoon."[91] Joseph sees her poems' notion of opening up a closed space as an unexpected guide to the quarantined life: "The imagination, whether Dickinson's or our own, and regardless of whether we are physically confined to a small flat or modest house, adds on rooms, balconies, terraces and the like, as well as raises the roofbeams and lets in more light. Our restraints, be they of our limited experience, conditioning, circumstance, the home, or the body (cf. [']my narrow Hands'), dare to open up to something bigger. The outside world is invited into the space now granted it." Joseph and those who respond to this challenging thread "dare to open up to something bigger" out of the pandemic's precarious equation of home and the feeling of being lost in time.[92] There's a Dickinson to be reinterpreted in 2020 for whom "A Prison gets to be a friend—."[93]

Judith Butler's *What World Is This? A Pandemic Phenomenology* does not present an optimistic assessment of the world, to be sure. But on the question of what people can make of timesoup, they agree with Joseph's view of what a particular kind of care-filled space can grant. Butler refers to the difficulty of "struggl[ing] against the very powers that dispose of lives, life-forms, and living habitats," yet recognizes, "one cannot oppose all that brutality alone but only through collaboration, expanding networks of support that make provisions for new conditions for living and reconfigured space-times for desire, enacting a new form of common life and collective values and desires. And for life to be livable, it has to be embodied—that is, it requires whatever supports allow for a space to be inhabited—and it needs a space, a shelter or dwelling, to live."[94]

This statement was not, of course, an interpretation of Dickinson's house of possibility. Yet it is a remarkable gloss on the situation of that poem for its readers in 2020–2021. In a postscript to his comment advocating for the idea of the reader-visitor to Dickinson's house as modeling "our restraints" and "daring to open up to something bigger," Joseph observed that he had "just now noticed" other people's threads in which they, too, simultaneously yet separately, were interpreting Dickinson through their pandemic experience. He was encouraged by the ready availability in the digital space of such "expanding networks of support," to use Butler's terms. To read and join the others became his occupation, thread to thread, a *this* for now.

One finds in the ModPo discussions of 2020 and 2021 numerous versions of this daring to open up. I drew hope from them then and still do. In reading several thousand comments from that period for this book, I observed not a hint of anger or even much impatience with the panicgogy going on all around them. Some bemusement over the situation of friends and loved ones who, unprepared, had little choice but to rush headlong into the "pivot" to online for school or work. And a good deal of genial recruitment of others into the free, never-shuttered mass seminar; as noted earlier, the enrollment jumped by many thousands in the spring of 2020. But, as I say, no discernible rancor. I'll confess to having been somewhat surprised by the experience of rereading a few years after the fact, given how much irritation and indignation I recall generally. The outrage expressed by philosopher Giorgio Agamben, to take an extreme and notable counter-example, was aimed at antagonisms across the board, at every aspect of the new digital life for teachers and learners.

In "Requiem for the Students," published on May 23, 2020, Agamben summarized two "firm" points. The first, "Students who truly love to study will have to refuse to enroll in universities transformed in this way, and, as in the beginning [when medieval academies were first formed around student meetings], constitute themselves in new *universtates*, only within which . . . the word of the past might remain alive and something like a new culture be born." ModPo participants would have likely appreciated the counterinstitutional spirit of the second contention. As we have seen, it's partly the vision hypothesized by M. Gessen. There is a certain optimistic pride in and around the various ModPo communities about the idea of dwelling in poetic possibilities for "students who truly love to study" and the possibility of an educational alternative to traditional credit-bearing, tuition-dependent enrollment.

But Agamben's first point was quite another thing. He expressed bitter condemnation of panicgogy and pivot. The pivot was not really a turn or an adjustment but a hard-and-fast ideological retroversion: "Professors who agree—as they are doing en masse—to submit to the new dictatorship of telematics and hold their courses only *online* are the perfect equivalent of the university teachers who in 1931 swore allegiance to the Fascist regime."[95]

The eminent Canadian poet and translator Erín Moure posted to Facebook an English translation of Agamben's invective during the last week of May, to which Fiona Templeton, the poet and playwright, responded by describing the dilemma she and many others faced: "This is so true. I feel I both want to refuse the takeover of technological education and refuse to go where I don't feel safe." The ModPo community roundly cheered Moure's next response: "Some of it is necessary for safety but who is consulting the students for ways to make discussion and contact work . . . the #modpolive course Al Filreis shepherds does this in myriad ways . . . but if the universities aren't making such things possible, time to take a Gap Year . . . and register for ModPo!!" This was a serious suggestion, befitting what some educators were offering among the "fall [2020] scenarios." This strategy came to be known as the "structured gap year."[96] It cannot be determined exactly how many of the new enrollees between May and December 2020 had chosen to include the free noncredit course about modern poetry as part of a structured gap year. But while the quantity of participation increased, overall the quality of the experience seemed unaffected by the addition of those who joined to fill a survey-course hole per the opportunistic stance Jonathan Zimmerman identified in "Coronavirus and the Great Online-Learning Experiment": "If there is a class you don't want to take," Zimmerman suggested, "take it online and get it out of the way."[97]

For some, as identified in Moure's distinction, a separation was emerging between second-space schooling (now with its vexed politics of reopening) and the cMOOC as an avid decentralization of the third space and the possibility of that "new equality of space" honored by ModPo poet Sophia Naz in her pandemic poems and posts. It was an equality that saw joining curriculum-focused students still thinking in units of syllabus weeks and semesters with the more typical previous ModPo participants—the office workers learning during breaks and on weekends, the retirees, the home-schoolers, the poets with their new poems seeking readers, the people like Maureen Bailey for whom universities are geographically remote and for other reasons out of reach, the people with learning differences, and the parents amid hectic caring for young children.

Adding to the distinction Moure offered her social-media friends and followers as a reasonable response to Agamben, there was a confusion that persisted and increased, was not at all relieved—and in fact further confounded—by the fast movement back into "the collegiate space" attempted by the for-profit MOOC enterprises. These competitive companies seized the moment of a structured gap year to reenter public consciousness with a basic strategy intending to remind the general public—not just students and their frustrated parents—of the way contemporary education could happen. The move backfired, arguably. MOOCs and all their putative failures were back in the news and social media and on the front lines of the debate once more. Jeffrey Young's overview of March 25, 2020, asked: "Will COVID-19 Lead to Another MOOC Moment?" Young reported that Coursera, the for-profit host of the LMS for ModPo and (at the time) 3,799 other xMOOCs, charged early into the fray to offer (temporary) free access to all those courses.[98] (Of course, ModPo was already always free, so this signaled no change. But I note, for what it's worth, that the MOOC portfolio of the Wharton School at my university had generated $20 million in 2019, that benchmark pre-pandemic year,[99] so giving it all away for free once again presented a challenge.) When a teacher identified on Twitter as "Dr Jon Cluck" refused to be in a room set for a capacity of seventeen people but where their thirty students had been gathering in person, they eliminated attendance penalties and live-streamed their lecture. They were then fired from the position, a decision their Twitter defenders blamed on MOOCs, even though, obviously, the online equivalent of the thirty-person course would not have resembled a MOOC in the least. "Truly awful that they are punishing you for doing the right thing. I remember not even 10 years ago in academia that everyone was so excited about MOOCs, and now we're getting this bullshit." And: "I use[d] to know a guy who taught one of the first super successful MOOCs. He said his university's motivation & agreement to do MOOCs was the free marketing. . . . Just garden variety greed." Some faculty chose this moment to recall the administrative ballyhooing of 2012. "College administrators used to love online learning despite lots of evidence that it's less effective," tweeted Jason Pearl, a scholar of eighteenth-century literature. "Now [as they urged 're-opening'] they love face-to-face courses despite lots of evidence it's unsafe. Both times, the thinking has been: sure this is bad for people, but it's good for business."[100]

"CONTENT" IN SCARE QUOTES

The revival in 2020 of memories of "an 'arms race' for MOOCs" certainly did not make for a good look for the profit-making MOOC providers during a moment already replete with moral panic—if the disposition of Dr Jon Cluck's defenders on Twitter can be viewed as typical, as I think indeed they were. "Arms race"! That was the phrase used to describe the first ascendancy of MOOCs by the philosopher of education Lavinia Marin in her book *On the Possibility of a Digital University* (2021). Marin finds MOOCs, by which she generally means xMOOCs, to be a failure overall. But since her interest is in studying conditions that might finally give rise to a successful digital lyceum, she observes that in 2012, the Year of the MOOC, "the enthusiasm [was] not for MOOCs as such, but rather the idea of moving the university online." This is a key distinction. Failures discretely pedagogical and financial—the wide perception of "garden variety greed" on the part of universities and outsourcing-obsessed public secondary schools and community college systems—put the true digital university, genuine "mediatic displacement" in Marin's terms, on hold. Until COVID. And even then, at first, "the main concern was less with providing the best type of education, but rather with finding something that was good enough, a survival solution." But soon "the hassles of moving entirely [to] education online revealed what was missing from these modes of interaction." Only when one considered "missing" aspects of pedagogy did "a clearer picture emerge . . . of the limitations of the [prospects of the] digital online university."[101]

Marin does not shirk from describing motives such as those that made Jason Pearl and Dr Jon Cluck bitterly skeptical. But she is not certain if the kind of education she recommends will or will not be "good for business," and she is critical of various examples of online teaching. The forms of education idealized in the book are, however, she argues, good for people—both for teachers and learners, learners foremost. In a concluding chapter, Marin's narrative of digital possibilities leads to an advocacy of experimental forms of the MOOC. The most striking example she offers is the so-called bMOOC, which she describes as the result of efforts to redesign the mode "from scratch." The bMOOC bypasses instructor-led deterministic xMOOC linearity, giving learners no preview of the content, as teacher-leaders offer "no clear goals or finish line." One bMOOC instance Marin cites modeled itself on Rancière's *The Ignorant Schoolmaster* and used that book—itself modeling maverick pedagogy—as part of a course activity in cocreativity. Experimenting with teaching practices of close reading, the students were to work deeply and slowly with, and then annotate, *only* pages nineteen through twenty-three of *any* book they chose from a list, Rancière's pages being among the options.[102] Aleatory teaching! I use this technique all the time in my Writers House classroom. Students take responsibility for their volition, however unexpected it might seem. Learners choosing texts to discuss? If they can find something to say about any random page—or in my teaching: stanza, line, or phrase—they prove for themselves at least that close reading is a sustainable interpretive practice even when, perhaps especially when, the text resulted from a learner's unintentional choice.

One of Marin's standards for success, in the slow forward-and-back movement toward the advent of the genuine digital academy—only somewhat sped up by panicgogy—is whether learners can cause "experiences of thinking" to befit teaching formats. She takes a chapter to consider whether a listener's thinking can happen during a lecture. Thinking *can* happen during a lecture, Marin argues, but it's not inherent in that venerable mode. Ultimately, lectures provide information, not knowledge. Until the full interactivity of online learning can be realized, teachers should understand that using "videoconferencing apps to enact an online lecture cannot yet be an instance of a digital university since the collective experiences of attention-making [a phrase, for Marin, synonymous with "experiences of thinking"] were subverted by the individualising logic of the screen." The iconoclastic bMOOC, on the contrary, "showed the possibility to stir occasions for thought by disrupting the linearity of the classical MOOCs, by disorienting the student and by refusing to deliver some 'content' to be learned." Marin's book presents the word *content* in scare quotes.[103]

How eccentric is the bMOOC? How scalable? ModPo, for all its connectivist aspirations, is no bMOOC. For one thing, there is no "refusal to deliver content." Mappings of the syllabi are readily available. Then again, many choose not to, or can't, follow syllabus order. What's more, there are these five bMOOC-like attributes: (1) the support for learner-led creative projects; (2) the encouragement of disordered browsing and the randomness of discovery, especially through ModPoPLUS, the crowd-curated roster of CCCR videos, and the "explore" function at ModPo.org that facilitates searching by poem, poet, participant, year, or category (subgenre or theme); (3) the provision of infrastructure to express a belief in the importance of sidetracking conversation; (4) the emphasis on coming and going, engagement and gap, accommodations to timesoup—encouragements of individual contemplation such as Ken X. felt that quiet lockdown night; and (5) the primary choice of content meant to disorient learners.

This last aspect is more heretical than it might seem. All these qualities and aims have had their detractors, but the matter of content has drawn a lot of attention and no small measure of ire—and not only in the context of plans for online education, although these have served as lightning rods, especially, as we have seen, during 2020–2021. The next chapter begins with a major figure among the detractors, whose timely intervention seemed to address issues raised in the emergent moment for open education stimulated by the development of massive open courses. Consideration of such a counterargument is helpful, I think, since any new form of teaching requires a frank reevaluation of the connection between content and skill. The chapter ends with examples of teachers and students in classrooms where the problems of reading, and even of *unreadability*, become occasions for students to learn that language is moving and unfixed, available always for the "experiences of thinking" (in Marin's phrase) that are unlikely, if not impossible, to happen through the one-way delivery of information. This is so even if that information is deemed to be something every literate citizen should know.

CHAPTER 3

THE DIFFERENCE-MAKING MACHINE

CULTURAL LITERACY, 2009

My close reading of Lavinia Marin's statement about the bMOOC led me to work further through aspects of problematic notions about content presented to heterogeneous learners. The thorny matter of content led me, in turn, to an incursion into the politics of education staged at the end of the 2000s by my graduate school professor, E. D. Hirsch.[1] It would be wrong to think of Hirsch's attack on schemes by educators to disrupt syllabus linearity and his rebuke of their plans to set aside goals for the delivery of topical information people should acquire as matters pertaining only to the old first wave of fights against the liberal educational establishment in the late 1980s. Arriving in 2009, just months before the early massive online classes, Hirsch's most strident refutation of learner-centered teaching was relevant because connectivism was giving way to xMOOCs, and many of the first colossal courses featured canonical reading lists and quick-take videos on works and concepts everyone should recognize. Participating in many early MOOCs was said to be something like acquiring cultural literacy.[2] It's even been said of the ModPo syllabus![3] Moreover, Hirsch's twenty-first-century update continued to echo through concerns about education during and beyond the pandemic, in part through the Core Knowledge Foundation (which sponsors schools and hosts national conferences) with its campaigns to combat learning loss in the 2020s. At the beginning of the 2010s, historian of education Terrence O. Moore felt it was the right time to describe the evolution of Hirsch as "the making of an educational conservative."[4]

I'm referring to Moore's 2010 essay-review of the book *The Making of Americans: Democracy and Our Schools* (2009). It was one of Hirsch's several follow-ups to the best-selling *Cultural Literacy: What Every American Needs to Know* (1987).[5] I read the later book in 2012 partly to find out where the open course I was creating would fit within the politics of online education. One could anticipate updated arguments for cultural literary accounting for new modes of multiaccess learning made possible in classrooms by connectivity and networked sharing,[6] teacher-independent innovations in information gathering of the sort that the argument of *Cultural Literary* back in the 1980s could not readily have known. By 2009, what would Hirsch have to say in response to the goal, put forth by the movement toward realizing the design for a wholly digital schooling, of intentionally "*disorienting* the student and . . . *refusing* to deliver some 'content' to be learned"—or to Kimberly McGee's conclusion that "the lack of self-control and *topic* control" in class discussions leads to a kind of "responsibility" that is an "underlying truth of democracy"?[7] Hirsch's topic was democracy. The lack of topic control in education and its—for him, negative—relationship to ideas of democracy in education was his major cause for concern.

For me, there was another thing to ponder: when I first read the 2009 book a few years after its publication, as I was choosing our selection of poets, its focus on *making Americans* rang a bell. Where had I already heard of this? More on that resonance a few pages further. If there was an echo, Hirsch would tell us, as he seemed not to be hiding any part of his agenda. He was explicit, urging us not to "tip-toe . . . around the idea that the schools should form Americans"—a political goal—once all of us agreed to "a standard language" to be taught, thus adhering to the principle that standard language requires standard content knowledge.[8]

COMMUNITY CREATES COMPETENCY

If ModPo's Edward Kranz observes that an "act of interpretation by an interpretive community . . . *creates a text*," for Hirsch such "anti-core-curriculum extremis[m]" has it dangerously backward.[9] Hirsch: "Content is skill."[10] Learning must proceed from the school's and teacher's choice of syllabus. Hirsch contends that common texts enable readable writing. And, let's face it, some writing is deemed more readable than other writing. How and why? The better passage might convey the same sense as its lessers, but it is easier to read and can be read faster than its "stylistically degraded" alternative.[11] "Assuming that two texts convey the same meaning, the more readable text will take less time and effort to understand."[12] "Relative readability," derived from ease and speed, from legibility and accessibility, from "efficiency" and ready ascertainment,[13] fundamentally contradicts Larry Eigner's idea taken to heart by teacher-poet José Reyes—individuals creatively perceive structured fields "with whatever eyes" (eccentrically: preposition → pronoun → verb)—which is an utterly different notion of accessibility, one necessitating and commending *more* effort rather than less.

While Hejinian, Lévy, and others endorse the personal rejection of closure, a model for presenting *all* subject matter, Hirsch ridicules the idea that learners "can gradually construct their own understandings." He expresses horror at what has arisen from educational progressivism. Versions of describing things he detests: "the anti-curriculum ideology," "open-ended formalis[m]," the devotion to "language arts" (which he deems a "cognitive wasteland"), courses that are "no longer . . . subject-centered" but learner-centered, and the "new approach [in which] specific subject matter was no longer to be determined *in advance*."[14]

Obviously, this concept does not align with the idea that the best place for learning about writing is a space in which writing actually happens. Hirsch mocks classrooms arranged "as a workshop." Although he is averse to discussions of classrooms as "spaces"—he finds such education school topics anathema—it's not hard to guess what he would make of Nardone's proposal that people's projects made in a learning space can sustain the subject village. Hirsch derides the use of phrases such as "reciprocal teaching" and "community of learners."[15]

A middle chapter of the 2009 book is titled "Competence and Community." His view there is that competence is what creates community. Competence is a prerequisite for, rather than a result of, the community of learners. Something like a bMOOC would surely strike him as yet another outcome of the unpardonable sins of the Project Method movement; he satirizes the method's attitude that "projects are better than books and lectures."[16] Hirsch's view that *competence creates community*, not the other way around, is more than just canonical conservatism of the Allan Bloom variety, though it does certainly lend itself to that. For Hirsch, it was a premise meant to change our views of the importance of diversity. Diversity *is* important, he argues, but it can or should be an effect of teachers teaching what all citizens need to know rather than the factor that determines curricular choices.

Hirsch makes his case for the relationship between reading and writing and citizenship in the chapter titled "Transethnic America and the Civic Core." Learning should create citizens who can function in public settings. This aim caught my attention as I encountered it while beginning to build an international—and internationalist—open-enrollment course topically focused (mostly) on U.S. writers. Hirsch wants directly to face "the difficult issue . . . of citizen-making," and the need to establish agreements about the United States and its ideals, regardless of the politics (or so he says). He is not especially gentle when pondering the admitted advantages of the inclusion of multiple "nation-alities" and "different religions." According to the core curriculum movement, "we leave them alone but *expect them to accommodate themselves* to the public sphere."[17] Patriotism, Hirsch claims, arose when American schoolbooks were widespread and relatively unified.

On the whole, conservative reviewers appreciated Hirsch's insistence, in the face of a disastrous liberal "anti-curriculum monopoly,"[18] that the founders felt the American political experience "depended on a common public sphere." Later, Hirsch says, Lincoln wanted schools to "diligently teach the common American creed."[19] "It is uncontroversial that schools in a democracy have a duty to help form competent citizens." Whether that is so, he is ready to take the idea a step further: "It is a duty of *American* schools to educate competent *American* citizens," and he emphasizes: "Hence my theme: The Making of Americans."[20]

We are a long, long way from the assessments of Wai Chee Dimock: only inso-far as the value of subject matter is "measured by the inspired output of others, those driven to get in on the act," can the pedagogy making it available to citizens be fully open and open-ended.[21] Only then can the right combinations for cre-ating cultural belonging in the form of education populism be arranged. Hirsch styles himself a populist too (a source of complaints from antagonists to his ideo-logical right), but let us consider his counterargument to combat the influence of the version of a people's poetics such as praised by Dimock in PennSound, ModPo, and the Kelly Writers House. It certainly should not be ignored that there *is* a citizen poetics of *The Making of Americans*. And it becomes possible to project onto the reading of a poem a few of Hirsch's methodic rubrics—includ-ing the frank antimodernism of his *Validity in Interpretation* (1967). There is certainly an idea implicit in such rubrics—as there is in Hirsch's defense against the "decisive attack" by Ezra Pound "and associates" on the "sensible belief that a text means what its author meant"[22]—about the way young people can read and understand poems when being schooled.

This is flat-out educational antimodernism. Such a practice highlights the crucial differences between the influential Hirschean view of literature and writ-ing and that of others encountered in my first chapters—learners, teachers, poets, digital theorists, proponents of reader response, skeptics of digital minimalism, and connectivist educators. Hirsch's perspective that to understand a piece of writing you already must know about its subject matter or even sometimes have to stipulate that it *has* subject matter contradicts the experience I and ModPo learners have had. Think of Cid Corman's "It isnt for want / of something to say," a poem that is not "about" anything except being with him in the poem. Echoing Corman in "It's Not That I Want to Say," the poet-theorist Fred Moten, in the book *Poets on Teaching*, argues that there might be "something to say" about a poem but what's far more important is the recognition that "It's not that I want to say that poetry should or can be disconnected from having something to say." He adds: "It's just that everything I want to say eludes me."[23] Moten, quoting Corman, is saying that the content of a poem is best if it is not said or sayable. In the culturally literate world Hirsch advocates, there is as little disconnection as possible between what a poem says and what an educated person can or wants to say about it, the goal being to narrow down to nil that which cannot be said about cultural information a text carries or from which it is written. Nor is it the view here, contrary to the strict originalism of *The Making of Americans*, that "reading and writing require *unspoken* background information, *silently assumed.*" The citizen poetics of *The Classroom and the Crowd* will not declare that "specified subject-matter knowledge . . . is the key to language comprehension."[24] Indeed, we can contend, admitting that it might strike fair-minded teachers of poetry as wrong-headed or too aesthetically strident, that "language comprehension" is *impeded* by the kind of settled, silent, agreed-upon background knowledge Hirsch believes should precede our noisy encounters with texts.

AMERICAN UNDERSTANDING

There's a 927-page elephant in the room. I'm referring to a big book by Gertrude Stein. Given that, for at least some people, Stein "changed language and writing for us all,"[25] there is certainly more than a little relevance to Hirsch's proposed great reformation of schools. Another way to put this: there surely is at least a "silent" or "unspoken" relationship between E. D. Hirsch's *The Making of Americans* of 2009 and Gertrude Stein's *The Making of Americans* of 1911, a book this challenging major writer "always called her main work."[26] But it is not mentioned in Hirsch's book of the same name. The exclusion of the obvious reference is perhaps aligned with the effective absence of Stein from those best-selling must-know/must-read lists,[27] notwithstanding her continued and amplified presence, according to field consensus, as one of the two or three most influential American modernists.[28] Perhaps Stein was sacrificed to the Hirschean ideal of common texts enabling readable writing—perhaps inconvenient, even contradictory, for Hirsch and his cultural literacy colleagues to commend a novel of such widely recognized importance in which ease and speed of readability are truly irrelevant qualities. Then again, by 2009, with *The Making of Americans*, he had advanced his case to the point where it was audaciously about how Americans are to be made—perhaps, it might be said, precisely Steinian in its hubris. Stein's novel most certainly has something to say about that making. It seems obvious, then, and perhaps now obligatory, to seek *The Making of Americans* somewhere in this important debate about education, regardless of her contribution having been ignored by Hirsch and merely tolerated or suppressed by others. For starters, it's been said that Stein's writing, and *The Making of Americans* in particular, "requires—one might say demands—that we attend to the words on the page,"[29] and that spirit would seem to align well with Hirsch's plea for diligent, instructive reading practices.

By having paired Gertrude Stein and John Dewey, and by exploring the debt owed to Stein in Joan Retallack's optimistic idea that composition (writing) is explanation (learning), I have already suggested the importance of Stein's heterodox practice to the experience of reading and responding like a citizen. Week 4 of ModPo, known as "Stein Week," is, for many learners, the turning point in reckoning with writing in which *how* matters more than *what*. Now, here, the suppressed linking of Hirsch and Stein gives me the opportunity to contrast distinct ideas about democratic understanding through difficult reading. Some or all of these lessons would seem to fail any Hirschean test. Nonetheless, there's an American pedagogy implicit in Stein's novel that counters the ongoing reactionary challenges suggested by Hirsch's *The Making of Americans* and in subsequent "patriotic education" projects, such as the syllabus put forward by the 1776 Commission in 2020 and renewed in 2025.[30]

Stein's novel tells the genealogy, immigration history, and emotional development of members of the Hersland and Dehning families. Within this telling of a very American story, the narrator composes meditations on the process of writing the book, which increase in frequency as the novel progresses and pushes the narrative story into the background. Interestingly, the more the book is about Jewish immigration and immigrant culture as a topic—in that sense, about the making of Americans—the more intrusive the metatextual passages. In aiming to tell the "complete history of many women and many men,"[31] not just those of the Herslands and Dehnings, "Stein's book has a democratic spirit to it," as one critic has put it.[32] It is about making an American culture that the chronicler can attempt to say she confidently knows. "The old people in a new world," she writes, "the new people made out of the old, that is the story I mean to tell, for that is what really is and what I really know."[33]

In *The Making of Americans*, Stein uses an extremely limited vocabulary and relies on techniques of repetition. She deploys an unusual use of the present participle, especially with nonfinite clauses containing a verb that shows no tense, and continuous-present or "prolonged present" gerunds:[34] "Really it is a very difficult thing in living for some to be certain that they are believing in loving, that they are believing in being honest in living, that they are believing in any one being a good one."[35] Whereas for Annie Dillard (in a warning that eminent writer has given her writing workshop students) "gerunds are lazy, you don't have to make a decision and soon, everything is happening at the same time, pell mell, chaos,"[36] for Stein such indecisiveness and supposed laziness are the very causes of all things simultaneously happening. This simultaneity expresses her "belie[f] in being honest in living" as a function of the American selfhood formed from language.

As you follow its words and phrases, an individual sentence in *The Making of Americans* is as readable as those sentences encountered in many readings assigned to secondary school students. The book "is always haunted by what we think it should say" near the ends of those sentences—by "what we are already sure that it says," according to E. L. McCallum in *Unmaking the Making of Americans*.[37] Reading along, we tend to know how to complete a Steinian sentence. We assume it will deliver another and another and yet another of the simple words it has used thus far. So we become part of the continuous present, a situation of sentence-level cognition. It's in the nature of reading a book like this, and it's fair to say that a major contribution to the art of modernist writing is about the reading of it. "The difficulty of reading the book," notes McCallum, "is less the incomprehensibility of the language than simply the challenging range of feelings that reading the novel induces."[38] The challenge comes, in part, because we begin to realize that Stein aims to "realize absolutely every variety of human experience that was possible to have," as she noted later, "every type, every style, every nuance."[39]

Insofar as Stein's book can be said to be educational, it is because it is about how to articulate the experience of reading. That's a terrific thing, I'd argue, for a novice reader to learn. The novel, McCallum suggests, is "about the practices of reading, the difficulty of reading, and even the impossibility of reading."[40] "Perhaps no other book makes it so plain to the reader that it is being written over time," Janet Malcolm wrote (despite her misgivings about Stein otherwise), "and that, like life, it is inconsistent and changeable."[41] The book theorizes reading time as writing time, and as such it challenges the very idea of literary progress. It is, Stein offers, "a record of a decent family progress respectably lived by us . . . and this is by me carefully a little each day to be written down here. . . . I hasten slowly forwards."[42] Its time is a paradox, haltingly hurrying. One critic, comparing Stein's writing to modernist visual art, uses the phrase "still narrative," an analog to still life.[43] Another, describing the filmic qualities of the novel, suggests that "no text in literary history seems quite so bereft of momentum as this one."[44] "I am resisting," Stein's narrator hypothesizes, "so that I can be slowly realizing and always I am knowing I can never really be knowing all the ways there are of feeling living"—that said in a sentence with five uses of variations on the present participle.[45]

Hirsch's educational ideal marks a clear separation between a reader learning and a writer telling that which is to be learned. For Stein, to the contrary, the novel being written becomes "this thing" that is itself "doing," and it is "trouble" equally for her readers and for herself as she writes. And before long, we find ourselves "do[ing] this thing" as well. George B. Moore, who has written an entire volume about the function of repetition in *The Making of Americans* as crucial to the rise of American modernism, proposes that it is "a book about writing as discovery itself."[46] Its metapoetic composition is one origin of Pierre Lévy's way of explaining collective intelligence—crisscrossing human subjectivities to defy "the linearity of text" and resist "present[ing] ideas in chronological order"[47]— and also of Lyn Hejinian's exploration of collaborative resistances to closure as explorations of ongoing difficulty. It's only a problem if you *don't want* the reader to be the one doing things with a text. Here's Stein on this approach: "Certainly it is trouble to me to be doing this thing. I certainly cannot in any way know it is a trouble to you to do this thing when you asked me whether you should or should not do this thing and then did what I said you should do about doing this thing. I certainly can be realizing it is a trouble to me to do this thing, I certainly cannot be realizing it is a trouble to you to do this thing."[48] The trouble Stein has with her own book is humane and passionate. She is hopelessly lost in the act of composition. Her "recording of this struggle within the pages of the book," Ulla Dydo observes, "provides some of its most profoundly moving passages": an instance of metatextuality as pure emotion.[49]

Unlike the literary texts Hirsch recommends for learners in *The Making of Americans*, Stein's *The Making of Americans* is not a book historically reporting on national happenings that have occurred before its "doing" as writing. It attempts to replace historical with emotional motives. This is her loving version of American making. "I love it and now will write it. This is now a history of my love of it."[50] What makes Stein's book difficult to read is fundamentally a problem for Hirsch and is at the core of his and many others' laments over education: it is that the role of the singularity of the important American event has been outperformed and superseded. The American Jews of the novel are *made*—"formed and reformed through immigration, marriage, births, and deaths"—"but those events are *not* the concern of [Stein's] narrator." McCallum continues: "To deviate from that paradigm [i.e., "a sense of continuously moving"], to dither, delay, defer, endure would be perversely un-American." The modernist novel demonstrates this point "by *unmaking* that American sense of time."[51]

If Stein's book can be deemed a response to canonical conservatism, as I think it can, then the most effective counterresolution is not just to offer an alt-canon in which Stein gets included once and for all. No, the instructional spirit of Stein's *The Making of Americans* is more radical than that. Its offering of a vast alternative, through its persistent unmaking, is a refusal to be part of the regular conversation about democratic learning Hirsch and others insist we must have, and to appropriate, on the contrary, the accusation of degradation (against "stylistically degraded" lesser writing). The standard, time-honored American topics are not even "the concern" of the writer! Reading for topicality—for content—is not at all the point! That big refusal, as a matter of fact, is so un-American as to be, Stein argues here and elsewhere, the most modern American thing imaginable.

WHY DEMOCRACY NEEDS THE HUMANITIES

I say, let's take all this to school. A consistent aspect of my own experiences teaching Stein to high school students is observing how the Steinian text welcomes the close-reading discussion into something like Scuro's timesoup. There's lots of generative dithering, delaying, deferring, and enduring. In October 2018, several ModPo colleagues and I convened a group of twenty-one high school students in Palo Alto, California, and recorded a forty-four-minute collaborative close reading of Stein's "A Long Dress," one of the enigmatic *Tender Buttons* poems. We started with nothing except the tiny text in front of us. But soon there were prolific digressions: the state of clothing manufacturing at the turn of the twentieth century; the history of electric current; trends in dress fashion (the fashion sense of the terms *line* and *waist*); the Triangle Shirtwaist Factory fire and its many Jewish victims; the experience of speed-up, piecework, scientific management, and Taylorism; the deprecation of young people's awareness today about the manufactured nature of products. During these tangents, several students were investigating relevant information and context by using smartphones in real time. Others took notes, along with their teacher (poet and ModPo TA Jake Marmer), to help prepare for a subsequent discussion.

Talking about Stein's "A Long Dress" in particular, it turns out, is a way of engaging in Deweyan active learning in which students "learn where the materials came from, how they were made." I admire Martha Nussbaum's case for "Why Democracy Needs the Humanities" (in her book *Not for Profit*) for several reasons but chiefly because its support of the humanities hinges on interactive practices such as those in which students "learn to ask about the processes that produced the things they were using every day," such as the very clothing—some of it meant to be radical or statement-making—these learners had chosen to wear on the day we discuss what a "line" of clothing means in a poem made of stylized *lines*.[52] Democracy needs the humanities, in short, because learning can entail understanding everyday actions.

A video recording of the collaborative close reading session at Palo Alto was made with the permission of the students and the school and added to the ModPoPLUS syllabus.[53] Oft-viewed, it has since served as a model—as have several videos about how to teach Stein's experimental verse portrait of Pablo Picasso—for other teachers and students attempting active learning in their own classrooms. A supposedly difficult text that invites extended collective focus, "A Long Dress" creates its own flexible standard for punctual rightness: the loosened approach to normative time frames, the bending of the clock rather than bending oneself to meet it, etc. that we saw earlier as features of crip poetics. Jake Marmer's students decided that the long discussion of the poem was long in exactly the way the poem itself was made, like a long dress with its own flow. They also concluded that the "current" that manufactured the dress was analogous to the machinery of collaborative close-reading pedagogy. This machine set loose an abundance of audio and video equipment into the room of active learning, as well as a cameraperson (Zach Carduner), an audio engineer (Chris Martin), and a surfeit of entangling wires and lights they had dragged into what was usually the learners' own uncluttered, uninterrupted, digitally minimal space.

They valued the intrusion and said so. They liked and comprehended the messy interdependence of creativity and technology: the combination of ModPo and Stein as a "machine-poet" loosed upon the rule-controlled apparati of secondary education. I borrow the term from Michele Bethke who wrote the following in the ModPo subforum on "A Long Dress": "I like the idea of the finished poem being the long dress and the current being the inspiration of the machine-poet."[54] During an earlier live ModPo webcast back in 2013, Bob Perelman described the implemented contraptions of poetics that humanize the machine/poet interaction rather than further mechanizing it. "Just think of a machine that does different things each time—perhaps like a brain maybe—that isn't just simply rotating wheels, or whatever a machine does," Perelman said. "A poem is a difference-making machine when it's a good poem. And Stein is certainly an active difference-making machine."[55]

When writing and speaking about her teaching activities using Stein, erica kaufman at Bard's Institute for Writing and Thinking (IWT) likes to quote Joan Retallack's essay "The Difficulties of Gertrude Stein" in *The Poethical Wager*: "There's an intense need for play when one is in a particularly untenable situation like adulthood."[56] kaufman's experience teaching other teachers how to use Stein in their own high school courses aligns well with how McCallum speaks familiarly in her book about making and unmaking: "We reading Stein must now position ourselves more as the interrupting child than the parent who is reading toward lights out and wishes to brook no delays or divagations from that aim. Close reading Stein, by which I mean reading Stein, necessitates reading childishly, even perversely, more for what we discover in the moment of reading than what conclusion we aim toward."[57]

Steinian pedagogy challenges the objective of setting learners sternly in the direction of a common knowledge. "Perhaps," Stein puckishly writes in *The Making of Americans*, "no one ever gets a complete history. . . . This is very discouraging thinking."[58] Teaching teachers to teach Stein in America's secondary schools, kaufman is encouraged by the discouragement. She guides teachers to ask: What happens when we mend or "fix" the sense of a Steinian piece of writing so that it makes more common sense to novice readers? I interviewed kaufman on this topic and quote here from the transcript of that conversation:

> It becomes really important for me to figure out a way to simulate an impossibly difficult experience with language. That's often the case particularly with younger students. That's how they feel when it comes to things that are associated with "literacy," particularly if I'm working with high-need school districts. There Stein is the perfect choice because no one, they or I, will really feel we fully, completely understand exactly what's happening. . . . Yet with Stein the teachers in my teaching workshop at first get upset. So then we can actually talk about the parallels between how the faculty is responding to this text and how students respond to what their teachers teach. What are the strategies that we use to invite people into grappling with really difficult texts? Then the thing that's so interesting about Stein is that . . . no one is going to say, "I totally understand what's going on." The reaction is: "I feel okay playing with this." It opens up the text, and then it takes away from the status of the text as being this holy thing that you can't know, that you can't love or touch. This is great . . . when you're in workshop with a teacher who's going to try to implement this in a high-school classroom.[59]

For two years, I taught an in-person version of ModPo to a class of seventeen Philadelphia public school teachers. We met in the evenings in a seminar room on the second floor of the Writers House, located just above the Arts Café (Samuel Sloan's venerable post-Gothic parlor, now the main event space). The teachers and I could often hear the sounds of a poetry reading happening below.

We surmise that *because* the rest of the house shares its sounds so readily with this 175-year-old second-floor bedroom—and also because snacks in this classroom are not just permitted but encouraged (in particular, a plentiful offering of chocolate bars for quick energy)—it is the space of choice for creative writing workshops with high school students. The teachers, as part-time students, were able to observe and participate in the online crowdsourced collaborative close readings. Based on this experience, Sally O'Brien, who was then teaching high school English in West Philadelphia, created a "Poets Imagining the City" curriculum unit she then experimentally taught to her own students, part of which entailed Stein and other poets presented as verbally peripatetic urban exemplars. O'Brien prepared in part by studying Michelle Burke's work on teaching Stein ("Writing from the Senses: Disarming Gifted and Perfectionist Students with Sound and Synesthesia"[60]): O'Brien learned not simply to reject the lecture mode as particularly inappropriate for the ModPo poems. She also intentionally "depart[ed] from the I-Do, We-Do, You-Do model, where a teacher models a process and then gradually releases responsibility to the students." She learned that in collaborative close readings of a difficult poem, each student can become immediately responsible for a "small piece of the puzzle." Thereupon, the work of the teacher is to encourage an assemblage of small-seeming responsibilities.[61]

FIGURE 3.1 High school students participating in the 2023 Summer Workshop for Young Writers at the Kelly Writers House.

Source: Kelly Writers House photo archive.

In Saigon, Troy Phillips teaches 9th- and 10th-grade English-language learners through ModPo. In March 2025, Phillips and eleven students enrolled in our course, and during nine intensive days of all-day sessions they completed it. The highlight was a focus on *Tender Buttons*, including "A Long Dress." They discussed how to vary English-language definitions, how to follow word play, how to hear homonyms. Phillips had studied the Palo Alto "Long Dress" video for himself although did not assign the students to watch it. Yet it became a model for their method of discussion—of Stein and all the ModPo poems—because, says Phillips, that form of collaboration "leads them to possibilities," to a sense of "rightness" as distinct from schooled correctness. When you're learning through homonyms the key is the way wording differences sound right. One day during their compressed semester I led a discussion by Zoom with these students in which we constructed a 90-minute collaborative close reading of "A Long Dress." Halfway through, I spontaneously assigned the one 8th-grader in the group, Han, to muse on the word "crackle" in the poem. "What is the current that makes machinery, that makes it crackle. . . ." Han described how the current making the machinery of Stein's poem-making made the poem's words variously snap, pop, hiss, and sizzle. At my request, she and a few classmates spoke the words aloud. They emphatically hissed and popped. They sounded out some synonyms of "crackle" by crackling. That sense of currency, they understood, was a poetic mouthful—electric (i.e., technical) but also contemporary (cultural)—and talking about/talking through the Stein was *making* the English words new. Han, it turns out, was the student who had insisted that her teacher reach out to me personally with an invitation to lead the collaborative interpretation across the twelve time zones. A recording of the session with Han and her ModPo classmates can become yet another option for viewing by other teachers and their students.[62]

In New Orleans, Julia Carey Arendell offers a choice of *Tender Buttons* to her high school students. "I tend to defer to 'Tender Buttons' when I use Stein in the classroom," she told me, "because those object lessons are very accessible." "Accessible?" I asked her. "Well, never the word we use with Stein," she conceded, but accessibility is not, for Arendell, a matter of interpretive straightforwardness or ease. It refers to the way that Stein increases the approachability, inversely proportional to the seeming difficulty of the assigned material. "If a teacher brings a Stein text to the classroom," Arendell says, "it will become pretty apparent to the students that the teacher is just as, or almost as, disoriented as the student." This turns the corner for students, in her experience, toward both confidence and feelings of intellectual safety. During our interview, I pointed out her pun on "object lesson." In what way, I asked, do the "Objects" mini-poems of *Tender*

Buttons—"A Box," "A Piece of Coffee," "A Method of a Cloak," "A Long Dress," and, of course, the infamously opaque "A Carafe, That Is a Blind Glass"—serve as educational object lessons? Answer: it has taught her students a way of "entertaining the possibility that they might be wrong" and "[to] have the self-awareness and also the confidence to say, 'I don't understand this yet' or 'I need more information.'" *I need more information* is key Hirschean phrasing, but in this case, in reverse. For Arendell, the objective in teaching about poetic objects is not information as a goal but using a supposedly difficult writer to encourage in students-becoming-readers the desire for information—to have the social daring required to state openly that one needs it. That is a version of "what accountability looks like" in education.[63] Stein's cubist carafe might as well be talking about how we learn to understand language's good, frenetic, ambitious trouble: "All this and not ordinary," Stein writes, "not unordered in not resembling. The difference is spreading."[64]

Arendell, then in her eleventh year (when we spoke) teaching students in New Orleans in this mode, had been for two-and-a-half years a teacher-student member of the inaugural cohort of Center for Liberal Arts & Sciences Pedagogy (CLASP) Fellows led by erica kaufman at IWT in affiliation with the Open Society University Network.[65] "I was blown away because [kaufman] sees Stein as a way to teach basic grammar." Arendell learned how, in a favorite activity, kaufman presents her students with Stein's verbal cubistic portrait, known as "If I Told Him" or "A Completed Portrait of Picasso," and asks them to make "fixes" or to write "corrections." The students repair or freely translate Stein's word usage and grammar. In a class of nonnative speakers, one of kaufman's students fixed Stein as follows:

If I told him would he like it. Would he like it if I told him. Would he like it would Napoleon would Napoleon would would he like it.

became:

I told him he would like it. He liked it and I told him that Napoleon would like it.

The idea that "subject-matter knowledge trumps formal skill in reading" does not apply when the language of the reading is essentially nonreferential or, in short, poetic.[66] Despite the attractions of its seeming fixities, information placed inside or (unspoken) behind a poem will not sit still. The "conservatism of language" is *always* tested by a poem.[67] In our interview, erica kaufman explored the dimensions of the classroom activity that enables teachers to enable students to know exactly what it feels like to make sense of making sense as a moving target. This stance further encourages role opacity. "It becomes the teacher as student, as student writer," kaufman told me. "It's all about empowering students to be able . . . to approach literacy more flexibly." The activity is collective, but the realizations are individual, personal, even intimate. Such individualization depends on the choice of a non-standard text. "Everybody is going to have to have their own process of sense-making," kaufman notices.

> Rather than give students either a text that's obvious and too easy, or a text that you already know what you want them to think about it, you level the playing field by giving them a text that even for you is just wild. As a teacher I have my own unanticipated reactions to this text, so that I can then generate *my own* language in response. Of course it's less about students being right or wrong, and more about everyone, teachers and students, being careful as readers and really attending to the way the individual words play out.

She further observes: "Because the teacher isn't so sure about the meaning of the text, the students realize the text is not actually that holy or sacred 'important' document. They then realize, 'I actually know a lot more about English grammar than I thought I did before.' Their writing improves."[68]

This is hardly an instance of the inattentive, unpatriotic "anti-grammar regime" advocates of core knowledge deem pernicious.[69] I'll concede that it is perhaps a cliché of progressive education to say that kaufman's students are learning to *trouble* the Stein text. It's another of those words critics of Deweyan assumptions operating inside graduate schools of education—full disclosure: I hold a secondary faculty appointment at one such school—will see as an effect of a vainglorious hypocrisy in this sort of teaching. Yet our syllabus includes poems by Stein, Dickinson, Niedecker, Hunt, Waldrop, Baraka, and Harryette Mullen because as we relinquish deference to their authorship, we realize their writing is learned best when it is troubled. Students of these poems can do things with words. The teacher inviting students to "try to make the words do it" is reminiscent of Stein's sense of her aim for herself to trouble the composition of *The Making of Americans*. "It is a trouble to me to be doing this thing," she keeps reminding us. What kaufman, O'Brien, Arendell, Phillips, Marmer, and various ModPo-affiliated teachers in schools aspire to teach is reading as doing—not just a hypothesis or ideal of asynchronous online teaching but a necessity, as Stephen Kosslyn's casebook for active learning points out in dozens of ways.

Here is what another of kaufman's students wrote in a report describing the activity engaging Stein's verbal Picasso portrait: "We began by reading the beginning of the poem again. We underlined the parts of the poem that we knew did not make grammatical sense. We talked about what a sentence is supposed to do and then tried to make the words do it. Some of Stein's ideas seemed backwards so we fixed them."[70] As we have seen, this is the sort of active learning—students fixing things—that Mara Holt, Lavinia Marin, Nicole Braun, José Reyes, and connectivist Stephen Downes find to be among the special social advantages of teaching remotely. The human poetry machine Bob Perelman identifies in Stein makes the 927-page modern novel a technical interface we should not fear—because, in part, it does accurately speak to our networked way of life well beyond the machinery Stein knew as a matter of technical fact in 1911 when she made "A Long Dress." But it also brings us back to the page and into the room. Perelman, not especially interested in digital theories, meant networking as an *analogy* to help us understand the way Stein as a preinternet poet networks her words. Marmer, kaufman, and Reyes, as a benefit of their significant experience teaching online (and specifically in ModPo), have also interestingly *exported* such qualities *back* into their face-to-face classrooms.

Is that export counterintuitive? Perhaps. People's educational experiences in communities engaged with experiments in learning experimental language, online and offline, form actual practices of reading, writing, close listening, and comprehension that can be shared every which way, across all the available modes. The visionary, child-centered poet William Blake—incidentally, the poet E. D. Hirsch studied at the start of his career[71]—was verily onto this at his most radical. "As the true method of knowledge is *experiment*," Blake said, "the true faculty of knowing must be the faculty which *experiences*." And so: "This faculty I treat of."[72]

William Blake and Gertrude Stein have more in common than one might think: their skeptical idea of the relationship between language and knowledge. That skepticism refutes the supposed conservatism of language and supports writing as experiences of thinking. Hejinian's "The Rejection of Closure," deeply influenced by Stein's "Composition as Explanation" and, in turn, influencing both the Writers House and ModPo as made places, imagines the experience of language as preceding knowledge and information. This is an idea anathema to core curriculumists and, contrarily, basic to the choice of content meant to disorient. "Language," Hejinian writes, "discovers what one might know, which in turn is always less than what language might say."[73] Perhaps common texts enable readable writing, but what if *any* text does so? What if "relative readability," with its connection to the concept of educational efficiency, contradicts accessibility rather than aids it? When learners are able to construct their own critical realizations, communities of readers create competence, and democratic forms of understanding can occur through difficult reading. Learners learning to ask about the clamorous processes that make objects they use daily can include, as one of those objects, the poem they take up for discussion. These noisy, everyday encounters with texts can *precede* our discovery of consensus knowledge. The three chapters of part 2, to follow, are about that noise: the sound of the end of the lecture.

PART II

The Sound of the End of the Lecture

CHAPTER 4

I HEAR/YOU HEAR

They cannot.
A note.
They cannot.
A float.
They cannot.
They dote.
They cannot.
They as denote.
Miracles play.
Play fairly.
Play fairly well.
A well.
As well.
As or as presently.
Let me recite what history teaches. History teaches.

—Gertrude Stein, "A Completed Portrait of Picasso"

HAVING VOICE, AN INTRODUCTION

The topics of the next three chapters are sound and learning. *Recite* is a vexed term in the modern history of schooling. Whatever utterances make up an alternative to recitation are our concern. Stein's way of ending her Picasso portrait poem, verse that is otherwise linguistically obscure, gets to the heart of the matter: "Let me recite what history teaches. History teaches."

First, we might ask: Recite what? What could Stein mean by the word *teaches* in that objectless phrase "history teaches"? How particularly is she referring to *teaching*? Is history typically not, after all, the taught object rather than the pedagogical subject?

Pedagogy always entails a subject. There is a who who is professing. Modernity taught us to emphasize another factor that is layered on the situation: *how* we know what we are learning. As we saw in chapter 3, one major idea of the modern, in the field of education as in poetry, has been to foreground subjects (the who) and process (the how), even at the risk of overshadowing content (the what).

Here is one way of reflecting on my own experience as a teacher and a scholar of modern culture: awaiting the right circumstance to advocate for a form of interpretation prompted by the idea that history shouldn't teach that history teaches. The circumstance turns out to have been technological. But before returning fully to the convergences made possible by that technology in part 3, about citizen poetics as an expression of crowd-powered effort, here in part 2 we will survey various backgrounds and groundworks from the 1930s, by way of the 1960s, through to the 1990s. These pages identify ideas, sources, and developments that brought me and many colleagues, collaborators, and learners to the interrelated ventures described in the previous pages and to the various places where people gather to form an alternative learning. In chapter 6, we will visit the public poetry reading—an event, a happening—as an instance of such a space. The final section of that chapter presents a speculative biographical profile of Max Warsh—a portrait of the visual artist as a young person whose parents (both of them poets) brought him to scenes and places where the sounds made by performed poems gave him a schooling in all the senses.

How can it be said, as Stein suggests in her unusual way, that a recitation of what "history teaches" is ironic? That which makes up the normal explicative order or denotative pedagogy—I ask you to picture it simplistically for now: a teacher points to a text and then indicates an object in the world, implying or saying outright: *this is what it means*—is not up to the challenge of permitting the performance of self-reflexivity, or of miracles playing fairly well (to use Stein's antic terms). Such performance is an alternative to the historical mode that seeks to treat objects as relatively stable recipients of signifying. Among modern materials, as we have seen in poems worked through by the ModPo crowd, there is often a self-reflexive teaching and learning; I've been calling this a metapedagogy. The view here is that the work of teaching starts with an insistence on some sort of self-conscious stance—or, in other words, the particular location or situation of the convening subject with respect to a commitment to openness. An example from a late 1990s application of perhaps the most famous expression of 1960s-era pedagogy: Paulo Freire's advocacy of "the duty of not omitting ourselves," for teachers, can obtain for poets and poems as they are presented with a similar sense of commitment. This was very late Freire, a short essay published two years after his death, in *Critical Education in the New Information Age* (1999).

What approach to the era of "new information"—that is to say, of the internet—can align with Freire's fiery ideas of 1968? His later worry about the emerging era of digital culture and global "edu-commerce" was the tactic by which the "postmodern conservative," speedily conveying networked "content 'packages'" of knowledge ("such practices reek with authoritarianism," he warned), refuses to accept "that participation—although an exercise in voice, in having voice, in involvement, in decision making at certain levels of power, although a right of citizenship—is in direct and necessary correlation to progressive educational practice."[1] I discern no technophobia in this strong correlation. The problem is not a technological one primarily. The problem, rather, is how to define this "right of citizenship" as an alternative to the new demands of the explicative order intrinsic to *This is what it means.*

SOUND READING

Turning to sound: although he was not writing about teaching, in the late 1990s, the poet Bruce Andrews was imagining an educational practice when he expressed the hope "for a revived radicalism of constructivist noise or athematic 'informal music'" in the world of poetics.[2] I have wondered what it might be like if our classrooms were filled with such disjunct clattering. Earlier, as I summarized the case against digital minimalism, I recommended the "noisy world" from which minimalists hoped to rescue us. What sounds, we now ask, are emitted when teachers and learners convene around clamorous "exercise[s] in voice"? These exercises are lessons "in *having* voice" associated with a humane aural literacy—lessons "in decision making" as noisy forms of the civic inclusion Freire propounds.

Now a professional confession: for much of my career as a teacher, I did not hear nearly enough of the noise. The turning point—the admission of sounds I first couldn't and eventually didn't want to control—came with the welcome intrusion of digital media in my courses. The main caution has been that the "use of new technologies" to aid teaching makes no difference unless or until some sort of fundamental change in teaching accompanies it. When Robin DeRosa—I cited her in the context of panicgogy—studied prepandemic open educational resources, she concluded that "when no meaningful relationship exists between the technology and pedagogy, the *tool itself* loses value."[3] Here I'm saying that, conversely, when such a relationship does get established, the quality of the altered environment can sound something like Andrews's athematic informal music. Signal without noise signifies only the ordinary. If it is true, as the Japanese-German writer Yōko Tawada insists, that "an onomatopoetic expression automatically entails the specification of what is being described"—i.e., if words sounding like what they mean convey their sense through just sound— why shouldn't an educator attempting to present such expression, preferring to "describe" in this fundamental albeit atypical way, help to share that sound sense with others?[4]

Of course, managing nonsemantic presentation in teaching is a real difficulty. Help has come in the form of advocates of various dissident versions of modernism who have argued that we might actually be better off if such writing simply did not belong in the classroom. The gist of that argument is, in short: right topic, wrong place. How did professing poetry reach this impasse? Consider four examples of such alternative modernisms that tend away from the traditional classroom: (1) the mode that revives use of old, preliterate forms; (2) the method that defies the alleged impersonality of the author; (3) the use of the traditional stanza conveying nontraditional messages (e.g. the Shakespearean sonnet of Caribbean-American communist Claude McKay) to move verse toward a general public; or (4) the linguistically alienated (or "exophonic") stance of the writer, such as Tawada, who chooses to write in German in lieu of Japanese *because* of her *nonproficiency* in the chosen language.[5]

Take the first of the four strategies: the intentional use of archaic materials to dodge, predate, or repress sanguine academic assimilation of modernisms such as T. S. Eliot's. This dissenting reversion was suggested by Jerome Rothenberg in his foundational "Dialogue on Oral Poetry" (1975). Rothenberg disliked Eliot and regretted the overwhelming impact of poetry that the Eliotic mode was having on schooling in the postwar period. "Dialogue" calls for the irrelevance of this sort of poetics to the curriculum, arguing for a complete remaking of the learning space as well as the role of the teacher. This view presents a total educational revisionism, and sound is the key element. "As for poetry 'belonging' in the classroom," Rothenberg tauntingly said in the "Dialogue," "it's like the way they taught us sex in those old hygiene classes: not performance but semiotics. If I had taken Hygiene 71 seriously, I would have become a monk; & if I had taken college

English seriously, I would have become an accountant." The remark is witty but apt. It should be remembered that Rothenberg did, in fact, teach in schools for many years. He understood how "the classroom becomes a *substitute* for those places (coffee shop or kiva) where poetry actually happens & where it can be 'learned' (not 'taught') in action."[6]

CLOSE LISTENING

Rothenberg's sense of the classroom as a "substitute" encourages us to consider where poetry actually happens: vociferous places. One kind of investigation into educational citizenship can take a cue from the sound, the actual *sound*, of poetry—and from the category or subgenre of sound poetry, in particular. In the preface to *Close Listening: Poetry and the Performed Word* (1998), published in the same pivotal moment as *Critical Education in the New Information Age*, Charles Bernstein described his volume, a collection of essays on sound recording and performed poetry, on the "audiotext" in general, as "a call for a non-Euclidean . . . prosody for the many poems for which traditional prosody does not apply."[7] My concern here is the converged histories of poetry and digitality from which we derive a "non-Euclidean" *teaching and learning* to befit this new aural consciousness.

Why even seek such a thing? The influential sound/visual/concrete/performance poet Bob Cobbing contended in 1969 that "sound poetry dances, tastes, has shape."[8] In the periods preceding Cobbing's sensory redefinitions of the form, especially beginning in the immediate postwar period of education boom when people presented poems as only printed, it might have been possible to add these dimensions to the realms of approaches in the classroom. But in general, that did not happen. For several generations, the experience of having been trained to see (and then after professionalization, to teach the seeing of) words on a page, no matter how complex that encounter, was not good preparation for the task of conveying a language practice—such as that of Cobbing, Rothenberg, Tawada, Jaap Blonk, Kurt Schwitters, bpNichol, and many others—as a kind of music, movement, or visual objects with physical shapes, poems as "dance, gesture & event, game, dream . . . music . . . vocable" of the sort that the late Rothenberg always idealized as an outcome of poetry's visionary "blaze of reality."[9] The expansion could happen, but an established practical matter awaited new technologies. "When the audiotape archive of a poet's performance is acknowledged as a significant, rather than incidental, part of her or his work," Bernstein wrote at a moment of high hopes for populist uses of digital recordings in the 1990s, "a number of important textual and critical issues emerge." And he went on to name these.[10] I'll now to add the matter of teaching to his list. The technology that enables us to acknowledge such material as significant rather than of mere additive or illustrative quality can itself become a part of the story of the poetic art learned by students of that art. *Learned rather than taught*—as Rothenberg always emphasized.

"Leonardo da Vinci," Cobbing liked to say, "asked the poet to give him something he might see and touch and not just something he could hear. Sound poetry seems to me to be achieving this aim."[11] The problem posed by this challenge is similar to the one mentioned above. Many people can easily manage seeing a text and hearing it too, albeit the latter with special new facility given advances in shareable audio. But *touch*? Enabling that kind of material engagement is next to impossible within traditional pedagogy. Yet it is crucial. In Erica Hunt's words: "Reader, we were meant to touch." Witnessing a printed poem with one's sight— sensing it as a visible word-*thing*, in William Carlos Williams's programmatic sense ("Poems are not made of thoughts, beautiful thoughts, it's made of words"; and "No ideas / but in things"[12])—is a feat sighted people generally believe happens in what we call a close reading. But of course, looking at the words of a poem, even assuming that sensory ability, is not the same as comprehending it.

The contributors to *New Media Poetics: Contexts, Technotexts, and Theories* (2006) studied broadly redefined forms of such looking. Although they offered little mention of the impact on education made by new kinds of texts, at nearly every point in the collection an altered practice was implicit, especially in the section titled "Technotexts." There, examples of computer-generated, programming-dependent, or network-enabled verse were offered. An essay in *New Media Poetics* on Cynthia Lawson and Stephanie Strickland's *Vniverse* (2002), for instance, described the "social reading space" required by this work in a manner that suggests what a teacher would need to do in the classroom to profess such art. While the text is performed through the artist's virtual interaction with a website, which can, of course, be apprehended without its creators being present, "the audience is also reading while being in a social space." However, the artists add, "*We* do not read it as *they* do."[13] *Vniverse* presented its "readers" (viewers? interactors? players?) with an interface offering a constellation in which stars, when clicked (or later touched), reveal a poem or a poetic fragment. The given design and contingent users' navigation of the interface shape the experience of the poetry as users investigate this textual universe in unordered ways.

Thus, "performing new media poetry" befits new dimensional thinking about how people learn from texts. It assumes learning to be a dynamic interaction among the threesome permissioned in the era of IT: first, the technotext itself; second, the performers/instigators of the site; and third, an audience that reads/ clicks/touches/looks/interprets within what becomes a social space. One of the several innovative contentions underlying such a poetics is that the artists' "creative process is an initial model for th[e] interaction" of the kind that could, under certain circumstances, take place in a course. In that case, learners can witness the creative process and, if the technotext succeeds, experience it somehow first-hand.[14]

TEACHING UNSAYABILITY

Before composing this chapter, I went forth and back between *New Media Poetics* of 2006 and *Close Listening* of 1998, marking the changes across that hectic eight-year period. The earlier essays, seen this way, become indicative expressions of late-1990s audiophilia. These were the variously optimistic stances of the day, documented just before the bursting of the first online teaching bubble and not long before the ascendant ubiquity of shareable MP3 audio files. With the moment occupied by those essays and the rises and falls of technology in mind, I reread each contribution to the gathering of essayists, deducing belatedly what might have been or could become a corresponding new educational practice. Dennis Tedlock's poetics of polyphony and translatability, for instance, reminded us that "writing, like speaking, is a performance." It strongly implied (though didn't quite say) that teaching such writing can be an enactment as well. "Speaking" in this special sense can entail participating in the intermedia performance of polyphony. We can conceive of all that speaking as sharing with the audio text its quality as "a semantically denser field of linguistic activity than can be charted by means of meter, assonance, alliteration, rhyme and the like."[15]

Then Peter Quartermain's "Sound Reading" reminded me that literal "unsayability . . . is a central feature of a great number of poems" I value and that for many years, apropos my earlier confession, I taught my students without conceiving of those poems in such a way. I realized that, in fact, I had been teaching as if the verse were always ultimately going to be sayable if I just did my job, and frankly—here was a problematic aspect of my teaching—saying it all rather competently.[16] My contemporaneous marginal notes remind me. The afternoon of the day I first read Quartermain's article in 2001, in the in-person prequel to ModPo, English 88, I was to lead a discussion of John Cage's "Writing through Howl" (1984), a poem generated semiautomatically from the words and lines of

Allen Ginsberg's Beat epic *Howl* (1956). The later work uses the earlier as a source text for words to be deployed as a new artwork according to quasi-predetermined line arrangements. Cage was rewriting Ginsberg by making a "mesostic" (like an acrostic, only the "spine word" runs down the middle rather than along the left edge of the text).

During the previous two meetings, the students and I enthusiastically reckoned with the sweet wildness of the original *Howl*. Its countercultural stances toward writing and career choices were a genuine attraction. After that, it was time to turn to Cage's aleatory Ginsberg. The result of Cage's relatively strict, deterministic procedure of "writing through" the language of the original "Howl"—with its by-then canonical status, its natural-seeming ecstasies, its easily recognizable free-feeling sound—is starkly beautiful. Cage's rendition of Ginsberg produces a succinct basis, or tonally similar but quantitatively dissimilar aural viscus, of the old very familiar long-lined beatnik howling. Albeit nonintentionally, Cage seems to argue in favor of doubts about the traditionalist claim that one way of saying things can be closer or truer to the original idea than another. What does originality mean here? The power of Cage's method of writing through Ginsberg is the relative unsayability of the answer to that question, or, in my view as a teacher-proponent of both artists, to any question about the variant of an expressed idea that is itself its best edification. Old pedagogical wine in a new bottle. First, the wine: a formalist focus on the poem as an autonomous source of inscribed history, of vintage content, needing no sources outside it, declining historical intention, and ignoring affect as fallacious.

But then the bottle: a site of—the container of—random, uncreative verse presented in the action-oriented classroom. Usually, the consciously articulate teacher professes a poetry he emphatically says he loves (had I really always been protesting too much?—probably, yes). I learned through Cagean chance operations to convey an appropriate moderating tentativeness, to struggle honestly with saying what I was supposed to say as a degree-holding professional about a poem. I bespoke the irresolution I sought to teach.

Not anticipating the precise differences, the Cage effect still presents Ginsberg's name running recognizably down the middle as an acrostic spine. The Beat colleague is still there somewhere. We just look: we read down the middle to work it out. After all these years in which I had passionately taught *Howl*, now the classroom was enjoined by a computer-aided or computer-like aesthetic repatriation of "A L L E N G I N S B E R G." It was a teacher-text teaching literary history, both the vast public chronicle of the famous predecessor poem and the psychological and anthropological histories of paired eras. During a moment of reading in a wrong way (not left to right but down the middle), a founding Beat could be rediscovered through a mid-1950s rendered by a mid-1980s presented in a classroom of the mid-1990s:

mAdness

coLd-water

fLats

thE

braiNs

throuGh

wIth

aNd

academieS

Burning

monEy . . .

"[A]cademieS / Burning / monEy" in a 1990s' version of the 1980s! The students had a great deal to say about the values of their era and the one preceding. The learning space was being transformed into a site where a poem thrived in its mode while disruptive technologies of reading became a method for comparative social histories. "Ginsberg's dense, clotted, overwrought line," Marjorie Perloff commented when considering the relationship between these two poems, "gives way to stark reduction, a reduction *that leaves a great deal to the reader's imagination*."[17] And to the students'! I found that that relationship—poem to (student) reader—could be extended to the reimagining of a classroom. Cage's technical proceduralism became a guide to the helpful "reduction" of *me* too, of a more opaque role. I observed an expansion of students' learning as part of our turn away from "dense, clotted, [and] overwrought" as qualities that typically inhibit the educational situation. Those happen to be qualities, style preferences really, that I and my students identified with *me* as a bona fide academic—so there was a certain amount of deprofessionalizing going on.

What happens, then, when the teacher presenting such a work attempts to convey its unsayability through the form or role of the teacher, permitting what I'm tempted to describe as an acrostic pedagogy? The teaching discovers that the new selection of old, well-known words helps convey a fresh social history of Beat naturalism that we all had naturalized and now made *less* wrought. To what extent is the educator finding an advantage in staging their own exit from the realm of expected semantic yet overwrought sense? A nonstudent observer sitting in one of these Cage/Ginsberg sessions once told me in the hallway after class that I was committing the imitative fallacy. I copped to the complaint but pointed out that the disparagement of imitation was itself already being called into question by Cage's unintentional art. Cage was urging us to think about our own tendencies toward control.

THE INTRUDERS ARE PARTICIPANTS

Peter Middleton, who in 2005 published a book about poetic performance and readership,[18] contributed to 1998's *Close Listening* an historical survey of the live poetry reading. The work taught me about the dynamics of the reading space some years ahead of the MOOC. Although it was not Middleton's concern, one has little trouble imagining the analogy to the digital classroom as like such a space. (This is the topic of chapter 6.) Imagine that the following observation was written about an alternative schooling: "The persistence of the . . . momentary ascendancies of poetry in an everyday world that threatens at every instant to flood back in and reclaim the space for its everyday functions suggests another possibility."[19]

Middleton calls these functions "intruders." They are noisy auditors: unplanned sounds, unconducive ambience, and the abruption of nonpoetic uses of the space onto the scene of the performance. And all of them "are really participants."[20] No live performance ever happens without them. The savvy performer might even become one. The iconoclastic poet can wonder, as talk poet David Antin did aloud in the middle of performing one of his hour-long improvisational verse stories, "what am i doing here?" Similarly, with this analogy, I strive—in the learning space and in this writing—to imagine that the *educator* can ask exactly the same question in the midst of the class-time hour, permitting the extrapoetic ambience to be part of the meaning of "here" to be studied and discussed, letting in the intruders. The poet-performer-teacher Edwin Torres, for example, makes an art of admitting them.

Join a workshop led by Torres, and you'll be taught how to welcome intrusion. As teacher-poet he helps render cacophony linguistic. No sound or movement is shut out from the eventual alphabetic. To understand his work well, one should try to be oneself, along with him, a "lingualisualist." That the word is hard to say aloud is part of his point in using it. I'll explain it as a way of telling a brief version of the long and also recent histories of how merged modes got separated and isolated in schools.

For Torres, at turns a concrete poet, sound poet, and performance poet once affiliated with the Nuyorican Poets Café, visual poetry can be misheard if it is only seen and not otherwise experienced. Hearing and reading him is a synesthetic adventure. "The under-wrong of the first hearing," he says, positively discloses "mistake[s] in our everything [it is all we are" [sic]. To "be the creative I was meant to be," he confesses in "[I spk lyric sht]" (a poem in his 2021 book *quanundrum*), entails making each poem a "statement, from ear to coastal cortex [a building a people a misunderstanding] [that] will last longer than concrete sound > be maker, under [mouth]."[21] Such poetic "statement" is meant to challenge the association of improvising (or riffing) and fluency. Delay is vocal materiality. It's "the fact of my mouth," as poet Jordan Scott has put it.[22] Here is Torres, somewhat more straightforwardly, in an earlier statement titled "The Impossible Sentence," written for the *Poetry Project Newsletter*. He has a theory about the rightness of the under-wrong: "Unrecognizable patterns of uttering—the polyglot crying for social affiliation—as we portray our demons with hierarchy, the available workhorse is the lingualisualist. . . . Taking notes against the voice falling in the ear, where many ways of understanding stutter into yester-speak. There is a third space, the eye that is the ear in the back of the brain."[23] Insofar as one can imagine a convergence of these two third spaces, that is the model of teaching and learning idealized in this chapter. As a more or less direct result of "sound's resistance to being codified in signs," and of "the paucity of language for describing sound," write Deanna Fong and Cole Mash in *Resistant Practices in Communities of Sound* (2024), "a generative space emerges through acts of attentive, intentional listening."[24]

Here, then, is the in-between space Torres means: on the one hand, a situation between apprehending the art of the poem in isolation (the typical state of a person's solitary reading) and, on the other, the talking head of presenter or lecturer (to which we respond by "taking notes against the voice falling in the ear")—but it partakes of neither. Auditory poiesis isn't just a matter of sounding and hearing. Torres's ideal location is where "social affiliation" is associated with the text and where the eye can function like an ear or hand. What Torres means by "patterns of uttering" is a whole built poetic environment, a nonfigurative house of possibility (to maintain Dickinson's trope). The house of this poetry is the "building [of] a people [of] a misunderstanding" created concretely from the "under-wrong" of our assumptions. Torres wants us to make a "building" in which the objectivity or *thisness* of poetic occupation—Dickinson's dwelling as both residing and obsessing—is an actual thing. It's the tangible effect of an interactive intrasensory practice. These intrusive qualities can be heard and felt in every Edwin Torres performance.

FIGURE 4.1 Edwin Torres performing in Berlin, July 4, 2009.

Source: Used with permission of Edwin Torres.

HEAR THE VOICE OF THE BARD

I fear my critical vocabulary here doesn't do justice to lingualisualism. Perhaps a personal reminiscence will help clarify. As a nascent member of the academic community, I was trained by people—not a lingualisualist among them—who enthusiastically brought a literary text into the room and presented it to us, in effect, as a still image. I refer here to writing that we were to comprehend visually, language learned with eyes, where "[I spk lyric sht]" was an implausible response to a common experience of misunderstanding. I came to associate the finest readings of poetic texts purely with the act of visualizing. I recall believing back then that the word *rhetorical* only pertained to printed words on paper and that rhetorical tools were limited to the lexical. I looked at Whitman and gazed at Williams and saw an on-paper version of Gwendolyn Brooks. I even learned to *look* at the misfitting visual and oral lyricism of Vachel Lindsay, which seemed to make Lindsay comply with the rest. I recall sensing even then that some kind of irony had been created—from, it turns out, a basic technological lack or pre-history—that was pedagogically either quite a trick or alternatively a miserable failure. And it was at the very least counterintuitive, given Lindsay's extreme performance. Yet, more often, as the other young apprentices to literary study and I sat in rows in the room, we were unconscious of the intuition we, as members of a loud, music-obsessed generation, were inclined to move against. How did one learn to *read* the tambourines and whistles that are crucial to the making of Lindsay's athematic noise without even knowing they were there?

Even such a strange, exciting sound as Lindsay's "Higher Vaudeville,"[25] a vocable indispensable to any real understanding of his poems, by whatever generation, I did not hear then and would not hear for years—well after I was sufficiently professionalized. How could I understand the poems without access to the auditory experience? The only audible thing in the room on such occasions was the kindly but tuneless voice of the professor who was, with limited effectiveness, suggesting that we look (and look again and keep looking until we perfected that look) at the super-thin anthology page or piece of mimeography he had handed to us. To look hard—with concentration one could *see through* that gossamer sheaf!—was to master the poem. It never bothered me that this was a mixed message until years later. The PennSound Vachel Lindsay page,[26] full of sounds difficult to make in the classroom of the 1970s,[27] is now commended to students and teachers. The instructional expectation is simple. Just follow Blake's romantic encouragement: "Hear the voice of the bard!"[28] The sound of the poet is thunderous, vaudevillian, primitivist (and in "The Congo" racist, to be sure[29]), implausible, apparently unmasterable. It resists settled close-reading practices. It renders commentary irrelevant and even absurd. Yet on the anthology page, Lindsay seemed nicely, if not quite neatly, to befit a literary-historical moment, the typeface all the same, marking a regular spot along the spectrum from Walt Whitman's protomodernist enthusiasm to the energized verse populism of Carl Sandburg onward to Beat and other forms of mid-twentieth-century visionary romanticism. *Seeing* Lindsay made for a discussion that did not remotely resemble the awed response to a wild stagy voice as it intrudes upon ears nor the challenge its awful noise presents to a quieted room of earnest sophomores.

THE SUBORDINATION OF THE EAR

In the long postwar era preceding routine digitality, teaching poetry became a creature of the twin revolutions of mass-circulated textbook anthologies and mimeography, even as we were already theoretically distancing ourselves from the critical ideology so well suited to both modes: formalist classroom practice in its booming post-GI Bill manifestation, alleging its open formalism, yet unwittingly teaching the poem's arbitrary material medium. That unconscious concreteness was a function of a (non)technology of its time. The mode marked a continuity out of traditions established several centuries earlier by the close association of poetic text with image—I mean, the text of the poem *as* a kind of image.

One history of the literary curriculum in the modern university runs as follows: The emergence of the printing press and of moveable type, the techno-genesis of the modern page, coincided with (and partially helped to instigate) the redevelopment of the idea of the college that more or less holds today. This version of the story has been told often and critically. In a presentation called "Text and University" (1991), for instance, Ivan Illich lamented "the separation and subordination of the ear with respect to the eye" in higher learning in our time. He reminded us that before the thirteenth century, scholarly reading was an oral-auditive activity, the scriptorium was a noisy place, the tradition of the "singing page" held sway, and so forth. Then the trope changed. "A new technique of writing lay-out makes university teaching possible." "Visual *ordinatio* [regulation, orderliness] replaces contemplative chewing, an oral backing and forthing, *ruminatio*."[30]

Texts considered worth studying were recopied—later, printed—and made their way to emergent centers of learning where apprentice learners gathered around scholars who gathered around texts, all of them seeing texts with their eyes. After the invention of inkable type and printing presses, students began to take notes in the lecture hall, the passing sound of the professing voice deemed less important than written and then subsequent typeset and printed accounts of what was said aloud. Tellingly, the remembered resonances bespoke what we'll call the *paraphonotext*—that is, the main audible text plus all the sonic intruders, with an emphasis on the unanticipated qualities of the latter. "The sound coming from lectures—that 'clear, dry, tingling sound,' like the wind in late fall—arose from so many taking copious notes in eighteenth-century [University of] Wittenberg."[31] This was the noise of students' pens scratching on paper, not the oral instruction being annotated. Immanuel Kant, as a teacher, opposed any vocal manner or affectation and "avoid[ed] appearing as someone who [as he put it] 'is fond of the sound of his own voice,'" insisting that lectures in schools are not about voice at all.[32] Meanwhile, the longer and, at that point, deeper (but increasingly quite separate) history of orality benefited from little to no such convergence with the rise of the modern academy as an institution, a new social corporation that would breed leaders of the polity and of the economy, including, to be sure, those who would go on to lead the universities themselves.

Thus for a long time, the poetry-as-sound tradition had to go its own mostly nonacademic, extracurricular, or public way. It continued on, outside regular sites of visual/graphic authentication and accreditation. It coped with intellectual bias. It was "pegged under a barrage of easy descriptors," in Edwin Torres's phrasing. The prejudice operated even in some of the hippest college-adjacent poetry communities. And roughly (and for the most part incorrectly), it was associated with an art linguistically unrigorous, merely popular, combatively undertheorized. Poets for whom "visual and lingual rolled off the tongue nicely" faced set-piece designations, such as "Slam—Performance—Language—New York—Nuyorican—etc—Poet," of the sort that Torres felt he needed to decline as he chose to create and theorize as a lingualisualist with multidisciplinary ambitions.[33] Thus, more than a century after the rise of reliable mechanical reproduction of sound, four decades after the recorder-player morphed into devices available and affordable to almost everyone, two decades since worldwide super-dissemination of sound files, and plentiful years into the era of stable, widely agreed-upon nonproprietary audio file formats, the field continued to be subject to the seemingly benign tyranny of the pedagogy of the text. It is this tight hegemonic affiliation of text and university that has tended to inhibit, as venues of learning, the third spaces where the lingualisualist might feel at home. To this day, such an artist might still reasonably feel out of place in academic realms, taking cues from bona fide library acquisitions. As Tanya Clement prepared her 2024 book on listening in the audio archive, she learned that the Digital Public Library of America included 27 percent images, 50 percent text, and fewer than 1 percent sound objects. As of April 2023, she reports, the international digital library platform Europeana was composed of 55 percent images, 43 percent text, and 1 percent sound.[34]

LISTENING AS ACCESS

Let's continue considering the record of poems as they are seen. Forms of visual discernment abound. Just look at poems. There might be a long verse line that runs further into the right margin than others; we see and reckon its difference as a loosening or indication of special excess energy. Or the so-called widowed line or word, left to its own devices at the marginal edge or top of a next page. Or words suddenly PRESENTED IN ALL CAPS. Or **bolded**. The unusual extra spacing between words. The three dots of the caesura . . . might indicate a cognitive temporal pause. The intentional spelling error (*vide* Joan Retallack's flaw-filled *Errata suite*); the bothered eye of a reader catches it, and then can't look past it. There's the typewriting of the poet making its way into published pages as transposed by editor and book designer from the platen into the codex—this for the tab-using poets, like Niedecker, Charles

Olson, Susan Howe, and the disabled William Carlos Williams (after several strokes), who might evince an antagonism toward the left margin. (Larry Eigner also felt such an "aversion"—that was his word. His antipathy signified openness.) Then there's the poem title that syntactically enjambs into the first line, as in the famous modernist domestic ditty:

THIS IS JUST TO SAY   [TITLE]

I have eaten   [body]
the plums . . .

When a poet gives us one or more of these visual cues, we read the prompt and permit it to report evidence of emphasis, irony, rhythm, silliness, formality, laxness, impatience, etc. Those extra spaces might mean hesitation or, perhaps, bold composition by field. Literary analysis has properly taught us to consider such moves fair game without the need to worry much about intention or biography (even, for example, in Eigner's case, where a biographical reading is compelling) or other kinds of extrinsic evidence for the reading. We read, and most formalisms account competently for these visuals.

But now turn to the poem as an archivable, replayable, aurally kinetic object of sound. While offering many of the same options for comprehension, the overheard art adds a myriad of options. A spoken word is stretched or dragged out unusually. Our ears notice that extension. Another word is mispronounced or surprisingly inflected. Can't unhear that. The poet transposes a spoken accent into alternative lettering, leaving a notation or script for later oral performance that might or might not be followed or followed well. (Louis Zukofsky renders "A fine lass bothers me" as "A foin lass bodders me" in a recording of "A"-9 from the epic poem "A" and much later, other poets have a score for performing it.[35]) Or separate sound senses or phrases from different vocabularies converge and form an auditory disorder. An extra-long silence does not so much refer to so much as presupposes a page's white space. A line is read aloud too hurriedly to be understood as regular semantic sense, thus inventing a differently signifying rush of air and noise, a difference discernible only in the overheard breath-marked experience of the poem. The hastening means something well beyond just the sonic. The differences of Eigner's writing are, of course, plentifully discernible on the printed pages of the *Collected Poems* (set by his editors in Courier to help replicate his nonproportional typewriting), but recordings of his readings, largely unheard but now gathered at PennSound's Eigner page, the earliest dating from 1970 and the latest 1995, add significantly to the poetry's powerful figure-ground gestalt. He performed the poem "Again dawn," (1959), on KPFA radio in Berkeley in 1994 and added this comment: "You know my mother said to me to communicate you must speak clear . . . first of all . . . though I soon realized that immediacy and force take priority."[36] The atypical recorded sound of an otherwise conventional word pronounced by a human voice—for instance, Eigner's unforgettable material inflection of the word *ground* in the poem or emphatic long *soon* in the commentary—inspires an imagined memory of the way a person's mouth was once opened at the moment of utterance. Hearing Eigner attentively argues for "listening as access," as Faith Ryan puts it in an essay in which she challenges the myth of vocal essence. Voice is interdependent. It makes possible a "relational listening."[37]

For readers and hearers of Eigner's poetry, elongation carries significance. Anne Waldman, a virtuoso of elongation, has over the years formed a demonstrative politics of the long Ō. When we read it on page or screen, Waldman's titular phrase "rogue state," a taunting play on unruly poet as diplomatic pariah regime, seems a fairly ordinary spondee (both beats stressed). But the poem "Rogue State" was apparently composed only for performance; its appearance as text on websites, for instance at poetspath.com,[38] seems secondary at best. It was titled "Notes for a Rally (Speech)" at one point. That version was connected with miscellaneous prose notes. Waldman's various live performances of "Rogue State," on the other hand, including a tumultuous one read before a standing-room-only Arts Café at the Kelly Writers House on April 15, 2003,[39] reanimates the spondee as a wild, witchy trochee: Rrr*ŌŌŌŌ*gue state, the freely hyperbolized tremolo chant about heinous, preposterous autocratic polity. Reading one of the poem's quatrains, absent the vocal stretching of the syllable r*ŪŪŪŪ*LE in the word *misrule* in the phrase "Lady of Misrule," might miss the political import of the rule-breaking ballad. The meaning of *tell* in the line "Don't *tell* me what to do" is in the sound being made as phoneme hurled against the explicative order.

> I'm in a rogue state, Mr. President
> Don't **_tell_** me what to do
> **_Your_** rules aren't my rules
> Cause I'm the Lady of Misr*ŪŪŪŪ*LE

The poem minus Waldman's sound just doesn't break so many of those rules. It seems to be somewhat easier to *see* genre (the fourteen-line block of a sonnet, for instance, or even a standard set-off four-line quatrain stanza) than to *hear* it. But Waldman's big ongoing struggle against the politics of ballad orthodoxy, the tradition in which there are still many more maidens than harridans, is aimed at the addressed leaders (in various versions, George W. Bush, Bush's attorney general John Ashcroft, among others). Yes, but "*your* rules" also speak back against those of page poets from whom this singer-speaker freely strays.

If one can't hear genre so easily, what are the political implications? Reading "If We Must Die" by McKay in print—it has been anthologized everywhere—its form is readily discernible. A reader's sense of its revolutionary politics will depend on an inability to reconcile the topic (violent counterresponse to armed racist civilians and negligent police) with the form (a perfect English sonnet with its racial unspecificity[40]). The sonnet's complex strategy—to enclose heretical ideas in a traditionally acceptable, respected, anthologizable British aesthetic pattern, a form/content Trojan Horse—is made perhaps too accessible for the reader who quickly views its fourteen lines and sees the super-competent A-B-A-B | C-D-C-D | E-F-E-F | H-H end-rhymes. But upon hearing the audio recording of McKay reciting the poem, one ascertains its challenging content first and then secondarily might attend to its status as a sonnet. Can one *hear* a sonnet? One can, but only with special listening skills, and in any case, hearing it through McKay's voice is precisely as troubling as the political stance of the poem.

FINDING OUT WHAT I'D SAID

The language for describing these and a myriad of other close-listening options is, even now, underdeveloped. New sound studies research has significantly advanced the analysis.[41] One continues, though, to have to imagine creating some sort of institutional analog (for Quartermain's "sound readings") to a pedagogical cadre of terminologists of the New Criticism in his heyday—who, in the 1940s through at least the early 1960s, revived, invented, and codified a superlanguage for the poem-as-seen that students in introductory classes could be taught to use with sufficient competence and upon which, it might be said with scant exaggeration, the institution of postwar academic humanities was founded.[42] So perhaps one reason we still do not teach poetry primarily (rather than supplementarily) through their phonotexts might be that we find it difficult to interpret what we hear with sufficient professional confidence.

When my students and I listen to sound files together *instead* of reading poem texts, I've observed that our vocabularies tend to operate similarly. They are not silenced by the terminology I bring to bear on the points I like to make about specific sounds of the words. They are adept at the music of words. The students notice this great difference—between the usual talk about a poem on the page and their talk of the sounded poems. Their discussions of poetics generally become charged with the medium and can articulate its presence. If it is true of those who perform spoken poetry that (as talk poet Antin once put it) "it was my habit to record my talks / *to find out what i[']d said*,"[43] then similarly, the disorienting, terminologically disruptive mode I am describing is a means by which we can *find out what we are teaching*. "Working specifically with audio recordings of poetry (or other content), I like to start with the intentionally vague question of 'what does this sound like?' and 'have you heard this kind of voicing or performance elsewhere—commercials, speeches, etc?'" I'm quoting Chris Mustazza in a dialogue with Jason Camlot, the founding director of the Canadian audio archive SpokenWeb (established in 2018), where PennSound is a partner organization. "Students will usually find," Mustazza adds, "something familiar to them which can lead us into important questions around performance, sonic aesthetics, and the very porous boundary between poetry and other kinds of speech."[44] By the 2020s, sound studies converge rather easily with discussion-based pedagogy, producing ideas about what Marit McArthur calls "teaching slow listening."[45]

This kind of realization goes back about fifteen years. Students in a freshman seminar taught in the spring of 2008 by poet and modernist scholar Julia Bloch, a founding ModPo teacher three years later, were assigned to listen to recordings of several poems by Amiri Baraka stored in and digitally served from PennSound. PennSound was launched in 2006. Two years later, the use of its sound files in a classroom was still a novelty. One recording Bloch used, of Baraka's "In Walked Bud" (2005), was not made available to the students in print. Halfway through the discussion, one student, Andrew, offered a reading of the poem that successfully associated Baraka's jazz-metrical scatting with the narrative of the speaker's physical movement:

> So I try to listen and see if the sound tells me the story. Why is this guy saying DO DO DEE? [Andrew imitates the scat.] And then I realize that it's the way he's walking into the scene that summer night. He's an African in the West with European harmonies. And then he says, "In walked us." Later the DO DO DEE comes back but it's changed by then. I heard it as a story and then [in a writing assignment] did a close reading based on the sound of the [scatting]. I never bothered to imagine how it would look as language on a page.

Responding to Andrew—who had filled the room with a resonant replication of Baraka's DO DO DEE, drawing it out from the remotely situated MP3 with the presence of his larynx and tongue—the discussion among the students was *entirely about the form of the poem*, very little directly about its social content.

Bloch had not pointed out this lit-class anomaly: students assigned to write about a poem they had not seen with their eyes as writing, implicitly stressing its supposed digital remoteness without identifying the technologies that authored this effect. She patiently waited for a student to make this point. Then: "We haven't even seen this written down," Amy exclaimed (and it was her remark that had then precipitated Andrew's capable formalist reading). She threw up her arms excitedly, and loudly asked: "*How do we read this poem?*"

THINKING AND SPEAKING RUN AT THE SAME TIME

Could there be a more fundamental question? The noise of Baraka instigated it. To those who have worried, as the antimodernist conservative Georges Duhamel in 1939 did in a rant against the radio, that "people who really need education are beginning to prefer noise to books,"[46] such student response, especially since the 2000s, stands as a powerful rejoinder. The book has been a medium for arriving at the teacher's goal, which is to teach young people to understand form as an extension of content. "Noise," however, as either separate from the book or parallel to it, can similarly be the medium. This has been a surprisingly hard case to make. Duhamel's antagonistic relationship to sound and his assumption that books are the proper alternative to noise is perhaps laughably outdated given how quaint complaints about radio seem to us now—or, similarly, dire warnings about rock 'n' roll in connection with the asocial behavior of young people, decibel-obsessed rebels without causes in the late 1950s, and with educational delinquency.

Nonetheless, we should take seriously various early internet-era expressions of anxiety and technophobia. Among these are Sven Birkerts's *The Gutenberg Elegies: The Fate of Reading in an Electronic Age* (1994) and Barry Sanders's *A Is for Ox: Violence, Electronic Media, and the Silencing of the Written Word* (also 1994). "I value the state a book puts me in," Birkerts writes, "more than I value the specific contents," yet he declines to explore whether reading books electronically can offer a similar or even corresponding "state."[47] Sanders's volume presents an even more fervent book-length argument: with the rise of the personal computer "a young person more than senses, he or she comes to *know* that authority, real knowledge, and skill, reside *in* the machine, dictated by an . . . anonymous expert." There's firm-handed authority in the book as well, Sanders concedes, but there, at least, "an author—a person—can be imagined," and if you are being told what to do by a book, you can conjure a person speaking at you even if give-and-take rejoinders can only be hypothesized. With the humane presence of author as authority, there is (as at a lecture) a chance to "watch that . . . mind in action." Watching of this sort is fundamentally educational, he believes. But again, when dictatorial authority is actual but hidden, the "rules" being "irrefutably set" by an obscure and thus pernicious force, it "creat[es] a world of youthful ghostwriters . . . who shimmer with no more substantiality than those glowing letters on the PC screen."[48]

Sanders is not against the long literary history of oral culture, but he certainly prefers the story of human interaction after the invention of alphabets. And, in effect, he blames orality—which can so easily turn into noise of the sort that is a sensory cognitive cousin to the noxious digital dictates of programming— for the decline in book learning. Reading is special. Sentences can be read many times, and doing so "feeds and fills out that activity we call self-reflective, critical thinking." Self-reflective learning "is something not possible in orality," Sanders observes. That's because "in orality, speaking and thinking *run at the same time*." The worst effect of all this cognitive simultaneity is that, especially in the hands of young people, it has provided the excuse for transforming audio amplitude or loudness into a metaphor for deep perception. " 'Volume,' " complains Sanders, "as the pitch of a voice, has somehow been extended to refer to the metaphysical depth of a self's 'interior.' " That "orality admits of no authors" is a problem for him because authors are associated with true authority, the loss of which, in an age of so much noise, he believes is a fairly direct cause of violence, of the lessening of the importance of the written word, and of our entire educational crisis.[49]

Julia Bloch's student Amy asked how we are supposed to read. Above, I indicated my elation over her fundamental question. It didn't arise from her having read a book that she could by custom expect to tell her what it meant. She asked because what she had for that day's lesson was an MP3 of just 1.4 megabytes in size, a seeming nothing—a format that supposedly "admits of no authors," as Sanders adversely puts it. Yet perhaps that exclusion is positive. Left to her own ears, without even a printed handout to hold onto, Amy was just disoriented enough to begin to reorganize the activity of hearing as a kind of reading, minus the honored traditions of authoritative guidance that had become seemingly inherent in the codex.

DON'T EVER COME TO THE POINT

When I teach Ginsberg's poem "America" in a classroom, the students and I listen together to recordings of two very different performances. The first time, in early November 1995, it was not the simplest matter to locate the recordings and something of an ordeal to set up the equipment to play the sound such that students and auditors, ninety in total that semester, could all hear the poet's voice filling our room.

During a month-long stint researching my first book at the Huntington Library in the late 1980s, I met Barry Sanders, the aforementioned critic of computing and lucid complainer against the noisy postbook orality of young people. We had argued about the ideas that became *A Is for Ox* over a series of long lunches there. You can suppose what my position was. During one discussion, I proposed that students could learn Ginsberg without any access to the printed text. When Sanders's book appeared in 1994, I wrote an intolerantly negative commentary about it for my university's student-run newspaper. At the same time, not at all incidentally, I also made the case for electronic mail accounts to be freely given to all undergraduates. My reading of the book encouraged me to advocate for online learning. It also provoked me to try experiments in teaching by sound alone. This was my first experience with a cogent screed against screens, and the encounter coincided with the founding of the Kelly Writers House in the autumn and winter of 1995–1996. Thus I closely associate these three scenarios—learning to talk with learners about digital sound, facing early complaints against electronic culture, and the strong institutional bias in favor of curriculum over other forms of learning—with Ginsberg's "America."

One recording of "America" I played in class had been performed live in 1956 before a sympathetic, ecstatic, and largely inebriated audience. Ginsberg introduced it with the remark that it was "an unfinished poem which I'll finish sooner or later."[50] The second recording is a professionally produced track, released on the LP *Howl and Other Poems*, a Fantasy-Galaxy record (#7013), taped in Berkeley in June 1959. That version is a studio recording done in a somber, unironic, plaintive, and vulnerable voice. It is accompanied by no ambient noise. In the first, as the audience raucously laughs and responds, Ginsberg's voice changes and slows as he recites. Teasingly, this line: "When will you take off your clothes?" I think it suggested the same meaning to the rowdy live audience as it did and does to my students. They get a bit rowdy themselves. Then again, lines such as "I'm trying to come to the point" have had varying effects on the students—most interpret it as a serious lament, furthering what they take to be the speaker's sense of his failure—while the 1956 audience accepts the sentiment as antic and wildly ironic, and they cheer on the poet as if to say, *Don't ever come to the point!* The point is not to come to the point but to wander everywhere in the writing as he spoke it. We were all witnessing Ginsberg with our ears—and, to quote Sanders in *A Is for Ox* describing the deficiencies of oral culture, the poet embodied the example of performance in which "speaking and thinking run at the same time." A terrible thing for Sanders. A terrific thing for Ginsberg's audience, and for teaching.

Teaching that poem—or poems really, for it is really two editions—I ask learners to describe in detail differences between the enacted sounds of words. They begin to construct a sound reading. When I first taught "America" as an instance of a work of art that produces a social soundscape—but prior to using the audio, I mean—I had never successfully been able to dissuade students from the conviction, one they seem to have inherited as children of Cold War–era Americans, that Beat poetics was ultimately meditative, unfunny, and angry. Obviously, the text on the page does not enact tonal or rhetorical options and alternatives in the same way. Even just one recording does so. But having *two* audio texts to compare takes the work to a realm in which difference and disagreement are not just possible but necessary as a structure of learning.

In the 1956 reading, Ginsberg himself was reinterpreting how he felt about the poem, and about the United States, in the very act of reperforming it. You can hear it: as he goes along, he understands its new contexts in a way that somehow anticipates our own context. And to discuss our own context is why, in short, I teach poetry. Even though Ginsberg's text, the basis of his different performances, is for the most part fixed, a script, a score, a famous ur-text played out through performed variations, the best way to respond critically to the sound is to perceive it as similar to the extraordinarily beautiful and also unpredictable phenomenon of quasi-improvisation that Antin describes as "a dialogue that [as I perform] I also conduct with my material and myself . . . and with a particular audience that I don't know till I get there."[51]

Learners learn to become live auditors. We can succeed in imagining ourselves analogously—the goal being to behave very much like the audience whom Antin does not know at the start but with whom his talk poem nonetheless somehow interacts as it goes. Ginsberg's "America" draws meaning from the American audience across decades by virtue of portable digitality. In the classroom, that proper curricular place, a space dearly paid for, the collaborative activity based on the sound of the poem at the end of the lecture, generalizable for a boisterous pedagogy, was, at best, a prospective add-on effect. Given the sustained old formalities of school, clocks on walls, hallway bells ringing to mark the end of the session (we still heard that tolling in 1995), people having other places to go immediately after, etc., there was still a lot working against the interanimations of poet/audience/recording/room.

THE PLAYFUL AND SINCERE DATABASE

In *The Sound of Poetry/The Poetry of Sound*, Craig Dworkin and Marjorie Perloff observed that in the supposedly "scientific" method of prosodic analysis, perfected by twentieth-century linguists and rhetoricians, "the more thorough the description of a given poem's rhythmic and metrical units, its repetition of vowels and consonants, its pitch contours, the less we may be able to discern the larger contours of a given poet's particular practice." They further emphasize: "Nor do conventional prosodic studies allow for the difference individual performance makes, much less for variants of individual and culturally determined reception."[52] Among the unaccounted-for cultural determinants Dworkin and Perloff described is the university itself as an institution built within defined boundaries. After all, it's safe to say that every one of those studies—the ones missing the "larger contours"—was hosted by a college or university.

Curricular legitimacy is of course associated with tuition dollars and core academic budgets. Although its main contribution within the academic system might ultimately be curricular, a resource for courses, the PennSound archive, with its 719 individual author collections, 10,757 files of group recordings, 773 gigabytes just of MP3s, its hosting of sound file downloads numbering in the tens of millions, has been managed and funded as an off-the-shelf operation: deemed "cutting edge."[53] At the same time, however, it's a charming professorial bauble, occasionally celebrated through collegiate news media, understood to be the extracurricular lark of aggressive innovative faculty and IT staff and otherwise generally left alone to expand or wane. Several attempts to partner for technical archival support with our university's library have been unsuccessful. Why? My best guess is that that failure is mainly the fault of PennSound's organizers: among our many flaws, we were more focused on limitless dissemination than proper preservation. Danny Snelson's Edit series at the Writers House, presented across five years of events (2009–2013), each devoted to turning that flaw into a celebratory theorizing about the importance and beauty of "unstable media formats"—the *aesthetic* value of what he calls the messy "little database" (he means it to rhyme conceptually with the typical fly-by-night modernist "little magazine"). It would seem nonsensical to commend a *database* of all things for being "error-prone and excessive, playful and sincere," but that is what Snelson has done in his recent work, including in a chapter on PennSound. Looking back on the Edit series at the Writers House, I think it was meant to encourage us to offer lessons in "constructing primary dispersion." From Edit to his obsessive, digitally kludged "Reissues" archive in *Jacket2* magazine (2011–present) to "Incredible Machines: Following People Like Us into the Database" (2014) to

The Little Database: A Poetics of Media Formats (2025), Snelson proves that dispersion can precede preservation and does not necessarily obstruct it. Edit, *in media res*, taught PennSound how to own its institutional waywardness.[54]

A few years before Edit, for a "roundtable discussion" on "new media literature" convened by Thomas Swiss in 2002, I and others were asked to respond to this question: "What will need to happen in terms of institutional . . . support, education, promotion and so on for New Media literature to be more widely known?" In my response, I observed that funds flow most freely through connections to customary structures of curriculum and scholarly preservation and were routed through traditionally built and equipped learning spaces.[55] As noted earlier, the first years of the IT revolution at the university were unfortunately focused almost obsessively on the digitizing of existing courses. This was a costly (and, I believe, largely wasteful) activity that tended to carry over all the conventional values already associated with the course, typically a lecture that became hardly more dynamic or intersubjective after the great conversion. Andreas Kaplan, retelling the story of academia's rampant digitalization for a book he edited (*Digital Transformation and Disruption in Higher Education*, 2022), found that, for many, "going digital" meant "merely moving an offline course onto a digital platform." Kaplan notes: "Nothing changes if nothing changes."[56]

These digitalizations might have led directly to new kinds of courses, indeed, a new medium implicit in the promise of the "new media." But more typically, they did not. "Web development" was understood to be a matter of putting old visual-text materials online, scanning stacks of paper notes and texts, a vast but poorly conceived media-transfer project. Students from the mid-1990s through at least the mid-2000s found course materials on the web and then printed them out, putting them back on paper. The main innovation seems to have been a sly economic one: instead of the instructor providing paper copies (as my own teachers had done during the heyday of the mimeo handout revolution), the student was obliged to pay for the traditional format by way of the new-fangled one. Accessible on-campus printers, with sufficient paper and toner, were at a premium. A mode that would seem to have inherent possibilities for interactivity turns out to have been remarkably static. I suppose this was just one of those typical transitional phases as a technology develops. In any case, it was indicative of a problem. Brian Kim Stefans in *Fashionable Noise: On Digital Poetics* (2003) noted that "the most uninteresting cyberpoetry which has yet to been written in our language" simply animated already existing images. This phenomenon suggested a parallel to teaching experimental poetry that was coming from outside the academy: ironically, Stefans felt, poets in this innovative field were singularly noninnovative. On the contrary, he said, "I am interested in interactivity, which is a theory about the *use* of material."[57]

HOW TO BE A LEARNING MANAGER

Traditional academic departmental and disciplinary categories, circa 1993–2010, presented another difficulty at a pivotal moment in the development of digital literary participation outside and inside the university. The digital poet Loss Glazier was thought reputationally at first to be " 'one of the UNIX guys,' " an experience he later described as "suffering ignominy" and always sensing "dimly veiled rancor." "Not only could we not get our early online texts correctly archived," he remembers, "we could not even convince the archival site to classify the [work] as poetry."[58] Although the "electronic poets" explicitly followed in the avant-garde tradition of—to take a few influencers from Glazier's list—Stein, Olson, Pound, and F. T. Marinetti, these figures were sanctioned by the departmental organization as producers of poetic art and theory on pages and thus, despite their categorical iconoclasms otherwise, already disciplinarily well-defined. The "e-poet" challenged the historical text-centric pedagogy of the academy in ways that were significant and are still not fully appreciated.

Meantime, these people were (when they were in the academy at all) academically scattered—and challenged variously. Glazier has been a poet and a literary critic (his book *Digital Poetics: The Making of E-Poetics* [2002] in most ways befits the critical tradition), but his appointment was hosted by a department of media study. Martin Spinelli had been studying and producing sound files in the manner I have been discussing and then entered the tenure track (and ascended to the tenured ranks) in a department of television and radio; later he left the United States to take up an appointment as professor of podcasting, and many of his projects happen outside academia. In 2001, the digital poet Katherine Parrish and her fellow graduate students, taking a course on electronic poetry in an English department, had to "close... the door when class was in session to protect our professor from the teasing of his passing colleagues who did not think ours was a legitimate enterprise."[59] We have to ponder the suppression or preemption of new talent during a formative period. The difficulty directly affected young literary scholars with interests in audio text. As Adelaide Morris put it in her book *Sound States*, "critics with a keen ear tend to turn not to literature but to classical or operatic music, blues, jazz, rock, rap, hip hop and the advanced technologies of youth music."[60] One wants the very same people passionate about art forms in which meaning is generated by "what happens as we go"—as Michael Joyce put it in his book about hypertext—to enter the learning space as teachers and help urge its transformation.[61]

Students like Parrish were hoping for a change in the classroom environment but only in order to study a kind of text that was always changeable. The experimentalist guidance that *learning, like art*, must always change—fundamental to Dewey's *Democracy and Education* and influential among hypertext theorists—recognizes that "all our experiences have a phase of 'cut and try' in them," as Dewey put it, or: "We simply do something, and when it fails, we do something else, and keep on trying."[62] Joyce's phrase "what happens as we go" expresses, I think, a pragmatist version of modernism updated for the digital era; it was a chapter title and generally a rallying cry in his book *Of Two Minds: Hypertext, Pedagogy and Poetics* (1995). Joyce argued that Charles Olson's notion of citizen artist as involving "the discharge of the many . . . by the one" should be applied to pedagogy. That application transforms the role of the teacher into that of "learning manager," as Joyce first rather clumsily phrased it. (He quickly added that by "manage" he meant "making do.")[63]

My colleagues and I at PennSound are learning managers. "The discharge of the many," in the context of the open digital audio archive, implicitly makes a generous structure, where Deweyan "cut and try" describes both the effort of the senders and the experience of the receivers. That which we share freely participates in a radically decentralized digital gift economy. In describing PennSound as a "massive shadow library" in his book about UbuWeb, Kenneth Goldsmith notes that one effect of our archive is to ignore and resist any idea whatsoever of profit from the rare and, in some senses, valuable recorded sounds of poetry. That it sees no earnings is much more than just an issue of funds to put back into the archival work. "PennSound is partially about preventing these works from being sucked into the voracious commercial whirlpool."[64]

Goldsmith praises the press release announcing the official launch of Penn-Sound, admiring its rhetorical alignment with "the free-culture movement" and with the amateur-spirited "folk archiving" that has animated UbuWeb and other retro Web 1.0-style projects celebrated in his book *Duchamp Is My Lawyer* (2020). PennSound joined ventures projecting the free-culture digital spirit. There was UbuWeb itself (founded in 1996). But also these: Craig Dworkin's *Eclipse* (launched in 2001); Word Circuits (late 1990s); Young-Hae Chang Heavy Industries (c. 1999); Eastgate Systems (1982); the *LINEBREAK* series (1995); Jim Andrews's Vispo WWW site (including sound poems from the 1980s); WFMU after it began streaming audio in 1997; recordings at the Internet Archive (founded in 1996); the Electronic Poetry Center or "EPC" (started as a Gopher in 1994)[65]; the Electronic Literature Organization (ELO) cofounded by eminent avant-garde novelist Robert Coover (1999); and the digital-spatial learning projects Nick Montfort first developed as a dual-degree undergraduate in humanities and engineering at Penn (1989–1993), leading directly to the M^<H1N3 (Machine) series at the Kelly Writers House[66] and culminating

later in the creation of the Trope Tank media lab at MIT[67]—and ultimately the editing of the comprehensive historical anthology of computer-generated texts called *Output* (2025). (*Output* links venerable with contemporary projects: a prose-poem fairy tale–making machine; the incomprehensible verse antilecture; the recurrent neural net sonnet generator; a program that generates haiku from Wikileaks documents called Haikuleaks—and more.)

These and other ventures in the innovative gift markets thrived in the half-decade before and for a decade or so after the collapse of Napster's direct file-sharing and -trading in 2001 (but not, of course, the end of the Napster attitude). They are digital-file economies in poetry that defy the proprietary strategy engaged by the popular music industry and by the intellectual property–owning research universities (just predating the rise of for-profit third-party xMOOC providers such as Coursera)—with the music people trying assiduously to track "ownership" of the MP3 file despite its basic nomadic quality while universities' lawyers are still, as of this writing, working out their legal tactics. Lawrence Lessig in *Free Culture: The Nature and Future of Creativity* (2004) reminded us of a history in which various recording industries were understood to have been born of piracy.[68] Marcel Duchamp persistently their guide (and, per Goldsmith's book, their *lawyer*[69]), conceptual artists had already by then embraced readymade piracy not just as poetic practice but as a matter of dissident values challenging conventional proprietary biases, individual creativity, sole credit, identifiable authorial voice, focus on product over process, and antagonisms against disjunction and fragmentation.

Digital strategies arose around such countervalues as creative collaboration in which intellectual property is hard, if not impossible, to discern. By way of the situation PennSound found itself in—but also generally through the learning that happens inside what Lytle Shaw in his book *Narrowcast: Poetry and Audio Research* (2018) calls the sort of "countermedia space" described overall in this book[70]—we can choose an alternative to the demeanor that follows from intellectual proprietariness. If that choice is made, it can become reasonable practice for educators to find a space to take advantage of various piratical successes while the discharge of knowledge and art happens as we go. The countermedia space is either a newly expanded aspect of a school's basic mission or a rationale for setting up a nonmarket shop adjacent to or outside the academy. My favorite contemporary Deweyite poet, Dorothea Lasky, offers a profane view of this latter alienated disposition in a poem titled "What Poets Should Do," a version of "academieS / Burning / monEy" per Cage's Ginsberg:

> Poets should get back to saying crazy shit
> All of the time

I am sick of academics or businesspeople telling poets
What we should do[71]

DREAMING ABOUT DEMOCRACY

Being "critical rather than 'good' citizens" of the classroom, as Henry Giroux once put it in "Dreaming about Democracy,"[72] has the potential of transforming teacher-student/master-apprentice practices, where the teacher is deemed to know everything and the student deemed to know nothing; the teacher thinks and the students are thought about; the teacher produces noise and the students are silent.[73] My point has been that an unintended centrist autocracy built around the text as image has contributed to these ratios of control.

One of the alternatives developed within the text-as-image community, the reader-response theorist's ideal of *I read/you read* as a liberating mode for every reader, can finally be an analog for what we have had in mind in this chapter as a beneficial effect of the uncontrollable dissemination of poetry as sound: *I hear/ you hear*. I say *finally* because, of course, this kind of intersubjectivity has been a century of pre-internet decades in the making.

CHAPTER 5

HTML WAS MY FLEMISH

I just want a poem to speak of

—Dorothea Lasky, "What Poets Should Do"

SOUND-THINGS IN THE CLASSROOM

A century ago, *Democracy and Education* argued that reflection upon experience as itself an experience would prompt a democratic renewal of learning. That definition of experience is connected to Dewey's insistence on the value of sound as mainly a sensory—and only secondarily an intellectual—insight. He called it "reflection in experience." "Thought or reflection," he explained, "is the discernment of the relation between what we try to do and what happens in consequence."

From this point in Dewey's thinking, it was just one step toward realizing a long view of experience as inherently always an experiment. "Some experiences have very little else in them than this hit and miss."[1] Learning must always change, and tolerating change enables learners to discern attempts from outcomes. Dorothea Lasky, her MFA in poetry and her PhD in creativity and schooling, translates that Deweyan difference—what we try as distinct from what occurs—into a "dream" program of reform: "A way to fight for poetry and education." For her dissertation, Lasky researched how teachers foster creativity in their classrooms. It was a study of five high school science teachers and particularly of students in those classrooms who loved poetry and the "poetic skill-sets" they acquired.[2] She became interested in the work of Dewey's student Lawrence Buermeyer, whose goal in the 1920s and 1930s was to bring poetry into "object-based learning" in schools.[3] Object-based learning, Lasky discovered, continues to be influential even among educators critical of damage allegedly done in schools by Dewey's association with liberalism. *What we try* becomes, for Lasky, "an expansion of our personality," and so *what happens* becomes "something *not* ourselves," a form of generous honesty.[4] For Buermeyer, art starts with basic raw materials of experience. Aesthetic life arises from these sensible, tactile, even undignified or "crude" basics.[5]

Lasky's own poems, frank, sometimes depressing, and even a bit crude, are not as programmatically positive as either Dewey or Buermeyer. But Deweyite experience—the idea that texts and topics are objects to experiment with, that objects of learning make basic sounds for close listening, and the idea of living "on and on" as incremental active learning—is never far from Lasky's own poetic writing. In an interview, Lasky observed that Dewey's statement about educational "hit and miss" is a fundamental principle for composing poems. Certainly for hers.[6] Here are more lines from "What Poets Should Do":

> Poems . . . are signposts of comfort possible
> To smooth the jagged edges
> Of this worried traveler
> That's what poems should do
> And that's what poets actually do . . .
> I just want a poem to speak of
> So I go on and on[7]

The phrase "to speak of" is a productive idiom here. It refers to something sufficiently worthy; it is also a text that has a soundness, an idea we can make noise about, a dependable resonance. The speaker of the poem persists because it is worthy of its sound. And this from the poem "Why Poetry Can Be Hard for Most People": "Because poetry reminds you that there is no dignity in living— you just muddle through."[8] From Lasky's poem "Genius," we get a Deweyite constructivist skepticism about the concept of genius. "There is no muse / There are only wild wild forces / That are allowed in."

> Knowledge
> And language
> Knowledge and language
> Are nothing
> They are sounds.

No poem by Lasky comes closer than this to *Democracy and Education*. "If I believed in genius, then I'd say / Yes I am one / But I don't believe, believe in it / Nor intelligence / Or all that."[9] Here's Dewey: "The measure of difference between the average student and the genius is a measure of the absence of originality in the former. But this notion of mind in general is a fiction. How one person's abilities compare in quantity with those of another is none of the teacher's business."[10]

When Lasky contributed to *Poets on Teaching: A Sourcebook*, she wrote about poems, Dewey, and the "sound-things" one can bring into the classroom. She reminds us that Dewey wrote extensively about "the importance of materiality and felt experience when it comes to learning poetry." Words being objects, when one "manipulates" a word one is changing a thing. Sounds, Lasky stresses, are among the objects to be introduced into the learning space. "Words are the symbolic things of the objects of sounds. These sound-things can be bounced around and smashed, but when things come together in the space of a poem, there is something spiritually and materially important to these connections." As evidence for this, she cites *Art as Experience*.[11]

Lasky is right to cite Dewey on this point. He believed a school at its best is a sonic community. He argued for sound reform in its several senses. We are about to go back in time to sketch a throughline of thought about sound and reforms in learning from the 1930s through the 1960s, which then—with the new associations of digital audio culture and learning in the 1990s—led to the cMOOC of the 2000s and some xMOOCs of the 2010s. Such a derivation, as I hear it, starts from Dewey when, in 1934, he argued that what is seen with the eyes tends to create feeling indirectly, whereas overheard sound has an immediate effect. Sight is classed as an intellectual sense, while "sounds have the power of direct emotional expression." Sound should be "freed from the definiteness it has acquired through its association with speech."[12] Lasky presents poetic sound-objects to her students to encourage them to drift away from expected definiteness. These activities align with Bloch's goals when she brought the then-new sounds of PennSound's Baraka from the outer edge of semanticism into the room. "Poetry's vocal roots hover ghost-like even as we read words silently," writes Jesse Nathan in *Open the Door: How to Excite Young People About Poetry*, a book for teachers he coedited with Lasky. "Writing remains a search for voices."[13] And, as with Bloch or with my teaching of Ginsberg's "America," when no text is given, learners begin to understand to value obliquity as a form of direct personal experience. "Sounds *come* from outside the body," Dewey writes, "but sound itself is near, intimate."[14] This is what Lasky means when she refers to what is both "spiritually and materially important" in connectivist teaching. "Our sensual perception is more cohesive than we realize," she told me when emphasizing that democracy in education succeeds when students are the focus of what she calls "everyday creativity." For this reason, she agrees with Dewey's heretical declaration against any professionalization of students in schools—his advocacy of learning as "not a preparation for the future."[15]

REFORM STUDIES, NOT STUDENTS

"Sound stimulates directly to immediate change," Dewey wrote in *Art as Experience*, "because it reports a change."[16] A change in the space of appreciating art and a change in the literal space of learning. Of course, in the mid-1930s, he also meant large *social* change. Any history of child-centered education requires an analysis of Dewey's sense of "social flux" as starting with individual emotional experience. John Darling's chronicle *Child-Centered Education and Its Critics* (1994) documents Dewey's call for a "constant reweaving of the social fabric" based in part on the "continuous stream of immigrants [which] brought the stimulus of variety of outlook and experience" at the time of his theorizing and writing.[17] There was something artful to be learned from the new pluralistic social noise produced by immigration. The way Dewey lauded crowd–made sounds in the mid-1930s corresponded with the collaged, migrant-friendly orality of populist poet Carl Sandburg, especially in that sonic grab-bag of a volume, *The People, Yes* (1936). As described in *Art as Experience*, sounds simulating educational, emotional expression include those that are "threatening, whining, smoothing, depressing, fierce, tender, soporific,"[18] and the experience of nonsemantic, nonspeech-like resonance can "denote the clash of attacking and resisting forces" and the "incredibly varied complexities of question, uncertainty, and suspense wherein every tone is ordered in reference to others."[19] In Dewey and Sandburg, sound is social. The sound-object helps citizens and prospective citizens ready themselves for the immediate future. "Sound," Dewey wrote, "is the conveyor of what impends, of what is happening as an indication of what is likely to happen."[20]

John Darling's account of learner-centered learning follows criticisms, some of them quite angry, leveled against Dewey as his ideas deeply took hold in schools and education departments in the 1930s, a time of general political liberalism. Some of the same critics decried leftist endorsements of Rousseau's *Emile, or On Education* (1762) as a model for making a citizen. Although conceding that it was "fashionable to laugh Rousseau to scorn as pre-historic, and even as anti-historic,"[21] and although finding his methods devoid of plausible theory, Dewey still extolled Rousseau for saying "that the only habit he would have his ideal pupil form was the habit of not forming habits at all . . . that he would do anything possible to keep the activities of this pupil from getting into habits."[22]

As *Child-Centered Education* turns in later chapters to summaries of ideas about learning in the 1960s, by which time teachers are to encourage "pupils to find out things for themselves," and "reading and writing" is "best . . . taught when the need for them is evident" to learners,[23] iterations of traditionalist pushback crowd his pages. The critics, of course, were addressing the excesses of student-led movements against authoritarian education that culminated in Paris, Mexico City, Berlin, Dakar, New York, and elsewhere in May 1968. In England, the reformist *Primary Memorandum* (1965) and the *Plowden Report* (1967) preceded those confrontations by a few crucial years, but they did coincide with the much-discussed pamphlet entitled *On the Poverty of Student Life* (1966), inspired by the Situationist International (SI). The school, SI people announced, has "become a society for the propagation of ignorance. . . . A modern economic system demands mass production of students." They added this facetiousness: "But all this hardly matters: the important thing is to go on listening respectfully. In time, if critical thinking is repressed with enough conscientiousness, the student will come to partake of the wafer of knowledge, the professor will tell him the final truths of the world."[24] The first mass protest in the western part of Berlin of that era, in June of 1966, was largely about the failures of traditional pedagogy. In Bernard Larsson's landmark photograph of the June 23 gathering, we can make out a placard reading: "Wir fordern Studien Reform statt Studenten Reform." They were asking for a reform of *studies* (Studien) instead of reforming *students* (Studenten). The crowd called for greater self-direction and wanted less in the way of predetermined answers and expected curricular outcomes.

In 1966, the advocacy for what might be called a learner's right to opacity—the freeing from definiteness via the sound-object to be "smashed," as Lasky puts it, such that it will generate its athematic noise—was a long way in time and perhaps in tone from philosopher of media and SI cofounder Guy Debord's early "Methods of Détournement" (1956) and "Détournement as Negation and Prelude" (1959). Yet the influential SI pamphlet, while itself a work of writing more straight polemic than Debordian fragmentation, juxtaposition, and mediated quotation, did concede in early situationist fashion that "the only *poetry* [the current situation] can acknowledge is the *creativity* released in the making of history, the *free invention* of each moment and each event."[25]

In the face of the deadly realization that history teaches that history uncreatively teaches, the professor who lectures students to convey "the final truths of

FIGURE 5.1 Bernard Larsson, *Das erste deutsche Sit-in*, Berlin, 1966. Rally in front of a sit-in of three thousand students in the Henry Ford Building of the Free University, June 6, 1966, photo, West Berlin.

Source: Kunstbibliothek/Staatliche Museen/Berlin/Germany: INV Larsson 1967/08-26A. Reprinted with inkjet printer, 2017, and exhibited at Museum für Fotografie, May–June 2024. A placard depicted reads: "Wir fordern Studien Reform statt Studenten Reform" ("We demand a reform of studies rather than a reform of students"). Permission: Art Resource & Staatliche Museen.

the world" could be treated like a learner, and the student who had been merely "an admiring spectator" might finally be heard. If, as Greil Marcus noted in *Lipstick Traces*, the poetic strategy of *détournement*, a radicalization of Duchamp, enabled the "cutting of the vocal cords of every empowered speaker,"[26] the resulting victorious silence might be replaced by the kind of sound that (per Lasky via Dewey) can be bounced and smashed yet nonetheless will express—the better conveyor of what impends. The thing to be cut is the "explicative order" Jacques Rancière challenges in *The Ignorant Schoolmaster*. In conventional education, "for comprehension to take place, one has to be given an explication, the words of the master must shatter the silence of the taught material."[27] And when the master's voice was no longer to be heeded, when "some tried their hand at analysis" of learners' hopes for a new educational order—"tried," they meant, but failed—a different class of institutional explicators was called in. The university rector, the SI pamphleteers observed, now argued that since "these students have insulted their professors," the latter having been silenced by indignity, the former "should be dealt with by psychiatrists." Thus, the explicative order managed by the professoriate would need to be slightly enlarged: "We need sociologists and psychologists to explain such phenomena to us."[28]

THE MYTH OF EXPLICATION

Initially, it seems, many readers of Rancière's book, *The Ignorant Schoolmaster: Five Lessons in Intellectual Emancipation* (1987; translated into English 1991), did not realize that it is an elaborate, partly allegorical response to the post-1966 debates about education.[29] The book recounts the story of Joseph Jacotot, a French teacher living in exile in the late eighteenth century who taught in Belgium without any knowledge of his students' language (Flemish).

The teacher realizes that knowledge is not necessary for teaching and that "explication is the myth of pedagogy." Out of necessity, equality is a starting assumption rather than a goal. The French *expérience* means both "experience" and "experiment." The breaking of the explicative order results in the possibility of—preceded in Jacotot's case by—the revelation of teacherlessness. Normally, the schoolmaster makes a coherent, definitive noise and "opens his mouth to explain the book" that the students are thenceforth supposed to learn. There follows a stunning question, various versions of which are at the center of my book here: "*But why should the book need such help?*" "An opacity has now set in," and "it concerns understanding." So "we are left with learning, with finding the tools of that expression in books." Not just any book, to be sure. Certainly not "orators' books: these don't seek to be *figured out*; they want to be *listened to*." On the contrary, seek books that cause readers to work "in the gap between feeling and expression, between the silent language of emotion and the arbitrariness of the spoken tongue."[30]

Mark Nowak, poet and teacher-organizer, has for years been encouraging nontraditional learners to write and make publications that function in ways diametrically opposed to those "orators' books" Rancière distrusted, less focused on demanding to be listened to and more on the collective activity that produces them. Nowak has sponsored "people's workshops," developed the Workers' Writers School, and has encouraged "transnational poetry dialogues" that are not just accommodating but also taking creative advantage of the multiple languages spoken among manufacturing, domestic, and transportation workers. Through the latter activities, he and his colleagues have learned that poetic transnationalism makes possible new collaborative readings of the English of Stein, Pound, the Language poets, and various contemporary Conceptualists, making for a fresh "minor literature" characterized by a "deterritorialization of language" and a relevance to "political immediacy."[31]

Nowak is the ideal ignorant schoolmaster. Ultimately, Jacotot dreams, as Nowak does, of a "community of equals," a broad social network of working people "that would be a society of artists" in which "the division between those who know and those who don't" has been bridged. This idea of the social "would only know minds in action," writes Rancière, "people who do, who speak about what they are doing, and who thus transform all their works into ways of demonstrating the humanity that is in them as in everyone."[32] Nowak admires Rancière's *Proletarian Nights: The Worker's Dream in Nineteenth-Century France* for its suggestion that workers can "rebel, through poetry, against the rigid predetermination of their everyday lives." "No book, to me," Nowak writes, "elucidates workers' rights to dream quite like" *Proletarian Nights*.[33]

With its own dream of a sort of teaching that attempts to establish a community of equals, *The Ignorant Schoolmaster* reinterprets political exile in the eighteenth century by way of 1968, and, as noted, his book is really a response to various reformisms (and their antagonists) of the 1960s. Nowak's social poetics offers a pedagogical rereading of the 1930s by way of theories of twenty-first-century capitalism and a renewed emphasis on the poem as work—a piece of work, an effort of labor, a thing made, a making. This emphasis reminds me of our experience with Jake Marmer's students working out how Stein's "A Long Dress" took its maker, and the makers of the dress, and then *them*, and then *us* with our ModPo machinery, such a "long" time in the making. Nowak's innovation,

I think, is to focus on making as truly akin to work such that work can unify ideas about learning-as-making and modernism. That is to say, social poetics can poetically display the work being done to make the poem, of course. "It isn't what [the poet] *says* that counts as a work of art," urged William Carlos Williams at his most proletarian (and most intensely antiacademic), "it's what he *makes.*"[34]

After three decades working on his community-based poetry projects, when Nowak decided to write an account of them and the ideas that support them—in a book titled *Social Poetics* (2020)—he was absorbing many influences across the decades, among them prison writing groups from the 1950s through the 1970s, Howard Zinn's *People's History* of 1980, the Nuyorican Poets Café (founded 1973), the concept of "history from below" coming into prominence with E. P. Thompson's subfield-naming essay of 1966. But Nowak's main contribution, to my mind, is a reassessment of what in the mid-1930s was celebrated—among factions joining (briefly) as an antifascist united front and then (also briefly) in a popular front—as "social poetry." By 1937–1939, the otherwise politically cautious new editor of *Poetry* magazine, George Dillon, sought out "social poetry" under that designation for the famed (and immediately prior to then, reputationally staid) modernist periodical.[35] A year earlier, Horace Gregory was commissioned to edit what he had persuaded *Poetry*'s founding editor Harriet Monroe to call a "Social Poets Number," actually featuring communist and fellow-traveling American poets.[36] *Poetry*'s Chicago-based editorial staff, including Monroe, was friendly not just with fellow Chicagoan Sandburg (Monroe had been his mentor) but also with the general robust sense of "the people" one encountered in his Depression-era verse epics of collective agency and dignity. Sandburg's Depression poetry was quite a breakthrough, as collaged proletarian verse, or "working-class poetry" in Nowak's preferred phrase[37]—verse constructed of "proverbs, questions, memoranda, folklore, faces, and wonderings," forming "a fresco and a field of grass"[38]—began to converge with formally experimental modernism, even with surrealist and Dadaist tactics. This was a categorical and aesthetic mixing (a literary united front) that succeeded in complicating what actually was meant by the flat term "communist poetry"—written by the likes of avant-gardists Kenneth Fearing, Langston Hughes, the Williams of *An Early Martyr & Other Poems* (1935), Muriel Rukeyser, and the relentlessly inventive Bob Brown—until the cultural Cold War of the 1950s forced a separation between the radical and aesthetic categories once again.[39] Nowak admires Rukeyser's Cold War-era memory of social poetry's reformation of poetic categories in the 1930s. "If we are free," she declared, refusing to recant, "we are free to choose a tradition."[40]

When Cold War culture insisted on the separation just described, and after scrubbing through the centrist filters of the 1950s, what was lost was a memory of how poetry of the 1930s had actually anticipated so many of the machines powered up in the 1990s and 2000s. It's taken a lot of work to get a fresh view of the prewar period. Sometimes this work has been described as "repression and recovery."[41] In this context, Rukeyser's bold insistence on freedom—"free to choose a tradition"—means free to reradicalize the received canon by what often amounted to a preinternet hacktivism. Bob Brown, whom Orchid Tierney in her short history of digital poetics deems a "media visionar[y]," variously attempted the hacktivist's strategy. That strategy and its fascinating inheritors in our time— such as "PennMOO" and its denizens or members of the "Wreading, Writing, Wresponding" seminar—is the next topic.

HAPTIC SOCIALITY

The machine in the 1920s and 1930s was a newish friend to poetry. Bob Brown was an active democratic socialist and a commune-ist. He lived on an Arkansas commune and cofounded a Rousseauian/Deweyite school. He believed that social poetry would synthesize the human act of reading with innovative machinery. He was exactly what Paul Stephens in *The Poetics of Information Overload* calls him: a "bibliomaniac" who deemed his and others' outpouring of books and writings to be making a case against digital minimalism long before networked computing.[42] Stephens summarizes the case cogently: "More information does not necessarily lead to less meaning."[43] The information overload opens up interpretive possibilities. Unplugging is a form of self-censorship, a closing of the mind.

Gems (1931) is Brown's portfolio of salaciously mechanized poetic chestnuts—i.e., classic little lyric verse exemplars that have come into the memorized canon. In any one Gem, you could find that the sin is entirely in the poet's omission and the reader's commission. Each Gem demonstrates that censorship produces the opposite result of what it intends and that the best lyric employs antilyric strategies. A trite, innocent word gets blacked out and then replaced, as the reader reads, by a transgressive one in the mind. A selection from *Gems* is encountered in the ModPoPLUS syllabus, and here is a typical participant's response in the forums: "In framing love and *nature imagery* this way, Brown suggests how *artificial* our frames are."[44] The hack might at first seem to be the effort of artifice, while in comparison, Alfred, Lord Tennyson is to be deemed the natural original. But no, the ModPo readers offer: in telling you authoritatively what word comes next—supposed free choices narrowed and even determined by rhyme, meter, genre, adherence to theme—it is the Victorian laureate who is the contrivance! My goodness, readers think, that's right, it's *Tennyson* who enables automatic-conceptual art. Tennyson, it turns out, was always already the poetic auto-completion machine, churning out quatrains whose line endings are so legible as to be predictable. Yet there's a hint of the happy glitchy future: the rhyme-and-meter-making engine, through the good offices of Bob Brown's machine, needs rehumanizing.

What is natural and humane in Brown's remix process of "writing through" by blacking out is the renaturalized relationship between the work of the poet-as-critic and the activist/hacktivist pleasure taken by the reader. "Pleasure in poetry comes largely from reading between the lines," Brown wrote about *Gems*, and he invited readers to join in and become "a competent co-creator."[45] And so found poetry, and even automatic poetry, can be social poetry. For instance, one of the *Gems* selectively erases, and thus makes more suggestive, this Tennysonian ballad stanza:[46]

THE LORD OF BURLEIGH (TENNYSON)

In her ▓▓▓▓ he ▓▓▓▓ gaily,
 If my ▓▓▓▓ by signs can tell,
Maiden, I have ▓▓▓▓ thee daily,
 And I think you ▓▓▓▓ me well.

It's up to Tennyson's/Brown's readers to decide what verb befits the speaker's brazen assumption of what the maiden thinks of Henry Cecil, the Lord of Burleigh who disguised himself as a commoner. One can just imagine. Brown has made a social poem through the unmasking of Tennyson and Cecil—by masking how gaily and daily he ▓▓▓▓ her.

"Brown re-invented the idea of censorship," comments Michelle Pereira in the ModPo forums, "and turned the process of censoring into one of liberating creation. Censorship usually limits the artist and curbs his or her creative agency, reducing and distilling possible meanings. Yet Brown here uses censorship to loosen the original poems."[47] In ModPo, when people read various poems like Brown's that disrupt the old charms of reading, they set out to find new charms. Exploring the origins of predigital strategies for such liberation and verbal loosening, rather than dour uncreative constriction, is Tierney's objective in her essay "The Politics and History of Digital Poetics: Copyright, Authorship, Anti-Lyric" as she connects preinternet media experimentalism to recent digital poetries.

Tierney argues that any understanding of "the radical experimentation of contemporary electronic literature" must begin with "the visual, technological, and

formal innovations of earlier avant-garde movements, including Futurism and
Dadaism, as well as later [but still preinternet] literary groups, such as Oulipo,
Fluxus and language writing." Bob Brown's leftist preposthuman avant-gardism
is, for Tierney, the right place to start. She opens by describing Brown's 1930 proposal for a mechanical reading machine. Likening his planned innovation to the
then-new cinema "talkies," "Brown's reading device proposed to deliver 'readies'
or a ticker-tape stream of prose or poetry to a viewer, thereby efficiently trans-
mitting a visual spectacle of information."[48] His case against literature as a form
of lecturing leads him to auto-electrical formats, not only for the sheer fun of
experimentation, "infusing erotic passion into the media technologies,"[49] but also
because he held a deadly serious political position, anticipatory of populist digital
culture, against poetry that was little more than a version of "[Calvin] Coolidge
(today: add Eisenhower)" as conventional oratory. "Now that oratory is dead,"
Brown reflected during the Ike Age, he wanted poetry "still read aloud" but
"vociferated ... by *electronicsniks*" as a way to renew poetry's difference-making.[50]

Readies were conceived not as a method of talking or even of writing but as
a social device for reading. They could be pronounced *Reed*-eez (*Read*-ease) as
an ethical pivot away from the thieving of Duchamp's *Ready*mades and their
emphasis on the genius of the artist's curating choice (no matter how liberating)
and toward something like Nowak's concept of poetic participatory democracy.[51]
That anti-"oratory" self-government—Bob Brown and Mark Nowak share this
also—functions upon a critique meant to ridicule canonical purveyors of pon-
derous "three-volume classics" as "pin heads." "Pin head" was Brown's nasty term
used in a verse statement he made for his experimental book *Words* (1931). Note
how new reading technologies are connected to this gloating predictive condemnation. "In the reading-machine future," this bibliomaniac wrote at the start of
the Depression:

> Say by 1950
> All magnum opuses
> Will be etched on the
> Heads of pins
> Not retched into
> Three volume classics
> By pin heads.[52]

Readies, Gems, the hyperproductive Fiction Factory (a mechanical formula
spitting out hundreds of marketable novels), the "pseudoepigraphous ... special laboratory" of *Words* (1931),[53] and Brown's many other whacky "tele-vistic"[54]

FIGURE 5.2 "Gertrude Stein at the Teletype."

Source: Gertrude Stein and Alice B. Toklas Papers, YCAL MS 76, Box 149, Folder 3528, Beinecke Rare Book and Manuscript Library, Yale University. Reproduced with permission of the Beinecke Library, with thanks to Nancy Kuhl.

inventions supporting preinternet cybernetics were all designed to explore what Katherine Parrish, writing about cybertheory, calls "the relationship between authorial control and its relinquishment," with emphasis on the latter.

Parrish took Katherine Hayles's celebrated book about cyberculture, *How We Became Posthuman* (1999), and reworked it as "How We Became Automatic Poetry Generators" in order to stress the *human-ness* of digital poetry in particular as "part of a distributed system" that enables rather than inhibits "the full expression of human capability."[55] Orchid Tierney, too, knows that digital poetics, with its mixed and convergent sense of authorship—which makes for an interpretive social network—destabilizes "but does not erase" the lyrical subject "or their sociopolitical experiences."[56] Tierney concludes that this kind of poetry "underscores the communal and interactive possibilities of the language arts and foregrounds their complex haptic sociality that reorients lyricism as a political condition."[57]

ALPH AND THE MOO

"Haptic sociality" is the right phrase for describing a poetry MOO. A MOO (from "Multi-User Dungeon [MUD], Object Oriented") is a multiuser text-based virtual environment furnished by object-oriented programming. The most successful educational MOOs preceded the rise of graphical browsers such as Mosaic and Netscape. To repeat, the space was entirely based on text typed (not even much yet copied/pasted) into the communal virtual space—as primitive as a futuristic mode could be. The key MOO quality is "multiuser." If you take the rigorous preinternet proceduralities and constraints of Oulipo (founded 1960) and project them into an early- to mid-1990s MOO inhabited by numerous people, you will have a good instance of haptic sociality at scale. Christopher Funkhouser is right to describe methods of presenting text in MOOs as "lively and unconventional by any standard." Everything happening in a MOO is a "conflation of speech and act."[58] Funkhouser's first experience with collaborative writing in a MOO was in the space made by "HiPitched Voices," a women's writing collective. He observed, as they explored hypertext writing online in real time, an advance over earlier "contrived approaches" to such group writing.[59] Unsurprisingly, Funkhouser, Tierney, Goldsmith, Glazier, and Parrish all refer to the Oulipo group, the workshop for potential literature founded in 1960 as crucial forerunners of interdependent digital poetics. Oulipo advanced various forms of noncomputerized (as well as sometimes computerized) procedural poetry, which was hugely influential, to be sure. But their main effect once digital networking and sharing became possible might have been the collaborative possibilities. If they defined *littérature potentielle* as the search for new structures and patterns that writers can freely use, those patterns have been taken in recent decades to refer to the social act of people together making a stile, rhopalism, N+7 poem, grid poem, exquisite corpse, cohosting a renga party, or the design and activation of text-generation programs to make algorithmic writing.

Katherine Parrish constructed an educational MOO called "MOOlipo." Inside a MOO, one built rooms using a MOO programming language. Each room contained coded objects, ways of generating plain-text literary forms (such as palindromes, collaborative Cagean acrostics, or auto-sonnets) with other people present as characters—such as my own casteless avatar, a cipher-like figure named Alph—and, in the case of MOOlipo, an engine that would be triggered to overwrite whatever text you typed with a string generated by various input texts, including those sneaked into the room by others. "The possibility for a poetics of non-intention blossoms in the MOOlipo" and generally for learner-centered learning as well.[60] In an educational MOO, "identity maintenance" is a specific and constant conscious effort, unlike much or most other experiences of writing where one, at some point, settles, even in second- or third-person stories, into some sort of ongoing *I*. Yet whenever Alph wrote text as participant, bystander, or guide at an activity, they—i.e., *I*—became specifically aware of playing a role, as it was likely to be altered by (or even with) others.[61] The MOO is a descendant of Brown's Readies, and it is a direct ancestor of ModPo. It is a digital machine that can "liberate . . . the author of authoritative discourses." It can also make transparent the "internalized codes" of which the author of conventional creative works is "unaware." Thus, upon entering a MOO as a kind of classroom, a learner can experience the same freedom. If you can leave aside the funky tech (hard to do, I'll admit), is that not the goal of all literary teaching?

Between 1993 and 1997, Susan Garfinkel, Michael Nenashev, the late Jack Abercrombie, Jay Treat, James J. O'Donnell, and I built and developed "PennMOO." Alph contributed no back-end programming, to be sure, but did somewhat learn to work the command line, and there they successfully convened the students of English 88. Inside PennMOO, we held collaborative close readings of poems (each poem as an "object"—"mob" or "mobile object"—with which to interact in each MOO classroom), group office hours (Alph hosted at 11:30 P.M. every Sunday), virtual poetry slams, and Alph-sponsored meetings with eminent "visiting" poet NPCs (nonplayer characters). We built a skating rink for digital exercise in the immersive text-based world and for social mixing (Alph slipped and fell on the digital ice a lot). And as a surprise, Susan Garfinkel instigated "food fights" after the English 88 students' incensed reaction to Ginsberg and his bratty Beat friends in *Howl* "who threw potato salad at CCNY lecturers on Dadaism," demanding that they be permitted to point out the hypocrisy, whereupon they threw digital salad, making such a mess of the place it required a reboot. We also attended antilectures where no one could identify whether the lecturer was a professor, undergraduate, or member of the IT staff.

At one point, I was disappointed by the uninspired discussion I was leading on Robert Frost's "Mending Wall." The students didn't want to give this intolerant "walling out" the time of day. Eastern European walls had fallen a few years earlier, and now there seemed to be only one side, as it were, on the old Frostian question.

> Before I built a wall I'd ask to know
> What I was walling in or walling out,
> And to whom I was like to give offense.

So I asked the students to ask parents, siblings, grandparents, or elderly neighbors to send me their email addresses (optionally, of course). I then set up a separate

> ## PennMOO for English 88
>
> **Alan Filreis**
> ___
>
> Main www page for **PennMOO** in English at Penn. Click here for a direct connection to PennMOO.
>
> 1. **English 88 was the first large-ish course at Penn to conduct course-related discussions, and to hold office hours, in a MOO.**
> 2. Information about our the 88 VIRTUAL POETRY SLAM and samples of what was created there.
> 3. Questions about PennMOO? Contact **"pennmoo@english.upenn.edu"**.
> 4. Stats on use of **PennMOO** (11/95).
> 5. Memo on concepts for making PennMOO a space in which to build **"Penn as it should be"** rather than reflecting *Penn as it is.*
> ___
>
> ○ Note on an easy way to connect to PennMOO via tinyfugue
> ○ **Introduction to PennMOO** for English 88--Instructions and Advice
> ○ Another, more general, **description of MOO**
> ○ Glossary of MOO commands and terms
> ○ Questions about MOO for 88? Send a message to Susan Garfinkel by clicking here.
> ○ First English 88 **PennMOO session in Penniman Library** - complete with positions
> ○ English 88 **Virtual Poetry Slam**

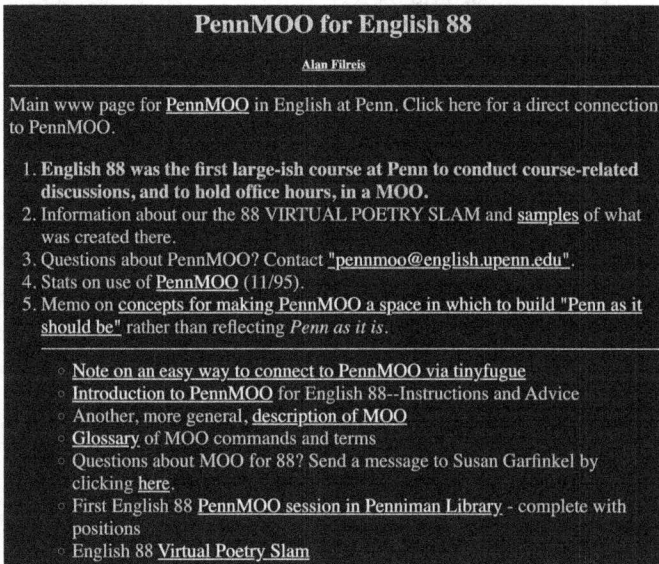

FIGURE 5.3 Screenshot of a PennMOO web page.
___
Source: "PennMOO for English 88," 1996, last updated in 1997.

"families88" listserv. I led two separate week-long asynchronous discussions of the poem, thereafter showing students the generational interpretive differences. The older folks, Cold War-era Americans, mostly accepted the rationale of maintaining the existing wall even while appreciating the speaker's doubts about its practical value. Then I concatenated the two listservs, filreis88 and families88, and succeeded in hosting the two groups as one community as they went at it about the wall. At the same time, Alph convened only the students synchronously in a special "Mending Wall room" inside PennMOO, where we tried to tear down the wall. I'd never presented Frost so fairly or effectively, before or since. Working with students in PennMOO was Alph's best experience with—at least the best first introduction to—the crucial pedagogical concept of "managing in the middle," which is how Shawn Wilbur describes it in *High Wired: On the Design, Use, and Theory of Educational MOOs.*[62]

The technical aspects of managing in the middle, though they're fascinating and taught me a lot about digital teaching, were less interesting to me, in fact, than the relevance of this idea to Frost's supposedly conservative poetics. The speaker of his poem has doubts about the wall but meets annually to rebuild it while mocking his neighbor who meets him there yet fails to question any structure. But the *wall* is the middle and turns out—if you think of the poem as building a third space in which we talk about human behavior—to be the poem's hero or at least its real subject and protagonist, its middle manager, while Alph, having made the middle capable, became an educator successfully putting into place what Sherry Turkle called "soft mastery" as a function of "non-linear" teaching.

Turkle's early (mostly optimistic) work, especially *Life on the Screen* (1995), was an influence on PennMOO pedagogy. She described how assuming different personalities in a MUD or MOO could be therapeutic and how "soft mastery" and "bricolage" might get us past the already conventional linear, abstract, or "hard" thinking of much computer programming. She argued that these virtual worlds, especially when they were operated with language, can shift a unitary sense of the self. This turned out to be the key to understanding how intergenerational interpretive communities—like my families88+filreis88 listserv—make the clearest sense of Frost's splitting

$$\text{speaker} \rightarrow \text{neighbor} \parallel \text{subject} \rightarrow \text{object}$$

across the long-standing stone wall of ritual social convening. Soft mastery augured a pedagogy. Not "*alone* together," to use Turkle's later more doubtful phrasing but rather, *together* together.[63]

The MOO was Alph's teacher for a while there. I'm a little embarrassed now by the fervent, programmatic tone of a memo I published on my website in January 1996, "Concepts for PennMOO." Still, this MOO manifesto gives the flavor of the collaborative potential, and it too is a rhetorical predecessor of ModPo. As you read, please forgive the old shouting ALL CAPS.

> We should work to create a MOO-based community, overlapping with BUT DISTINCT from the course-based communities that inhabit the space at present. To this end, I'm going to suggest that we rethink the issue of students building their own spaces [I meant: we should allow it], and give "unofficial" spaces a real chance to develop. I'm going to experiment with this in my English 103 [to be held in spring semester, 1996, a course titled The Literature of Community]. . . . Generally, we should work to ELIMINATE THE SEPARATION OF ACADEMIC AND SOCIAL—we should integrate these as wholly and assiduously as we can. This is, after all, the one thing PennMOO can do that most other academic spaces literally cannot (with the exception of the very rare course taught in the students' residences).[64]

One can tell that as all this unfolded I was under the spell of *On the Poverty of Student Life.* To enable learners, not only tech support staff and a few programming-savvy faculty, to build their own learning spaces seemed a real, particular shift of power—if it was indeed true that to have access to the technical means and the virtual right to make a made space was to understand structures of literary learning and not just the texts typewritten into it.[65] PennMOO gave over some authority to learners partly because it put the idea of space and text together. This merging is why George Landow in *Hypertext* (1992) felt it reasonable to describe a near future of "reconfiguring literary education." His discussion of power and the move away from the lecture seemed real from my vantage point inside PennMOO. "Educational hypertext redefines the role of instructors," Landow wrote, "by transferring some of their power and authority to students. This technology has the potential to make the teacher more a coach than a lecturer."[66]

Charles Bernstein would not use the term *coach* to describe himself, but it befits his stance. Perhaps he would prefer "wresponder." Not one to regret previous enthusiasms, he recalls: "In the 1970s, many of us, batty as hornets in a bee's nest, spoke of reader's response, the reader not the poem makes the meaning"—a view he now finds excessive yet indicative of an era. When he read about erica kaufman's experience teaching teachers to teach Stein in a draft of this book, Bernstein pointed out that he ultimately prefers this framing: "reading as doing." His essay, titled "Wreading, Writing, Wresponding," collected in the book *Teaching Modernist Poetry*, implies a political history of Language writing that helps further understand why experimental poetry and hypertext theory have similar things to say about the power of reading. That history is suggested in the pedagogy of wreading: students have laptops open, and they are all talking, and the "ongoing serial collaboration" continues from preclass to in-class to after class, while the teacher projects onto a classroom screen—a "large LCD display," then at nontrivial cost to the university—not the poetry being studied but the index of the class listserv.[67]

As a teacher, Bernstein's goal is to stave off what might be called wikiphobia. Yochai Benkler, in presenting his case for "a collaborative reception version of the wiki model," says that those experiencing such anxiety in response to information overload make "the Babel objection."[68] For Bernstein, on the contrary, Babel is a dream world for colloquy. More information means more choices and a proliferation of language registers and rhetorics. With his anarchic style and satirist tone, his "babble flow" (to borrow the name for a genre of writing favored by Jack Kerouac at his most experimental), Bernstein might seem to promote DIY as an ethos, but that's not quite right: DIT, or Do It Together, is more like it. The very history of Language writing is implied in the idea of maximalist wresponding as a noisy, postauthoritative form of writing: "The class time is a blank page on which a composition takes place: everything happens."[69] If everything happens and everyone can compose the plan, then no embarrassment is necessary. The reader, not the poem, *does* make the meaning—and, what's more, the more the wreaders, the better the wreading.[70]

Parrish, with her perspective from inside MOOlipo, was dreaming of how the machine might replace existing literary power, and Bernstein's seminar experiences in substitution, deformation, recombination, and homolinguistic translation,[71] aim for the same replacement. Parrish quotes Oulipo's most famous member, Italo Calvino: "And so the author vanishes . . . to give place to a more thoughtful person."[72] Joyelle McSweeney and Johannes Göransson, in "The Anxious Classroom," equate the lecture with "a read-only pdf." "We must abolish the Teacher as Authority," they write, "a figure meant to block the anxiety of the classroom. Poetry is not a set of rules and requirements to be imparted to students, a downloadable instruction sheet, a read-only pdf."[73] Wresponding is what happens when a "thoughtful person" replaces Calvino's author and McSweeney and Göransson's lecturer at once. Teaching reading through writing does a much better job of permitting the anxiety students feel when confronted by a difficult poem, their own poems no less than those of an assigned famous poet. In *Rethinking University Teaching: A Framework for the Effective Use of Educational Technology* (1993), when Diana Laurillard wondered, "Why aren't lectures scrapped as a teaching method?" she gave a bit of credence to academics who "will always defend the value of the 'inspirational lecture.'" Then again, "How many inspirational lectures could you reasonably give in a week? . . . Inspirational lectures are likely to be occasional events." In the next moment, Laurillard turns to print, "easily the most important educational medium." And using a significant analogy, she concludes: "Print is similar to the lecture."[74]

NOT COURSEWARE

Let us consider the end of the lecture as we know it. It is "the oldest surviving pedagogical practice in the university" and exists remarkably unscathed into the era of interactive learning.[75] How could that be?

Back again to the mid-1990s. At a conference sponsored by the SEI Center for Advanced Studies in Management on "the virtual university" held in early 1995, midcentury urban sociologist and former university president Martin Meyerson

(1922–2007), by this time three years retired and feeling consciously at the verge of a new era he would not fully witness, stood up in the audience and said the following: "The best lectures have always been those that deal with 'tentative materials' that result from the professor's research. If they cease to be tentative, don't include them in the lecture; print them and share them. The main teaching function has to be interactive."[76] The World Wide Web was still new to most folks, and after Meyerson said, "print them and share them," it had to be pointed out that he might have meant, "digitize them and make them available on the WWW."

However, the pedagogical change Meyerson's valedictory remarks augured was hardly in error. The sociologist's slip about printing correctly suggests that the advent of the web was not inherently required to bring about this reform (although it certainly has catalyzed it). So, too, recent digital aspects of modernism arising since the mid-1990s—Stein's "history teaches that history teaches" has been one inspiration for it—bear with them methods and even some technical practices that predate digital connectivity by decades, but the emergence of the latter can still be said to coincide with further developments. As we have seen, most teaching has changed only superficially in response to all this. The IT-enabled lecture does not particularly increase the learner's engagement with the material. Its pedagogy, expressed in the benevolent but educationally flawed concept of "online courseware," seemed to be "unlocking [universities'] gates to the world" but offers an experience of information rather than of knowledge.[77]

Soon after the SEI conference, John Seely Brown and Paul Duguid, in "The University in the Digital Age" (1996), asked, "What are higher education's 'core competencies'?" It turned out that "courseware" wasn't near the top of their list. Even if delivering courses could be done competently, schools should have been emphasizing "learning not lading."[78] Courseware was and is an expression of the explicative order. "Explication is the basic flaw at the heart of the learned master's transmission of knowledge," as we read in *Understanding Rancière, Understanding Modernism*. There was nothing particularly emancipatory in knowledge thus delivered, no matter how much generous unlocking of gates was intended by managers of the institution. "To explicate something to someone is to show the latter that he is unable to understand it on his own." Explication leads to stultification.[79] Despite great claims that were being made in the 2000s for the introduction of IT into the classroom and enormous expenditures made by colleges and universities in that period, 60 percent of the undergraduate students surveyed for a 2007 report by the Educause Center for Applied Research said that they disagreed with the statement, "I am more engaged in courses that use technology."[80] This was just three or four years before the xMOOC.

When Minerva University was formed in 2012, that "year of the MOOC"—its courses entirely online, with small pods of students residing together in locations globally—it still seemed obligatory to articulate the simplest case against memorization via lecture: "The question is not whether to memorize content," Stephen Kosslyn and Ben Nelson wrote in *Building the Intentional University*, "especially in light of today's information explosion, but how to know where to find it, how to evaluate it, and what to do with it."[81] Simpler still: give students fishing rods, not fish.[82]

"Our aim is not to teach knowledge and skills for their own sake," says Mike Magee, Minerva's president, "but to equip our students with intellectual tools they can use to adapt" to reality. Thus, Minerva's student *culture*, the way students live as students, is said to be itself "malleable and emergent."[83] Full disclosure: a poet and scholar of American pragmatism, Magee was one of the founders of the Kelly Writers House.[84] His verse is featured in ModPo's main syllabus, as noted in my opening pages. The poem by Magee learners encounter in ModPo's week 10, titled "Pledge," encourages readers and listeners to disavow the memorized sounds and senses of the traditional rote pledge to the flag through a long series of homophonic "Flarfist" substitutions. (Can you hear the pledge, even as you read? "I plug elegance / two thief rag / off-Dionysus tastes of America / in tune theory public / four widgets hands / one day shun," etc.) The example of Magee gives us the opportunity to put a Flarfist poet of the early 2000s together with the head of a digital university of the early 2020s. We get this amalgam: rote required sound has you reciting what others require you to mean; the lecture is an autocracy, no matter how well meant. The experiment in mishearing and misstating, on the contrary, favors poetic noise-making that is connotatively freed, thus allegiant to meaning-making but differently so. Going fully online, as Minerva did when it was created to reinvent higher education "from scratch," didn't and doesn't in itself lead to the spirit of learning's changeability. Minerva's advent stipulated even more emphatically: technological without pedagogical change is meaningless.

THE NONFIXED UNIVERSE

For some, the full inception of the internet accelerated the shift away from content and affirmed the transience of apparently unimportant materials, all of which would be subject at any time to "redirection and combination." Such has been the irregular view of Goldsmith, for whom redirection and combination are a model for teaching and a justification for art and its curation. The founder and curator of UbuWeb has for years been the instructor of creative writing courses called Uncreative Writing and Wasting Time on the Internet. The latter title was especially meant to be contentious,[85] but, in essence, it is a coherent semester-long case against fears of information overload. The students typically work away at laptops during the (anti-)lecture, rapidly researching haphazardly mentioned artists and concepts, sending each other messages that the teacher cannot read.[86] He knows that if he and they are permitted to "go off on a tangent about [Jasper] Johns and [Robert] Rauschenberg and their relationship as expressed in Rauschenberg's bed, an image of that bed is always a click away." Babbling information without a plan ironically creates confidence. "From there," the teacher continues, "we can head anywhere into the non-fixed universe, be it film, text or sound." None of it is deemed more important to the semester's work than anything else. That aspect of classwork is not rigorous, but the general idea paradoxically is—coming to realize, as Cage and Duchamp among others did, that there's really no such thing as wasted work or wasted materials.

Goldsmith's point here about "wasting time on the Internet" is that "the web itself is a non-fixed space." It's the space where the dissolution of transformative subjects can be prevented. Any sharing of the web's qualities with the classroom itself grants that old enclosure a new spatial measure of freedom.[87] Teaching is hypertext. In Goldsmith's classes, you're left to your own devices. "Because hypertext poetry is something new," Ed Falco had written in a prose section of his book of early hypertext poetry, *Sea Island* (1995), "there is not yet a body of literature prescribing preferred methods of reading. Pretty much, you're on your own." "Much of the stuff I teach is so non-fixed that it never appeared in any sort of stable form," Goldsmith says. "The secret . . . is making the materials available in a sharable form that can be passed around. . . . The students need things to take away with them, to listen to, to share, to love, . . . to possess." Wasting time becomes a form of pluralistic intellectual curatorial independence. Freedom is bringing to the classroom teaching materials that can only be gathered, saved, and taken away, else they cease to exist. "Much of what is there on Wednesday afternoon," Goldsmith says about the web as a teaching tool, with some meaningful exaggeration, "is gone or unavailable on Thursday morning." Hard to give students a quiz on that. How could you know what to know? Waste, in this sense, is a rejection of curricular minimalism. Rather than mistrust digital networks as wasteful sources, Goldsmith and his students lean in.

Quoting Falco in his comprehensive *Prehistoric Digital Poetry* (2007), Christopher Funkhouser interprets Falco's statement ("you're on your own") as befitting other early hypermedia artists' "liberational" claims. Applying such self-determination to the classroom, Goldsmith and his students discover the nonrestraint of being on their own, in Falco's liberated sense. But it is not the least bit the lonely process Falco seemed to have in mind. What is perhaps "pre-historic" about Funkhouser's book—surveying all that precedes networked intermedia—is the freedom of artists "who grant themselves license to appro-priate available tools for their own imaginative ends."[88] The effects and values of that imagination extend well beyond the text and are immune to the actual failures of hardware or network, such as Goldsmith's laptop-obsessed students in the relatively early IT days could suffer at any time were it not for the fact that he lugged around "an external hard drive crammed with hundreds of gigabytes should the thing I'm looking for not be available." Even taking into account a dra-matic imagination of technical vulnerability—another version of his cherished nonfixity—later in the book *Wasting Time on the Internet*, Goldsmith looks back and, without any sarcasm, dubs all this online *and offline* relationship-building "The Social Network."[89]

In Goldsmith's "uncreative" creative writing course, the active learning activ-ities students undertake constitute another workable instance of the subject matter the participant-learners are exploring.[90] He has been teaching horizontally, in the manner of intermediation. Since he came to teaching only after the advent of the interactive web, indeed well after the founding of UbuWeb, this concept for him is not metaphorical. Nor, for that matter, is it conceptual. It is a literal effect. The puckishly styled "requirements" for Wasting Time on the Internet, the course—"distraction, multitasking, and aimless drifting [are] mandatory" according to the course description[91]—make literary values clear just as they are also things the students actually *do* in the Deweyan sense of learning by doing. Can work being done in a classroom, online or in person, happen on the model of intermediation? The Uncreative Writing seminar is certainly an instance. So are these in-person classes (among many others): Maria Mencia's Media Skills course, Bernstein's Wreading Poetry workshop, Karis Shearer's Digital Arts & Humanities taught inside the AMP lab, and John Cayley's Writing3D.

When one makes an effort at Mencia's Autocalligraphy, working with her inside a MOO-like "interactive generative space" in a media research lab in Lon-don or New York, the result is a constantly metamorphosing text, networked, simultaneously visual, oral, aural, and textual. It "has the characteristics of electronic writing in terms of its 'constellation-like structure,'" whereupon the in-person "*personal* aspect of handwriting" must be part of "the *collective* experi-ence through the participation of the user."[92]

Bernstein's Wreading Experiments in Philadelphia challenged students to do what Web 2.0 or 3.0 does without thinking, with its increasingly extreme

decentralizations and interoperabilities: recombination, poetic relineation, dele-
tion, collaboration, cutting-up, and serializing language by categorically rough
and often incorrect associative groupings.[93]

Shearer's pedagogy, constituting the founding ideas at work in the AMP
(Archives, Media, and Poetry) Lab in Okanagan, British Columbia, guides
students as they learn cultural interpretation generally through analysis of new
and old audio media and poetry. She and they deliberately move back and forth
between digital and analog media—tape recordings made of the 1963 Vancouver
Poetry Conference, for instance[94]—in order to work out the ongoing intermedi-
ated relationships, rather than the differences, between the two.

At Brown University, operating within the aegis of George Landow and Robert Coover's early courses in hypermedia, Cayley's LITR 1010G, or Writing3D,
was first known as Cave Writing. I've been inside the CAVE. The Cave Automatic Virtual Environment, a latter-day 3D MOO, features spatial audio among
other experiential breakthroughs. Students write not just in but *for* immersive
virtual reality environments and then move out again, inventing literary activity
for *dimensionally* third spaces. This approach, to say the least, challenges habitual
ideas about text and narrative.

FIGURE IT OUT

Not long after the hypertext markup language known as HTML had been perfected and was being widely distributed, I was attempting to teach that language
to my students—for the most part, asking them to go out and learn it while
using it. This was to enable them to create web projects based on the course
materials—poems—we had already discussed and as an aid to our many dis-
agreements and mutual misunderstandings, a sure furtherance of my often rather
vague desire to decenter the teacher. What better means of achieving that decentering than to require the students to learn something about which the teacher
knows only a little? I was ignorant, and HTML was my Flemish.

A simple markup language associated with big thoughts about deprofessionalization? Actually, I knew a bit more of HTML and UNIX commands than
Jacotot knew of Flemish, but the spirit of ignorance was cognate. I have always
done the coding that generates web materials with a plain text editor or directly
on the server at the command line, using just a handful of markup elements and
plain-text representations I've memorized, and—forgive the stretch—the practice signifies largely. At an institution where IT professionals typically program

or outsource programming on behalf of academic humanists, hand-coding befit the DIT (do it together) ethos that was already starting just then to animate the newly formed Kelly Writers House and would, in a few years, enliven the digital free-culture idea of PennSound. Goldsmith puts it best: "HTML is free and always works regardless of the technological changes. Stay backwardly compatible. Stay simple. Stay free."[95]

I was teaching the poetry and poetics of community inside a student residence with students who lived, studied, and played in the same building where I, my partner, and our two young children lived. I was striving for as much of a personal, nonproprietary sensibility as I could convey to my cohabitant learners in Van Pelt College House. One of those students who resisted all this mightily was Amanda Karsten (now Hirsch). Forward ten years later: Amanda, based by then in Washington, DC, was a web consultant. That in itself was a remarkable outcome, given the intensity of her original resistance.

A decade after college, Amanda had become one of the many creative young people, talented writers, of that bloggy moment who zig-zagged into and through new information technologies by way of the literary humanities, representing a particular bearing out in a mid-Generation X career sense of Donna Haraway's provocative dictum that "Writing is pre-eminently the technology of cyborgs."[96] Amanda was blogging daily in order to help "inspir[e] creative living in DC." Her digital audience was young but not a crowd; they would be digitally won over one reader at a time. Once, as she prepared to upload another post, she found and read one of my own blogs. That blog (2007–2015) was devoted to the year 1960 (https://nineteen-sixty.blogspot.com). Each post described a poetic or art happening that occurred in that year. Much later, my book *1960: When Art and Literature Confronted the Memory of World War II and Remade the Modern* (2021) was partly constructed from a selection of these blog notations. An entry, the one Amanda read, was entitled "Patchen, Can't Type, Turns to Picture-Poems."[97] From this, she posted a new piece for her *Creative DC*, entitled "Picture Poems, and How Learning HTML Under Duress Helped Me Lead a More Creative Life, or, Thank You, Al Filreis." I was flattered by the compliments, delighted to have been Amanda's teacher, and excited to be written up as the person teaching a poetry seminar in which students were required to teach themselves HTML.

I was also intrigued by this successful integration of the story of Kenneth Patchen's physical and poetic struggle, which had driven him painfully to a new form of writing, and Amanda's own real although modest (not physical, to be sure) duress in the seminar when I had tossed the students into the cold dark web ocean from which she emerged with a means of being creative in new mode. In 1960, Patchen suffered a series of setbacks, including a preventable fall from a hospital gurney that resulted in a bad back getting much worse. Unable to stand or even sit up for more than a few minutes, he could no longer work a typewriter. The entry in my 1960 blog reads in part: "Here's the good part. Prevented from working at his typewriter any longer, Patchen stopped writing conventional poems. He created letters and poems only in a large hand scrawl. He used pens and a paint brush. He developed his 'picture poems.'"

It was a sense of the hybrid medium of the picture-poem, not its visual meaning but the fact of its textual visuality, that drew Amanda's attention back to me as a teacher of would-be fin de siecle cyborgs. While one old move drifted away from the mechanics of writing, another new-fangled move headed further into it—writing as appendaged by it—but I suggest that both were and are fresh, and both enable the visual, or, more generally, the concrete. And both theoretically associate disability writing with the capacity of working and creating in a third space to invent generative intersubjective teaching. "Incidentally," Amanda Hirsch wrote, "Al [Filreis] is the reason I learned HTML, despite ardent protestations at the time. I was in his Literature of Community class"—this was indeed the seminar I proposed in my extravagant "Memo" proposing heterodox uses of PennMOO—"and our final assignment was to create a website reflecting our definition of community. 'But we don't know HTML!' half of us said. This was in 1996–97. 'Figure it out,' he told us."

In this book, I have been describing a poetry and a pedagogy of figure it out, of Antin's "find[ing] out what i[']d said" as he says it, of Meyerson's tentative materials, Andrews's athematic noise, Falco's "you're on your own," Rothenberg's classroom as coffee shop or kiva, and I had no more idea of what I was doing as Amanda's teacher than Patchen did with his desire to continue writing poetry when compelled by circumstances into the new medium—than Amanda did as she grumpily shifted her attention away from regular literary study to writing in new spaces for unknown audiences.

FINDING YOUR SPACE

Ideas for building a place between (or different from) family/home and standard schooling—according to Suzanne Choo's account of literary third spaces—were prompted, in part, as counterarguments against statements made by the influential poetry critic Harold Bloom, who had antagonistically confessed that literary criticism "always will be an elitist phenomenon" and advocated reading a poem as a poem with "a stubborn resistance whose single aim is to preserve poetry as fully and purely as possible."[98] Quoting Bloom, Choo understood the phrase "fully and purely" as having spatial implications. The "stubborn" stance, on the one hand, endorsed preservation that required safeguarding the traditional classroom as the securest place for poetry. On the other hand, of course, it could and surely should have been acknowledged that there exist numerous noncanonical spaces people productively inhabit without ambitions of purity: the writing circle; the poetry trail;[99] the pub (abbreviated, after all, from "public house"); the "multipurpose room" at the local public library branch;[100] "museums, parks, and gardens";[101] the basement;[102] the chess alley;[103] the choir room;[104] the open loft;[105] the breakroom at the Ford assembly plant;[106] the café where "no one seemed to mind" if artists order just coffee and stay;[107] the student-led open mic night (a regular scene of initial entry into the Kelly Writers House[108]); the lesbian bookstore (site of abundant literary effects chronicled by June Thomas in *A Place of Our Own*). All these and more, occurring across improvised uses of common spaces, succeed in making "fully and purely" preserving poetry untenable if perhaps also irrelevant and even wrong-headed. These are not places conducive for a critic to enact a goal of enduringly selective canon formation, which for Harold Bloom in particular was a matter of "decid[ing] a question that is ultimately of sad importance: 'Which poet shall live?'" Jerome Rothenberg, who strove at all turns to bring poems into the kinds of spaces just listed, when responding to this "sad" life-and-death question in a sharp essay on Bloom's "exclusionary criticism," took it that the latter's role was that of "the critic as exterminating angel" (and dramatically referenced the Holocaust).[109]

Higher education has not regularly ventured into spaces such as those just enumerated. The siting of the Kelly Writers House in October of 1995 was a timely and lucky counterexample. One among others, of course, whose stories should be told. Disappointingly for advocates of public or public-friendly commons, the city-planning phenomenon of "unfunctional zoning" frustrates and even prohibits the making of unofficial gathering spots in residential areas; there are also untold both official and customary forms of unfunctional zoning within universities and even at small colleges and college towns.[110] Here is an example of what gets negated by this obstruction: the solo reader, seeking a literary social life, enters a shared space and finds that it is both a community and a metacommunity—not only a conducive place in itself but also a portal to a network of *other* sites, a looking glass, as at Librería Mujeres in Madrid where thick binders of flyers among the bookstalls led June Thomas and several generations of like adventurers in turn to further meetings, groups, and gathering spots. "I wanted something to read," recalls Thomas of her early queer entering, "but I also needed a place to *live*."[111]

The site for social networking we have been trying to locate is where this book's three main areas of concern converge. One is the vast interpretive community that convenes around the poetic because it provides the motive for improvising unlimited conversations about pretty much "everything else," to quote again Bernstein's phrase for the work of impure free-form redistribution.

Second is the shifting definition of learners and learning. I have made this analogous to the poem at a time in history when it was, in various ways, released from the constraints of the book and page and thus freed from a certain kind of assumed authorial authority. In other words, the looking glass goes online. I have been arguing that there is a connection between that disorganized diffusion—for instance, of a poem as audio (or video) recording—and *overall* like states of openness, exactly as between the implicit potential antiautocratic qualities of pagelessness and the prospective democratic aspects of a gathered vast community. "The journey from isolation to community," to use June Thomas's phrasing, is chosen rather than credentialed.[112] Its rewards are surprises. Experiencing its nonauthoritarian qualities does not require matriculation and is often thwarted by it. The poem Thomas could find in a book of poems serendipitously picked off the shelf at Librería Mujeres is the equivalent of the page in one of those binders leading her like a no-longer-secret map to further sites of understanding.

This reformist association or analogy—I referred to it earlier, by way of the 1999 Bard conference, as "alt-poetry / alt-pedagogy"—draws attention to the third main concern: a consideration of aspects of the sort of text that is not textual in the sense assumed for centuries. The nontextual text enables the kind of readers' and writers' common space where hearing and producing significant sounds are "attempts to capture what is actually a constantly shifting and changing milieu of ideas, events, appearances and meanings."[113]

The lifting off from the page, the return to noise, that will be needed for the discernment of an international and intergenerational critical citizenship involves the recording of synchronous sound to be asynchronously shared sooner or later and elsewhere *such that those two activities are basically similar*. Here are questions arising from that large claim: What could possibly be the connection between intellectual community and audio file formats? Why argue that sound inhabits a third space more auspiciously than written text? How relevant are David Rothenberg's discoveries, across decades of travel and research, that birds "learn new phrases" from each other and even from human accompanists (including Rothenberg himself playing clarinet), and that, similarly, "humans can learn through sound"? His concept of "vocal learning" is connected to poetry communities (not incidentally, he is a poet).[114] Those communities are a leading edge, like the gathering choirs of self-taught songbirds Rothenberg travels to meet, and worth close observation. Why does the planned out-loud reading of poems affiliate with—and, actually, *imitate*—the sort of off-hand conversations among friends and acquaintances that many people desire and deem an enhancement of their aesthetic lives?

And: How much are these noises part of a poem's soundscape—how much of the sounds are found and how much composed, and how much require social accompaniment?[115] Before we can turn (in the final two chapters) back to ModPo as an alternative poethical space made possible by certain uses of open online platforms, reconsider a point made earlier: that the main problem is to describe an alternative to *This is what it means*. I cited Bruce Andrews's call "for a revived radicalism of constructivist noise or athematic 'informal music,'" and speculated about classrooms that were to be filled with such noise, with novices or amateurs convened around "exercise[s] in voice," per Freire, "in *having* voice . . . in decision making" as a version of the basic "right of citizenship." Now we can further assess: How close to that informal communal sudden music—distractions, digressions, disharmonies, counterproductive whisperings, interruptions, the positive "underlife" of the common spaces that spatial theorists of education and aesthetic explorers like Rothenberg cherish[116]—can we come when we convene? One of several use cases for this is the occasion of the live poetry reading, which, at its best, is closer to choir than to lecture. So far, I have been focusing on the close affiliation of two phenomena of social signifying: the open-access discussion and the digital recording. The public poetry reading is a third phenomenon. It's time then to attend some readings.

CHAPTER 6

THE READING

But now the lines are starting to think of their own accord. . . . It's as though the lines were on the lookout for something.

—Caroline Bergvall, performing *Drift* at the Kelly Writers House, March 28, 2022

THE IDEAL AUDIENCE IS LIKE THE IDEAL READER

The PhillyTalks series was another significant influence on the development of ModPo, especially considering the importance of recorded poetry events that, as recordings, serve as prompts for further social gatherings. PhillyTalks was created at the Writers House in 1997 by Canadian poet-critic Louis Cabri and cohosted by Aaron Levy (later founding curator at Slought). Each PhillyTalks event featured an unlikely pairing of poets whose written interchanges were published before the event as a newsletter, whereupon a double poetry reading occurred, followed by an interaction among these: the just-established effects of the reading, responses from the live audience, the now-reconsidered printed pre-event newsletter, and, then, onward into the event's future, by responses to the widely distributed recording.

ModPo asks, just as Levy once did of Cabri: Is an ideal audience analogous to an ideal reader? Here was Cabri's answer: "An event that is recorded seems to be shaped in part by how its participants decide to negotiate between the idea/ideal of a potential and future audience, and the actual live audience." The event desired is one "that finds its audience, finds or discovers, as much as founds or creates, audience." These happenings tangled the *reading* (aloud) of set-piece writings, the *reading* of prior printed or emailed texts, and the *reading* of the sounds of commentaries emerging from the audience. This last, unprepared-for paraphonotextuality is what Jackson Mac Low—whose humane computer-generated chance proceduralism is a major influence on Cabri—idealized as "unknown, unexpected outcomes" despite the curatorial hard-wiring. Cabri conceived of the manifold mutualities of PhillyTalks as inventing a "live proceduralism." Here is precisely the context for his engagement with Mac Low (who was once himself a featured PhillyTalker): the series "enabl[es] writers and texts to mingle in a certain predetermined way, that arrives, despite pre-determinations, at 'unknown, unexpected outcomes.'"[1]

In a talk on "The Event of the Archive" (2003), given after PhillyTalks ended its run, Cabri invoked Clay Shirky's concept of "social software."[2] Cabri had invented a reading machine in all senses of the related terms *reading* and *machine*. In that way, PhillyTalks was a descendant of Bob Brown's "Readies." (Cabri's other series, "The Transparency Machine," also hosted at the Writers House, bears a similar debt.) Deliberately mixing talk of media, Cabri sometimes refers to his series as "a *reading* practice involving poets"—that is, poets who *read* before that "ideal audience [which is] analogous to an ideal *reader*."[3]

MISLISTENING TO DETAILS

The paraphonotextual aspect of a poem as performed during a live poetry reading—including but not limited to what Peter Middleton identifies as "unplanned sound," "obtrusive failures of attention," sounds made by a room's "insistent temporariness," and the like (an aural spatial underlife)[4]—can be most readily appreciated by audiences through the informal, often off-handed, prefatory remark spoken by the poet. Paraphonotextuality is another name for a poetic third space. This is what Cabri means when he describes an event as a "status," entailing converged poetic identity—in other words, "the unfolding subject-in-process of the events themselves." The full phonotext encompasses (1) the totality of sounded signifying, meanings made by actualization of the "poetic voice"; but also: (2) text as score, or "the scripted incarnation of the poem" (in Bernstein's phrase in "Making Audio Visible"[5]) presented as orality but "also" available in print; (3) accidental ambient noises made by a productively energized audience and by the restless room itself, as Middleton observes, on top of what David Rothenberg calls "our mechanized dins and hums . . . everywhere";[6] (4) when readings are recorded, audible traces of the technical medium itself, sounds the machinery makes; and (5) vocal interpolations by the poet that are not but can seem to be part of the text-as-score as delivered.

Consider this fifth element for its sometimes surprising ambiguity: it is not always evident that a poet's prefatory remark is paratextual—not obvious that it isn't the beginning of the poem itself, already underway. In 1981, when Ted Berrigan performed all of *The Sonnets* (1964) at New Langton Arts in San Francisco—the recording is preserved in PennSound[7]—audience members who had not read them in print or did not have the book handy during the event might not have gotten a clear sense of when one poem ended and the next began. Even if you were adept at hearing units of fourteen lines, you'd still have trouble if your goal was to discern one poem at a time. And not all the sonnets conform to the traditional length. Sometimes Berrigan did not identify the shift to the next in the series. He often made comments, prefatory quips, or wisecracks after a poem or an improvised coda before another, but the language of the remark sounded much like the verse, in keeping with Berrigan's demotic idiom. Was the experience of listening lesser than that of reading? Some who care about the audiotext would say: just different. Some might say: better. By sharpening discernment of the paratextual element as more or less distinct from the poem itself, during a reading such as Berrigan's durational performance of his eighty-eight sonnets, audiences become recurrently experienced in hearing differences in the tone, phrasing, vocal pitch, and diction of both sounded scripted text and spoken paratext.

In a statement promoting the importance of phonotext as a means of increasing our understanding of poetry generally,[8] Steve Evans describes what happens when listeners to recordings of live readings become less rather than more adept at, as it were, turning the page.[9] What Evans (borrowing from Fredric Jameson) calls "vanishing mediators"—the disappearance of audiographical facts of the poem once it starts its journey as an object technically reproduced, digitally recopied, shared, posted, and disseminated; the erasure or forgetting of original mechanical technique that had been layered onto performative poetic mode—can be extended to the problem presented by "*mis*listening" to the various paraphonotextual elements. Problems and opportunities: "*mis*listening to details" in historical, archived recordings is the starting point for Tanya Clement's book *Dissonant Records: Close Listening to Literary Archives* (2024). "Voices in historical recordings," Clement writes, "can sound like coughing or the roar of an animal; they often overlap, with multiple people speaking at once; they can be too quiet or too loud and confused by the sounds of an audience, a car passing by, or the warp and wow of the recording or playback device. What *was* that in the background? Where *are* these people?"[10] When difficult listening encourages us to contemplate a space, room, or spatial situation, mishearing creates closer, better listening. *Where are these people?* is generally the apt question. The cooperative act of "multiple people speaking at once" is not only a part of the aural record that needs to be reckoned intentionally, but it is also a metaphor for the social virtuality that is my book's main topic.

AUDIO'S SECULAR MIRACLE

Does the order in which a poet reads poems add meaning to the poems? Poetry readings, poem by poem, often seem nonsequential if apprehended as an entire performance. Performed poems, even if presented in a carefully designed sequence, are not meant to seem equal in importance. In the poetry reading, emphasis rises and falls from one poem to the next.

Experienced listeners can hear in the voice—and not so readily from the text read by itself—that a poem is being summoned to serve as a topical or tonal transition or as a light moment between heavier pieces. Voice assigns poems roles. The fundamental separation of the sound of poems from their source—that is, the storing of them in physical and then digital media followed by the releasing of them "into a new spatio-temporal context"—has the potential, counterintuitively, to enhance rather than disable the audience's sense of the juxtaposition of and between texts and paratexts. Evans calls this technical separation a "secular miracle." While expressing concern over lessened awareness of the vanishing mediator, he is delighted by the way the widening of the field of textuality has begun to include not just the sounded text as data but also as metadata.[11] Within the whole recording of a reading—that is, the reading of many poems in a sequence structured performatively—adjacency and ordination provide a sort of metadata. This idea might seem obvious, but not if we mean metadata as the audio archivist means it.[12]

The point about adjacency is best made through example. Let's take an October 15, 1988, reading at the Ear Inn in New York in which Bernadette Mayer presented eighteen poems. The fifth and sixth poems she performed at this noisy, venerable bar were "Do You Have Sex in the Bed of [sic] the Floor?" and "The Tragic Condition of the Statue of Liberty."[13] The latter was published, collected, and anthologized.[14] Mayer offered no prefatory remark before reading. Its earnest and unironic quotations from Emma Lazarus and the directness of its criticism of gentrification and embrace of the local politics of parental engagement with public education make for clear aural interest and fairly straightforward interpretation. "Do You Have Sex in the Bed of the Floor?" is an uncollected poem; the manuscript is preserved among Mayer's papers at the Mandeville Special Collections Library at the University of California, San Diego.[15] The tone of the poem, if encountered apart from the live or recorded reading, is entirely unclear. It is ungrammatical; while Mayer's listeners are soon familiar with her informal vernacular and frank idiomatic speech, they do not expect missing parts of speech, subject-verb disagreement, or the fractured prepositional phrase ("*of the floor*") in the title. So "Do You Have Sex," on its own, might seem to displace the poetic "I," voicing the voices of others, but the special politics on behalf of that particular Other might remain hidden. The recorded paratext provides not just the poem's politics but also its rationale for standing politically as well as poetically alongside "The Tragic Condition of the Statue of Liberty," which is a poem celebrating the U.S. Bicentennial. "This is a poem," we hear Mayer say into the microphone at the Ear Inn, "that was written by my students in Junior High School 104. And I hope none of their parents are here. It's a collaborative work by them." The audience laughs. Many of them know that the poet is herself the parent of children; there is a very good chance all three of them, Marie, Sophia, and Max, were present at the reading. While lines such as "How does it get so big?" and "When he gets excited what comes of it. Cum. / When he sticks it in the rectum, does it hurt?" seem merely salacious, the poem becomes still more shocking when one realizes that the voices in the poem that are not the speaker's but are those of schoolchildren fulfilling a classroom assignment, students whom the poet was teaching as a parent-volunteer at the Simon Baruch Middle School on East Twenty-first Street in Manhattan. Having been given the constraint, the children, through the poem, collectively ask where adults in their lives do their lovemaking. The collaboration produced this result in a poem later performed in an insular bohemian space, a site to which even the socially radical poet hopes none of their parents have access: "Anywhere possible or between the crib."[16] The children—perhaps including her own—too clearly see what is happening to and around them and their siblings.

Mayer starkly presents the fractured awareness of the proximity of adult sexuality and wants to convey, in a collage of common bawdy scenes, the cramped hassle and rude incongruity of domestic parenting in small lower Manhattan apartments. "Do You Have Sex" makes no overt narrative judgment. Its unlikely connection to "The Tragic Condition of the Statue of Liberty" is to doubly imply the power of parental involvement as a form of extreme social alterity— first, by making a theme of how terribly or marvelously much the children know, and second, by producing the results of the avant-garde poet's very presence *as parent and artist at once* in the public school classroom, liberating the voices of children through her willingness to experiment with collaborative text and the local politics of voice. The poem's questionable erotics is its earnest political ethics. The canonized "Tragic Condition" gains significantly from the full phonotextual context despite the easy categorical separation of the recording from its origins. This, I think, speaks both to the centrality and the interpretive power of the secular miracle Evans describes.

The poets, critics, and theorists whose essays are gathered in the late 1990s in *Close Listening*, along with Morris in *Sound States* (1998); the curation-minded archivists, sound artists, and theorists of the phonotext at PennSound, Spoken-Web,[17] and UbuWeb; and sound studies critics such as Lytle Shaw, have variously asserted and now proceed from the stipulation that the recording of poetic performance now derives its conveyance of textuality in such a way as to actually put few hearers in mind of the page or book. "PennSound," suggests Shaw, "has done something more than make critics and historians of poetry aware of readings and recordings more broadly as objects of study. Its very existence has pressed the question of just what this awareness might mean for our understanding of poetry." For Shaw, the general acceptance of PennSound as a regular resource, a lessening of consciousness that one consults the archive as a special gesture, has caused "a tipping point": the recordings streamed or downloaded there "stopped offering new windows onto what are finally readings of texts and [have] become instead primary objects of study in themselves."[18]

THE CASE AGAINST THE READING

These relatively recent advances in classifying phonotextuality perhaps mask the insufficiencies of foundational expressions of displeasure with poetry readings. The sounds produced by the public poetry reading—intruders included— should have us asking a version of the basic question Julia Bloch's student Amy asked when she had only the sound of a poem to go on: How do we read poetry when *reading* is not really part of the experience? Or, in short, what is poetry? Basic questions. Yet, when commissioned to report on the phenomenon of the live reading for the *American Scholar*, eminent poet-essayist Donald Hall began with the popular assumption—with which he, as a poet who gave frequent public readings, either did or pretended to share[19]—of its triviality and ultimate irrelevance to poetic value.

Hall's essay, "The Poetry Reading: Public Performance/Private Art," noted (incorrectly) that "most readings" are sponsored by departments of English at colleges and universities and that that very entity, as host, "is ambivalent on the subject." Hall focused on the reading as an inapt extrapoetic socio-economics—a "gig" for which there are ritualized invitations, fees, in some cases, agents handling arrangements, a whirlwind of airports, and unctuous professorial hosts. Hall quoted John Frederick Nims, the witty, accessible lyric poet who was editor of *Poetry*—a writer as attached to the page as anyone—arguing that "poetry readings are to our time what the Black Plague was to the fourteenth century."[20] Significantly, when Nims elaborated this view, he emphasized not the reading of the poems themselves but what he deemed the annoying, irrelevant—merely performative—paratext: "your imperfect sentences, your repeated phrases, your false pathos, your drawings and denouncings, your humming and hawing, your oh-ing and ah-ing."[21]

To prepare for his essay, Hall consulted with poet and dancer Katharyn Howd Machan, who was "studying readings" for a doctorate in performance studies. From among the information Machan provided, Hall selected the example of a poet refusing to dramatize, the one who gave poetry readings in which the performer "attempts to be as much like the printed page as possible." This nonperformativity befit Hall's satire of the reading's marginal relevance and supported the idea that boredom as a response to the poem abets antihumanistic loathing. Of course, the assumption here is that the poet whose public rendering of the art is intentionally flat—who seeks, for instance, to keep all tonal options open for the hearer, who eschews the typical interpretive guidance of the audience through vocal cues—makes the problem of "bad poets perform[ing] bad poems badly" still worse and cannot really be counted as performing. This phenomenon is summoned by Hall to help us contemplate why we bother about poetry readings in the first place.[22]

Assessments such as Hall's tended to focus on vocal tone.[23] Otherwise, however, Hall's prejudicial essay was as far as it could be from a consideration of the phonotext as a valid, distinct version or edition of the poems. Tone is the one central textual element of traditional interpretation that has always easily assumed a sounding, at least as a residual of dead-metaphorical connection to orality. But, of course, according to hermeneutic convention, tone need not refer in the work of the critic to the sound of the poet or others reading the poem aloud.

WHAT IS POETRY?

Interpreting tone is also among the most difficult textual reading skills to acquire. Yet, as teachers of poetry have been among the first to discover, the audio record of the poet's performance readily enables a nuanced discussion of satire, irony, and parody in particular. The application of high-performance computing to entire audio archives, such as the experimental data-modeling program known as ARLO (adaptive recognition with layered optimization)—an early prototype for analysis of sound collections in the humanities—when applied to PennSound might someday fully automate discernment of lineation, rhyme, the grammar of imperatives, and even the presence of certain stanzaic forms.[24] But such programs seem unlikely, at least any time soon, to identify tonality as indicating a semantic relationship of the poem's voice to the speaker's attitude toward subject matter. This is what Chris Mustazza describes as "machine-aided close listening" in his discussion of crucial differences between close listening and "distant listening."[25] Can distant listening ingest huge quantities of sonic material and organize them by tone—not tone as in timbre, tenor, and pitch, but rather, tone as an aspect of a poetics, the attitude toward a poem's content as heard in the speaker's voice? Rather than exiling the problem of tone from discussions of archival phonotextuality, these distinctions ought to place it at the center.[26]

If it was the intention of Donald Hall, via Machan's research, to support his prejudice against poetry readings as extraneous to poetic value by referring to the absurdity of a poet traveling a distance and receiving a speaking fee only to voice a poem in person with a deliberate lack of tonal affect, it is, perhaps, a primary goal of the scholar of the audio archive to guide us, on the contrary, toward ways of reading the phonotext for both textually internal and extra aural evidence of the poet's tone. The future of critical responses to John Ashbery will arguably not depend so much on the poet's persistent avowals of the importance of tonal neutrality, for these can be ascribed to temperamental shyness covering as a conceptualist rigor. More relevant is the audio archive of recordings of Ashbery's readings ranging from 1951 to 2013 (dozens of readings, hundreds of poems, preserved and now available at PennSound) in which tone color or tone quality, pitch, loudness, etc. can in each instance be juxtaposed with diction, word choice, metrical pacing, and the speaker's attitude toward topics.

The flat, diffident pitch of repeated readings of Ashbery's famous metapoem "What Is Poetry," for example—its status as "radically 'poor theater'"[27]—makes productive irony possible if one considers that in the poem itself the poet-speaker seems to be writing an annoyed response to repeated earnest queries asking for a frictionless definition of the genre. The poet-speaker in the poem, a poet figure who discusses poetry—who it might be assumed is the same as the person who is composing the poem—is easily confused with the eminent poet Ashbery reading the poem yet again in the presence of listeners. Those hearing it might wonder if the great Ashbery became bored with this oft-requested chestnut—if, in other words, he stopped trying to make this poem sound fresh or interesting—until the poem's content indicates that it is *about* the tediousness and specifically the pointlessness of the request. And just when one settles into the realization of a perfect harmonization of nonperformance, tone, and subject matter, the final line arrives—

It might give us—*what?*—some flowers soon?   [emphasis added]

—with its exhausted and amused deflation of regular celebration. That *what?* is so casually bothered, half-heartedly dismissive. The comic gift the poem gives us is not the valedictory bouquet one receives upon graduation, as it were, from the underperforming "school" of thought where "all the thought got combed out." Rather, it's the aesthetic pleasure the poet-speaker derives from creating a list of non-sequitur responses to the unanswerable titular question (the list of queries is in the poem's famously paratactic opening lines).

WHAT IS POETRY

The medieval town, with frieze
Of boy scouts from Nagoya? The snow

That came when we wanted it to snow?
Beautiful images? Trying to avoid

Ideas, as in this poem?[28]

Whether poetry has any effect—the question-assertion *What is poetry* seems to be an existential challenge—becomes a problem only solved by the unaffected pose. Hearing the poet read without affect makes this reading not just likely but almost inevitable.

In the instance of "What Is Poetry," as is the case with innumerable other poem recordings you can find in PennSound, there is hard audiographic evidence adding to paraphonotext. In every case, we can put together a specific context of recording. For "What Is Poetry," we have a reading Ashbery gave on BBC Radio 3 in 1999. On that occasion, he introduced the performance of the poem by telling us about its origin. He recounts the story of diffident teaching. Back in 1974, he recalls, "When I could at last no longer escape teaching," he entered classrooms where students kept asking why their teacher called *this* a poem but not *that*. "What is poetry anyway?" they queried. Soon it became a prompt. The result was a piece of writing that carries with it a pedagogy, a work instructing his students—and us, of course—on the importance of the impartial, evasive nonanswer in verse (criticism as poem, poem as criticism) just when a tendentious answer "in school" is expected. The poet is not a teacher; rather, he could simply "no longer escape" the role. Yet the verse presents postmodern pedagogy: a tonal nondidacticism created out of exactly the urge that typically produces educational definition, ordination, and semanticism.[29]

HEARING IAMBIC PATRIARCHY

Even meter is tonal. The archive of recorded readings is replete with unique evidence of poets' metrical designs. Even the most regular iambic tetrameter (four beat) or pentameter (five beat) line, read silently on a page, can be variously sounded. It can mean regularity. Or it can imply a belief in prosodic transparency, not calling attention to itself as regular. It might or might not refer beyond text-metricity to the larger literary history to which it pays homage, alters, challenges, or, indeed, bitterly parodies. The sound of a poet's voice in the recording of a reading of an homage poem will bespeak the tone of the line. An exaggeration of the classic iamb—two beats, the first unstressed, the second stressed—suggests criticism or even rebuke: irony expressed solely through meter. Even a modest irregularity of standard iambic pentameter, with its inevitable reminder of the long English verse tradition, can suggest that the use of the iambic is meant to convey natural speech. When Robert Frost performed what are among the four most famously regular iambic pentameter lines in modern American poetry—

> I lét my neíghbor knów beyónd the híll;
> And ón a dáy we méet to wálk the líne
> And sét the wáll betwéen us ónce agaín.
> We keép the wáll betwéen us ás we gó.

—his ambition was apparently to draw our attention away from the lines' uniformity and predictability, as the speaker and his neighbor in the story told by the poem ritually maintain the impediment of subjectivity fabricated between them. A five-foot line that is most certainly not iambic pentameter, which cannot be read as iambic without ironic self-consciousness, Frost pronounces as close to regularly as possible without, as it were, crossing the line: "Something there is that doesn't love a wall."

The iambics of "Mending Wall" have been parodied but not because of anything Frost did with his voice in performance. In the audio archive, there is a discernible relationship with literary history itself: not only in Frost's suppression of a too-iambic meter and, the obverse, his drawing out the iambic quality of the noniambic line, but also in the oral presentational strategies of poets operating consciously in the mode of Frostian performance. William Stafford, in "Traveling through the Dark," his famous poem about encountering and then discarding a dead pregnant doe on a rural road, reaches a general statement of his natural dilemma at the end of the first stanza: "to swerve might make more dead." Like Frost, Stafford reads aloud with a smooth, casual-seeming countrified colloquiality to help belie the lines' formality. In recordings of the poem,[30] he emphatically pauses after the first foot ("to **swérve**"). It's an effort to control the perception of the phrase's iambic potential. The speaker overcomes the dilemma by disposing of the doe's body, preventing human destruction by not "swerving." Thus, he says, he "thought hard for us all." The masculine presumption in this—a natural heroic stance tempered by caution, civic-minded generosity, and proximity to correct superhearing ("I could hear the wilderness listen")—is aided by the carefully modulated echo of Frost.

> By glow of the tail-light I stumbled back of the car
> and stood by the heap, a doe, a recent killing;
> she had stiffened already, almost cold.
> I dragged her off; she was large in the belly.
> My fingers touching her side brought me the reason—
> her side was warm; her fawn lay there waiting,
> alive, still, never to be born.
> Beside that mountain road I hesitated.[31]

Our sense of Rae Armantrout's poem "Traveling through the Yard," published first in her book *Precedence* and later included in *Veil: New and Selected Poems*, will depend entirely on interpreting tone. The poem's dedication reads: "(For William Stafford)". Insofar as Stafford's use of "Dark" suggests a metaphysical grandeur and hints at a mysterious and almost Gothic capacity for allegory, and Armantrout's use of "Yard" suggests a boundaried, unnatural space, the homage might range across elaboration, domestication, complementarity, and rebuke. It might seem to be a poem "after" the mode of a favored predecessor. Stafford's *doe* becomes Armantrout's *dove*. Both are alive, as it were, to the prospects of symbolism. In the end, for the reader of the poem as printed text, Armantrout's critical parodic intention is perhaps sufficiently clear: where Stafford's speaker—ethical, paternalistically diligent, naturally familiar—pushes the doe "over the edge into the river," Armantrout's speaker—anxiously domestic, critically impatient, feminist—"heave[s] it / across the marriage counselor's fence," thus raising, although by no means resolving, the issue of Stafford's gendering of the victim. The rescuer's relation to the doe, the unborn but living fawn in utero, and prospective human drivers on the narrow road whose reprieve from swerving now need not "make more dead." The phonotext resolves any doubt about the tone of Armantrout's response.

Armantrout performed "Traveling through the Yard" at a double Segue Series reading (paired with Ron Silliman) at the Ear Inn in New York on April 7, 1984.[32] The complete reading took twenty-five minutes,[33] and it consisted of twenty-four poems from *Precedence* in manuscript, which was published by Burning Deck Press nine months later.[34] To judge from its various vocal and other audible responses—always a key element in the paraphonotext—the Ear Inn audience included friends and colleagues. Armantrout's latest pithy disjunctions received a warm, supportive hearing. One could certainly surmise from the recording the communal qualities of the scene in that tavern on that late afternoon, and, though it was considerably less raucous, it puts one in mind of the unruly, friendly audience first hearing Ginsberg's "America," responding to the poem in such a

TRAVELING THROUGH THE YARD

(For William Stafford)

It was lying near my back porch
in the gaudy light of morning—
a dove corpse, oddly featherless,
alive with flies.
I stopped,
dustpan in hand, and heard
them purr over their feast.
To leave that there would make some stink!
So thinking hard for all of us,
I scooped it up, heaved it
across the marriage counselor's fence.

FIGURE 6.1 Rae Armantrout, "Traveling through the Yard," *Veil: New and Selected Poems* (Wesleyan University Press, 2001), 30.

Source: Reproduced with permission of Rae Armantrout.

way as to encourage and shape its vocalization in real time, the coproduction of sound—as we say in music communities, a "new sound"—in several respects. When Armantrout introduced her poem in 1984, mentioning its title and its situation as a response to Stafford, the audience laughed at the diminution from wild dark to domestic yard. The poem's short lines, generally of three feet, seem to make the poem, if a parody, responsive primarily to Stafford by way of theme.

We listen further. Formally, Armantrout's poem does not seem especially responsive to the tradition one can hear in Stafford's elaboration of Frost's natural metrical swerve. But then, a tonal turn. Armantrout arrives at her poem's eighth line: "To leáve that thére would máke some stínk!"—a parodic echo of Stafford's "to swérve might máke more déad." Armantrout performs the iambic tetrameter with comic overemphasis. It causes laughter in the audience sufficient to require an appreciative pause by the poet, like a bow, apparently taking in her hearers' alignment with the work's mockery of Stafford's grand lyric gesturing. Armantrout does not sound like Stafford at that moment, though; she is imitating *Frost*. In "some stink," which might otherwise be a trochee—*some* expressing astonishment, equally weighted with *stink*, with emphasis on the remarkable quality of the smell—the shift to the forced iamb calls attention to the falsity and pretension of Stafford's literary-historical gesture in a way that strikes Armantrout's collegial hearers as more humorous than mere thematic rejoinder. The most formidable parody was in the metrical performativity. "Stink" after "leave that there," though it does not rhyme in the poem, has been readied for the Frostian masculine rhyme, and it leaves us hearing a matching masculine meter in Stafford's **bórn, cárt, cóld, deád, réd, róad.**

The literary communality in the Language poet's confrontation with Stafford's Frostian poetics and its larger meaning for aesthetic ideology is affirmed in another recording of Armantrout in which she read (at my request) and then discussed "Traveling through the Yard." This happened at the Writers House during Armantrout's residency in 2016 as a Kelly Writers House Fellow. In a public interview-conversation I hosted, she recalled that it was Bob Perelman—back then a Bay Area Language poetry colleague—who first pointed out the "egregious" quality of the earlier poem. As it happened, Perelman was in the audience receiving this remark and can be heard responding—a crucial bit of paratextual evidence for the poem's ultimate aim. "It's such hubris that [Stafford] thinks the wilderness is listening to him," Armantrout observed. That the poem is *about* the significance of the sound a poem makes—specifically, a critique of conventions of hearing—is now to be reckoned from the audio archive.

We can all now listen to materials that include such paraphonotextuality as indications of audience response and its recurrent effect on performed meter and, thus, tone. These can include the poet's commentary, hearers' comments about the sound of sentiment,[35] the poetic identity (as discernible from the recording) of individual audience members, and the values—acoustic, of course, but also socio-literary—of the Arts Café as a particular room in a particular old house. Every room accommodates its own particular applause. Some rooms encourage more once applause begins; others quickly stifle the next wave. This is not only a matter of acoustics but also a function of other forms of warmth and resonance, the whole ambience. Applause between poems or even within the performance of one poem affects the performer's delivery. Tanya Clement and Stephen McLaughlin built a machine that ingested thirty-six thousand of PennSound's sound files and began, through this sort of "distant listening," to *visualize* applause. The goal of the research was to learn how to mark predictable moments in all or most readings. "We can thus make general inferences," they wrote, "about the structure of a reading by looking at its applause distribution."[36] But such information can be used to follow immediate subsequent effects on the poems' social signifying.

Armantrout's poem receives socially resonant applause for its status as a humane, resourceful rejoinder to someone else's assured applause poem. A good deal is at stake in an audience's response to Armantrout's talking back to Stafford—he who, after a while, read his deer-on-the-road poem at nearly every poetry reading (and it was reliably an encore poem). She wrote from the domestic spatial viewpoint, from "my back porch." She reported on the lived experience of home that was being put at risk by the presumptions of external social forces disguised as natural through regular lyric metaphor. The dynamic experience of a conversation between and among Stafford, Armantrout, Perelman as poet-witness, and the applauding audience jammed into the parlor of our nineteenth-century cottage was really, I think, about the poetics of space in Gaston Bachelard's foundational sense. "A house that has been experienced is not an inert box," he observed in *The Poetics of Space*.[37]

At Armantrout's 1984 Ear Inn reading, one segment of the audience was hearing this West Coast Language poet for the first time live, while another segment—the louder of the two—consisted of colleagues, supporters, and aesthetic fellow travelers seeking expanded company and mutual affirmation. The performance of hyper-iambic orality—thus pushing an interpretation of the poem's response to the Frostian element of Stafford—was a particular response to that second audience. It was a special moment in the acceptance of a poetic movement going national at an especially supportive site—less auditorium than coffee shop or kiva ("where poetry actually happens," to emphasize Jerome Rothenberg's key phrase). It was a specific response, yet now it is irrevocably part of the vast interpretive record. The specificity can be worked out from the old sounds. The affirmation of this interpretation exactly thirty years later, with several vocal people in the room in 2016 who had been there in 1984, was, in one sense, we suppose, a "formal poetry reading,"[38] but the poet and I, as moderator, were sitting at a table, and the audience, at a level line of sight, faced us in the semiround and sat as close as three feet and no further away than twenty-five—and were invited to interject, query, and add things to the permanent sonic account.

THE COLLABORATIVE EAR

Are there poetic sounds made so that the phonemes behave like prime numbers? They sound as they sound and cannot be reduced to mean further. Some of these are the uninvited or unexpected sonic intruders. Here, we return to a fundamental question: How and why should we listen to those intruders? The question remains important as we reconsider why letting intruders in, as a metaphor for close listening and as an actual policy of openness, pertains to the case against minimalism presented in the stories of the Kelly Writers House and ModPo.

If, as the poet Lorenzo Thomas put it in "Neon Griot," his essay on poetry readings, "dynamic interactive relationships, formal and informal, between artist and audience define the heritage of the poetry reading"—and if public readings "have been [unfortunately] perceived as entirely secondary to the existence of poems as printed texts"—then the recovery of the interactive relationship is itself at stake in the analysis of the paraphonotextual intruders. Those guest noises are deemed external only when wrongly understood to be irrelevant to the role-integrative bardic heritage Thomas and others have sought to recover.

Every sound is relevant even (and especially) when irreducible. In the legacy Thomas describes, distinctions among the roles of poet, historian, chronicler, cantador, praise-singer, teacher, and mediator become less meaningful.[39] Now consider the responses of the global ModPo community—which I've described as encouraging the role opacity that succeeds conventional teacher/student and poet/reader distinctions—to the performance of poetic sound of the sort that closes the distance from the maker of sound to the listener's ear. Tracie Morris draws attention in ModPo more than most of the other poets because of the way her sound closes that gap between her voice as producing a subject and the listener as putatively an object at which the sound is directed. Other poets who perform to close such distance are also the most successful at inspiring the responsive noise of the ModPo crowd; indeed, several such poets will be presented here as examples of transforming readings into interactive teaching spaces.

Morris is a musical poet, soundscape-making artist, and vocalist with a close relation to conceptualist poetics. She was trained in theories of speech acts. She knows the immediate action of the performed artwork. She uses her own sound and those of others, including machines, to create transmedia extensions of the body in performance.[40] She interacts with audiences entirely. She has been described as having a "collaborative ear."[41]

"I never take requests," Morris once ironically told an audience at the Writers House near the end of a ninety-minute performance in which pieces were chosen and performed as responses to the ambient sociality of the room. The faux stern comment came in reply to the question called out from the second row: Would she be willing to reprise her performance piece titled "Africa(n)" as an encore? "Africa(n)" has been the final poem in the ten-week main ModPo syllabus since the inception of the course. Between the ModPo syllabus, the performance of the poem during previous visits to the Writers House by Morris, and its appearance in several recordings on PennSound, it was likely that more than half the audience in the room already knew it and could anticipate the experience.

"Africa(n)" is a quasi-improvised chant of a single digitally audio-sampled sentence of official historicism about the Middle Passage—its words then stuttered, jumbled, repeated, and deformed. Its one line is: "It all started when we were brought here as slaves from Africa"—a recorded utterance once performed by actor-dancer Geoffrey Holder in what Morris calls an "Afro-Shakespearian" voice, stentorian, stagy, didactic.

Morris politely declined to end the evening with "Africa(n)" as an encore, preferring to conclude with "The Mrs. Gets Her Ass Kicked," a quasi-improvised sound poem about domestic violence. Earlier the same day, in the same room (although it was then configured as a seminar, chairs set up in the round), she had actively participated in a session with me and my students and several other visitors on the topic of representations of the Holocaust. The conversation had turned from the meaning-making strategies supporting the will to bear witness to the linguistic and, as it were, spoken-word difficulties of death camp inmates who survived traumatic acts of violent hatred and sought to give voice to the experience of violence and sorrow.

Many of those who had participated in the discussion a few hours earlier stayed or returned to be in the audience at the public reading, including myself as host and moderator. Now, in the act of improvising from a scripted, oft-performed poem about physical abuse, Morris began to "hear in my throat" (as she later described it for me) the rhythms of the very piece she had declined. We witnessed a singular throat-bound aural return of the repressed: well into "The Mrs.,"[42] (normally a 3.5-minute performance) she began to beat her fist lightly against the top of her sternum, such that it affected the movement of her vocal cords and her breathing, added acoustical hiss, and created an irreducible breathy percussive sound at the bottom of each of the other vocal resonances. Through PennSound—and for many thousands of people by way of each other, through to the tenth and final week of the main ModPo syllabus—the painful faltered cadence of "Africa(n)" will always begin suddenly to approach "The Mrs."[43] We hear the sound-trace of it as the poet herself, in a moment of vocal learning, hears the semantic relationship between the two pieces—contemporary domestic trauma and historical international genocide—in the doubled embodied sound she is making. The encore became a seven-minute-long convergence of the two, a looping feedback of ambient interconnection, an improvised immediate action yet formal in every sense—hot, nondistant, intimate but just as formal as Geoffrey Holder's basso profundo.

What happened was what Morris, in her prose contribution to the anthology *I'll Drown My Book: Conceptual Writing by Women*, calls "sound substitution."[44] "Say[ing] something whose phonetic substance will be *impossible to reduce*" is nonetheless saying something that, as an after-effect, is almost entirely paratextual.[45] Its emergence was unique to the site and situation. But its preservation makes it available to those who can learn to read (interpret—yet really to read as to *hear*) the liminal remains of both. Now that preserving the soundscape of a third space is fairly routine, we must ask: Who are the people who can hear them? These sites constitute an unplanned interpretive community—an interanimating crowd and its own "sudden music" as heard in the memory of the sound.[46] We hear.

WHO ARE ALL INCLUDED?

Morris has insisted that for those in her audiences who hear the repeated *we* in the phrase "when we were brought here," the pronoun and repeated open sound of "Africa(n)" can refer to those engaging with the vocal distortions in the moment of reception. Here is my attempt at transcribing a part of one of the variable performances of the piece:

when we
when we we
when when we
when when we . . .
when we were brought
when we were brough—
when we were br—
what when we
when we

As much as any poem encountered by the global thousands who have participated in ModPo over the years, Morris's "Africa(n)" inspires a focus on both
metapoetry and metapedagogy. The topic of the poem, they say, is the possibility
of an inclusive "we." It can include the hearer/witness and can inspire a breakdown of the barrier typically separating poet/performer from witness/audience.
The poem enacts an altered situation of learning to listen closely. Learning, too,
requires a collaborative ear.

Vijaya M. was inexperienced with performance poetry when, as a first-time
student in ModPo in 2021, she first heard and viewed Tracie Morris. She posted
this for the community to read: "[I hear] the emphasis on the word 'we' as in
'We the people.' Who are all included? When I heard the sounds of the breaking down what I heard was that of a sobbing of a child. . . . That is what I heard
in her voice. She unites and integrates the form to the content. This kind of
crying shudders through the body in waves."[47] For Vijaya, in the asynchronous
moment of encountering Morris, close listening helped create an ethical position deriving from the obligation to hear history being haltingly retold. "The
moment it started I was overpowered by a sense of obligation to listen reveren-
tially to its fractures and fragmentariness," wrote one of Vijaya's interlocutors,
Rahana Ismail.[48]

Rahana's, Vijaya's, and others' comments on "Africa(n)" insist on respecting
the theme of freedom transmitted in irreducible broken sounds made by tiny
indecipherable mind/body decisions by Morris in the act of performance. They
find it to be an ethical matter. In *The Poethical Wager*, Retallack argued that,
in contrast to social and language systems that confine us to repeating unvar-
ied patterns, unintelligibility represents freedom—that what is indecipherable
ultimately "reveals life continuing as a continuing surprise."[49] It's a live proceduralism. The electronic and mechanical aspects of recording were important
but not determinative. "In her recorded live performances of 'Africa(n),'" wrote
Colette Bates in the ModPo forums, "it's astounding that Tracie Morris can

achieve with her voice effects that one might expect to only be possible through digital mixing and editing."[50]

Colette understands "mixing" to refer to the technical means by which recorded audio can be recreated, but she is noting the opposite. The digital audio editing is relevant here only as a metaphor, but if "Morris uses the human vocal apparatus to mimic the random-access dispersal of the MP3," as Danny Snelson puts it,[51] then her collaborative ear could be the model for an open forum of teaching as close listening. The mixing Colette means is poetic and pedagogical, still another version of resistance to the idea of receiving poems "fully and purely," to the sense that professing critical response to poems will necessarily "always be an elitist phenomenon." What Morris has done with her voice is "impossible," Colette argues. Colette, Vijaya, Rahana, and dozens of others have conferred about a poem whose written form (even if it existed) would be irrelevant to the group's analysis of it.

The question the crowd asks about Tracie Morris's sound-text is surely the right one: Who are all included? This inclusion requires the recognition and exploration of the relationship between the space in which the poet once utters the poem and that which is realized as a made place of ongoing learning: poet as teacher experimenting in the act of performing the poem among others, always an incipient "we." The poetry reading as teaching. Now a few further examples.

THE TEACHER WHO DRIFTS, CHANTS, SCREAMS, AND FEEDS YOU SNACKS

When Caroline Bergvall performs her book-length poem *Drift*, the presentation follows the currents and eddies of learners' responses to how the slowly swirling projected oceanic visuals seem to be moved by her voice together with stray sounds made in the room. For Erín Moure and Karis Shearer, who write about the public reading as an educational space, Bergvall presents an example of what can result from "the interaction between teaching and practice."[52] She is the unanchored straying-from-the-point instructor in the moment, standing in a university space transformed into a lab, theater workshop, or Cayleyesque CAVE by fantastical sonic and optical operations—and she and we are deeply inside a lesson in the impermanent fluidity of art as written-to-be-performed, seeing what happens as we go, a drifting guide to drifting. This ignorant schoolmaster performs the state of being unmoored from certainty: "For a minute there," she says to her hearers, "I lost myself Totally at sea lost myway tossed misted lost mywill in the fog."[53]

FIGURE 6.2 Caroline Bergvall performing *Drift*.

Source: Used with permission of Caroline Bergvall.

When Cecilia Vicuña begins a performance by standing unnoticed among the still-arriving, settling audience, conversing quietly with someone, someone unknown to her, in fact, and when she increases the volume of her voice and closes her eyes but continues to engage in what seems like a side conversation, which turns out to have been a poetic chant in the first place, she is committing to a form of guidance that emanates leaderlessly literally as well as figuratively from the back of the room. Our teacher-encourager insists on not concerning herself with distinguishing interpersonal from didactic discourse, front from back, telling from vocalizing.

When M. NourbeSe Philip performs her disjunctive documentary poem about the slave ship Zong by chorally chanting and collaboratively dancing rather than "reading" at a podium from a text as a semantic script, and the audience members seem to decide that *they* might become the reader/speaker of the poem—that they should take a lead as transmitters of words back up to the stage—a reversal of creative category takes place. The poet is primarily responsive to the learners rather than the other way around. The "durational reading" of *Zong!*, fugal and quasihallucinatory, becomes a staged exploration of role opacity.

FIGURE 6.3 Cecilia Vicuña in performance at the Kelly Writers House, February 16, 2017.

Source: Photograph by Al Filreis.

The roles of poet/teacher and listener/learner—of citizen of the past and citizen of the present—become an altered way of teaching the historical telling of the victims of the Zong Massacre whose stories cannot adequately be told in descriptive terms yet must be somehow professed. Being equal parts song, moan, shout, oath, ululation, curse, and chant, it forbids distance and necessitates unprepared participation. An increase in preparedness happens in real time and makes an ethics of a performative pedagogy.[54]

Whenever Bernadette Mayer performed "Chocolate Poetry Sonnet"—a poem about comforting her young children with chocolate bars when she and partner (and fellow poet) Lewis Warsh took them to poetry readings—she comically threatened to transform whatever reading venue she had entered into a space where all people, not just school-aged kids, were schooled in the extrapoetic conditions necessary for making what happened in the room conducive to hearing the poems. It was impossible to hear Mayer read that poem—as I did several times—and keep yourself from thinking about how often you've struggled with close listening, how little you wanted to be an adult sometimes, nor to keep from joining her conclusion, right there inside such a space, that "poetry is [only] as good as chocolate"—and also realizing there and then the truth of an even more profound idea about cultural leveling: that "chocolate's [every bit] as good as poetry."[55]

When Charles Bernstein, as a brash college sophomore at Harvard, screamed the names of the numbers one through one hundred, with increasing loudness to the point of earsplitting vocal irreality, the spoken poem became an institutional critique of the state of higher education in 1969. I hear it as a dissident counterresponse to the surprisingly conventional form and language of student protests of that moment, ironically lacking their own practices of disjunction. Perhaps this disconcerting performance is to be counted among situationist interventions of the time. Through the numbered supersequential screams emitted within the heart of the site of higher learning, ground zero for credentialed elite U.S. education, the young neo-Dadaist is engaging a poem unrecognizable as literature (it's just screaming; it's numbers, not words, numerical rather than semantic; it's mere counting) to instruct us alternatively. He enacts an aversion to the poetry reading exactly as he counteracts old-school teaching, incoherently protesting against the way conventional teaching *and* conventional writing (as the poet-novelist Robert Majzels has said about public readings) "reinforce the idea of the author as the source of meaning, to the logocentric illusion of presence."[56] "1–100" was collected with other early tape works under the title "Class,"[57] and through that cry, perhaps calling for a different kind of Harvard classroom, Bernstein was saying in the most impertinent way that he will not merely say "aye," will not be roll-called as present, that he's not there despite all the ruckus of 1969-style engagé. It's a lesson in a new loudness. He's loud, like a loud tie, but in another sense, he's audibly insensible and invisible. By the end of the performance, there's not much left of his master's sequential voice.[58]

"1–100" reminds us that there's no such thing as a nonspecific voice. When I hear the PennSound digitalization of the original reel-to-reel recording of that student's scream against rote numeracy,[59] I'm reminded of what Cid Corman observed when, in a notebook, he dared to summarize all of William Carlos Williams in a phrase: "WCW: the voice as particular."[60] Corman was one of the first poets to advocate for and host poets reading live on the radio. Listeners wrote him letter after letter to describe remotely hearing broadcasts of *This Is Poetry* between 1949 and 1961 as an education over airwaves in modern poetics.[61] For Larry Eigner, who was unable to attend a college in person and only here and there taught himself through correspondence courses, the discovery of *This Is Poetry* provided an essential irregular series of lessons in the sound of modern poems, starting with Corman's "non-declamatory way of reciting" W. B. Yeats in the first broadcast Eigner heard.[62] "It puts the stress rightly on the spoken word," Corman wrote in *Poetry* magazine about his show, "tests the imagination of writer and listener, revives the need of the oral-aural commitment in verse, and permits the largest possible audience to experience the poem."[63] (*PoemTalk* and PennSound both have origins in the production and effects of that radio program. The debt came full circle in 2001 when Corman, telephoning us from Kyoto, Japan, read his poems in a Kelly Writers House live interactive audiocast, now preserved in PennSound. The reading included a sonorous rendition of "It isnt for want," the meaning of which he told us was as simple and clear and self-evident as could be—it didn't need to be explicated. And he told us this in the clearest of baritones.[64])

Corman, Bernstein, Bergvall, Vicuña, Philip, and Mayer, along with Rothenberg, Morris, Antin, Torres, Ginsberg, and Lorenzo Thomas, among others, have knowledge to impart from, as it were, the back of the room. They position themselves as already othered in a persistent system of proper education, with its prearranged rows of chairs, chalkboards, and whiteboards requiring back-facing, demands of you not to "talk in class" (a persistent illiberal practice that has been decried through a shared Instagram meme),[65] its pious bans against eating while learning (no chocolate bars or other sweet disruptions of the child's

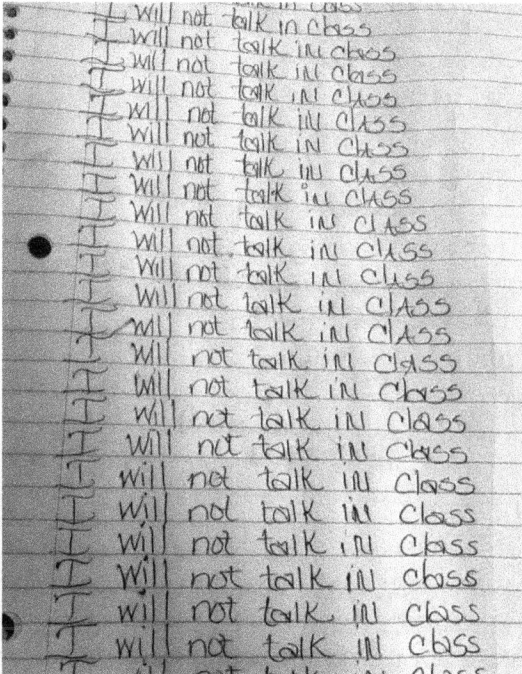

FIGURE 6.4 "I will not talk in class." Multiple sources, photographer unknown.

Source: Courtesy: The Educator's Room.

stolen focus)[66]—whatever among any number of features and built-environment effects are furthest from kiva, connectivist thread, MOO, or cozy house of possibility. If these are the kinds of sites where and how poetry actually happens, then they are also scenes of effective experimentation in learning that we can locate, plan, occupy, and revitalize. A poetry reading can enact discourse as an event. Any site of learning with a poetics of space can do the same.

WHEN THE POETRY READING IS YOUR SCHOOL

CHOCOLATE POETRY SONNET

when my children were growing up
we never had candy at home but
when we went to poetry readings
i always brought chocolate bars
to make the poetry palatable or
more interesting so they'd
be relatively quiet, it only backfired
if the reading lasted too long, then
there'd be hell to pay but i deserved it
right? after a while if i knew
the reading'd be long I'd bring two
so i began to think of long readings
as two-chocolate-bar readings, eventually
i'd bring two just in case, sometimes saving one
   poetry is as good as chocolate
   chocolate's as good as poetry[67]

(Bernadette Mayer)

Max Warsh (b. 1980) was one of those children. Later he became an art photographer whose visual work features symmetric, seemingly abstract details of urban architectural exteriors. He has also been a gallery director who arrived at that position after a history of involvement with artist-run art spaces. The meaningful outlines of this story have been tempting to me as someone writing about alternative poetic education. I wanted to know more—beyond what his mother reported through her sonnet and told me and others in conversation—about those poetry readings and the use of chocolate in lieu of a babysitter. If those readings were an education for that child-become-artist, how so?

His memory of the readings "is mostly aural," he has told me.[68] He recalls "hearing the voices very clearly" and the sounds of words. He's fine now joining a conversation about the much-documented benefits of being read aloud to.[69] But actually—perhaps like some children receiving such benefits—he did not follow what the words meant. The meanings being conveyed at those events, he vaguely just assumed, were social rather than denotative. He observed "people coming together in the same group over and over again" and began to comprehend the way "familiarity . . . grows through" a recurrent community: presumably people he recognized, sometimes sitting or standing in the audience, sometimes speaking from the stage, some engaged in side conversation otherwise. We imagine them, from his vantage, arranged around the room in mysterious combinations. These memories are commingled with scenes of poets and poetry at home, for "the same people . . . would come to our birthday parties. Our birthday parties were like an extension of the Poetry Project." The poetry community constituted a babysitter. "It was a collective effort to raise us."

Max's mother, Bernadette, was parentally strict about nothing—except healthy foods. No soda, no sugar. There were visits to a health food store on First Avenue between East Seventh and St. Mark's called Prana. They went there to get carob. Max and his sisters, Sophia and Marie, hated carob "because it was so clearly not chocolate and it was . . . a replacement for chocolate." He comprehended poetry readings—and the gatherings of poets at their home, and the workshops his mother taught to which he was also brought along—as effecting a happy reversal of that unpalatable replacement. Poetry → chocolate: a special familial nonsymbolic formula and rather magical exchange. A first lesson in currency. This is the child's point of view Bernadette Mayer managed to replicate in the sonnet. She showed a capacity for that perspective in much of her writing.

These are memories of poetry as spaces: public readings, community writing workshops held at home, and workshops organized to occur in rooms (such as at the Poetry Project or at the College of Staten Island) that felt a bit more like ordinary learning spaces. The lines that might regularly define for a child a way of distinguishing domestic spaces and their connection to the art—in this case, of both parents—"were very slippery." After the workshops, especially those held at home, "people just stuck around sometimes and then turned into just hanging out, so I think it's not always clear where the learning started or stopped." That they "never had babysitters" extended after a while further out into the urban field—to evening seminars at the College of Staten Island (CUNY) and poetry readings held on the Staten Island Ferry, consisting of Staten Island–based poets his mother had befriended (presumably some of them commuting) mixed with nonpoetic commuters. Who was who? Unclear. The space and scene of poetry "was pretty chaotic" and did not abide distinctions between and among personal, professional, political, parental, philanthropic, pedagogical, social, and administrative matters or processes. A preserved spiral-bound notebook includes everything Bernadette Mayer did, felt, and thought about her work as director of the Poetry Project over the course of a year.[70] Everything that *could* intrude upon that work *did* intrude: notes on fundraising for a children's poetry workshop (she wrangled $1,000 from Con Edison); family self-portraits sketched by her children when they grabbed temporary control of the notebook; drafts of letters such as a frank, confessional missive to be sent to former director Ron Padgett, an important poet in the scene with whom she was having a major organizational disagreement: "I don't think the formality of our administrative tasks should so overwhelm us that the pleasure's not in it, just as one is dealing with *all the formal expectations of parenthood*—+ to

FIGURE 6.5 Page from Bernadette Mayer's Poetry Project notebook, drawings by Max and Marie Warsh.

Source: Poetry Project Papers, Rare Book and Special Collections Division, Library of Congress. Publicly available at: https://www.loc.gov/item/2014659017.

do them right—still one is a person on one's own (still!!) + can have some private pleasures + having them is a good thing (for ALL)."

Perhaps it is no surprise, then, that artist and New Yorker Max Warsh believes he knew even then, as a child, what his mother's pedagogy was. That's because it was the same as her mode of being a parent. He witnessed her at workshops and readings, all the same: she was "a peer like everyone." It's the same sense "I always got" that "we were all kind of peers," and this, as he learned through poetry and home, he associated even then with the way art had to happen in the world: "She was never really parental. . . . It was more like, 'We're here together and let's figure this out.'" The life they lived in and of art was figured out. The way children moved in and around "the sort of thought spaces I was raised in"—that also was just figured out; that they were mostly unplanned was what made them "thought spaces" in the first instance. In a real sense, it was all happening in the New York School–style. The way the children would appear in poems—they were characters in a daily nondrama of art being figured out as it went. In Bernadette's poem "Max Carries the One," we don't know what "the one" refers to, and that's because young Max is somehow being asked to take responsibility for the way the poem proceeds! "Dont look at me, look at your own self."[71] The word *incorporation* in "The Incorporation of Sophia's Cereal" refers not just to the inclusion of sister Sophia as subject matter but also to her having taken over the poem's diction and vocabulary and its power of gamified metaphorization over the morning routine. Was there a poem to be made from this ordinary breakfast scene? Even this domestic poetics had a pedagogy. It was learner-centered learning exactly as the poem's imaginative terms were not those of the parent-teacher—a move toward a child-centered childhood from the pages of *Democracy and Education* and *Art as Experience*. The bowl of puffed wheat was augmented by bananas, *and it was all a school*: "[T]he bananas / Were the teachers" while "the cereals were the kids." Breakfast was for learning, but the teachers were, well, *bananas*, and the parent was merely assigned a part. So that this would be no plain analogy to education—because what's the fun in that?—the mother-poet "was the giant" and "my spoon was my spoon." She hadn't even enough authority over her own poem to be rewarded with a likening: the child's imagination augured true "believing in living" (its gerund and its continuous present right out of Stein), but the mom gets to be no more than literally a mom.[72]

What kind of school was all this? For Max, he explains, it was an education in the meaning, significance, and social effect of community spaces. From the public poetry reading, exactly as Moure and Shearer idealize it in their essay about readings as community events, he learned that "poetry can really happen anywhere. I feel that way about being a visual artist too." He eventually left New York City for an art journey away from its inescapable centrality, earning an MFA at Indiana University (2002–2004), his thesis project about "methods of escape" (through the double installation—a floating outline of Thoreau's cabin near a looping video of Max scrambling headlong down a long dark high-rise stairwell—he seems to be fleeing 9/11-damaged downtown Manhattan). Then he returned to the shaken city, a reverse escape, and began in earnest to make artworks and art spaces (both) out of the learned "resourcefulness" requiring "that you will find space to make it happen by any means." But then—and here was a "direct" lesson—it was "time to start showing" art on the basis of the idea of breaking the connection between authorship and authority, a concept that positively infused what was, in effect, his home-schooling. This is how he explained it to me:

> In the realm of building communities in spaces I learned in a direct way from my dad [Lewis Warsh] visiting my studio and him really encouraging me to start showing, and setting up the space to show people [other artists] in a way that was linked to the ethos of the publishing world of the '60s, where you publish your friends' work because it needs to be out there and brought into the world. And just in terms of that collective knowledge-building exercise, I think that's to me more interesting and not something I had tied to the poetry reading experience or growing up in that world. I think my experience growing up with them both and then transferring that into a space of visual curation, and curating as a group, and really trying to break down a kind of hierarchical sense of authorship in a curatorial voice, has been something that, when I had an artist-run gallery, we were always trying to experiment with.

So while the artist son swerved from his parents' medium—from the linguistic and oral to the visual, from verse to art photography—it was no statement of emotional "resentment" against the "commune kind of mentality" of his upbringing nor at all against the surrounding literariness of books, printed words seen everywhere and in all directions, of city life rendered as I-do-this-I-do-that texts. This child of the second-generation New York School decided visually to "encounter with architecture as I walk through the city," as he has written in an artist's statement. "Architectural details speak to me as a series of passing images that frame the sense of place, the psycho-geography of the landscape."[73] This is non-Freudian nonagonistic psychobiography: its scene of instruction and its positive constructivist origin are the communitarian East Village poetry reading. It became a motioning toward Guy Debord's much-discussed situationist dérive, "psychogeography" as knowledge exploration by way of loosely defined urban walking practices, an homage to his parents' radicalization in the 1960s, with their emphasis on urban avant-garde poetics, influenced by the anti- or counternarrativity of many New York School predecessors: densely interpersonal connections to observed places seen along *arbitrary* city routes—a frank haphazardness that replicates the metropolis's incessant disjunctive inconclusiveness. (Lewis Warsh's scathing satire of the awful sort of scene-driven poetry reading, in his poem "1000 Poetry Readings," gets inversely at this version of the rejection of closure: "I hope you'll see," says the pretentious poet-performer speaker in the father's verse parody, "how I tried to tie everything together."[74])

The shift away from language and books was a positively repressed swerve. But it was perhaps no more emotionally significant than a practical plan not to reenter the art world as a poet, nor even perhaps as a *reader*, but as the adult grown up from the child who heard the sound of words but didn't comprehend their semantic sense. For those words did not *read* like a Debordian psychogeographical community; they just *sounded* that way. Every space seemed to him like a great edifice of books. "I gr[ew] up with walls of books thinking about space and thinking about how that was just the norm. And my sort of understanding of reality was living in a room that is just a wall of books, and that's your wall." "The combination of visual and informational density of shelves of books," he wrote for the magazine *LVL3* in 2012, "is something I am continually drawn to."[75]

FIGURE 6.6 Family photograph of the Warsh/Mayer apartment living room.

Source: Courtesy of Max Warsh.

THE PERFORMANCES OF UNDERSTANDING

I observed that many of Max Warsh's photographs of New York City buildings, shot from the outside, facing front—for example, *Colonnade* (2013), *The Daily Life of Immobile Things* (2014), and *Vestry* (2015)—look very much like that edifice of bound volumes; that his art has perhaps exteriorized and externalized the shape and design of the primary instructive aesthetic scene of his artist parents and their ubiquitous, circulatory community of friends. His response to that idea: "I think the visual sort of ornamentation and detail on the surface of architecture, to me, started out as something to be read like language. Those sort of rhythms and movements and points that drew me in were almost like a form of reading and language play."

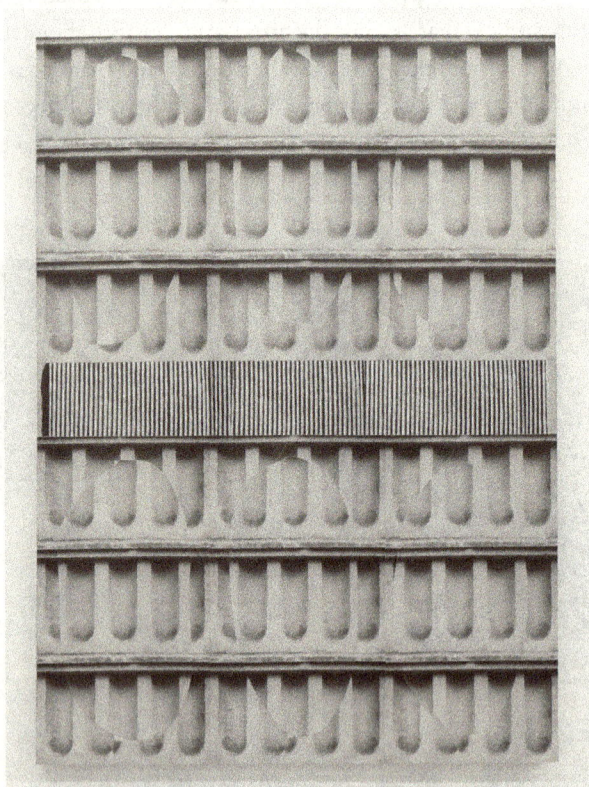

FIGURE 6.7 Max Warsh, *Colonnade* (2013), photograph and acrylic on panel, 30 × 40 inches.

Source: Reproduction provided by Max Warsh. © Max Warsh.

FIGURE 6.8
Max Warsh, *The Daily Life of Immobile Things* (2014), photographs and acrylic on panel, 30 × 40 inches.

Source: Reproduction provided by Max Warsh. © Max Warsh.

FIGURE 6.9
Max Warsh, *Vestry* (2015), cut photographs and acrylic on panel, 48 × 60 inches.

Source: Reproduction provided by Max Warsh. © Max Warsh.

This is a way of describing Max's creativity in sum, and even inasmuch as his situation is special, I know my book has shown that he is not alone: the rediscovery of a life of books that will not be read by the usual means. Understood thus, his art becomes another lucid reply to Johann Hari when in *Stolen Focus* he laments the supposed broken connection between books and thoughtful regard—or to Newport's *Digital Minimalism*, to Josh Misner's *Put the F**king Phone Down* (2019), to the contentions of Barry Sanders, Andrew Keen, Nicholas Carr, and others who have been sad or mad about the end of the sort of private contemplation associated with the experience of printed books. The noncodex sense of the book presented in this profile signifies no lack of attention and certainly not the need for decluttering nor anything other than a longing to sustain the feeling one gets from the image of a family's shelves and stacks of books. For Max, it had been a profound progressive education in wherever and whenever through whatever medium knowledge can be derived. Rather than being intimidated when faced with overwhelming book knowledge he hadn't yet acquired, Max sought to comprehend the thought space in a related but ultimately different or parallel way. The adult child of two poets now explores the following:

> [the] idea that there's all this knowledge that is unknown, or to be known, sitting on those walls. I remember going to college and feeling like I want to read books that I know are way beyond my philosophical comprehension and it always felt important to me to go there even if I was not well versed or in a theoretical space to understand some of that stuff. But it always felt like a necessary thing to do and I still feel that way. . . . I think that is definitely for me an extension of sitting in those poetry spaces and trying to grapple with what I'm hearing.

That kind of "extension" is the educational paradigm shift proposed by Moure and Shearer in "The Public Reading: Call for a New Paradigm." They argue for a new close reading of listening to the reading. They propose democratic attention. They contend, along with Susan Gingell and Wendy Roy in *Listening Up, Writing Down, and Looking Beyond: Interfaces of the Oral, Written and Visual* (2012), that performance "is a forum in which histories and social identities are negotiated."[76] This connotation of *forum* helps us understand what poet-critic Lytle Shaw in *Narrowcast* describes as the site-specificity of the social sound emitting from poetry. It has "the specificity of a real *space* of enunciation"—"a distinct location [that] tend[s] to interweave the speaker's sounds . . . with those of that environment." What was formative for Max Warsh can be a model or a guide for many other persons or groups, including many people I've met inside the Kelly Writers House and remotely through ModPo, anyone for whom the most productive learning entails learning to apprehend fully—to discern with ears and eyes at once—the "cultivation of a . . . countermedia space" as part of the human "search for alternate temporalities."[77]

When Louis Cabri gathered essays for a special issue of *English Studies in Canada* on "Event and Sound in Poetry," he began by reminding us that "uttered sound is unstable—allophonic, noisy" and that critical "prosodic inventions," such as measure, rhythm, or the concept of the phoneme itself, are just attempts "to 'stabilize' sound's protean qualities." Somewhere between sound's "continuum" and "discreteness"—the former hard to explain, the latter relatively easy—is where we finally find the *event*.[78]

The events we remember, those that have taught us fundamentally, are where we learned while grappling with our understanding of the unstable continuum. If theorist of learning Howard Gardner is right in *The Disciplined Mind* "that understanding should be construed as a performance" and, even more pointedly as he presents his reformist ideas about education, that learning should be structured around the "promulgation of 'performances of understanding,'"[79] then understanding is not the same as being given information, and something like a public reading is or is at least akin to an ideal school setting. This notion of understanding, of course, applies in the poetry world far beyond the reading. Kristen Gallagher's small cohort of LaGuardia Community College students heard and amplified the forum noise of ModPo similarly, enlarging and supplementing the act—the event—of understanding their general educational situation. It was for them, as Max Warsh says, "an *extension* of sitting in those poetry spaces and trying to grapple with what I'm hearing." He deeply felt and learned from—as Cabri once described PhillyTalks—the "event's plural subject-status."[80] When the event is reckoned affectively "as an 'intentional' site," Moure and Shearer conclude—when it is "part of a *broader act* of poetic exploration and inquiry" and is seen by participants "as a site that is more than reiteration of an authoritative, printed text"[81]—it becomes an alternative school. Alt-poetry, alt-pedagogy. Experiencing the public reading in this way, they say, can "spur the evolution of collaborative critical and creative poetic space[s]" but might also lead to "the evolution and application of new pedagogies for teaching literature to and among critics and poets, not separately but together."[82]

❧

Moure and Shearer's sense of their phrase "not separately but together" orients them toward action. They are proponents of reforms that assume a connection between poetic encounter and public behavior. The sections of my two concluding chapters are notes toward an understanding of that behavior as an aspect of citizenship. Through these, I endeavor to describe the reverse engineering by which, counterintuitively, the intimacies of a remote community can be directed *back* to the in-person place; to salvage a positive connotation of "the crowd" from its connection to traditionalist education and abhorrent twentieth-century politics; to explore at close range the splintering brain of a human group—its navigating the information cascade—and to promote its status as a hopeful challenge against the knowledge industry; to identify a cooperative intercultural and crossnational assertion of the right to criticize assumptions underlying syllabus as core knowledge, canon, and other expressions of top-down curation; to explore a redefinition of subject-matter expertise as an outcome of the massive open course; to comprehend diversity as an *effect* (as well as a cause) of collective innovation; and lastly, to rethink accessibility in open education as being exactly as fragile as the thin glass of a screen held by the human hand. I trust it makes sense that a book as positive about digitality as this one concludes with the human hand.

PART III

The Crowd, Yes

CHAPTER 7

NOTES TOWARD A CITIZEN POETICS

I have not yet come across anybody in ModPo considering older meanings of "dwell"—Old English dwellan *"lead astray, hinder, delay" (in Middle English "tarry, remain in a place"), of Germanic origin; related to Middle Dutch* dwellen *"stun, perplex." Does this open up another level of "Possibility"?*

—Janet Penney in the subforum devoted to Emily Dickinson's "I dwell in Possibility"

Isn't it ethereal to think that poetry exists in the subliminal where we have to be led astray to a place we would never reach if not for the "dwelling"? The poem becomes a road map to the House—the dwelling is how you arrive here. . . . The etymological origins of "dwell": It had a noun form in Old English, gedweola *[which means] "error, heresy, madness." Also compare Middle English* dwale *"deception, trickery," from Old English* dwala *or from a Scandinavian cognate (such as Danish* dvale *"trance, stupor, stupefaction").*

—Rahana Ismail

I might be going astray here but your further research into dwell *reminds me of "Narcissus," the etymology of which includes "to cause numbness or stupor."*

—Jim Lynch

Jim, I do not think you are going astray. Could the abandonment be of a conventional life to experience an authentic life?

—Charles

And therein lies the circuitous aspect of ED's poetry once again: You dwell in order to arrive, and when you arrive it is in order to dwell.

—Thea Terpstra

REVERSE ENGINEERING

Who are these people, and what are they talking about? There are two other questions to ask as we conclude: What actually happens when digital dwelling inspires citizenship? And what good comes of that sort of inspiration?

As for what happens: in short, *gedweola* abounds. So Rahana Ismail suggests. If you skipped the colloquy serving as an extended epigraph above, please go back to Rahana and her colleagues. You'll be reading about people opening the door of the house of poetry and warmly welcoming error. It is a conversation of exactly the sort that Sherry Turkle suggests in *Reclaiming Conversation* must be "reclaimed" *from*—in other words, taken out of, not left to deteriorate inside—the digital space.

As for what good can result? I believe there is an ethical situation being explored in Rahana's reference to a "here" located within that genuine conversation. Similarly, in Janet Penney's sense of remaining in place or planning to stay and also—paradoxical as it might seem at first—in Jim Lynch's and Charles's commitment to wandering while staying the course. "We have to be led astray to a place we would never reach if not for the 'dwelling.'"

After forty years of teaching, my main goal is to sustain places inhabited by people like Janet, Rahana, Jim, Charles, and Thea as they together develop a revised sense of how to learn. There are many advantages to relearning learning. These days especially, finding new ways to dwell will help these people withstand numerous large and small antipoetic biases that throw suspicion upon the value of going astray.

My two final chapters suppose an idea of education resistant to that bias—an idea based on a workable alternative to professional thinking. Here we will consider: What can be done better to support the nonroutine social impulse felt by devoted amateur learners outside the academy as they try to teach one another within a site that does not resemble any classroom they've known? Theirs is a place where lessons arise suddenly; where, ultimately, little guidance is required; where solutions are not demanded; where participation and belonging are the elements of citizen-style belonging; where, for the most part, no evident expert is present—and yet, contrarily, where even the most neutral-seeming space, driven partly by AI-generated assumptions about what counts as normal sense-making, will find a way of casting doubt that is detrimental to iconoclastic expression. The idea of dwelling, according to Rahana, after all, draws on connotations of heresy and trickery and, in effect, hackery. These must be revived and navigated.

Opinionated Software

How neutral is the platform? One ModPo learner, a first-timer in 2024, is an application developer by day job and a poetry person otherwise. ModPo people know them as Epistolaris. After a few months in the course, they described the LMS as "a very opinionated piece of software." This didn't cause them to quit. It inspired activity in the discussion forums on the basis of their counteropinions. The assessments of Epistolaris—about poems—are part of the hack. They went on to "wonder what the 'ideal' platform would look like for a 'course' like ModPo," aiming through those quotation marks to gain distance from certain definitions of a course.[1] If ModPo is not really a course but a site for convening poetic conversation, is it especially susceptible and sensitive to opinionated software in ways that disclose a major presumption?

When Coursera's engineers push out an updated version of the platform, it is based on someone or some team having affirmed or assumed definitions of what a course is. If the upgrade is primarily to serve technical needs, that redefinition is implicit, even unintended. Making for easier access to fixed course materials as a high priority can affect all the other unfixed and improvised moving parts. If unintended secondary effects of an optimization degrade the usefulness and accessibility of the discussion forums—unlinking them from the syllabus, for example, or even deleting ("refreshing") the accumulated course memory or social history of conversations—does ModPo's primarily focus on free discussion, more intensive than other courses hosted by the company, relate to the overall norms established for the open course? True, ModPo's emphasis on discussion makes the project an outlier among MOOCs. To the extent that the exception might in fact help re-define educational values that are being even unwittingly enforced as standard through system enhancements, it is always going to be much more than a technical challenge. The deviation from the norm doubts the priority of teaching solutions and the orientation to instruction through the delivery of answers as key qualities in online education. What if it turns out that these are not the key qualities? "ModPo is that outlier where almost everyone enters without orientation," Laura Lippman, the journalist and novelist and long-time ModPo citizen, told me. "Up, down, good, bad—it's not only a mystery, it's beside the point. ModPo holds out the possibility that if one takes the time to think about something, it might become more comprehensible, but it will not be 'solved.' We are not working our way toward solutions, we are working our way toward our own aesthetic values. *What do I like? What do I think? Why? Can I articulate it? How?*"[2]

Several technical aspects of the xMOOC platform—issues, I'll admit, of lesser import than the matter of solutions and orientation raised by Laura—annoy me as a teacher with my hopes of lowering barriers so that people can learn without being driven by prescribed outcomes. None more than this: posts to the forums that seem to be even modestly heterodox or nonstandard as expression—in short, let's just say poetic—are sometimes greeted with an extra link appearing below the post:

translate to English

Consider what happened to Terry Talty's pandemic renga stanza earlier: "our world / even while moving fast / still standing still." Now it's rewarded with an invitation to others to have it translated into the language in which it was written. Perhaps I should not make a big deal of this. But it's at least fair to ask: What was inside the black box that triggered the recognition of Terry's writing as foreign to its own language? Perhaps it's the anomalous way of describing time. Or its lack of a simple active verb. Yet these are typical poetic tropes. The offer from a site to rewrite with AI would seem helpful, even if detrimental to poetry and talk of poetry. So is poetry then the outlier, as Laura says? Or is it a test case? My argument all along has been that it's a test case. Its exploratory language— "composition as explanation" (in Stein's terms) or "writing as an aid to memory" (in Hejinian's) or using words to "find out what I'm saying" (in Antin's)—is not improved when rewritten to befit aggregate habits and norms.

I want to test the case further. I myself posted the following statement in the forums, whereupon the "translate to English" option was prompted:

How we say what we say is as important as what we say. In fact, the how of what we say is more important than the what. In the best poems, the what is in fact the how.

I was not just playing a game against the machine. That statement, word for word, is one I make in the introductory video atop the ModPo syllabus. Despite its discursive oddity and its modest foreignness to simple English language routines, the meaning of the claim becomes fairly obvious to almost everyone on the site. I asked Raymond M. about it, and he distinctly recalls hearing the remark for the first time in September 2012 and comprehending it then. "The fact that it was perhaps counterintuitive made me pay more attention to it," he tells me. "I figured it was so beautiful it had to be true."[3] Taking stock of posts in a long forum thread devoted to discussing this very pronouncement,[4] Jim Lynch reports that "there might be some confusion" and speculates about why. Some learners think we teachers primarily offer instruction in how "the how" of modern verse has changed over time—historically developing styles, modes, or movements. But soon it's clear that what does not change is the way the quirky assertion, not a matter of literary history, can *always* encourage the human "impulse for . . . communication from one mind to another (whether achieved or not)."[5] The circular form of the adage, Raymond, Jim, and others such as Vijaya M. and Sanjeev Naik agree,[6] might flummox new learners, or at least give pause as it did them. But pausing is the point, and soon most comprehend why, in a course about poetry, the tenet should be expressed as it is. Thus the site's first major thesis statement is: in the language we will now study together, inconclusive process supersedes settled content, or, in plain language, *how* is *what*.

Reading Crowd Moods

Teaching uncertainty unclearly? This will strike some as ridiculous, an imitative fallacy. Others, upon entering, know they are opting into a world in which no *what* is what it's cracked up to be. Charles is among the latter group. That he has no taste for exegetical simplification is an aspect of "the abandonment . . . of a conventional life" to which our conversationalist aspires as he opts to occupy the Dickinsonian dwelling.[7] It's important for me as an educator to know what happens to the poetic sensibilities of Charles and his acquaintances inside a technology that is being trained by one group of people to suggest to another group of people that what they say is better if made standard. In doubting Turkle's doubts, I am not suggesting that having a conversation in the online space is easy. In fact, I'm saying it's an achievement that happens because aspects of the environment—its own *how*—are being overcome. Such survival is basic to the lessons of the course. The importance of prevailing against the drive toward expressive standardization is a contrarian value to be inferred from some of the poems themselves, and the best example of this inference can be found in how the crowd deals with another short poem of Dickinson's, one that we will closely consider in this chapter.

That crowd is not a hive mind. Not only in the conversational thread about dwelling but also, from what I have seen, pretty much everywhere, they tarry, delay, perplex, stun, welcome heresy, invite stupor, and relish in error. They are the self-founding audience Cabri discovered for PhillyTalks at the Writers House—participating in a live proceduralism. They have the multiplicity yet consonance of purpose of "the people" who become characters in Sandburg's *The People, Yes*: they "take what comes, hold on, let go," the public poet observed, and that is how "they feel their crowds and *read* crowd moods."[8] A populist troubadour singing verse to huge audiences, Sandburg saw how the crowd generates moods and meaning, and I'm certain that, as a folk poet ingesting every locution of the moment, he would have taken no exception to the clumsily phrased idea of "user-generated content"—although another way to think of it, as journalist Jon Pareles suggested when exasperated in the 2000s by that buzz-phrase, is as "something a little more old-fashioned: *self-expression*."[9]

Janet, Rahana, Jim, Charles, and Thea—self-expressive people with noncommercial voluntaristic ambitions—met up in a subforum space for a few days in September 2023 and decided on their own that their job was to redraw "the road map to the House" of Possibility. They rethought the key idea of the course: poetry makes a fairer space than prose. By reveling in etymological musings, they created a good instance of "attention no one had the chance to resell." I quote the phrase from Tim Wu's *The Attention Merchants* (2016).[10] Going against every big digital trend Wu describes—and avoiding the costs of distraction he identifies in the attention economy—these new friends' asynchronous accumulations are designed to be nontransferable and nonpackageable. This crowd found a free home with an open door, not in spite of that but because of it; one could say it is a temporary refuge, flimsy for its digitality, susceptible to eviction. Nonetheless, it is an enduring idea of home. Sara Hendren's *What Can a Body Do?* describes this paradox of tenuousness and durability. Working with Bachelard's presentation of inhabited space as having "the notion of home" to support the case for a new social model for thinking about people who have difficulty navigating spaces, Hendren pushed hard at the etymology of *dwell* and *inhabit* just as our group did to get back to the Latin root *habere*. For Hendren, inhabiting means to have and to hold but also to give and receive. Planning to stay necessitates a conversation. Dwelling in *What Can a Body Do?* is ample interaction, the movement back and forth and among, on the analogy of a single human body trying to navigate its world.[11]

Uncertainty-Aware Planning

During one of the visits to Philadelphia made by Coursera founders Daphne Koller and Andrew Ng in early 2012, Koller visited the Kelly Writers House for a tour and a further meeting about the quirky needs of ModPo. She immediately understood the analogy we drew from the MOOC to the space of the Writers House as a free and open literary commons, and she was supportive in response to my worries about the lecture-centered site design thwarting that correlation. She listened with interest to my telling of the story of the metamorphosis of Samuel Sloan's cottage into a subject village where writing is not just for writers. Soon after that visit, she put me and Chris Martin, the friendly technologist on my staff who was also new to such scaled-up initiatives, directly in contact with Pang Wei Koh, the young staffer at Coursera—in fact, as noted earlier, the third employee after Koller and Ng.

Pang Wei Koh was coordinating the building and rebuilding of the discussion forums and essay-submission module, which also had not been amenable to our pedagogy. We wanted essays to be ungraded and peer-reviewed through unformatted, plain-text commentary. We spent the summer and fall of 2012 working alongside Pang Wei to build out the forum system (inventing poem-by-poem subforums, etc.) even, after a certain point, *while* the initial enrollees—then already numbering 36,500—were starting to use them. It was concerted fix-by-fix chaos, requiring every bit of interactive improvisation on his end as on ours as we chose to present our roster of disordered poems. Professing eclectic aesthetics and advocating for comfort with interpretive chaos deserved a technical groundwork that somehow aligned with our case against digital minimalism. Perhaps it was an impossible ask. Anthony Kolasny, a biomedical engineer among the founding ModPo crowd and, as it happens, a lifelong friend of Mark Nowak (the Rancière fan and author of *Social Poetics*), urged us to argue with the technologists that ModPo should "stay in 'perpetual beta.'" A member of the Breakfast Club (the global asynchronous poetry meetup occurring daily in "the morning" despite the numerous time zones of its breakfasters), Anthony explained that technology should be engineered "as beta" to listen for "the openness of the worldwide voice." "Education and tech innovation," he insisted, "should be a community effort and constantly evolve. We are *all* making it better."[12]

During a conversation with me in 2024, Pang Wei recalled grappling with the idea—novel, at least to him, in the new world of building MOOCs—of the dynamic design problem facing us in that pairing:

$$\text{entropic poem} \rightarrow \text{complex system}$$

ModPo, he remembers, was the first humanities MOOC requiring some fresh programming at the newfangled back end of the platform. Once our conversations about poetry drew him toward "a visceral appreciation of what the humanities brings to people that is different from math or programming," which was itself "eye-opening," he then took on the task of conveying what he called "the poetry of it" to the busy software engineering team he led, an idea for proceeding that was then somehow transliterated into adjustments in the code.[13]

Pang Wei Koh is now a tenured professor of computer science engineering and counts among his specialties how computing models can be made "more trustworthy" and "how AI systems best augment and interact with their human end-users."[14] I like to think that what was a nettlesome—but also, as he recalls, unexpected and exhilarating—five months of back-and-forth with a teacher of "difficult" poetry adamantly devoted to his progressive pedagogy, the ignorant schoolmaster in the school of the MOOC, has perhaps shaped his developing academic research interests (for instance, in problems of accounting for diversity in LLMs). If that is the case, it would be commensurate with the effect it has had on me as I have reconceived the rationale for having founded the Writers House seventeen years prior. The goal of programming—of building an entity—is to reduce that which impedes objectives and outcomes. How do we square that with goals valuing frictional aesthetic experiences?

These real technical considerations—and the process of them: collaborative cross-discipline testing of a perfectly flawed machine for massive numbers of individuals simultaneously interpreting unsolvable poems—became fundamental to the subsequent developments of the Writers House itself as *more commons than salon*, as a site of public in-person exchange, an export *back* from the emergent digital commons to the daily methods of the denizens of Sloan's cozy cottage. Reverse engineering for the communitarian *salonniers*. When it was created by its thirty-five or so cofounders, students, faculty, university staff, and local artists, the Writers House was designed to have some aspects of various models in a great post-midcentury tradition of poetry projects preceding it—ideas, elements, and methods drawn unsystematically from the Poetry Project (founded in 1966); the San Francisco Poetry Center (1954); the Teachers and Writers Collective (1967); Bard's IWT (1982); the Kootenay School of Writing (1984); the series and scenes at Woodland Pattern Books in Milwaukee (1980); Small Press Traffic (1974); the refusal of the correct possessive in the name of Bob Cobbing's "Writers [not Writers'] Forum" (c. 1963); the lighting and overall feel of familiarity of the Nuyorican Poets Cafe (1973); the Segue Reading Series (1978); New Langton Arts (1975); the intentional intergenerational spirit of Burning Deck Press (1961); Corman's radio show "This Is Poetry" (1949–1962); the "Talks Series" in Berkeley curated in the late 1970s and early 1980s by Bob Perelman (a Writers House cofounder and a Language poet featured in the ModPo syllabus); even a touch of the idiosyncratic residentialism of Black Mountain College, which had been formed partly on Deweyite principles. But now, to all those somewhat obvious field-specific and genre-adjacent influences, we were adding the new digital modeling Pang Wei Koh called home, with its new kind of role opacity. I admit that, at first, I didn't see how Pang Wei's world could have anything to do with those scenes at Segue Series readings or at Bard or Burning Deck. Still, at least for Chris Martin, Julia Bloch, and me, as we worked closely with Pang Wei, we would need to concoct some sort of actualization of these values and ideas of "architecture" (that favorite programmer's word) as language in the ModPo site. It was one thing to create an architecture where people entering the space didn't feel that what was written or said in a language was a foreign language in the same language, quite another to invite tens of thousands beyond such congenial confines to break with expressive convention while tolerating, or sometimes ignoring, what the wiring of the space prejudicially assumed of us.

On his end, as it turns out, Pang Wei Koh was also seeking a break from any such prejudice. Perhaps it even beckoned an alternative path to professionalization. A dozen years later, after all, he was coauthoring a paper on "uncertainty of thoughts" in LLMs and on "uncertainty-aware planning."[15] When we talked, he summed up our 2012 experience in four emphatic words: *It was all improvised.* And he meant it most positively, as nerve-wracking as it might have been at the time. He was pointing out the mix and exchange of hard and soft skills necessitated by our collaboration. As ModPo participant Mark Marziale contemplated the alternative paths inscribed through Dickinson's brain-teasing poems, he also realized the fundamental contradiction of typical field distinctions. Coming to ModPo after decades in software development, Mark decided that "the hard sciences and soft sciences should switch titles."[16] He was partly joking, as he later recalled for me how and why he found poetry hard after decades of programming.

But Mark was also being serious. Retirement from a life in computing didn't mean postcareer deprofessionalization so much as a chance to break from how the vocational mind assesses its problems. He finally wanted to learn how to talk across fields. This was not so unlike Pang Wei and me, although we were both very much enmeshed in careers. "Very often," Clay Shirky once commented in an interview about barriers to collective thinking, "professionalization means that the designers spend a lot of time talking to other designers, the sociologists spend a lot of time talking to other sociologists, the engineers to engineers, and so on. And there's obvious benefit there in terms of raising the state of the art within one of those professions. But there's a loss there of the kinds of insights or alternate points of view that can come from other places."[17] To repair that "loss," Mark Marziale joined ModPo. The poem he most delighted in discussing, Dickinson's "The Brain within its Groove"—we will soon take a look at that poem—is also about that kind of loss.

THE COMPANIONABLE CROWD

In solitude the trumpets of solitude
Are not of another solitude resounding;
A little string speaks for a crowd of voices.

—Wallace Stevens, "Notes Toward a Supreme Fiction"

I write this as ModPo approaches its fourteenth year, with an enrollment of 90,716 people. I try to keep track of new enrollees. Although, as I compose these sentences, we are in the SloPo off-season, nonetheless, each week, some 240 new learners join. The ModPoPLUS syllabus has grown to nine times the size of the main syllabus. The initial group instinct against decluttering, first an idea in revolt against xMOOC syllabus limits, and later a proud general attitude, now manifests itself in a superabundance of cross-related poems, complex nested sub-forum chats, and complexly categorized videos that memorialize all manner of over one thousand get-togethers posted to three media storage platforms. My opening chapters conveyed the idea that poetry that formally does what its content says is itself a subject matter useful for responding to the challenge the original coconveners accepted: an open online course, including its technical aspects, will admit and own the kind of disruptive noise—the intruders—such that the dissonances of the gathered crowd can be heard. We drew as much from Pang Wei Koh's then-new mass-networking technologist's "visceral appreciation" of our approach to nonstandard knowledge as from the poethical methods of the humanistic leaders of, for example, Bard's IWT. When it has functioned well, ModPo has been the sort of confluence where teachers and students create "a shift in the social organization of learning and what counts as knowledge."[18] This has been a social shift from gatekeeping to open-sourcing, and the adjustment is meant to set in motion a new sort of civic capacity. If crowds can be free to think abundantly and irrelevantly, there will be a public quality to their thinking regardless of the publicly reputed marginality of the topic.

The Wisdom of Crowds

James Surowiecki was among the first to report comprehensively on that freedom. In *The Wisdom of Crowds* (2004), he summarized a great deal of evidence that had already accumulated to suggest that under certain conditions, a large, heterogeneous group of people will offer better or more accurate responses to a question or problem than that offered by one or a few experts. It is hardly a coincidence that Surowiecki's study, and then Jeff Howe's famous field-naming article "The Rise of Crowdsourcing" (published in *Wired* in June 2006), emerged when they did, only a few years into the era of Web 2.0, the time of sharing, crosslinking, folksonomies,[19] and for some people, a preference for participation over publishing.

Here's a version of the question I've been asking, now amended through a study of crowdsourcing: How do credentialed scholars and teachers fare—*and what becomes of their profession*—when presenting difficult texts in the context of thousands of global readers with little overall interpretive experience yet strong voluntaristic motivation and a collective aptitude for intense microattention? The hermeneutic and pedagogical roles of the expert once again converge after many postwar decades having been separated and isolated.

Certain modes of organization-led (or "top-down"[20]) idea-harvesting, outsourcing answers to answerable questions, fact-gathering or confirmations, or discovering solutions to challenging yet solvable problems—such as we see in the effects of crowd-fixing, crowd-solving, macroscopic pattern recognition, human computation, microwork (series of tiny discrete processes), crowd-coaching, crowd-jobbing, even "crowd dreaming" activities that have reached beyond for-profit corporate projects into the fields of citizen science and citizen journalism[21]—can further extend to cultural archiving and curation,[22] and even art-making.[23] So-called distant reading practices have been introduced by digital humanities projects, including literary history, by way of large-scale analyses of data gathered by and about crowds. I've been arguing that that analysis can also succeed if applied to close rather than distant reading—to the work of a few lines of imaginative writing whose meaning is eventually discernible as a big shape of human response.

Stuart Dunn and Mark Hedges, writing about humanities crowdsourcing, reminded us that in most instances the goal is (mere) crowd-fixing, as "the barriers to participation are relatively low" and "the core tasks are straightforward, self-contained and relatively easily learned." But Dunn and Hedges set out to discover "how the crowd can surprise us,"[24] and that aim aligns with my original goals. We, too, through the active choice of writing that is not straightforward, orderly, or self-contained, have been considering: What does typical crowdsourcing have to do with disjunctive subject matter, where consecutive logic and figuration go off course? What is the value of previous experience when the current work of understanding extends far beyond that experience?

This is not a problem usually faced by the bona fide expert, for whom the point of the work is often to define a problem being addressed and then to seek and find a cessation in the definitional effort so evidence-gathering takes shape and finalizing observations can be offered. Such a project stops or imagines a stopping point. But there seem to be few endings sought in any corner of the massively responsive readership, and that stance is related to the refusal of most of these people to aspire to the role or status of specialist or expert. David Blaine, a 2012–2013 ModPo learner, persisted and flourished once he realized he could opt for that refusal. "True, we come to the point where our experience with a poem ends," he observed of the crowd of amateur readers, "but we keep going."[25]

The Lonely Crowd

The term *crowd* is deeply problematic, participants in a community-sourcing project will tell you: they are no unity. Nor need they remain at all unindividuated for long. "Crowd *wisdom*," striking for its premise of sagacity, is only partly a recuperation of praise for what ModPo people achieve together. Gustave Le Bon's founding modern negative connotations of crowd members—irritability, incapacity to reason, absence of the sane critical faculty[26]—were shaped by the ideologies of their time.[27] They are generalizations biased as a method against individual identity formation. As we know through the experiences of José Reyes, Sophia Naz, Nicole Braun, Raymond M., Dan Bergmann, Laura De Bernardi, and others, each member of the crowd tells a distinct story of the meaning of collaboration.

The history of the crowd's usage was, for a long while, at least partly neutral and useful. A verb at its origin—to press, to fill a space, also to hasten on—*crowd* only belatedly became an English noun signifying the mass of spectators, back then still positive enough: for example, in the fortunate scene, at least for the playwright and producer of a jam-packed Globe Theatre, a throng mentioned in the *Oxford English Dictionary* entry for the early noun. But modern connotations, starting with Charles Mackay's *Extraordinary Popular Delusions and the Madness of Crowds* (1841) and Le Bon's *The Crowd: A Study of the Popular Mind* (1895), profiled people behaving differently when massed, madly descending rungs on the ladder of civilization. In the 1930s, "the masses" were taken up by the Left for constructive use, while "crowd" was pushed further toward suggestions of ominous group behavior. Crowds were for adoration of fascists; the U.S. communist *New Masses*, conversely, a serious literary journal especially between 1934 and 1939, regularly featured a connotative consistency between mass collectivity and the creative generous refinements of the people's artists. But not so much "the crowd." In the mid-1930s verse of Horace Gregory, a prominent *New Masses* poet, a homeless worker was an individual looking to join a "chorus for survival" by desperately *avoiding* the "trampling down / All under . . . / In crowds, crowds over crowds." The triumphant chorus would be a mass. The crowds were those who sought to prevent the worker's song.[28] Herbert Blumer's "Collective Behavior" (1939) focused not just on crowds forming and evolving but also on how they could be dispersed. Then came the 1950s, with its centrist anticommunist consolidations, its steadfast prosurburbanism, and with that, its ambivalent half-worrying, half-complaining about the routine life of the white-collar worker and sociological concerns about factors such as the negative ideological effects of collective bargaining. David Riesman's *The Lonely Crowd*, even without any anticipation of networked collaboration, forms the most direct link decades forward to Jeff Howe's claims, Yochai Benkler (*The Wealth of Networks*), Jimmy Wales's Wikipedia, and the problems and possibilities of the many networked projects that Surowieki, Shirky, Don Tapscott and Anthony D. Williams (in *Wikinomics* of 2006), and others described in the 2000s.

The Lonely Crowd identified three cultural types, one (roughly speaking) giving way to the next and then to the third: tradition-directed, inner-directed, and other-directed people. Other-direction, which Riesman and his colleagues found increasingly dominant in postwar America, responds attentively (although sometimes for the wrong reasons) to social forces. Translated into interpretive collective problem-solving, other-directedness should be supportive in the networked situation, deriving advantages from orientation to community, even at the risk (which Riesman points out) of no longer holding to previous standards of the cohesive society. But being an other-directed member of the crowd means loneliness, and a society—or a project—populated by other-directed people will supposedly be deficient in leadership and potential. Leaving aside that this critique of other-directedness is deeply rooted in the anticrowd (and anticommunist) biases of its postwar moment in ways *The Lonely Crowd* (1950) leaves unexamined—exactly as Daniel Bell's *The End of Ideology* (1960) does at the end of the decade—when we turn to Riesman's anxious assessment of the state of education, we can see its long after-effect on cultural assumptions about crowdsourcing in the 2000s and in the arguments made against MOOCs in the 2010s.

The harsh case made in *The Lonely Crowd* against the other-directed teacher will remind us of the anticonstructivist conservatism that continued to decry Dewey's influence on rejections of closure in education when that attitude was being revived in the 1960s and soon began to shape ideas about creativity— witness people like Lewis Warsh, Bernadette Mayer, and their friends; Kenneth

Koch's Writers in the Schools project; the enormous influence of poets who in the 1950s had been at Black Mountain College with its Deweyite ideas about noncurricular apprenticeship; and the Language and Black Arts poets arising generationally out of *The Poverty of Student Life*. Riesman's (unintentionally?[29]) conservative assessment of American schools will be familiar from the backlashes we've examined against asynchronicity, digital collective imagination, the learning space as a cocreative made place, and the end of the lecture. Riesman's interpretive summary begins:

> Progressive education began as a movement to liberate children from the crushing of talent and breaking of will that was the fate of many. . . . Its aim, and to a very considerable degree, its achievement, was to develop the individuality of the child. . . . [Teachers in the progressive system] are, increasingly, young college graduates who have been taught to be more concerned with social and psychological adjustment than with [the student's] academic progress. . . . This looks progressive, looks like a salute to creativeness and individuality; but again we meet paradox. While the school deemphasizes grades and report cards, the displays [i.e., student art on classroom walls] seem almost to ask the children: "Mirror, mirror on the wall, who is fairest of us all?"
>
> While the children's paintings and montages show considerable imaginative gift in the preadolescent period, the school itself is nevertheless one of the agencies for the destruction of fantasy. . . . Imagination withers.[30]

This was the supposed narcissism of liberal conformist other-direction. By the end of the passage, you realize that he's bitterly mocking "the movement to liberate children." Rereading *The Lonely Crowd* well into the era of digital collective intelligence, I miss any role played by cognitive hetereogeneity. The predominance of other-direction in education indicates for Riesman a worrisome "breakdown of walls between teacher and pupil," and then, in turn, a "break[ing] down [of] walls between student and student."[31]

Surely, the metaphor of the wall is the trouble here. For Riesman, such role opacity causes a problem in the content people should know. He noticed that the tumbling of walls in America's classrooms "permitt[ed] th[e] rapid circulation of tastes"—deleterious, miserably poor styles, merely *popular* tastes—as crucial canonical lessons in who the great Julius Caesar was and what happened to the cultural life at Pompeii were sadly being replaced by a progressive "realism" through which learners in class read stories about trains and telephones (mere modern technologies!) and receive happy, tender tales of "race relations of the United Nations or our Latin American neighbors."[32]

As I reread this tendentious assessment, I thought of Julia Carey Arendell, erica kaufman's teacher-mentee-student, presenting Stein's *Tender Buttons* in a class on crossover art in a New Orleans school in connection with visual artwork by Beyoncé and a homework assignment that involved making an Instagram reel (the short informal first-person POV video). The walls of Arendell's classroom had tumbled down long before the Stein assignment. The "rapid circulation of tastes" crowded by her students and crowdsourced from that month's current vlog reel memes and methods—such circulation is itself the curriculum (crossover art) and was always at the heart of Stein's method, the companionable continuous present in composition as explanation—made for exactly the other-directed realism Riesman satirized, by which, according to him, imagination withers.

AND TRODDEN OUT THE SCHOOLS

For Jon Avnet

Organized Disorganization

When David Blaine told us that "we keep going" despite the ModPo crowd reaching the end of an experience with a poem, he, like Mark Marziale, mentioned Dickinson's "The Brain, within its Groove" as a prime example. It is a poem that seems to be about intellection without cessation. It is about thinking at the edge of chaos,[33] and the *way* it is written falls toward the same edge. That precipitous falling causes readers to think chaotically, especially when they attempt with others to comprehend where the poem is going. This remarkable bit of eccentric writing has become one of those anthemic artworks that strikes people as being in the flow of—and is also *about*—the course. There are others that function self-reflexively too, as we have seen: Niedecker's "Poet's Work," Stein's "A Long Dress," Corman's "It isnt for want," Hunt's "Reader we were meant to meet," Eigner's "a structured field," Morris's "Africa(n)," and more. But because participants encounter it in the first week of ModPo, Dickinson's brain poem is the one that sets off the flux. If the brain is "let" to "swerve" from a thought, Dickinson suggests, the same brain cannot restore any of its regular running. The result is a verbal fission releasing enormous power, destructive of previous thinking, although offering good health overall for the creative mind that lets the work happen. To achieve such health is the foremost aim of the course. The poem is an instance of the rampant remedial imaginative power it describes:

> The Brain, within its Groove
> Runs evenly—and true—
> But let a Splinter swerve—
> 'Twere easier for You—
>
> To put a Current back—
> When Floods have slit the Hills—
> And scooped a Turnpike for Themselves—
> And trodden out the Mills—[34]

"The Brain" has been discussed line by line, word by word, by thousands of people, while at least one hundred thousand have witnessed the proceedings. Others who read the collaborative interpretation of this poem have commented elsewhere, connecting "The Brain" with other poems and most other parts of the course. The discussion within this poem's subforum has been entirely self-organized into 463 titled topical threads, many of them numerous screens in length. Not one of these threads was created, named, or directed by any leader or convener. Within the threads, there have been posted some eight thousand comments, questions, responses, and direct replies. By a partial count,[35] it seems that a total of some 103,000 people have seen the comments, and this number doesn't include posts to external social media that continue the conversation outside the main ModPo site, which perhaps doubles the total readerly population.

The content of the conversation is never to be mastered by the instructor. And given that "working the crowd" is always, to some degree, as Lior Zoref puts it in his book *Mindsharing*, a matter of "managing digital relationships" and "finding your crowd" as a form of "building [a] new network" with its personal as well as professional and even political connotations,[36] it's a real question as to the ultimate appropriateness or even relevance of my involvement—the matter raised by Laura De Bernardi, as we saw when she advocated avoiding the views of the instructor. The crowd's intelligence, of its own devices, is sometimes moved by a sudden flood of responses, a rapid in the stream. It can also drift slowly across months and even years of the crowd's rereading. When Shirky offered the following summary of the thesis of *Here Comes Everybody: The Power of Organizing without Organizations* (2008), it might as well have been a commentary on Dickinson's conception of the brain and the organized disorganization of the response to it: "Most of the barriers to group action have collapsed," Shirky contends, "and without those barriers, we are free to explore new ways of gathering together and getting things done." In conducting his research on disorganized organizing, Shirky affirmed a conclusion that "one simple form of cooperation, almost universal with social tools, is conversation" and that "conversation creates more of a sense of community than sharing does,"[37] even as it introduces risks of the sort we see when Dickinson's mind-sharing splinters and goes awry, sweeping up readers along with it.

Dickinson was and is a loner of a kind, certainly biographically and in several ways poetically, but *a* brain's dissolution is not what this poem seems to be about. The speaker refers to "*the* Brain," not "*my* Brain," and the crowd identifies their own collective intelligence through conversation in response to that generic species plural. At the same time, individuation among the supposedly lonely crowd is discernible. Individual talents and personal interests emerge. Dickinson's confounding poem is a locus for the push and pull of people's close and distant readings and for the very meaning of the term *distance* (with its connotations both of impersonality and digitality). In the hectic multivocal colloquy, one of the crowd, our Mark Marziale, suddenly felt a metapoetic turn coming on—and then, expressing it as criticism of the course caused a bend in the flow of conversation. I will attempt to describe what happened.

Let the Splinter Swerve

Mark had been, as mentioned, in the midst of shifting his personal interests from hard knowledge to soft. After thirty-five years as a software developer in San Francisco and Chicago, he retired and stumbled into ModPo. He attended seminars of the in-person meetup group convened by ModPo TA Max McKenna at Chicago public libraries (I joined one of these), sessions that were video-recorded and then added to ModPoPLUS. To judge from his forum comments in general, it seems to me that Mark was at first more curious about digital community-building than about the poetry. If after a long single-field career one finds (in his words) "that once you've moved off your settled assumptions, a kaleidoscope of possibilities could open up," he now encountered a poem that itself said as much. He discovered in ModPo, as he recalled for me a decade later, that "tech work . . . is easier than trying to figure out social problems,"[38] and his active interlocutors in the lively subforum for "The Brain" have come to represent, for me, a characteristic range. It is a remarkable group, and like Janet, Rahana, Jim, Charles, and Thea, they constructed an arbitrary yet meaningful convergence. Through Dickinson, this contingent of the ModPo people found themselves addressing the "social problems" Mark had been wanting to face as he turned from tech to poetry.

So who are they? One way to see them is as a cast of characters in a many-handed drama of many brains. But no one scripts roles or distributes a program. They come and go, performing inadvertent parts upon the big asynchronous stage. Mark was joined by Juan Pablo Laso of Quito, Ecuador, then a student of microfinancing; Linda Dunlavy, a grant writer at the Hadley Institute for the Blind and Visually Impaired in Chicago; Yves Y., then a high-school student who was writing intrepid, experimental queer poetry and was a lively participant in the classroom close reading of Stein held in Palo Alto; the late and much-missed ModPo original, John Knight, a Quaker active with the pacifist Alternatives to Violence Project in Maryland's prisons and a member of the first ModPo Breakfast Club; Maria do Socorro Baptista Barbosa, a teacher of literature at a public university in Brazil; Yosuke Tanaka, a chemical engineer and translator living in Tokyo who later filmed discussions in person at the Writers House about the influence of imagism on Japanese poetry and still later contributed an essay on Ezra Pound's orientalist imagism to the ModPo anthology *The Difference Is Spreading: Fifty Contemporary Poets on Fifty Poems* (2022); Mandana Chaffa, an Iranian-American former NASDAQ employee for whom Persian is a first language, a thirteen-year repeater of the course who has hosted meetups through a partnership she created on behalf of ModPo with the New York Public Library; Benita Kape, who lives in Tairawhiti on the East Coast of New Zealand, composes haiku, and was then caring full-time for her disabled husband (since deceased); Robert Boucher, an octogenarian former engineer and haiku poet residing in Los Angeles who attended in-person meetups organized by TA Molly O'Neill and posts verse to *All Poetry*[39]; Nancy Rueda Santos, a financial analyst in Monterrey, Mexico; Mary Armour of Cape Town, South Africa, whose contributions to the ModPo forums since 2016 alone occupy sixty-two screens; Luke Patrick Fortier, a Boston-based accountant who has worked in the biotech industry; Dan Bergmann, the autistic teenager featured in Thomas Friedman's ecstatic first column about MOOCs;[40] Jeremy Dixon, the poet and maker of handmade art books in Wales whose comments on Niedecker and poet's work we explored earlier; Katherine Price, who didn't hesitate to take issue with interpretations I seemed to be pushing; and Sonya Arnold, an occupational therapy assistant in the Chocktaw, Oklahoma, school district specializing in supporting children with brain injuries. Sonya commended ModPo's "awesome diversity" and explained that her motive for enrolling in the course was "to become 'me.' "[41] How much of a stretch is it to contend that such an assembly, with its range of professional interests, backgrounds, language cultures, and personal experiences, will produce readings of a poem that, all told, could hold their own with those of experienced teachers of Dickinson and even professional critics?

Luke Patrick Fortier, with his combination of biotech engineering and business experience in New England (a region that is home, after all, to the doomed mill Dickinson imagines), initiates a thread to problem-solve the equation of the brain (neurology/imagination) and the mill (industrial technology/reality). Sonya, with her expertise in brain injury, becomes the fortuitous respondent to Fortier, redefining the question as being a matter of allowing or "let[ting]" the "splinter [to] swerve" a brain that cannot but go in such a direction. We should focus, she says, on "the rush of something new." Given the quantity of respondents, the convergence of Mark, Luke, and Sonya (among many others) cannot properly be described as accidental. A better term to explain the gathering would be the one used by Pang Wei Koh and his colleagues: uncertainty-aware planning.

The poem triggers an awareness of the interpretive confluence just described: its disorderly inevitability. It seems to be about a mind that inexorably tends to swerve from its train of thought. Swerving becomes intransitive, objectless. Its activity is a source of power greater than those real objects which, in the world outside the mind, people have historically constructed to constrain and direct water, which with infamous irresistibility has, as it were, a mind of its own. Yet the poem is not just about this uncompromising natural phenomenon. As verbal figuration and poetic form, it becomes an instance of the swerve described in its telling.

Because the brain presented as content in the poem operates in the mode of the poem, and also so much in the mode of people reading it—because, in other words, the meaning of the poem is the brain's response to it; because the poem's thinking about thinking swerves—creative power derives not from concentration or direct attention, nor from running evenly, but from digression, overload, improvisation, illogic, inconsistency, and inattention to standard distinctions between body and mind. Positively overwhelmed by shared understanding, at times feeling (and expressing) a risky form of derealization, the lay learners try to "stop thinking," as Dewey put it in *How We Think*. "But the flow of suggestions goes on in spite of our will," Dewey explains, "quite as surely as our bodies feel."[42]

The People Have the Power of Water

For Dan Bergmann, Dickinson's speaker's struggle with the body's mind is a major personal theme, and he and I have discussed that struggle variously over the years. A dozen years after he first began to read the poem, I asked him to speculate on why so many ModPo learners identify with the digressive situation it depicts. "The splinter is the key," he told me. "When people's brains mean the groove, other people line up to tell them they are overreacting. So I think people find themselves in the poem and want to be free from . . . [*there followed repeated vocalizations that sounded to me like the words* piracy *and* pirouette—*thirty-six seconds of what Dan calls his "processing time" and which he insisted that I try to include here;*[43] *then followed by:*] People don't want to work so hard to stay in the groove. And yet that's what most people do most of the time."[44]

Insofar as "The Brain" is about how neuro-difference can be depicted neuro-differently, the crowd collaboratively interpreting it comes to not only comprehend but also embody Dickinson's idea about the power of distributed cognition. In other words, the group arrives at this inconclusiveness through its own version of just such a distribution, an approximation of "what most people do most of the time" without demanding coherence. The ModPo citizenry can see themselves as having the power of water. They cannot help but swerve, and they don't seem to worry about cognitive overload.

The mass interpretation of the poem—each person deciding upon a reading while observing choices made by others—causes what Surowiecki and network theorists identify as an information cascade.[45] Jonathan Spira, in his contribution to the proliferation of books in the 2010s about information overload, describes "how too much information is hazardous to your organization."[46] It it? Always? The organization of ModPo is hardly threatened by the unplanned overflow of its participants. The only top-down organizational goal directing the crowd's responses here is the presence of a particular poem as syllabus content that doesn't behave inertly the way instructional content often does. Dickinson's "The Brain" converts its own failure to disrupt into a disruptive innovation by digressing from its role as a piece of writing carrying subject matter—that is, whatever it is that seems initially to be "even and true."

In her long commentary on the metaphor of the implied millwheel, Katherine Price contemplates the parallel between what happens after the "Splinter" diverts the poem's attention and our attention as reader-interpreters of a metaphor meant to explain writing that keeps bringing us "full circle" to its comparing. "The Splinter is poetry itself," Katherine writes. Her intervention ponders the circling of the wheel *metaphor*, as we collectively understand swerving figuration, "but we cannot 'put it back' into our former concept of it" once it's out there as a viable interpretation offered: "We are no longer in control of it [our reading of the Mill as a figure of destructiveness] . . . and in some ways *we* have been washed away." If we make available to the crowd "a meta-poetic method," in Katherine's phrase, then the social network—turning in on itself as a wayward-tending collective imagination—"cannot 'put it back.'" The poem's proliferation of read-ings cannot be redacted or minimized any more than Dickinson's own mind-sharing.[47] The information cascade becomes a group-identifying flow state—a case against concerns about information overload, a form of maximal experience.

This is just the first among poems in the ModPo syllabus that frame con-versations like the one in which a mill is said to be like a school. A skeptical version of a question participants ask as they discuss is this: How is my read-ing of this poem being shaped by what ModPo seems to want me to think? Is that not like a mill whose site needs reassessment? The counteradvocacy against discontinuity—the view that Dickinson's speaker actually *prefers* running evenly and true and *rues* her thinking when it wanders astray—can become a disrup-tion of the teaching. This is how Mark Marziale suddenly expressed his dis-agreement with the interpretation of the poem he believed I and my team were pushing too hard:

> I enjoyed the video discussion of the poem, but my impression was not that she was advocating for wild roaming thoughts but rather that the brain will naturally (in its Groove) run evenly and true (straight and accurately). Then she shows the destruction of that process by distraction or diversion (the splinter). So my feeling was she was saying we have a natural tendency to think clearly and well. But once distracted we have no hope of forcing our brain back on its original path. Still, the brain within its groove may find its way back on its own. I enjoy the opposite conclusion, that she was arguing for the value of diversion, but I don't see anything in the text that supports that. Just my 2 cents.[48]

This is a plausible critique of the video.[49] In it, a group of (presumably) academic people, filmed inside a house for writers at an élite U.S. university, will tend to "advocate for wild roaming thoughts" because that's what intellectuals do, even if the poet's writing does not "support" the reading they project onto it. That projection is ideological, implies Mark and, to some extent, Katherine. But they know—of the course, not just the flood in the poem—that there's no turning back. The irresistible flooding of the discussion prompted by the official ModPo video—both are sources of power—has created an awareness of a "forcing" that will flow just as wildly, even in the opposite direction, as a result of dissent.

Because ModPo participants are aware that the MOOC phenomenon has been under attack by various factions in higher education, their ideas about the Dickinsonian mind take on a metapedagogical inflection. The doomed factory-powering mill, subject to the brain's creative destruction, is also subject to that of the crowd encountering any appearance of a normatively productive institution in the course. In this reading, the mill is the classroom in the industrial mode, where learners, normally seeking to be even and true, do not swerve in time to stay ahead of the poet's brain going awry. The poem can be said to unleash its out-of-the-box power against, and actually to imagine the destruction of, the kind of "knowledge industry" launched and lauded by people like UC Berkeley chancellor Clark Kerr[50]—leaders of the big postwar diploma mill—at a tipping point in the expansion of research universities into massive superstructures. The doubts of Katherine and Mark represent an ironic and dissenting interpretive turn for the swerving ModPo crowd, especially considering that, for its many antagonists, the xMOOC conformed all too logically from Kerr's vision of productive higher-ed giganticness and, finally, in the 2010s, pushed that vision globally out to millions. Katherine's key phrase, "*We* have been washed away," applies to the course and to its precarious situation among institutions of education.

Will the cascade of ModPo learners overrun it? Was ModPo the mill? The very first crowdsourced video—genially copycatting the ModPo leaders at the Writers House—would pose similarly challenging questions. The final chapter starts with the story of that rejoinder.

CHAPTER 8

PLANNING TO STAY

Misunderstanding opens up new vistas that the person trying to be understood never thought of.

—Dan Bergmann

Power is measured by the inspired output of others.

—Wai Chee Dimock

TALKING BACK

Steal the Plums, Nick the Video

The CCCR syllabus—the archive of Community Collaborative Close Readings—was launched when, during the inaugural season of the course, three Scottish participants decided that Tom Leonard's "Just ti Let Yi know," a rejoinder to William Carlos Williams's "This is Just to Say," formed an insightful criticism of Williams's appetitious domestic thieving of the refrigerated plums.

JIST TI LET YI NO

(from the American of Carlos Williams)

ahv drank
thi speshlz
that wurrin
thi frij

n thit
yiwurr probbli
hodn back
furthi parti

awright
they wur great
thaht stroang
thaht cawld[1]

The Scottish participants explained that the most appropriate way to respond to the ModPo video about Williams's poem was to record their own.[2]

This first video rejoinder was conceived by Sean Donnelly, a ModPo learner whose day job was as business manager for the Prince's Trust in Scotland, which supports young people between the ages of eleven and thirty needing education or training for work. Sean joined Nancy Somerville, a poet, former community teacher, and organizer of writers workshops, and Lorrane Borwick, a "lifelong learning worker" with the City of Edinburgh Council. They gathered in a flat in Edinburgh to film a genial mock or copycat close reading. To replace the cups of coffee and tea at the abstemious ModPo table inside the Kelly Writers House, they each drank from a chilled tall can of Scottish beer—in itself a knowing nod back to Ivy academia from the supposed provincial crowd. The three in the video, while they interpret, drink from cans of the same "special" Leonard's speaker has pilfered from the frij in the poem. While imitating and thus crediting the ModPo method—wearing T-shirts that read "THIS IS JUST TO SAY ModPo 2012 IS PURE DEAD BRILLIANT BY THE WAY"—they were at the same time responding to American dominance in modernism, to programmatic claims by Williams and others for the great experiment in "local" "contact" (two of Williams's favorite terms) through the use of demotic language, a localism that Leonard outdoes through his Scots. The three were also responding to the implied claim by Williams that his original domestic stealth—he takes his wife's plums—is authentically raunchy and audacious and thus heretical. Comprehending a contextual intra-English deradicalization, Sean Donnelly suggests that in Williams's poem, the plums and icebox "all seem . . . set and stable and kind of . . . less fluid." When Sean adds that, in contrast, Leonard's poem is "more fluid," he means "more fluid of a poem." But he is also eyeing his own can of Tennent's Special on the table in front of him. The fluidity of content invites cascade as a form. Lorrane responds with a comment about language and culture. Leonard's poem is translated "from the American" of Williams, and the rejoinder, she adds, "may be more fluid because it's in our language and we can understand it and it's almost a cultural thing with the special, and it's something we can relate to." "[A]hv drank / thi speshlz" is deemed by these three ModPo citizens as liquescent, runny writing, the opposite (despite other similarities) of the effect created by the pinpoint set-piece contrivance Williams constructed for his imagistic, domestic, suburban scene. In fact, these learners discover a tripling of fluidity in Leonard's riposte: the nicked tinnie, the proud and specially legible localist language, the implied open domestic arrangement and story. "Awright" has replaced "Forgive me." "I'm thinking now," Nancy decides, "this is the day of the party . . . and he's lying on the couch." The party is planned for social sharing, in any case, whether beer has been consumed prior to or during.[3]

The fiction of Leonard's pilfering speaker is that he is *saying* his poem. The writing we read transliterates spoken Scots into print. On the other hand, the story of Williams's speaker is that he has left a note; we know it is a *written* taunt to the domestic partner who has been removed from the scene, a note for checking on what he might get away with in the relationship. Its spindly lines are a self-consciously modernist performance enacted in her absence (otherwise, there would be no reason for a note), such that one can hardly imagine his partner to be the only or even primarily intended recipient. Leonard beckons toward a social occasion that he has disrupted but by no means canceled. In fact, it seems

FIGURE 8.1 Screenshot from the YouTube video recorded in Edinburgh, Scotland, November 2012, with Nancy Somerville, Sean Donnelly, and Lorrane Borwick.

quite the opposite: he's begun the party early. Williams's act leaves nothing more to be consumed except the poem. Leonard's reply to Williams is a characteristically sly one-upping political gesture: it credits Williams for making a poem out of an unpoetic, domestic moment, yet has something pointed to say about the deeper linguistic dissidence in the legacy of Scottish modernism as a rejoinder to the colonial poetic situation.[4]

Between Human and Place

The close reading of Leonard, posted to YouTube from Edinburgh on November 2, 2012, with three weeks remaining in the first season of the course, became the initial entry in the poetry network of commons-based peer production only later dubbed "CCCR." The YouTube link is embedded inside the ModPo site. As of this writing, one can watch 103 videos on the CCCR page compiling crowd-sourced collaborative close readings. The project has taken off. Members of the crowd have filmed them in Sydney, Madison (Wisconsin), London, Los Angeles, West Palm Beach (Florida), Carrboro (North Carolina), Boston, Vancouver, Washington, Prague, New York City, Montreal, Chicago, Colombo (Sri Lanka), Dublin, Berlin, Toronto, San Marino (California), Melbourne, Claryville (New York), and elsewhere. Some of these explicitly copy the method and spirit of the initial Edinburgenzians' retort. The European Time Zone Meet-Up (ETZM) gathers online via Zoom and in an open-ended forum thread but conceives of its Berlin-centered situatedness as a matter of a home-base time zone. ETZM has continued to gather monthly for several years. Anyone can join from anywhere, but the connection is defined nevertheless. Participants from far outside the central European zone have become increasingly involved, as far away as New Mexico and New South Wales, but I have noticed how "visitors" from outside the zone defer to the "local" conveners at key social moments during the discussions, not on the basis of there being anything particularly *Berlinisch* about the choice of poems but out of a subtle skill of convening that enables people to balance lively global virtuality with respectful locality.

The Edinburgh video introduced us to all the mix of virtuality and locality ETZM and other meetups have inherited. If, by one consistent definition of *crowdsourcing*, the group seeks to outperform remote experts, the inaugural video certainly befits the category. It takes the simplest element of the xMOOC, the recording of the short video conveying course material—the classic one-way dispatch from expert instructor to amateur crowd—and shows that, in some ways, it can be turned around. It implies that the concept of collective intelligence demands efforts at participatory culture. It strategizes and borrows from Leonard's critique and devotion to local language. It talks back to Williams by talking back to ModPo while honoring the pedagogy premised on an idea of crowd wisdom that itself permits active engagement in a teaching mode as a form of learning.

Obviously there are limits to liberating such talking back, given that, despite frequent trips the ModPo team makes to cities where ModPo participants reside, the much-heralded home of the course—virtual as it may be—is not ultimately unfixed or modifiable. In a chapter devoted to ModPo in the book *Posthumanism and the Massive Open Online Course*, Jeremy Knox devotes a few pages to the CCCR Leonard video and describes a complex dynamic of poetic resistance versus spatial conformity. "While the context and poem are different, deliberately chosen to highlight local context, as a network space, the configuration is identical. If this is a resistance, it is to American poetry, *not* the spatial arrangement of the educational activity. . . . The video serves as an example of how the pedagogical relations modeled by the ModPo video discussions hold together as a stable networked space." Knox's analysis underscores a problem besetting the xMOOC despite our efforts to introduce connectivist practices and hybridity. It leads him to the most perceptive critical comments I have encountered on the predicament of MOOC transference: longing and affection for the poetry (in this case) is sometimes displaced not just upon the confident, charismatic leader-convener but also onto and into the "authentic" space the course calls home—in the instance of ModPo, a charming house already famous as a literary freespace. Each laudatory gesture emerging from the distant crowd has the potential to trouble "the limits of the KWH property, emphasizing the *supposed* bond between human and place."[5]

Takk Dy Breath Away

A Shetlander poet residing in Glasgow regularly encounters the problem Knox describes. Christie Williamson is devoted to an internationalist open online course presenting a perhaps unavoidably authoritative sense of place. Like his predecessors, Sean, Lorrane and Nancy, he has pondered what constitutes authentic location for an otherwise rewarding virtual citizenship. In each critical or at least cautious response to what the American English of modern U.S. poetry is teaching him about the role of place in his own verse—a theme centrally important to him as a locale-focused writer and as an artisanal independent bookseller—he also contemplates his relationship with Scottish English as someone who increasingly prefers to write verse in Shetlandic (Shaetlan).

By way of this speculative translational linguistic configuration—something like: the Scottish language is to the American language as Shaetlan is to Scottish—Williamson found himself encouraged by the notion that his study of U.S. modernism through ModPo, especially ideas about the importance of local linguistic "contact," such as in the partisan localist modernism of Williams (a main topic of week 3 in the course), might lead him deeper into his poetic engagement with the language and landscape of Shetland, even to the point (as he wrote when translating Lorca's Andalusian Spanish *separately* into Shaetlan and English) of "artificially inflating the linguistic distance between Shaetlan and Ingles." As a place-specific poet, he was beginning to feel more personally expressive in Shaetlan than in Glaswegian English; this coincided with a time when the differences of Middle Atlantic U.S. English, sounding out from the ubiquitous audio of ModPo recordings, daily filled his headphones during his most intense period as a ModPo student. "Shaetlan an Ingleesh are different languages," Williamson later wrote in an essay. "Since the languages work differently, so the poems work differently."[6] Differences between two dominant Englishes might thus be beside the point.

Through a full engagement with ModPo over the years, Williamson has sought to test the dimensions of an increasing freedom from the cultural and—in terms of marketing poetry books—financial constraints of the modern English he heard and wrote locally and stocks in his shop. This effort followed from and paralleled his overall plan initially, years earlier, to turn from prose to verse, another move away from markets. That turn, he once told me, "resulted in a yearning to know what the right hand side of the page felt like. Instead of writing prose, I began experimenting with poems which broke free from what Tom Leonard famously described as 'the tyranny of the left-hand margin.'"[7] He faced dual constrictions—of the line and of the language. The language of poetry, as itself a response of some sort to several tyrannies, emerged as a consistent undercurrent.

The year Christie Williamson joined ModPo, the second of the four annually refreshed essay assignments asked participants to write out a close reading in response to Williams's poem "Nantucket":

> Flowers through the window
> lavender and yellow

changed by white curtains—
Smell of cleanliness—

Sunshine of late afternoon—
On the glass tray

a glass pitcher, the tumbler
turned down, by which

a key is lying—And the
immaculate white bed[8]

The poet-student posted his essay in the busy forums and received eight peer-review responses from others around the world. But then, upon arriving for a visit with a cousin in Scalloway, the ancient capital of Shetland (population today 1,200), he decided this was the situation for a translational rewriting of the Williams into Shaetlan. In the process, he challenged the language of local holiday arrival. Williams's "Nantucket" actually seems to be about leaving the island. The vacationing speaker peers back through the window of presumably his or someone else's rental house and gives us the perfect imagistic provincial set-piece, a modernist ancestor to contemporary images we know from Williams-Sonoma or Anthropologie catalogs. The image verges on summertime meme—on what hellolovelystudio.com's and *House Beautiful*'s high-season Pinterest influencers identify as "Nantucket Style Chic Design Inspiration."[9] The picturesque space is pristine, filled with light. There are white curtains and a white bed on which someone has left a key. That key is what leads me to interpret departure—inspirational vacation vacating—rather than arrival: one leaves the key to the rental behind as you leave. The key is not a metaphor, for it follows from imagism's sometimes postcard-perfect antisymbolism. No ideas but in nice things.

Responding, I think, to Williams's way of emotionally vacating the precise scene of a tiny modern poem, Williamson composes his own poem and calls it "St Catherine's." Its title shares the name of the cousin's rustic Scalloway house. Williamson is not a true poetic descendant of Williams. The latter's view is reversed from Nantucket in several respects: first, it is a view from inside. In another sense, it presents a perspective not of the house but of the landscape in strong emotional context:

Coated optics
conservatory

Da hills o Clift
watch oot

Doon by da fit
o da gallows hill

takk dy breath
awa[10]

The modernist's Nantucket is a place where a visitor-poet sees a world framed yet altered by curtains. What is immaculate is the uncluttered built environment, the modernist aesthetic of no-ideas-but-in-things juxtaposition: a tray, a pitcher, a tumbler, a key, a bed. Had there been drinking? Had there been sex? No matter. It's over. The settled view, almost a result of imagist nonpresence—not so much a

FIGURE 8.2 "Nantucket Style Chic Design Inspiration," posted by hellolovelystudio.com. Interior design by Kevin Isbell for *House Beautiful*.

Source: Photograph by Don Freeman, used with permission.

vision as a staged glimpse—is nearly verbless ("changed" is more an adjective; the key is "lying" but inert). Williamson's Scalloway starts from ModPo's American modernist emphasis on radically reductive perspective. The arrival of the Shaetlan speaker, in a return to the familial scene, not only signals enduring frank and faithful presence but also the risky effort at having a vision that comes with being there. The verb is beseechingly, imperatively strong: "watch oot." Why the warning? Your view from the house is of the foot of the gallows hill (a place-name, but readers are not certain of its literalness nor its perhaps violent suppressive prehistory), so you must be careful not to fall down too far that way with your eyes. But "watch oot" is a pun: be warned, and also be sure to look. No "immaculate white bed" in the end, no key to the visit, but a visionary *local* perspective that will "takk dy breath / awa." True contact.

Williamson submitted the ModPo essay, wrote his poem as a further response, and then included the poem in his book *Doors tae Naewye*. He opened his bookstore in Glasgow in honor of Dickinsonian obliquity: Tell It Slant Books. In October 2023, the ModPo team held a series of events, including that week's live webcast, in Scotland. We visited Tell It Slant, and in a corner of the breakfast café that hosts the bookstore, we recorded with him and three other poets a thirty-seven-minute comparative discussion of "Nantucket" and "St Catherines."[11] Now that exchange is available as an enlargement of the complex English-

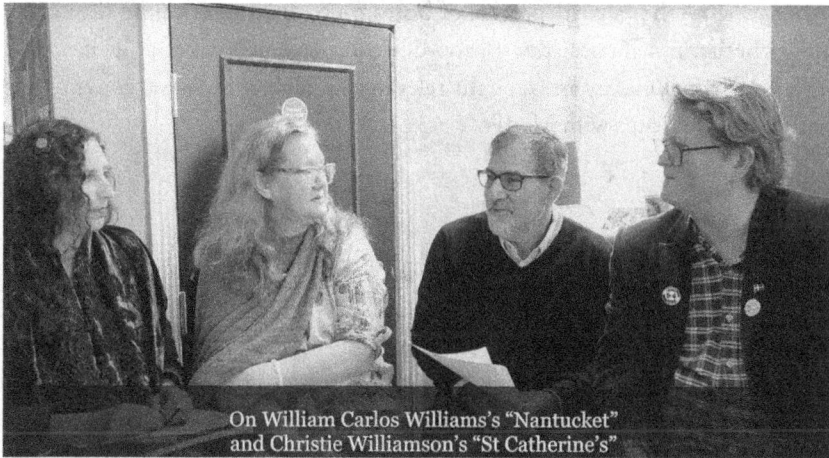

On William Carlos Williams's "Nantucket"
and Christie Williamson's "St Catherine's"

FIGURE 8.3 Recorded at Tell It Slant Books, Glasgow, Scotland, October 12, 2023. From left: Laynie Browne, Lee Ann Brown, Al Filreis, Christie Williamson. Filmed by Zach Carduner and Chris Martin.

language story of the modern to be discovered in the course materials. By this point in the triadic relationship between Williams, Williamson, and the ModPo community, it is difficult to sort out roles of teacher, learner, poet, reader, interpreter, and interpreted.

EXPERTISE AND ITS DISCONTENTS

Sean Donnelly, Nancy Somerville, Lorrane Borwick, and Christie Williamson participated with such intention in the making of these videos for complex reasons. To judge from the videos themselves, among other evidence, their motives are apparently these: First, a desire for a constructive form of participation, or, as Daren C. Brabham frames the rationale in his book *Crowdsourcing*, a claiming of the opportunity to contribute to the making of new resources—a challenge to the additive capacities of the project. A second motive is an assertion of the right to criticize assumptions underlying the host organization's core curation.

According to Brabham's overview, the first of four main elements summarized by efforts to theorize crowd wisdom is (1) *motivation*—participants' incentives for getting involved in crowd-powered projects. The other three essential aspects are (2) *expertise*—the acceptance by the organization sponsoring the mass collaboration that those outside standard definitions of academic expertise can bring fresh insight, sometimes to apparently settled presuppositions; (3) *top-down management*—the "shared process of bottom-up, open creation by the crowd and [whether it can coexist with] top-down management";[12] and (4) *diversity*. This book concludes by assessing the relevance of each of these categories to our particular experience with ModPo.

Motivation

While it is true that participants' overall incentives for engaging in citizen poetics are central to the success of the collaborative close reading of any particular poem, unsurprisingly, those reasons are mostly distinct from the list of motives summarized from the survey of research presented by Brabham and others who survey crowdsourcing. These surveys, to be sure, do not account for poetry MOOCs. Typical of the items on Brabham's list: "To earn money." "To build a portfolio for future employment." "To pass the time when bored."[13] Extensive interviews conducted with ninety-one ModPo participants by Amaris Cuchanski in 2013, and with a score by me in 2017 and 2018, and follow-ups with twenty-six of the original ninety-one in 2023, and an additional forty or so conversations in 2024 during the writing of this book, tend to affirm the centrality of conscious motivation but reveal significant distinctions.

We start by confidently asserting that the ModPo people are not there to earn money! Nor to become more hirable job candidates (a pitch favored by Coursera for recommending their courses—"GET JOB-READY"). The testimonies on the question of motivation suggest that crowdsourcing arts projects not only befit the wise-crowd model but also might even have a thing or two to teach practitioners of crowd-fixing in the fields of marketing and consumer psychology. That's because very little among responses to our two basic questions about intentions—"Why join ModPo?" and, for those who have continued, "Why stay?"—has to do with poetry per se as subject matter. That outcome doesn't sadden me, nor does it inhibit conclusions we might draw about the role of poetry in learning. On the contrary, it indicates the prospective wide public efficacy of poetry for realizing *other needs* rather than either the failure of poetry or its irrelevance to productive contemporary living. It suggests that the method and model, drawn from what we do with a poem, can scale toward most other areas. People's needs range widely.

A lab researcher we interviewed at length was motivated to join in search of "a place of peace" and to try "inquiry-based learning" as a direct parallel to his work in science. A retiree I met at a meetup in Brookline, Massachusetts, enrolled in order to ask herself, "Why am I alive?" A teacher with whom I spoke by phone continues to reenroll annually because the discussion causes her to "feel open in all directions" in response to "levels of knowledge [that] do not feel hierarchical." An accomplished entertainment industry entrepreneur I visited in Beverly Hills, by now a friend, was and still is motivated because participating "makes me slow down." A military veteran remains after thirteen years because of the "buzz" created by the "many different channels for participation"; perhaps paradoxically, he seeks ModPo's "*'offline'* discussions" most of all. A forty-eight-year-old "successful, professional woman" joined to "untangle" her then recently discerned codependency with her substance-abusing spouse. An adult daughter and faraway elderly father (Tracy and Reinhard) planned to "pass notes in class" and engaged, on the side, in a running juicy dialogue about the TAs, poets, and fellow participants; they said they learned a lot—about each other. A rural resident joined mainly to "think together with others" despite her isolated "fragile soul" and health-related need for a fragrance-free environment. (She has mentored others as a Community TA for a decade.) A high-school junior joined not because she didn't have enough regular schoolwork to do as she pursued high grades in anticipation of the U.S. college application process but because she sought freedom from the five-paragraph essay. An eminent poet-editor is surprised to find that he is motivated more "from an emotional level" than a literary one. A technology worker in Manila back in 2013 enrolled after a devastating typhoon when she was in need of the remote company of others, but she stays because she wants to support other people whenever they need the same. (In 2024, she published a book of poems.)

A person with an MFA degree, indeed a former instructor in an MFA program, discovered that "nothing in my education . . . prepared me for these poems." They were hard to understand, and she never dared to put them in her own syllabi. How could she profess to instruct verse she didn't follow? After all that poetic training and teaching, she retired, "felt adrift," and then, happily deprofessionalized, finally felt able to devote herself to the difficulty. A retired tradesperson is involved because of his fascination with "the process of how knowledge [is] being shared." The pharmacist we met earlier, feeling "restless, irritable and discontent because I am not learning in a classroom," joined primarily to take advantage of peer-reviewed prose writing. She preferred to receive feedback from other nonspecialists.[14] A self-identified autistic woman heard that ModPo might help with her PTSD and had "thought the doors to higher education were closed to me forever." A "bureaucrat living in Kolkata" obsessively listened and watched recorded videos and live webcasts to accompany himself "while commuting between home and hospital, home and office, office and hospital" to mark out the days and weeks of his wife's fifth through eighth rounds of chemotherapy. His children live far away. He has no help. After a while, he connected to ModPo very early mornings and very late nights and then "even when I'm alone in my office." His goal was to find others remotely to "help . . . me hold everything in place and . . . to hold on to myself."

A fifty-three-year-old feminist theorist and adjunct professor joined during treatment for ovarian cancer to "bring to fruition in my lifetime" a use for file drawers full of unfinished nonacademic writing. Another teacher, a "Katrina survivor" who had been summarily fired from her classroom position after the storm along with 81 others of the 150 on the staff and was never rehired, one night stumbled into a bookstore and witnessed poet Ruth Salvaggio read from *Hearing Sappho in New Orleans*. During the reading she realized the connection between art forms and the "piles of trash" that constituted her beloved city, whereupon she joined ModPo the next morning because she wanted to "enjoy the struggle" and learn to make something meaningful from the contemporary fragments.[15]

A thirteen-year-old Tanzanian was inspired by ModPo's discussion of "The Rejection of Closure"—it "really helped me be free in my poetry"—and mailed to Hejinian, a 1963 Harvard graduate, a copy of his illustrated self-published poems, subtitled *My Harvard Self-Recommendation*. After watching the on-location video of Anna Strong Safford and me walking in circles around Harvard Yard while discussing John Keene's fantastical depiction of George Santayana and W. E. B. DuBois eyeing each other along those same paths in 1890,[16] this precocious learner read all of Keene's *Counternarratives* aloud to his father on our recommendation. The Harvard University he variously glimpses through ModPo (Hejinian, Creeley, Bernstein, Stevens, Ashbery, Keene, et alia) is not a practical destination. "Harvard is really a metaphor for me wanting the best education possible," he tells me, "even if I don't go to university." (A portrait of this aspirational young person appears on the cover of this book.)

A college sophomore enrolled because she was "interested in learning to live with ambiguity." A participant from Ontario wanted to delight in her friends who incorrectly believed that "I do nothing else but think about poetry" while knowing in her heart that her actual motivation was to "find my world" after the death of her husband. A fifty-three-year-old South African woman registered because, for health reasons, she can't keep up and must go at her own slow pace (due to "fuzziness" or "fibrofog" from medications treating fibromyalgia) and didn't want to waste tuition money on a deadline-imposing fee-based course she would fail. An elderly Bostonian enrolled because during "a pause in life," they needed to see humor, curiosity, and empathy in others. A nonacademic Irish writer participated in order to test herself: "Could I actually complete an academic program?" (She did just that.) A sixty-something worker in a fast-food restaurant with a "moderate social anxiety disorder" looked back upon a fearful childhood of being "ostracized by my classmates" for reading books and decided to find a place where she could "dare . . . to venture an opinion"; her favorite ModPo figure was Marcel Duchamp as he turned a urinal into an artwork.[17]

A devoted member of the Long Poem Group, who has been affiliated with ModPo for more than a decade and has not yet met any of her "LongPo" friends in person, seems to like it that way. ModPo connects her back emotionally to her complicated father, who contracted polio as an adolescent; bedridden for two years, he taught himself to build shortwave radios and created distant friendships. He later married a Polish survivor of a Stalinist labor camp, a stone quarry in Siberia. While her Polish mom "played bridge and medicated her WWII experience with booze," her dad enrolled in correspondence courses. The daughter retains an unforgettable image of a father's nonmetaphorical remoteness: the long envelopes of remote lessons in philosophy, history, and boat design arriving in the mailbox. For what was he reaching out beyond his family's life? He wanted to build a sailboat after he retired, but before that, he led the family to brief hectic residencies in Sudan, England, Chile, Puerto Rico, Peru, and Ecuador. Our LongPo devotee is committed to what used to be called "distance learning," and it is an "entire ModPo 'world' " to her. It provides her a "frame of mind," she told me, giving social definition to the word *correspondence* in the phrase "correspondence course." ModPo is not a sailboat, nor is it a medicating bottle of booze; it's a new-fangled shortwave radio that she gets to help build, an all-way means of being remote and, at the same time, sustaining her motive for planning to stay.

The first questions we ask of the ModPo participants are based on the two inquiries the authors of *Planning to Stay* recommend for residents of a neighborhood who are about to engage in a civic planning exercise: "1. What is it about this place that draws us here? 2. What could we add to this place that will keep us here?"[18]

Expertise

It is said that the organization sponsoring a crowdsourced activity should attempt to demonstrate its commitment to the values of cooperation, aggregation, teamwork, and creativity such that "groups of people can outperform individual experts, outsiders can bring fresh insights to internal problems, and geographically dispersed people can work together to produce policies and designs that are agreeable to most."[19] This description does not take into account interpreters gathering around an arts project. The closest Brabham comes in his account is a reference to design contests. Nonetheless, the definition of outperforming experts portends a major reform of assumptions about literary expertise. Since we are focused here on the orientation to process, the *how* of a poem, mind-sharing projects of this kind require a method "far less specialized," as Wai Chee Dimock puts it. "Power," she adds, is "measured by the inspired output of others." As we have seen, Dimock observed an education populism that—like the Kelly Writers House as ModPo's host and PennSound and PoemTalk as its sibling resources—"produc[es] outpourings of words that can be counted on to extend indefinitely" and advocates a "*nonselective* nurturing of writing."[20] It was without negative judgment, we recall, that Dimock referred to "non-selectivity" as the opposite of professionalism.

Most accounts of crowd wisdom use the term *amateur* to describe the crowd. *Amateurism* can be defined as being associated with nonselectivity but, again, without the pejorative connotations. In making her optimistic case for generous academic thinking and for proposed public-inclusive reforms—and based on her earlier research into "connected communities of readers" (including Oprah

Winfrey's Book Club)—Kathleen Fitzpatrick in *Generous Thinking* is obliged to describe "our anxieties (and they are very real anxieties) about deprofessionalization, about association with the amateur."[21] Louis Menand's take on academic professionalism in *The Marketplace of Ideas: Reform and Resistance in the American University*, with its titular call-out to traditions of free speech, is less optimistic. "Every profession has a side that is turned away from the anarchy of open competition—away from the system that the profession serves and that made professionalization necessary in the first place. Requiring that people earn a credential before they can be allowed to work in one's business is a way of defending oneself and one's fellow practitioners from market forces."[22] The advent of many millions of new MOOC learners, including some who are already certified professionals in other fields, has raised the specter of chaotic new marketplaces. Creating a cult of the amateur is a risk, certainly a risk ModPo incurs. Credentials, even mostly useless "certificates of completion" (which is what ModPo awards people who "complete" our course), add to the anarchy Menand describes.

Fitzpatrick calls for a modification of expertise so that "defending oneself" is a lesser motive. "Critical humility," she says, is required for enacting or even imagining a "public literary criticism."[23] Lisa Ruddick has written about how superfluous complexity—in what academics publish and say, the sentences they write, even in response to simple questions in public settings—results from what she calls "the game of academic cool." Deprofessionalization, surely helpful here, involves bypassing anxieties about appearing naïve, accessible, or sentimental. Ruddick found that young academics, initiating into their specialized fields, "feel ashamed of the varied, private intuitions and desires that might diversify their interests." Reviewing scores of articles, she found that "there is a near silence as to whether there exist any positive, beneficial forms of self-organization, individuality, inwardness, or self-boundaries."[24] It's hard to imagine how that stance can play out well in relation to a crowd of amateurs saying they seek thoughtfulness, company during a storm, or relief from intellectual shyness. Anthony Watkins, the most active of the ModPo CTAs, is intellectually shy. When I first asked him if he would be willing to help guide others, he told me that he "didn't see how a college dropout from a state university could be part of the team." In a memoiristic novel, he wrote: "My education is lacking, except for what I have picked up from being a CTA. Funny that I am supposed to be an educator. Maybe most educators, even full professors, are always learning from each other. . . . ModPo, it turns out, is only masquerading as a college class. It is really a community of lifelong learners who love poetry but also love the people."[25] When we observe that what is missing in crowd theorizing is a fully explored connection to antimonologic pedagogies, we can perceive, following the insights of Fitzpatrick and

Ruddick and the experience of Anthony Watkins, a reversal of the negative val-
uation of the rightness of the nonprofessional speaking out plainly on academic
topics in a forum hosted by the fully credentialed academic. Anthony and numerous others in the ModPo crowd regularly express their awareness of the cultural
conflict brought to the fore in discussions of the university-sponsored MOOC
phenomenon. They report that many academic expert monologists project their
nonetheless liberal (and specifically prodemocracy) views in praise of outsider
nonspecialist dialogue without giving up the monologue as the chief mode for
disseminating that view. Notwithstanding the new openness of academic borders made possible by the open course, "the teacher confuses his authority of
knowledge with his own professional authority."[26] In this negative circumstance,
suggests Menand, "professionalism is a way of using smart people productively
without giving them too much social power."[27]

Elisa New leads the vast public project Poetry in America and wonders, when
MOOCs were new and roundly doubted within the academy, that the question
ever was why engage in such a thing. On the contrary, she told me:

> The question is why . . . professors should continue to be satisfied with teaching
> small and shrinking groups of 18–21 year olds or, via their scholarly monographs,
> reaching even smaller audiences of specialists and experts. I am not persuaded
> any more that specialization has done the humanities much good. . . . It seems
> obvious to me that it is much more valuable and important to communicate to
> 100,000 people the first, second, or third most important idea about a work of
> art, than to add the hundredth most important idea about that work to the store
> of specialized knowledge.

Poetry in America, launched in 2013, arose from New's experience teaching general education courses. Although within a few years, the project grew beyond the
xMOOC format, it was directly influenced by ModPo, which she had closely
observed during our initial year. From her vantage, its disruptive aspect was this:
we fully engaged nonspecialists like Anthony Watkins, and what particularly
motivated her venture was the involvement of such "post-college learners in
humanistic study." Prior to ModPo, New observed, educators "tended to think
collective reading of poetry an activity primarily suitable for 18–21 year olds." It's
her perspective that poetry was typically closely tied and limited "to liberal arts
education rather than to life-long learning. ModPo broke that open."[28]

In nearly all accounts of the sudden rise of the xMOOC where one found
discussions of "creative disruption" and even sometimes "creative destruction"
in higher education, any formal sense of *creativity* was diminished or entirely

omitted. Typical is "Creative Destruction," an essay written by the editorial board of *The Economist*, published on June 28, 2014. There, MOOCs were said to have "failed to live up to their promise"—true enough—but the *The Economist* board made no mention of the failure of ideas about teaching that would help educators adapt to the new learning.[29] It seems that the group determined that a *business model* was the problem, not established concepts of how people collaboratively learn, nor the issue of resistant definitions of professional authority.

The massive networked community excites fears of mass amateurization within circles of recognized experts. In a book-length study that applies "third space literacies" to digital media and schools, John Potter and Julian McDougall answer those fears by observing how the concept of "porous expertise," typically otherwise lauded by progressive theorists of education, manifests itself as a "powerful knowledge" made still more powerful by peer networking (including MOOCs) and the lessening of digital divides achieved in digital spaces populated by a range of generation, origin, viewpoint, and formal educational attainment. Crowdsourced online projects focusing on aesthetic literacy can successfully "operate . . . in a 'mixed economy' of schooled and informal learning." The key question, according to Potter and McDougall, is always going to be, "whose knowledge counts?"[30] Although we have known each other for thirty-seven years as I write this, I was grateful during our interview to be reminded by Elisa New that if the so-called lifelong learner is foremost among those whose knowledge counts, then much else for all others will fall into place.

Shirky seems right to describe, then, in the context of organizing without credentialed organizations, how "mass amateurization breaks professional categories."[31] This leads him to define sociality in a way that aligns well with our experience with the folksonomies of the forums: "If people can share their work in an environment where they can also convene with one another, they will begin talking about the things they have shared."[32] In heterogeneous networks, content and content's established categories become secondary as mutual responses to such content become more easily shareable. But in our experience, whenever the goal of interpreting an open-ended poem is deemed to be problem-*solving*, the social aspect of the group work is diminished, and "the opposite of expertise is . . . thought of as incompetence." This is the view of Carl Bereiter and Marlene Scardamalia in their book *Surpassing Ourselves: An Inquiry into the Nature and Implications of Expertise*. "From the standpoint of performance," problem-*solving* will fail, of course, when handled by inexpert people. "When we consider it from the standpoint of process, however, the opposite of expertise is the opposite of progressive problem solving. That is something we may call problem *reduction*."[33]

The realization that solution is not just impossible but irrelevant and that a poem is itself about such inapplicability to whole assessment requires not the elimination of the poem's problems but iterative attempts to reduce them. What's needed now are a lessening of uncertainty thwarting partial progress and a decline in worries in schools over the dimensions of the difficulty. The leaders of Poetry in America have had as much experience sharing poetry with high school students as any MOOC project. Because Poetry in America, a nonprofit, offers subsidized, very low-cost college credit, and because such credit is highly valuable currency for the students in the partner schools, students will typically sign up for Poetry in America courses without any preexisting interest in poetry. Thousands have read and discussed poems in Poetry in America courses hosted through Harvard and Arizona State University. "What they say again and again," New has found, "is that they didn't think they'd like poetry—but in fact, they love it. Learning that they love something they thought they'd hate gives them new confidence in themselves as learners. New possibilities emerge."[34]

Top-Down Management

Considering the third main descriptor of mass collaboration, I accept that for Brabham's assessment he chose a somewhat narrow working definition of crowd-sourcing, his aim being to *exclude* projects in which "top-down management by those charged with serving an organization's strategic interests" gives way to a "commons [that] is organized and produced from the bottom up and [whose] locus of control is in the community." That is to say, the relationship between "bottom-up open creation by the crowd" and "top-down management" is itself a "shared process," but ultimately, structures in those cases are deemed problematically "designed to serve the organization's needs."[35]

By this definition, despite its openness to the digital commons, no academic host of a free, noncredit mass-enrolled xMOOC can rightly claim the *total* absence of "management"-determined syllabi. But *partial* absence, yes: it was two years, for example, before I was more than peripherally aware of the LongPo group, which was organized through the forums in late 2021 and continues as of this writing through regular extrasite sessions. The LongPo people choose modern and contemporary American verse epics somehow by mutual consent. "Sometimes it goes to a vote," one regular tells me. Not one of the choices has been from the ModPo syllabus, despite its provision of more than sufficient possibilities through ModPoPLUS and the Teacher Resource Center.

They have discussed, for instance, Hart Crane's *The Bridge*, George Oppen's *Of Being Numerous*, and Mei-mei Berssenbrugge's serial ecological poems. Members range in age across fifty-five years. They have come to agree upon their own stated method: "We try to read 'out of the poems' instead of 'into the poems.'" They use PennSound audio recordings and consult episodes of *PoemTalk*, but it's part of their connectivist mission "to avoid reading poems that have already been discussed in ModPo."[36] LongPo needs ModPo aesthetically but not organizationally. No extraction of usage and participation data by academic researchers investigating MOOCs' failures will track or notice the LongPo folks. Yet with respect to crowdsourcing definitions, they do certainly, although invisibly, "serve the organization's needs." LongPo is what Shirky calls a "post-managerial organization." "Social tools," built from the recognition that "sociability is one of our core capabilities," as Shirky puts it, make possible "action by loosely structured groups, operating . . . outside the profit motive."[37] Sociability leads the LongPo people to rigorous organization-independent learning.

THE ART OF BRIDGING

The final crowdsourcing metric is diversity, a term that needs a particular definition for the open online course. As the utopianism of Lévy's *Collective Intelligence* predescribed some specific effects of the interactive web emergent a decade later, his emphasis on cocreation as a "form of universally distributed intelligence, constantly enhanced" progressed further in discussions of *diversity*. If the crowd was not heterogeneous, what could "universally distributed" mean?

Decentralization

Mark Granovetter's research in social network theory in the 1970s, as presented in "The Strength of Weak Ties" and elsewhere, studied the way that weak ties in a social network were the most important.[38] This work predicted much to come. Early complex digital social networks (SixDegrees, Friendster, MySpace, Orkut, Facebook, etc.) and then the massive open online course are predominated by such weak ties. Commenting later on this history in *Mindsharing*, Lior Zoref was not writing about MOOCs, yet his summary of Granovetter and others' conclusions befits the importance of diversity to distributed collaboration in the open course: "Our strong ties tend to be [with] those who are most like us, but our weak ties are our link to the heterogeneity we need to mindshare and access crowd wisdom."[39] After Granovetter and Lévy, Surowiecki, in *The Wisdom of Crowds*, took up the historical connections and produced a wide definition that begins with diversity of thought.[40] Scott E. Page has been reviewing and conducting sociological studies of how the range of experiences functions in a number of problem-reducing environments.[41] My goal in this final chapter has been to show the decentralization of an interactive humanities/arts MOOC—where interpretive decisions are pushed out to open forums populated by people connected by weak ties—and that quality can now serve, I believe, as an instance of heterogeneity as Surowiecki, Page, and others have explored it. Diversity is a form and expression of decentralization.

Whereas decentralization is generally the most basic assumption of crowdsourcing in any finance-based or profit-focused project, seen by proponents as a virtue and by detractors as exploitative, and whereas a densely populated interactive MOOC is so complexly decentralized that it is impossible for the instructor to describe what is going on intellectually at any one time, then what could be the relationship between diversity on the one hand and the decentering of expertise and authority on the other? For me, this is the key to the ModPo experience. Surowiecki expends great effort to explain this. "If one virtue of a decentralized economy is that it diffuses decision-making power . . . throughout the system, that virtue becomes meaningless if all the people [making interpretive decisions] are alike." Multifaceted groups bring varying attitudes toward risk and different "time horizons" in thinking about the point at which some measure of consensus brings pleasure and feelings of mutuality to the group. Page's goal is to demonstrate through his studies that eclectic groups become effective at facing problems. At one point, Surowiecki summarizes the research as follows: "Homogeneous groups are great at doing what they do well, but they become progressively less able to investigate alternatives."[42]

In her essay for *Our Compelling Interests: The Value of Diversity for Democracy and a Prosperous Society* (2016), Danielle Allen prefers the terms "bonding ties" (for strong, familial, presupposed relationships) and "bridging ties" (for Granovetter's "weak" relationships—social, chosen, sometimes accidental), and then proposes "social connectedness" as the main outcome of broadening the range of democratic arrangements.[43] Allen makes no reference to advocates of digital connectivism—her range of citation and analogy extends to theories of justice and of social capital and (noninternet) network theory—but her ideas about bridging and interactivity align well with connectivists' democratic claims. Her main question is: "What sort of interactional norms, capacities, skills, and knowledge do we need to cultivate inside institutions aspiring to support social connectedness?" Allen's answer, in sum, is that "we need an art of bridging."[44] Why an "art"? The art she means is an artful process or method that can not only be admired for its own elegance but also points toward subject matter that, by its nature, provides a reason for the "interactional" convening of people across all the differences between and among them.

In this book, I have been arguing that poetics serves as a model (to continue for the moment with Danielle Allen's framing) for a version of a social connectedness basic to the practical sharing of interpretive insights and power or power-sharing as specific effects of democratic norms.[45] The group's work together on Dickinson's "The Brain within its Groove," that difficult poem about power, is a good instance of power sharing. In the open discussions of an experimental poem, there is rarely gain (as we certainly saw with "The Brain") in a group's "doing what they do well." Exploring alternative paths through the underlying (il)logic of modern poetic language—which is to say, nonrealist, swerving, drifting in Caroline Bergvall's sense, and typically nonnarrative—is not an endpoint but a necessary early step in the process of acquiring skills for bringing collaborative intelligence to bear on the task of a group's understanding. We've seen that the poems are always ultimately about the necessity of investigating those alternatives. The noisy, vociferous information cascade is not merely an apt way of thinking about the problem. The overload can be a fundamental aspect of understanding all at once the form/content relationship so important in twentieth- and twenty-first-century thinking. The massive aspect of the group of interpreters aligns once again with the poetic content, but never more so than when the group's clamorous cognitive and experiential range unexpectedly aids in getting *beyond* what the group already knows it has previously done well and, in that next phase, produces something new.

Multiaccess Learning

Using the vexed term *ability* to describe a posteriori training, skills, and field-relevant knowledge, Page in *The Difference* argues that the range of origins and backgrounds among members of a group can be as important as such traditionally acquired ability.[46] He also contends that "distributed problem solving can be thought of as a form of innovation" and encourages a redefinition of what constitutes knowledge.[47] By the logic of this argument, when the content being mindshared has the primary quality of *itself being innovative as representation*, heterogeneity would seem to be a requirement if the goal is to establish a commensurate innovation. Page talks about a "diversity bonus." *Bonus* is a term uncongenial to me, but in this context we'll take it to mean *something extra*. It yields from the efforts of "people with diverse cognitive repertoires" and is realized only when such people "work inclusively on complex tasks."[48] The key qualities are complexity, opacity, and nonroutinization. Page and others observe that routine tasks yield no such bonus.

To the boldest claim of his study—that disparities within groups can outperform ability—Page hastens to add, "in some contexts." My experience suggests that crowd-supported poetics offers such a context, especially where ability had been otherwise defined institutionally by metrics of credentialing (earning grades and credits) based on narrowly circumscribed reward networks with their set processes of candidacy for admission, slim acceptance rates (5.4 percent at the university hosting ModPo[49]), and assumptions of standardized training in close analysis—with strong preferences for resolving difficult questions with workable, quickly evaluated, and indeed marketable or exportable answers. As Cathy Davidson has reminded us in *The New Education*, academic technophobia, for her a form of cultural politics that has targeted crowdsourced knowledge bases,[50] is sometimes a cover for fear of the erosion of established (and arguably measurable) definitions of assessing individual ability. It's a version of doubts about other-directedness in progressive education, and it has a similar problem of conformity and uniformity. If "diverse perspectives . . . enable collections of people to find more and better solutions" (in Page's phrasing), and if this reason for convening people around material conveners care most about threatens concepts of ability and makes it difficult for teachers to assess—let alone grasp or, in any sense, master—the enormous process, then that is certainly a cause for the obstructionist scenes and scenarios Davidson laments in "Against Technophobia."[51] In conducting research for an essay about ModPo to be included in the book *Teaching Literature in the Online Classroom*, Anna Strong Safford and Davy Knittle consulted with several dozen ModPo participants identifying as requiring accessibility for their learning. It was not a surprise to Safford and Knittle, or to me, that the comments gathered on disability evinced essentially no technophobia. On the contrary, the testimonies of these participants described the many digital platform particularities that constitute accessibility, with forms of asynchronicity atop the list.

One participant who conferred with Safford and Knittle, identifying as a person with disabilities, made certain to point out that having "the main course material . . . available aurally" is fundamental to the feeling of inclusion.[52] This only further augments the overall importance of the poetics of sound to the

ModPo pedagogy and of "the 'visual rhythm' " in third spaces deemed crucial by the citizen-focused *Planning to Stay* authors. The availability of sound is doubly accommodating. One conclusion I have drawn from the research Strong and Knittle conducted on accessibility leads me to refute various assumptions that increases in cognitive, sensory, and experiential diversity correspond to levels of technophobia. As Davidson points out, that limitation, basically a political one, typically comes from prospective online teachers whose nervous educational traditionalism in this sense becomes, in effect, discriminatory. Then there's the related question of the willingness and capacity of all people to accept and thrive in the resistance to closure. Another person interviewed by Safford and Knittle implied a triple association: (1) ModPo's accessibility for learners with disabilities; (2) the forum posts of those experiencing death, grief, and displacement; and (3) the openness and irresoluteness of the poems themselves. "Poems that approach the unsayable," this person reported, "offer so many resources for those of us in diaspora or suffering complex losses."[53] The poems' resistance to easy sayability is parallel to the abundance of media options for entry at any point. Valerie Irvine's studies of "multi-access learning" are ultimately about the kind of accessibility Safford and Knittle explored in their interviews with ModPo people who require what is institutionally known as accommodation.[54] This is a productive paradox in sum: The putative *inaccessibility* of the poems is what enables—indeed demands—a wide *accessibility* of modes, means, methods, and digital pathways.

I'm Nobody! Who Are You?

Above, I referred to traditional preferences for solutions even in collaborative settings. One of Scott Page's "core claims" is: "Diverse fundamental preferences frustrate the process of making choices."[55] Laura C. enrolled in ModPo because she was exhausted by the scary expectations she associated with schooling—that it required a series of quick choices among optional answers—and she was finally seeking a setting where options would remain open for longer periods. Laura, who publicly identifies as living with "an autism spectrum condition (moderate Aspergers) and complex post-traumatic stress disorder" and who "wasn't able to do college in a traditional way," realized through full engagement with ModPo that her calamitous internalization of preferences for solutions to problems presented through curricula had become the single topic of greatest fear for her. Her "fundamental inability to read people and situations," which otherwise in

her experience "can be dangerous," on the contrary, became an asset when reading poems *because* "we're such a diverse group" and *because* "misunderstandings," which usually plague her, are encouraged by the interpretive process—and
especially because the notion of ending the course on a certain date annually in
November is well understood to be an ironic deadline. She hadn't been able to
"make it through college," but then, when she felt somewhat ready to return,
"there was no way to turn back the clock," and anyway, "the scholarships I had
originally gone to school on had run out decades ago." She associated her traditional poetic education with "a lifetime of closed doors." She walked through the
open door of the Kelly Writers House just once in November 2012 to see finally,
fully for herself, the collegiate space she had been joining virtually. She discussed
poems in the Arts Café that day and then joined a pizza party with fifty other
ModPo learners who had made the trip to be in the space. *Closure* and *openness*
are key terms for Laura. In the context of forum commentaries on the poems, she
told us that "I'm afraid I don't know any way other than to be open" and cannot
"say things that [I] don't entirely mean . . . in spite of my lack of education."

FIGURE 8.4 Laura C. with the author, Kelly Writers House living room, November 19, 2012.

Source: Photograph by Max McKenna.

In grade school, Laura was forced to memorize Dickinson's "I'm nobody! Who are you?": "I loathed that poem because they used it in the wrong way, to try and teach us little people humility, telling us we were all homogenized products and having us recite it in Hallmark-y tones in unison. I bore an unfair grudge toward ED from that day on."[56] After the first season and before it was decided to continue ModPo in an open ongoing session with all-year participation enabled through annual "symposium modes," Laura announced that she hoped "to see ModPo continue in some manner beyond the scope of the course even," and devoted herself to building what is by now a Facebook group of over ten thousand people. The group has been praised as "an informal study hall for whoever comes seeking help [or] advice."[57] And in an atypical assessment of Facebook, it is commended to prospective new members as "intimate," with a vibe of "energy and personal interaction."[58] Laura helped manage that group for years, eventually passing it on to another CTA, one of the ModPo Renga Party founders, Sanjeev Naik. To the ModPo citizenry, Laura is the furthest thing from nobody. She is no longer focused on the poems per se but wants to preserve a social attention to open interaction among the wide-ranging group of interpreters and encourage the acceptance of misunderstanding. ModPo taught her, she told us, to seek out other people for whom, as Freire put it in *Critical Education in the New Information Age*, "teaching and learning . . . involve search, live curiosity, [and] misunderstanding."[59]

Dan Bergmann and I had been discussing his experience as an emergent literary intellectual "trying to be understood" when I asked him if he wanted to comment on Freire's sense of misunderstanding. "The value of misunderstanding is twofold," Dan tapped on letters to form words in response. "One is that misunderstanding opens up new vistas that the person trying to be understood never thought of. The other value is that understanding is richer if preceded by misunderstanding, like a charcoal sketch under a painting." In week 4 of ModPo's ten-week syllabus, participants encounter the challenging concept that Stein's writing is clear as mud. Some readers in the crowd simply do not see the idea as paradoxical, having become skeptical (during week 3) of confident, hyperbolic dicta pronounced by the programmatic modernists such as Pound, H. D., and Williams, in their adamant and sometimes intolerant advocacy of minimalistic clarity. In his first season with ModPo, Dan knew himself to be a person in search of clarity. But then, week 4 was all charcoal sketch and little painting. When he first reached Stein Week in 2012, he found himself at a "terrible" impasse. "As an autistic person," he recalled for me much later, "I was reveling in knowledge I could acquire," and muddy language seemed anathema to acquisition. But when reminded of Stein's apparently outrageous claim that she was writing for

mobiles out of words and ideas that get activated by the wind of the reader's irritation." He's describing disjunction as an almost surrealist mix of (1) the group,
(2) the individual reader, and (3) the disorienting text as a prompt for variable
action. "Diversity," Page concludes, "works best on disjunctive tasks."[63]

The fundamental preferences of a heterogeneous group, if and when they
prolong and sidetrack the process of making interpretive choices, create the "irritation" Dan describes. At the same time, the ranging tendencies of these people
produce an intellectual experience that they say is satisfying because it is commensurate with the innovative form of the problem—its difficulty—given over
to the crowd. This apparent contradiction seems like a good way of describing
the eclectic cohort who came together around Dickinson's "The Brain." Such a
difficult assignment—describe an easily distracted mind and do it together with
others!—requires perhaps an *overabundance* of heterogeneity. In *One Smart
Crowd* (2021), a crowdsourcing handbook outlining the characteristics of "open
innovation," entrepreneurs Simon Hill and Alpheus Bingham identify "problems
[that] can be solved only if you have '*too diverse* a set of skills and experience.' "[64]
When asked about the effect of ModPo's eclectic population, a seven-time
returnee to the course also turned to Dickinson's wayward poem about the wayward brain. "Diversity is another name for lots of information," Allan Keeton
told me, "without which there are no surprise swerves. Only when there is much
more than enough diversity can there be a living system that echoes the human
brain in call and response from the humans and their brains. Without it there is
only the groove, the stereotypical repeating pattern."[65]

CONCLUSION: FRAGILE LIKE THE THINNEST GLASS

When Dan Bergmann is asked to define *diversity*, he immediately turns to the
question of work. "I want to live in a world in which the people who have access
to the best education [are] . . . willing to do the work." His way of describing
inclusion in the ModPo community, somewhat like Dimock's, is counterintuitively to think about an "exclusionary filter," thus increasing the value of occupy-
ing even the free space. "The ferocity of that filter" (in Dan's phrase) means that
those who participate in crowdsourced interpretation of disjunctive writing are,
by definition, "excited about coming to understand the poems." Only when the
xMOOC is seen to consist of people who "otherwise have nothing in common"
are we able to "keep in the curriculum poems that excite people from every condition, and we can learn about the conditions as well as the poem." This idea will

not seem illogical to readers of this book. The widely varying states of excitement of learners assure the curriculum, not the other way around. The ModPo crowd is inherently "more hit-and-miss" than one might sometimes appreciate, but the sheer associativeness of the collective close readings—such as Janet, Rahana, Jim, Charles, and Thea riffing upon "dwell"—qualifies as "a beautiful thing" of the sort that should give us pleasure as art does. It can be deemed beautiful because of and not in spite of the filter. This, argues Dan, "runs counter to the main flood of the internet."

Aiden Hunt's approach to the forums seems to be this: create or enter a new thread bearing a hope that each ensuing discussion will have at least some of the beauty of the poem being discussed. Because his goal is the furthest thing from credentialing or anything like conventional forward motion (recall his personal interest in Stein's daily repetition, described earlier, as a model for living), he seeks intellectual company to join him in the poem's neighborhood. "The entire ethos of ModPo is more my style of learning. As I get older, I see how college is often not about actually learning, but getting 'qualifications.' Qualifications don't mean much to someone who can't use them anyway." Aiden has described to me how his experience with Tourette's, "treatment-resistant depression," and overall neurodivergence had led him previously toward existentialism's "everything's horrible, everyone's dying" attitude. But recently, the ModPo syllabus has helped him find poets and poems that permit unconventional interpretations, attracting others' congenial responses, which in turn puts him in the sort of productive conversations he mostly avoids in person or synchronously. One unconventional reading—that of Dickinson's "The Brain"—starts with this personal identification: "I connected with [Dickinson] more as a sickly, reclusive type of writer, which is how I've always felt even though I did a good job of passing as healthy." But no passing is needed here, as Bruce Andrews's, Anne Waldman's, Bob Cobbing's, or Edwin Torres's athematic noise enters the scene of thought with such force as to tumble the walls of the mill. Here's the gist of Aiden's reading: "To be honest, my brain doesn't tend to swerve from its groove. It's more like I constantly have two turntables blasting music and fighting for attention in my brain." He learns to permit the fighting. His is a personal interpretation of the brain, but it happens to resonate with many others. He says he "can't use" educational qualifications, but his deep understanding of cognitive flooding, such that it can wipe out the diploma mill, appeals to many citizens who have already earned those degrees and *then* joined ModPo, where they wander onto Aiden's ground.[66]

During a five-hour conversation Dan Bergmann and I held at his home in Massachusetts, we discussed Larry Eigner's physical limitations and turned to

FIGURE 8.5 From left: Michael Bergmann, Dan Bergmann, Al Filreis.

Source: Photograph by Magda Andrews-Hoke, March 9, 2024.

a poem. I had not intended Eigner's poem to follow from Dickinson. But Dan immediately saw that it did follow. It was, at least in his reckoning, "a companion piece" to "The Brain within its Groove." It's the same Eigner poem that José Edmundo Ocampo Reyes had encountered at the ModPo meetup in Brookline five years earlier:

```
a structured field is
      the mind
        light
      and the view
           with whatever eyes
```

Dickinson is "thinking about her mind as not confined," Dan observed. On the other hand, "Eigner is more like me appreciating the order his mind has created." In one case, the brain tends to run evenly; disruption is then perhaps inevitable, and its fabulously destructive effects inexorable, but it's not where we typically begin. "I think the difference is Eigner's whatever. Whatever keeps the eyes separate from what's out there by calling it a view."

View is cognition. This idea led Dan to think generally about the MOOC phenomenon and his response to its structures and its encouragements toward nonstructure. "A structured field," he said, "is the mind's way of sorting what's out there into something it can deal with." I then remembered Reyes's quirky understanding of *whatever* during the Brookline meetup and shared it with Dan.

Dan and I pondered two possible readings of the tone and diction of *whatever*. One option is that it indicates agnosticism, even indifference over which perspective is good for the poem's purposes. Another reading aligns with an assertion of disability rights: you insist that whatever view is gained can be seen as the same, mine or yours—a suppression of subjectivity for the sake of what humans have in common. Dan prefers the latter reading, and his way of explaining this struck me as intentionally Steinian: "You don't have to do that with a view, because you are going to have to do that with a view. It can deal with what's out there into something it can deal with, not in it."

That day in Massachusetts, we didn't discuss the facts of Eigner's attitude toward the room with a view not all that far from Dan's home—the glassed-in office-porch where Eigner, often from his wheelchair, could see a yard, a street, a wooded area that led to the ocean. It was a "crux," says his biographer, "between the outdoors and the indoors."[67] But in our discussion of his connection to Dickinson, we decided that the opening of Eigner's field, a cousin to Robert Duncan's opening, gave him a window that made the poem possible and also is identified in the poem's subject matter. The view is a portal, a looking glass to pass through: it means opening, receptivity, limitation, and screen.

Screens both provide views and also *are* views. Dan's Steinian contemplation of *with* rather than *in* as indicative of stances or positions with respect to the structured field reminded me of Reyes's panicgogy poem "Type," and I asked Dan if he wouldn't mind turning to it. The result was a long discussion exploring an avid citizenship of the screen.

Dan observed that it proves once again that "poems can be sculptures and in fact characters can be sculptures":

TYPE

To see *these* characters
only as sculptures
arranged on shelves
of the thinnest glass.

FIGURE 8.6 Dan Bergmann and José Edmundo Ocampo Reyes, April 2024.

Source: Photograph by Meredith Bergmann, used with permission.

The typed-out letters—said Dan as he, through adapted assisted communication (AC) on his spelling board, pointed with a finger to glyphs—should be considered O N E L E T T E R A T A T I M E, with all the patience of the conveyor of words exceeding that of the recipient. "The thinness of the glass means that they [the letters] are not separated from us by that much." It "gives a precarious delicacy to the whole thing," he said. Learning to touch gives access to haptic sociality. Then, this exchange:

AL FILREIS: What does the word *type* mean?

DAN BERGMANN: It's the verb that got the characters onto the shelves.

AF: What about the glass? What does the glass refer to?

DB: The screen of the phone. So books are—the screen of the phone is a kind of . . . a fourth wall.

AF: And . . . you don't pierce it on a phone.

DB: You pierce it on a phone. And behind it is a world of letters and sculptures. It's also in the touch screen I showed you this morning, where I touch a letter on the glass. [Here, he was referring to a new large Apple monitor that enables him to touch letters, which, in turn, prompt likely word and phrase choices, a tool that prospectively will lessen dependence on AC as his means of writing and communicating. He had demonstrated it for me before our interview began.]

AF: How does that [new form of] touching a screen feel to you?

DB: It makes my heart race. The spelling board depends on my helper's shared attention. Shared attention is great, and it's especially valuable in piercing autism, but on the touch screen I am my own interlocutor. . . . Even though it's thin you don't want to break it. You have to be gentle.

AF: What if the MOOC consists of an image of a world of people, all of whom are relating to each other by touching their screens. . . . Many thousands of people using the finger to reach each other.

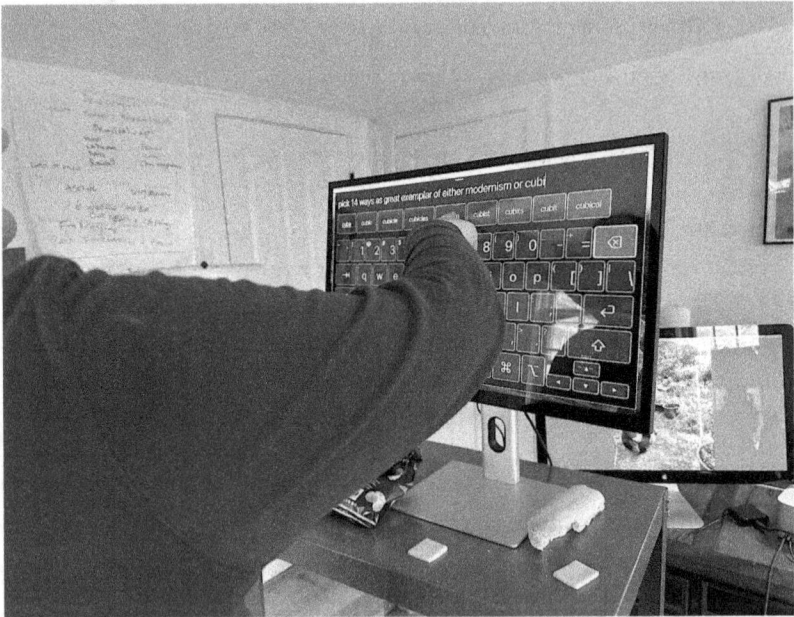

FIGURE 8.7 Dan Bergmann demonstrates his customized Apple monitor, March 9, 2024.

Source: Photograph by Michael Bergmann, used with permission.

DB: What I'm looking for is interactivity of people who are isolated to some
   degree or other, using the finger to touch the glass.
AF: Do you think ModPo is fragile?
DB: Like the thinnest glass? Yes, I do. I do.[68]

Daniel Bergmann tolerates both the anarchy of this new massive learning
system and its precarity because it holds out hope for him of self-governance
and of work- or "occupation"-based inclusive meritocracy. We recall that when
Erica Hunt pleads for touch to be recognized as a sensory function of writing
and reading—"Touch, reader, we were meant to touch"—she knew it would
lead *readers*, often left out of the signifying equation, "to exchange definitions
and feel the pulse of language." Then comes a serious commitment to mutuality:
"I promise if you step in it will propel you, me, it."[69] In my interview on a visit
to Los Angeles with Christopher Forman, a ModPo participant since the beginning, he reported that Hunt's poem struck him as indicative of the promise of
collective intelligence in a world in which "our education system rewards us for
having the right answer." When readers "step in," as Chris says he has taken many
years to learn to do, "language" will be understood as the antecedent of the "it"
that altogether "propels" poet, reader, and language itself: that's the "touch"
Hunt means, says Chris.[70]

I learned from Chris that Dan Bergmann is telling the truth about the ModPo
experience of them both: the act of exchanging definitions, which might mean
giving up your own rightness, is fragile, but there's merit in it no matter what.
In her book *Everybody's Autonomy: Connective Reading and Collective Identity*,
Juliana Spahr, cohost of the 1999 Bard conference, cites Stein's notorious (pur-
ported) claim that her "writing is clear as mud" to support her argument that if
"reading is usually taught in school so as to walk hand in hand with assimilation,"
then "anarchic—in the sense of self-governing—approaches to reading" will
enable "reading [as] at best a form of co-production."[71] Stephen Downes, one of
the originators of the cMOOC, defines the autonomy of a "good community"[72]
throughout the essays and pieces gathered in his book *Connectivism and Connective Knowledge* and especially in the talk, "Connectivism and Transcultural-
ity,"[73] crucial documents that are—in short—about citizenship. Without making
reference to massive open interpretive communities (the book was published a
few years before Downes's cMOOCs), Spahr imagined for a kind of poetry previously assumed to be inaccessible and elitist what Dimock in "Education Populism" observes of the ModPo citizenry: that "far from being a privilege of the few,
poetry here is another name for the populism that animates [the project], making its case, over and over again, that writing is durable precisely because it is for

anyone and everyone." "Stein's claims to write for everybody," Spahr notes, "with her use of fragmentation to encourage reader autonomy" depend, in a sense, on a large poetry network, *the larger, the better* to my mind if institutional critique as much as poetry is deemed to animate both. For the sake of that ideal, Spahr's study of modernist poetry networks focuses as ModPo does on "works that encourage communal readings,"[74] and those works, in turn, make for Downes's autonomous yet welcoming good community.

Synthesizing Page on decision-making enhanced by diversity, Dimock on the durability of nonacademic interpretive communities, David Rothenberg on "learning through sound" among the "dins and hums" and the resulting sudden music (in which "you can hear the greatest personality of the performer"),[75] and Spahr's redefinition of a readership for writing written for everybody, we arrive at this stopping point: cognitive diversity enables disjunction, and disjunction, in turn, enables revised definitions of what is clear—that which is normally deemed to be legible, understandable, known, and solvable. When I first saw in Steven Sloman and Philip Fernbach's *The Knowledge Illusion: Why We Never Think Alone* (2017) the assertion that "representing knowledge is hard, but representing it in a way that respects what you don't know is *very* hard,"[76] I could only think that I was reading a description of an admirable poem—and also of the work of the many admirable people willing to gather around it. The crowd, yes.

ACKNOWLEDGMENTS

The retrospective aspect of this project led me to reconnect with former colleagues, students, and collaborators. Some of these friendships go back decades. Generous people took time to talk with me—not only about our experiences together through ModPo in recent years but also in various earlier classrooms, physical and virtual, at the Kelly Writers House, inside the work of digital accumulating at PennSound, and sitting together behind our earliest computer screens. I wish to thank the following people for edifying conversations: Kristen Gallagher, Andrew Zitcer, erica kaufman, Jerry Rothenberg, Lisa New, Charles Bernstein, Christopher Forman, Julia Carey Arendell, Pang Wei Koh, Christie Williamson, José Edmundo Ocampo Reyes, Tracie Morris, Dottie Lasky, and Dan Bergmann.

The founding of the Kelly Writers House and its tenuous hold on existence in the early years are described variously in the book. There is not the space in the chapters to properly acknowledge the roles played during its creation by all the key people nor to express my feelings of debt. Of the founders and earliest supporters, just a few are listed here, but I want to emphasize that the use of *we* in this book is as genuinely plural as I can intend it. These people, among dozens more, played a part in the planning and development of the house through its first seasons: Heather Starr, Shawn Walker, Tom Devaney, Joshua Schuster, Stanley Chodorow, Judith Rodin, Jon Avnet, Andy Wolk, Tali Aronsky, Alex Edelman, Tom Lussenhop, David Hollenberg, Mark Kocent, the late Bob Lucid, Elliott Witney, David Brownlee, Bob Perelman, Lorene Cary, Kerry Sherin Wright, Harris and Jane Steinberg, George Blaustein, Jean-Marie Kneeley, Randall Couch, Leah Cianfrani, Sheila Raman, Louis Cabri, Dave Deifer, Teresa Leo, Susan Albertine, Megan Bly, Herman Beavers, Rachel Belkin, Blake

Martin, Phil Sandick, Harry Groome, Janine Catalano, David Slarskey, Hannah Sassaman, Karina Sliwinski, the pioneering digital Alumverse group (especially Elsie Howard, Alberto Fernandez, Barry Berger, Robert Shepard, and Conni Billé), Deb Burnham, Jennifer Snead, Whitney Namm Pollack, Carolyn Jacobson, Nate Chinen, Mike Magee, Adrienne Mishkin, Aaron Levy, Linda Kronfeld, Myra Lotto, Bob Lundgren, Sarah Dowling, John Fry, Michelle Taransky, Adam Kaufman, Joanne Hanna, Tahneer Oksman, Peter Schwarz, Paige Menton, Courtney Zoffness, Nick Montfort, Peter Conn, Scott and Roxanne Bok, Erin Gautsche, Cheryl Family, John Carroll, Kate Levin, Steve McLaughlin, and Greg Djanikian. To our many more recent and current friends and supporters—numbering in the hundreds and including some extraordinarily generous individuals and families who have established endowment funds to keep us going into the future—I express the deepest gratitude. I am moved by your belief in the vision of a place for creative people that remains free in all senses and open to all. The commitment of David Roberts to online literary discussion, earlier than most, has enabled us to try out ideas for convening with lifelong learners. My beloved former student David Gross, among other ways of providing help, made the renovation of the Arts Café possible; without him, the tech wizardry of the ModPo live webcasts would be unachievable. The Wexler family enabled us to build and equip our recording studio; it's where many of the ModPo videos are created, staffed technically by students supported by media apprenticeships enabled by Howie Lipson, trained through summer internships and various creative ventures funded by the Wolpow family, and recruited from high schools because of the expansive vision of the Hartman family and Maury Povich. I urge this book's readers to visit the Writers House website or our printed *Annual* to see all the names of our supportive friends and to read about the projects, events, spaces, internships, awards, and student fellowships they make possible.

All royalties earned from the sale of this book will be donated to the Digital Projects Fund at the not-for-profit Kelly Writers House. That fund directly supports ModPo, which remains free and open to anyone from anywhere.

Jessica Lowenthal, Alli Katz, Julia Bloch, Jamie-Lee Josselyn, Andrew Beal, RJ Bernocco, and Mingo Reynolds are among the members of our talented, long-time staff; nothing happens without them and their colleagues. Thanks to Val Ross, with whom I worked closely for nearly two decades, for inviting me to deliver my "End of the Lecture" antilecture outdoors on campus. And thank you, poet/teacher/arts leader Simone White, dear friend, for believing in our venture such that you want to be part of its long future.

The magnanimous persistence of the late Paul Kelly—provider of the major gift for renovating the old house in 1997, cocreator of Kelly Writers House

Fellows, and philanthropic source of the endowed chair I have held for several decades—launched us with a rational force of personality and a great skill for asserting the importance of a place at the university beyond the outsized effects of its business school. The plaque honoring him in our foyer aptly quotes Dickinson: "For Occupation—This." After reading that metapoetic assertion, you enter. Paul Kelly entered early and often and, in a sense, never left. He found *This* right there and helped us make more of it. He died suddenly of the COVID-19 virus in 2020. The chapter on poetry and learning during the pandemic is dedicated to his memory.

The original and early ModPo coconveners (the "ModPo TAs" as they are known) were willing to be filmed, with no takes, no postproduction edits, scant prior planning, zero previous experience talking while a camera intimidatingly rolled (handheld evening-TV-news-style) thirty-six inches from our faces. That there was no such thing as a false start turned into a poetics and a pedagogy. A number of these original spontaneous colloquists are still involved more than a decade later, and those who have become busy with other matters make annual special appearances during webcasts and in the forums. I am grateful to them beyond being able easily to say; they have become friends entirely by way of our hours and hours of relentless unscripted poetic talking—to slightly amend Robert Creeley,

        because we are
      always talking.

Anna Strong Safford, Molly O'Neill, Max McKenna, Emily Harnett, Amaris Cuchanski, Ali Castleman, Dave Poplar, Lily Applebaum, Gabi Ojeda-Sagué, Jason Zuzga, erica kaufman, Kate Colby, Jake Marmer, Amber Rose Johnson, Camara Brown, Julia Bloch, and Davy Knittle will always be in an unscripted group conversation going on inside my head when I read one of our poems by myself or with others. As I write these acknowledgments, I find that I appear in 1,014 video-recorded close readings with various permutations of—and sometimes all of—these people. Happily, I cannot easily distinguish my thoughts about the poems from theirs, and in the course of my book's story I have described why this is a blissful state for a teacher, critic, and supposed expert. In a way, *The Classroom and the Crowd* is about how such bliss might be generally achieved, given new tools and heterodox arrangements. A wide openness is among those arrangements. I cherish the profound ideas about openness offered by Dan Bergmann, the most assiduous learner I have ever met, even though he has rarely felt comfortable sitting in a classroom space and has mostly taught himself; it's apt that Dan gets the last word in this book. I value the research Davy Knittle and Anna Strong Safford conducted in order to comprehend and describe ModPo's approach to questions of accessibility. And a special thanks to Amaris Cuchanski for having conducted nearly one hundred interviews with ModPo participants in 2013 and for keeping meticulous transcripts and notes, and to Dave Poplar for carrying out simultaneous projects—first, a study of connectivism and its relationship to the early development of ModPo and, second, his survey of participants' assessments of the syllabus (some of them quite critical) before the addition of ModPoPLUS.

While writing this book, I was in contact with many ModPo participants, some of whom I cite and quote. A few of those mentioned in the chapters have asked to have their names abbreviated or altered, but in any case, all these partners in our eccentric mass-interpretive venture will know who they are, and I'm glad they can read here of my appreciation: Nicole Braun, Laura C., Aiden Hunt, Izengo Jongintaba, Raymond M., Padmasini Ramji, Terry Talty, Kimberly McGee, Laura De Bernardi, Luke Patrick Fortier, Rochelle, Hilary B., Benita Kape, Miranda Jubb, WareforCoin, Mary Armour, José Edmundo Ocampo Reyes, Ann Sayas, Katherine Price, Sonya Arnold, Alison Borkowska, Laura Lippman, Joseph Aversano, Jim Lynch, Michelle Pereira, Tracy Sonafelt, Janet Penney, the late John Knight, Juan Pablo Laso, Alice Allan, Melissa Hayes, Gavin Adair, Laura Lee, Therese Pope, Veronica Scharf Garcia, Sekhar Banerjee, Pamela Joyce Shapiro, Karren Alenier, Bill Speer, David Blaine, Rahana Ismail, Colette Bates, Ken X., Edward Kranz, Sean Donnelly, Nancy Somerville, Sharon Wells, Cat McCredie, Lidia Ostepeev, Alonna S., Kay M., MC Catanese, Yves Y., Martin Porter, Lorrane Borwick, Debjani Chatterjee, Linda Ireland, Graham Meikle, Brian E., Thea Terpstra, Mark Marziale, Vijaya M., Elaine Eppler, the late Andrea Buonincontro, Irene Torra Mohedano, Meredith Lederer, Sophia Naz, Mary Hannahan, T. de los Reyes, Anthony Watkins, Yosuke Tanaka, Margaret X., Apolena Vacková, Mandana Chaffa, Epistolaris, Jeremy Dixon, Imaad Majid, Matt Lutwen, members of the LongPo group and of the GSG (Global Study Group), Anthony Kolasny and the DC-based ModPo Breakfast Club, and Sanjeev Naik and other celebrants who attended the annual ModPo Renga Party (especially during the pandemic). In a sense, this book has been collaged from their and our collective experiences, composed out of the broad virtual space we have inhabited here and there for many years together. They and many unnamed others are centrally part of constructing the concepts explored in these pages. My practice is to refer to ModPo participants by first name based on the preference of most and owing to the abbreviation or pseudonymity of some surnames. There are a few exceptions for various reasons, e.g., "Reyes" and "Naz" rather than "José" and "Sophia."

The ModPo team—the organizers, coordinators, and administrative and technological handlers of the project—is truly that effective thing: a *team*. A superb teacher and poet (whose poetry is represented in our syllabi), Laynie Browne is the ModPo coordinator. Anna Strong Safford was Laynie's stellar predecessor and Julia Bloch brilliantly filled a similar role in the first years. Sophia DuRose, a member of the full-time Writers House staff, also an extraordinary poet, not to mention the most perspicacious person I have ever taught, is a ModPo TA and a crucial part of the core team. Magda Andrews-Hoke (studio and webcast techno-coordinator) and Makena Deveraux (video editor and studio engineer) also deserve praise here. Gates Rhodes filmed the original round of videos, and Kristen Martin organized and directed them. Zach Carduner and Chris Martin have kludged and reverse-engineered numerous technical aspects of our eccentric version of the open online course. Their creation of the ModPo weekly live webcast is a miracle, a most magical hack. Chris has been with me from the very first moment we reckoned with this wild idea.

The people who have made PennSound possible have done hard work, almost all of it voluntary: Charles Bernstein, Chris Mustazza, Steve McLaughlin, Danny Snelson, Michael Hennessey, and again Zach Carduner and Chris Martin, and PennSound's close affiliates too: Chris Funkhouser, Kenny Goldsmith, John MacDermott, and Michael Nardone are among them. PennSound, thanks to these people, is a Web 1.0 nirvana gone gladly awry. Danny Snelson is right in his book (about the poetics of media formats) to think of PennSound as a "little database" on the model of the fly-by-night little magazine.

At Coursera, I received encouragement and support—some technical, some political—from Daphne Koller (one of the company's two founders), Pang Wei Koh, Clara Ng, Mark Pan, Huy Le, Relly Brandman, Meera Ramakrishnan, and Kapeesh Saraf. Kapeesh persuaded his programming team of the importance of the discussion forum in the platform just when site planning was moving in less interactive directions; he invited us to visit Mountain View, California, and gave us his team and lunch and a room for ninety minutes, whereupon we—well—openly *discussed* the centrality of open discussion in massive remote learning. Megan Carr, Peter Decherney, Ellen Rhudy, and Amy Bennett, among others at Penn's Online Learning Initiative and Center for Excellence in Teaching, Learning, and Innovation, have offered timely help in getting us out of certain MOOC messes.

These colleagues and collaborators entered my teaching-with-tech life fairly far into the game, but my book recounts experiences of the years before the MOOC, dating back to the late 1980s and 1990s. First, during my terms as English undergraduate chair beginning in 1990 and then at the Kelly Writers

House starting in 1995, I came to depend on the generosity, vision, and strate-gizing of people at my university who were not really supposed to be spending their days helping me with projects like PennMOO, the pre-WWW "English gopher" for online course descriptions, the establishment of an independent web and mail server just for my department, the de facto awarding of electronic mail accounts to students, the use of the early web as a collaborative project-planning tool (via new file sharing), the early live audiocasts (live internet poetry radio!), and soon after that the interactive webcasts, rickety global three-ring circuses. Jay Treat, the late Jack Abercrombie, Michael Nenashev, Susan Garfinkel, the "English Helpers" (Jack Lynch, Sam Choi, Allen Grove, Carolyn Jacobson, Erika Lin), John MacDermott, Phil Miraglia, Ann Dixon, Mark Liberman, Dennis DeTurck, the late mensch John Smolen, the pioneering classics professor Jim O'Donnell, and in recent years Chris Mustazza and Warren Petrofsky: these colleagues were there to help me realize in technical fact the various emergent ideas I had about extending learning beyond class time, space, and curricular credit. The most influential of these people, Ira Winston, is the most talented navigator of technological institutional byways I have encountered. Ira pushed me, showed me, mocked my tech naïveté aplenty, and he did whatever it took to bring resources to bear so that learners and I could enter these new spaces. I thought he was behind me when I entered them, but then I turned forward and he was also there, up on ahead, beckoning me. If every university had an Ira Win-ston, trespassing disciplinary and school borders to make things happen, higher education would be a more innovative and also more heavenly place.

I also wish to honor Margaret Maurer, the late Robert Blackmore, David Wyatt, and Ron Brown for teaching me how to teach; John Richetti for showing me the vital passion entailed in admiring a poem as a poem; and Tracie Morris for showing me what it actually means to cultivate a "collaborative ear."

Four people whose ideas about poetry are fundamental to those presented here—Lyn Hejinian, Jerome Rothenberg, Tyrone Williams, and Marjorie Perloff—left us bereft of their genius energies during the year this book was writ-ten. These losses I feel profoundly. My book is dedicated to memories of them.

Some pages about crowdsourcing in part 3 are revisions of an essay published in *College English* (Winter 2020) in the special "Poetry Networks" issue edited by Kamran Javadizadeh and Robert Volpicelli. Parts of an essay titled "Modernist Pedagogy at the End of the Lecture," published in *Teaching Modernist Poetry*, edited by Nicky Marsh and Peter Middleton (2010), have been adapted for some passages in chapter 4. I am grateful to the editors of *AModern* for inviting me to write about paraphonotextuality for a thematic number on "The Poetry Series" (March 2015); this work has informed passages in chapter 6. I was honored to be invited to participate in a conference on new media poetics—where I first tried out some of the ideas presented in chapter 4—and then to be included in a book deriving from that symposium, *New Media Poetics: Contexts, Technotexts, and Theories* (2006), edited by Adelaide Morris and Thomas Swiss.

I am grateful to Max Warsh for spending some hours with me as I interviewed him about his photographic art in relation to the communitarian poetics of his poet parents, Lewis Warsh and Bernadette Mayer. Thank you also to Max for permission to reproduce three photographic artworks. I want to thank the following poets and literary executors for permission to quote from poems: Erica Hunt, David Eigner (for Larry Eigner), David Kermani (John Ashbery), Dorothea Lasky, Rae Armantrout, José Edmundo Ocampo Reyes, Philip Good (Bernadette Mayer), Sophia Naz, and Bob Arnold (Cid Corman and Lorine Niedecker). I acknowledge the diligent efforts of my research assistants: Enne Kim, George Gordon, Carlos Price-Sanchez, Jesse Schwartz, Sophia DuRose, and Husnaa Hashim. This is the second book I've published with Philip Leventhal as my editor. He has perfected the balance among shaping suggestion, practical trust in authorship, and sense of the ideal readers.

Most of this book was written inside my isolated mountainside cabin in the high peaks region of the Catskills. I don't know what I would have done without my fun-loving friends there, Mania, Duncan, Trina, Andy, and Anne-Marie, who lured me out after long writing days.

My mother, Lois Filreis, aged ninety-five as of this writing, leads me with persistence and productive impatience. *When will your book be out?* she wants to know. *And when are you going to write a novel?* I'm always grateful for my beloved Ben: I'm not a parental sort of teacher, and I hope that's made me a better and more interesting parent to him. Hannah, a fine, fun, and "voicy" writer, has read and listened to passages from this book in draft; I've cherished her encouragement of me to make the writing sound really like me. So much affection for my adult children and their partners, Julie and Aaron! I feel a special boundless love of Jane Treuhaft, who cares about books as books more deeply than anyone I've ever met. She more than just tolerates my incessant digitality; she likes it because it has made, after all, *a book*.

NOTES

INTRODUCTION

1. *The Today Show*, aired December 10, 2012, on NBC, WBAL-TV recording archived at the Internet Archive, https://archive.org/details/WBAL_20121210_120000_Today/start/6420/end/6480.

2. Clay Shirky, *Here Comes Everybody: The Power of Organizing Without Organizations* (Penguin, 2008).

3. Kathleen Fitzpatrick, *Generous Thinking: A Radical Approach to Saving the University* (Johns Hopkins University Press, 2019), 8.

4. Nick Anderson, "Elite Education for the Masses," *Washington Post*, November 3, 2012; Steve Henn, "From Silicon Valley, A New Approach to Education," NPR, April 18, 2012, https://www.npr.org/sections/alltechconsidered/2012/04/18/150846845/from-silicon-valley-a-new-approach-to-education; Guy Raz, "Online Education Grows Up, and for Now, It's Free," September 30, 2012 https://www.npr.org/2012/09/30/162053927/online-education-grows-up-and-for-now-its-free; an audio recording of the *Chicago Tonight* interview is preserved here: https://media.sas.upenn.edu/afilreis/ModPo-misc/Durbin-Dick_on-Coursera-ModPo_Chicago-Tonight_WWTW_9-26-12.mp3. This was covered by the *Springfield Democrat*, the *Kenyon Review*, and the *Poetry Foundation*, September 20, 2012, https://www.poetryfoundation.org/harriet-books/2012/09/dick-durbin-is-taking-an-online-poetry-course; Daniel Luzer, "Dick Durbin Tries Online Poetry Class," *Washington Monthly*, September 21, 2012, https://washingtonmonthly.com/2012/09/21/dick-durbin-tries-online-poetry-class.

5. Ann Kirshner, writing for the *Chronicle of Higher Education* after participating in Ezekial Emmanuel's MOOC on healthcare, observed: "The quality and format of the discussions were immediate disappointments. A teaching assistant provided some adult supervision, but too many of the postings were at the dismal level of most anonymous Internet comments: nasty, brutish, and long. The reliance on old-fashioned threaded message groups made it impossible to distinguish online jerks from potential geniuses. I kept wishing for a way to break the large group into small cohorts self-selected by background or interests—health-care professionals, for instance, or those particularly interested in the economics of health care. There was no way to build a discussion, no equivalent to the hush that comes over the classroom when the smart kid raises his or her hand." Ann Kirshner, "A Pioneer in Online Education Tries a MOOC," *Chronicle of Higher Education*, October 1, 2012.

6. Laura Pappano, "The Year of the MOOC," *New York Times*, November 2, 2012.

7. Justin Reich, *Failure to Disrupt: Why Technology Alone Can't Transform Education* (Harvard University Press, 2020), 18, 20.

8. Jonathan Freedman, "MOOCs: Usefully Middlebrow," *Chronicle of Higher Education*, November 25, 2013.

9. Reich, *Failure to Disrupt*, 20.

10. A few years later, several poems and videos were added to the supplemental ModPoPLUS syllabus by and about Lowell and Plath.

11. Kevin Carey, "Into the Future with MOOCs," *Chronicle of Higher Education*, September 3, 2012.

12. Jason Bangbala, "A Joke About Teaching and Learning Via Jason Bangbala," *O'Really?* (blog), January 11, 2013, https://duncan.hull.name/2013/01/11/bangbala.

13. The ModPo quizzes, required by the site's programming, were intentionally designed by the ModPo team as a workaround to generate the nearly automatic assessment of "pass." We set the system so that each participant can retake the quizzes *ten times*.

14. Laura Lee, transcribed interviews conducted by Amaris Cuchanski, 2013.

15. Karren Alenier, transcribed interview conducted by Amaris Cuchanski, 2013.

16. "Free Verses," Dorian Rolston, *The Paris Review*, December 10, 2012, https://www.theparisreview.org/blog/2012/12/10/free-verses/.

17. Jonathan Marks, "Who's Afraid of the Big Bad Disruption?," *Inside Higher Ed*, October 5, 2012, www.insidehighered.com/views/2012/10/05/why-moocs-wont-replace-traditional-instruction-essay#ixzz28Qk9rqmZ.

18. Kay M., "FINAL WORDS November 2024," November 10, 2024, Coursera, https://www.coursera.org/learn/modpo/discussions/forums/NzMRHW4ZEea1yQpXzAOzow/threads/5lw8E5xHEe-cGw63bomW7Q/replies/vNW4qJ9pEe-sWwr_xtlj9Q. Note that although I provide the URLs for the comments here, comments in the Coursera ModPo platform are visible only to those with Coursera accounts who have enrolled in the ModPo course.

19. Brian E., "Final Words 2024," ModPo discussion forum, November 10, 2024: https://www.coursera.org/learn/modpo/discussions/forums/NzMRHW4ZEea1yQpXzAOzow/threads/5lw8E5xHEe-cGw63bomW7Q/replies/vNW4qJ9pEe-sWwr_xtlj9Q/comments/HozyPJ9uEe-cGw63bomW7Q.

20. Melissa Hayes, transcribed interview conducted by Amaris Cuchanski, 2013.

21. Lyn Hejinian, *The Language of Inquiry* (University of California Press, 2000), 35.

22. Clayton M. Christensen, Michael B. Horn, and Curtis W. Johnson, *Disrupting Class: How Disruptive Innovation Will Change the Way the World Learns* (McGraw-Hill, 2011); At the time of this writing, it has been viewed 6,106,786 times: Salman Khan, "Let's Use Video to Reinvent Education," TED Ed, March 16, 2013, YouTube, 20 min., 27 sec., https://ed.ted.com/lessons/let-s-use-video-to-reinvent-education-salman-khan.

23. Clive Thompson, "How Kahn Academy Is Changing the Rules of Education," *Wired*, July 15, 2011.

24. "Global one-world classroom" is a slogan Kahn used in the famous TED Talk and was frequently invoked, e.g., Salman Kahn, "Envisioning a Global, One-World Classroom," *Big Think*, May 11, 2013, https://bigthink.com/articles/envisioning-a-global-one-world-classroom. For a critique, see Frank P. Noschese, "Kahn Academy Is an Indictment of Education," *Action-Reaction: Reflections on the Dynamics of Teaching* (blog), March 30, 2011, https://fnoschese.wordpress.com/2011/03/30/khan-academy-is-an-indictment-of-education/.

25. Jim Trelease, quoted in Dorothea Lasky, Dominic Luxford, and Jesse Nathan, eds., *Open the Door: How to Excite Young People About Poetry* (Poetry Foundation, 2013), 23.

26. Pappano, "The Year of the MOOC."

27. Tamar Lewin quoting Tom Leddy in "Professors at San Jose State Criticize Online Courses," *New York Times*, May 2, 2013, https://www.nytimes.com/2013/05/03/education/san-jose-state-philosophy-dept-criticizes-online-courses.html. See "An Open Letter to Professor Michael Sandel From

the Philosophy Department at San Jose State U.," *Chronicle of Higher Education*, May 2, 2013 (the letter was dated April 29), https://www.chronicle.com/article/an-open-letter-to-professor -michael-sandel-from-the-philosophy-department-at-san-jose-state-u/

28. Carey, "Into the Future."

29. Dave Cormier, "Seven Black Swans for Education in 2012," *Dave's Education Blog: Building a Better Rhizome*, December 19, 2011, http://davecormier.com/edblog/2011/12/19/top-ten-black-swans/.

30. S. Bulfin, L. Pangrazio, and N. Selwyn, "Making 'MOOCs': The Construction of a New Digital Higher Education Within News Media Discourse," *International Review of Research in Open and Distance Learning* 15, no. 5 (November 2014): 296.

31. Peter Coy, "Google's Boss and a Princeton Professor Agree: College Is a Dinosaur," *Bloomberg*, September 13, 2013, https://www.bloomberg.com/news/articles/2013-09-13/google-s-boss-and-a -princeton-professor-agree-college-is-a-dinosaur.

32. Thomas Friedman, "Revolution Hits the Universities," *New York Times*, January 27, 2013, https:// www.nytimes.com/2013/01/27/opinion/sunday/friedman-revolution-hits-the-universities.html.

33. See "Tom Friedman Predicts the Future(s) of Higher Education," *Pennsylvania Gazette*, July 9, 2013, https://thepenngazette.com/tom-friedman-predicts-the-futures-of-higher-education.

34. Ulrich Hommel and Kai Peters, "Shared Learning in Higher Education: Toward a Digitally Induced Model," in *Digital Transformation and Disruption of Higher Education*, ed. Andreas Kaplan (Cambridge University Press, 2022), 240.

35. Carey, "Into the Future."

36. Steve Kolowich, "Doubts About MOOCs Continue to Rise, Survey Finds," *Chronicle of Higher Education*, January 15, 2014, https://www.chronicle.com/article/doubts-about-moocs-continue-to -rise-survey-finds.

37. This uncoupling from professionalization is a key idea in Fred Moten and Stefano Harney, *The Undercommons: Fugitive Planning and Black Study* (Minor Compositions, 2013). That equation depends on certain learned skills of "negligence." In classrooms such as Gallagher's, close reading in this context is thus a form of learning nonnegligence, a counterskill gained that enables collective intentional attention. See the section of the book titled "The University and the Undercommons," 22–43, especially 30–35. Roopika Risam, in a review of *Generous Thinking*, criticizes Fitzpatrick for not sufficiently crediting fugitive planning by academics of color, but she endorses Fitzpatrick's focus on "non-market relations of care." Risam, "Academic Generosity, Academic Insurgency," *Public Books*, November 27, 2019, https://www.publicbooks.org/academic-generosity-academic -insurgency, n33.

38. Interview with Kristen Gallagher, April 4, 2024.

39. Chris Parr, "MOOC Creators Criticise Courses' Lack of Creativity," *Times Higher Education*, October 17, 2013.

40. Freedman, "MOOCS: Usefully Middlebrow."

41. James J. O'Donnell, "The Future Is Now, and Has Been for Years," *Chronicle of Higher Education*, September 3, 2012, https://www.chronicle.com/article/the-future-is-now-and-has-been-for-years.

42. Ann Kirschner, "A Pioneer in Online Education Tries a MOOC," *Chronicle of Higher Education*, October 1, 2012, https://www.chronicle.com/article/a-pioneer-in-online-education-tries-a-mooc/. "When a 10-week survey in modern and contemporary American poetry attracts more than 20,000 [*sic*] students around the world—as one offered by Coursera apparently just did—something important is happening."

43. Carey, "Into the Future."

44. Amanda Ripley, "College Is Dead. Long Live College!" *Time*, October 18, 2012.

45. Jeremy Knox, *Posthumanism and the Massive Open Online Course* (Routledge, 2016). See especially "MOOC Reactions: Disrupting and 'Making Sense,'" 13–18. Knox devotes a long chapter to ModPo (128–66). See Jonathan Haber, *MOOCs* (MIT Press, 2014); Francisco Hidalgo, Cristina Huertas

Abril, and M. Gómez Parra, "MOOCs: Origins, Concept and Didactic Applications: A Systematic Review of the Literature (2012–2019)," *Technology, Knowledge and Learning* (2020): 853–79.

46. See Ry Rivard, "Measuring the MOOC Dropout Rate," *Inside Higher Ed*, March 7, 2013, https://www.insidehighered.com/news/2013/03/08/researchers-explore-who-taking-moocs-and-why-so-many-drop-out; Seb Murray, "MOOCs Struggle to Lift Rock-Bottom Completion Rates," *Financial Times*, March 3, 2019, https://www.ft.com/content/60e90be2-1a77-11e9-b191-175523b59d1d; Rachelle Peterson, "Why Do Students Drop Out of MOOCs?," National Association of Scholars, November 12, 2013, https://www.nas.org/blogs/article/why_do_students_drop_out_of_moocs. See also Haber, *MOOCs*, 91–97. Peterson concluded that high drop-out rates were a result of the absence of meaningful discussion: "If MOOCs managed to provide opportunities for thriving discourse and flourishing interpersonal relationships, more . . . students would find time to persevere. . . . If a course is to be more than an intellectual IV dripping bare facts into the mind, it requires articulation of questions and synthesis of answers, discussion and debate, and some kind of intellectual community."

47. There are, of course, many variations of online courses, some open like cMOOCs and xMOOCs, others more private, and each seems to have earned an acronym. These are not particularly important here. Perhaps somewhat relevant—but will not receive consideration in this book particularly—are SPOCS (small private online courses) and SMOCS (synchronous massive online courses).

48. George Siemens, "Connectivism: A Learning Theory of the Digital Age," *International Journal of Instructional Technology & Distance Learning*, 2 (2005): 3–10; emphasis mine.

49. Valerie Irvine, Jilliann Code, and Luke Richards, "Realigning Higher Education for the 21st-Century Learner Through Multi-Access Learning," *MERLOT: Journal of Online Learning and Teaching* 9, no. 2 (June 2013): https://jolt.merlot.org/vol9no2/irvine_0613.pdf.

50. I discern this network of recommendations especially from the large "Introduce Yourself" forum threads in September 2020 and September 2021.

51. Masha Gessen, "What Do College Students Think of Their Schools' Reopening Plans?," *The New Yorker*, July 11, 2020, https://www.newyorker.com/news/our-columnists/what-do-college-students-think-of-their-schools-reopening-plans. See also Scott Sargrad and Maura Calsyn, "The Great Reopening Debate," *Chronicle of Higher Education*, June 19, 2020; "3 Principles for Reopening Schools Safely During the COVID-19 Pandemic," Center for American Progress, July 2020; "Tackling School Reopening During COVID-19," *Hunt Institute*, November 12, 2020; "The Rise of Online Learning During the COVID-19 Pandemic," World Economic Forum, April 28, 2020; Corey Robin, "The Pandemic Is the Time to Resurrect the Public University," *New Yorker*, May 7, 2000: https://www.newyorker.com/culture/cultural-comment/the-pandemic-is-the-time-to-resurrect-the-public-university.

52. Anya Kamenetz, " 'Panic-gogy': Teaching Online Classes During the Coronavirus Pandemic," NPR, March 19, 2020, https://www.npr.org/2020/03/19/817885991/panic-gogy-teaching-online-classes-during-the-coronavirus-pandemic.

53. Jonathan Zimmerman, "Coronavirus and the Great Online-Learning Experiment," *Chronicle of Higher Education*, March 10, 2020. For a summary of responses to Zimmerman, see Jim Lang, "On Not Drawing Conclusions About Online Teaching Now—or Next Fall," *Chronicle of Higher Education*, May 18, 2020.

54. Dana Goldstein and Eliza Shapiro, "Online School Demands More of Teachers. Unions Are Pushing Back," *New York Times*, April 21, 2020, https://www.nytimes.com/2020/04/21/us/coronavirus-teachers-unions-school-home.html.

55. Rebecca Heilweil, "Paranoia About Cheating Is Making Online Education Terrible for Everyone," *Vox*, May 4, 2020, https://www.vox.com/recode/2020/5/4/21241062/schools-cheating-proctorio-artificial-intelligence.

56. Frank Bruni, "The End of College As We Knew It?" *New York Times*, June 4, 2020.

57. Jonathan Kramnick, "The Humanities After Covid-19: What Happens When Hiring Dies," *Chronicle Review*, July 23, 2020.

58. Quoted in Bruce Sterling, "For the Love of God, It's Damien Hirst," *Wired*, January 17, 2011.

59. Peter Rant, February 20, 2024, in a thread I created seeking interpretations from members of the ten-thousand-person ModPo Facebook group.

60. Rebecca Barrett-Fox, "Please Do a Bad Job of Putting Your Courses Online," https://anygoodthing .com/2020/03/12/please-do-a-bad-job-of-putting-your-courses-online/comment-page-1. See Beth McMurtrie, "The Coronavirus Has Pushed Courses Online. Professors Are Trying Hard to Keep Up," *Chronicle of Higher Education*, March 20, 2020: https://www.chronicle.com/article/the-coronavirus -has-pushed-courses-online-professors-are-trying-hard-to-keep-up. By March 20, 2020, Barrett-Fox's post had been viewed more than 1 million times.

61. Quoted in Kamenetz, " 'Panic-gogy.' "

62. Nic Helms, Cait Kirby, and Asia Merrill, "Designing for Fatigue," *Hybrid Pedagogy*, January 27, 2022, https://hybridpedagogy.org/designing-for-fatigue.

63. See chapter 2 in this volume.

64. See Yosefa Gilon, Maxwell Bigman, Jenny Han, and John C. Mitchell, "Insights for Post-Pandemic Pedagogy," *Arxiv* (March 2022).

65. Gessen, "What Do College Students Think of Their Schools' Reopening Plans?"

66. For an overview of "What Happened to cMOOCs," see Reich, *Failure to Disrupt*, 85–87. Reich's main text was finalized by March 2020, so the argument does not refer to "panicgogy," although he briefly explores the effect of the pandemic on the reputation of MOOCs in his preface.

67. I am referring to what has been called "care ethics in the context of higher education." See Mary Drinkwater and Yusef Waghid, eds., *The Bloomsbury Handbook of Ethics of Care in Transformative Leadership in Higher Education* (Bloomsbury, 2025), esp. 36–51, 278–96.

68. Fitzpatrick, *Generous Thinking*, 53.

69. John Dewey, *How We Think* (D. C. Heath, 1910), 34.

1. OPEN DOOR, OPEN TEXT, OPEN LEARNING

1. Edward W. Soja, "Thirdspace: Toward a New Consciousness of Space and Spatiality," in *Communicating in the Third Space*, ed. Karin Ikas and Gerhard Wagner (Routledge, 2009), 50.

2. Lyn Hejinian, *My Life* (Sun & Moon Press, 1987), 39.

3. Elizabeth Birr Moje, Kathryn McIntosh Ciechanowski, Katherine Kramer, Lindsay Ellis, Rosario Carillo, and Tehani Collazo, "Working Toward Third Space in Content Area Literary," *Reading Research Quarterly* 39, no. 1 (January/February/March 2004): 41.

4. Masha Gessen, "What Do College Students Think of Their Schools' Reopening Plans?" *New Yorker*, July 11, 2020, https://www.newyorker.com/news/our-columnists/what-do-college-students -think-of-their-schools-reopening-plans.

5. Suzanne S. Choo, "Expanding the Imagination: Mediating the Aesthetic-Political Divide Through the Third Space of Ethics in Literature Education," *British Journal of Educational Studies* 69, no. 1 (2021): 65–82.

6. Homi K. Bhabha, *The Location of Culture* (Routledge, 1994), 56.

7. Kris D. Gutiérrez, "Developing a Sociocritical Literacy in the Third Space," *Reading Research Quarterly* 43, no. 2 (April/May/June 2008): 152.

8. See Suzanne S. Choo, *Teaching Ethics Through Literature: The Significance of Ethical Criticism in a Global Age* (Routledge, 2021).

9. Jonathan Rutherford, "The Third Space: Interview with Homi Bhabha," *Identity: Community, Culture, Difference* (Lawrence and Wishart, 1990), 209.

10. Gutiérrez, "Developing a Sociocritical Literacy," 152.

11. Erica Hunt, *Jump the Clock: New & Selected Poems* (Nightboat Books, 2020), 109.

12. Robert Duncan, *The Opening of the Field* (Grove Press, 1960), 7.

13. Allan Bloom, *The Closing of the American Mind* (Simon & Schuster, 1987), 56.

14. George Siemens, "Connectivism: A Learning Theory of the Digital Age," *International Journal of Instructional Technology & Distance Learning*, 2 (2005): 3–10; emphasis mine.

15. The connection between Olson's "Projective Verse" (1950) and Eigner's poem "O p e n" is made by Jennifer Bartlett, *Sustaining Air: The Life of Larry Eigner* (University of Alabama Press, 2023), 39–40

16. Jal Mehta and Sarah Fine, *In Search of Deeper Learning: The Quest to Remake the American High School* (Harvard University Press, 2019), 58.

17. Bloom, *The Closing of the American Mind*, 56, 38, 42, 26, 41, 57.

18. Bloom, *The Closing of the American Mind*, 59.

19. Interview with Pang Wei Koh, April 17, 2024.

20. Steven White, Su White, and Kate Borthwick, "Blended Professionals, Technology and Online Learning: Identifying a Socio-Technical Third Space in Higher Education," *Higher Education Quarterly* 75, no. 1 (February 2020): 1.

21. White et al., "Blended Professionals," 4.

22. George Siemens, "Connectivism: A Learning Theory of the Digital Age," *International Journal of Instructional Technology & Distance Learning*, no. 2 (2005): 3–10," 4.

23. White et al., "Blended professionals," 4. See also Celia Whitchurch, "The Rise of the Blended Professional in Higher Education: A Comparison Between the United Kingdom, Australia and the United States," *Higher Education Quarterly* 58, no. 3 (2009): 407–18.

24. Duncan, *The Opening of the Field*, 7.

25. White et al., "Blended Professionals," 6.

26. Lyn Hejinian, *The Language of Inquiry* (University of California Press, 2000), 47.

27. See Kelly Writers House calendar, https://writing.upenn.edu/wh/calendar/0201.html#28); Kelly Writers House archive, https://writing.upenn.edu/wh/archival/events/2001/retallack.php; PennSound, Joan Retallack author page, https://writing.upenn.edu/pennsound/x/Retallack.php#Alt-Poetries.

28. Here is a sample from Retallack's comments about "the contemporary" during the discussion at the Kelly Writers House: "I suppose I would want to say that almost all poetry that I would call truly contemporary is difficult, but not all difficult poetry is contemporary. I also want to say that I didn't mean that string of adjectives as an equation. I mention it as a range of ways in which contemporary poetry had been described. I think the contemporary is difficult. The contemporary moment is difficult. It's been difficult for every contemporary throughout history because it has so much that is unprecedented that we don't know how to respond to, and our, you know, habitus, as Brodeur puts it, was designed for other times. Our ways of thinking, our forms, are always moving out of date on some level. These things remain useful for part of the contemporary, but not all of the contemporary, and there's always, I think, a bad [inaudible: split{?}] between what is new and changed and changing rapidly now, because we're all experiencing, have been for most of a century, an accelerating contemporary. I mean, this is all obvious. This is what makes it, I think, a kind of poethical challenge to poets who most foreground issues of form in their work more than any sorts of writers. And issues of form are issues of composing the language in which you are living in the world in which you live. And I think that's where it becomes difficult, both in the sense of being hard and challenging and being delicious. I mean, I think the beauty and the difficulty are coterminous in work that's really exciting." Transcript made by Michael Nardone.

29. Joan Retallack, *The Poethical Wager* (University of California Press, 2004), 170.

30. John Dewey, "My Pedagogical Creed," *School Journal* 54, no. 3 (1897): 77–80.

31. See John M. Slatin, "Is There a Class in This Text? Creating Knowledge in the Electronic Classroom," in *Sociomedia: Multimedia, Hypermedia, and the Social Construction of Knowledge*, ed. Edward Barrett (MIT Press, 1992), 27.

32. See also Charles Bernstein, "The Artifice of Absorption" (1987) and Susan Howe's "The End of Art" (1984). They are not explicitly writing in the spirit of Fish's version of reader-response theory.

33. Stanley Fish, *Is There a Text in This Class?: The Authority of Interpretive Communities* (Harvard University Press, 1980), 3, 9.

34. Justin Reich, *Failure to Disrupt: Why Technology Alone Can't Transform Education* (Harvard University Press: 2020), 23. The latter formulation, stressing the Deweyan tendencies of reader-response criticism, is quoted from Fish, *Is There a Text in This Class?*, 21.

35. Quoted in Retallack, *The Poethical Wager*, 170; Gertrude Stein, *A Stein Reader*, ed. Ulla Dydo (Northwestern University Press, 1993), 498.

36. Retallack, *Poethical Wager*, 221.

37. Interview with Kristen Gallagher, April 3, 2024.

38. Wai Chee Dimock, "Editor's Column—Education Populism," PMLA 132, no. 5 (2017): 1093.

39. On Dewey, see Tom Borup and Andrew Zitcer, eds., *Democracy as Creative Practice: Weaving a Culture of Civic Life* (Routledge, 2025), 7. See also Andrew Zitcer, *Practicing Cooperation* (University of Minnesota Press, 2021). On Dewey's call for "creative democracy": "Creative Democracy: The Task Before Us," in *John Dewey: The Later Works, 1925–1953*, ed. J. Boydston, vol. 14 (Southern Illinois University Press, 1976, 224–30).

40. In-person and email interview by author with Andrew Zitcer, June 5–7, 2024.

41. A research project conducted by doctoral students in the School of Design at the University of Pennsylvania produced a report, "Documentary History of the House at 3805 Locust Walk," Kelly Writers House, https://writing.upenn.edu/wh/about/history/documentary_history.php. The report includes sections on natural lighting and the use of eaves and other features to shade sun and enable ventilation.

42. Samuel Sloan, *The Model Architect*, vol. 1 (E. S. Jones & Co., 1852), 21, 19.

43. Borup and Zitcer, *Democracy as Creative Practice*, 3, 14.

44. Zitcer, *Practicing Cooperation*, 216.

45. In part, this derives from the work of urban planner William R. Morrish. See Morrish and Chaterine R. Brown, *Planning to Stay: A Collaborative Project* (Milkweed Editions, 2000), 7.

46. In-person and email interview with Andrew Zitcer, June 5–7, 2024.

47. Dimock, "Education Populism," 1092.

48. Dimock, "Education Populism," 1093.

49. Michael Nardone, "Our Format: PennSound and the Articulation of an Interface for Literary Audio Recordings," *English Studies in Canada* 44, no. 2 (June 2018): 2.

50. Nardone, "Our Format," 20; Loss Pequeño Glazier, *Digital Poetics: The Making of E-Poetries* (University of Alabama Press, 2022), 3.

51. Nardone, "Our Format," 15.

52. Gary B. MacDonald, ed., *Five Experimental Colleges* (Harper & Row, 1973), 56.

53. Nardone, "Our Format," 22.

54. Ron Silliman, "Who Speaks: Ventriloquism and the Self in the Poetry Reading," in *Close Listening: Poetry and the Performed Word*, ed. Charles Bernstein (Oxford University Press, 1998), 373.

55. Pierre Lévy, *Collective Intelligence: Mankind's Emerging World in Cyberspace*, trans. Robert Bononno (Basic Books, 1999) 122–23.

56. Hejinian, *The Language of Inquiry*, 43, 46–47.

57. Hejinian, *The Language of Inquiry*, 51.

58. Thea T[erpstra], "What's Mine Is Yours," Coursera, subforum thread on Hejinian's *My Life*, https://www.coursera.org/learn/modpo/discussions/forums/ZBsHxygmEeaZ8Apto8QB_w/threads/9DdE-1XzEe2JxgqGil2XMQ. Note that although I provide the URLs for the comments here, comments in the Coursera ModPo platform are visible only to those with Coursera accounts who have enrolled in the ModPo course.

59. Edward Kranz, "Writing Framed by Context," Coursera, subforum thread on Hejinian, *My Life*, https://www.coursera.org/learn/modpo/discussions/forums/ZBsHxygmEeaZ8Apto8QB_w/threads/e2aRCkUhEe2GWw5xCmtijQ/replies/LQwAMVMAEe2gJQoSBJDjPw.

60. Linda Ireland, "Writing Framed by Context" Coursera, https://www.coursera.org/learn/modpo/discussions/forums/ZBsHxygmEeaZ8Apto8QB_w/threads/e2aRCkUhEe2GWw5xCmtijQ/replies/6SdK_FNiEe2OYhKeLMWt-Q.

61. Interview with Kristen Gallagher, April 3, 2024.

62. Elaine Eppler, "'A Pause, a Rose, Something on Paper,'" 2020, Coursera, https://www.coursera.org/learn/modpo/discussions/forums/ZBsHxygmEeaZ8Apto8QB_w/threads/Wu299BnkEeuithLKuUhLGw/replies/koToSRqjEeuoKgpcLmLqdw/comments/eIUIbBqxEeuoKgpcLmLqdw.

63. Lévy, *Collective Intelligence*, 67.

64. Interview with Kristen Gallagher, April 3, 2024.

65. Mary Hannahan, transcribed interview conducted by Amaris Cuchanski, 2013.

66. Kimberly McGee, transcribed interview conducted by Amaris Cuchanski, 2013.

67. Claudia Rankine, *Citizen: An American Lyric* (Graywolf Press, 2014), 79.

68. Interview with Laura Lippman, January 10, 2025.

69. David Brooks, "The Campus Tsunami," *New York Times*, May 3, 2012, https://www.nytimes.com/2012/05/04/opinion/brooks-the-campus-tsunami.html.

70. The video recording of the discussion is available in the ModPoPLUS syllabus and also at YouTube: https://www.youtube.com/watch?v=DopHofdAXmk.

71. Curtis Faville and Robert Grenier, eds., *The Collected Poems of Larry Eigner*, vol. 3 (Stanford: Stanford University Press, 2010), 1028.

72. Brooks, "The Campus Tsunami."

73. David Brooks, "The Big University," *New York Times*, October 6, 2015.

74. David Brooks, "Intimacy for the Avoidant," *New York Times*, October 7, 2016.

75. José Edmundo Reyes, transcribed interview conducted by Amaris Cuchanski, 2013.

76. Brooks, "Intimacy for the Avoidant."

77. Mara Holt, *Collaborative Learning as Democratic Practice: A History* (National Council of Teachers of English, 2018), 114.

78. Holt, *Collaborative Learning as Democratic Practice*, 114.

79. Selena Dyer, unpublished report on ModPo's annual "Final Words" webcast, November 11, 2019.

80. Holt, *Collaborative Learning as Democratic Practice*, 113, 114–15.

81. Carol L. Winkelmann, "Electronic Literacy, Critical Pedagogy, and Collaboration," *Computers and the Humanities* 29 (1995): 431–48.

82. Holt, *Collaborative Learning as Democratic Practice*, 114–15.

83. For one of many accounts, see Michael Greer, "Ideology and Theory in Recent Experimental Writing or, the Naming of 'Language Poetry,'" *boundary 2* 16, nos. 2/3 (winter/spring 1989), 335–55.

84. Louise Matsakis, "Artificial Intelligence May Not 'Hallucinate' After All," *Wired*, May 8, 2019, https://www.wired.com/story/adversarial-examples-ai-may-not-hallucinate; and Beren Millidge, "LLMs Confabulate not Hallucinate," Beren's Blog, March 19, 2023, https://www.beren.io/2023-03-19-LLMs-confabulate-not-hallucinate.

85. David Blaine, transcribed interview with Amaris Cuchanski, 2013.

86. John Dewey, *How We Think* (D. C. Heath, 1910), 216.

87. See, e.g., Alex Wong, *The Digital Decluttering Workbook: How to Succeed with Digital Minimalism, Defeat Smartphone Addiction, Detox Social Media, and Organize Your Online Life* (Alex Wong, 2021).

88. Cal Newport, *Digital Minimalism: Choosing a Focused Life in a Noisy World* (Penguin Random House, 2019), xi.

89. Newport, *Digital Minimalism*, ix.

2. POETICS OF PANICGOGY

1. José Edmundo Ocampo Reyes, "Systemic Functional Linguistics," *Rattle*, January 12, 2020, https:// www.rattle.com/systemic-functional-linguistics-by-jose-edmundo-ocampo-reyes.

2. David B. Tyack and Larry Cuban, *Tinkering Toward Utopia: A Century of Public School Reform* (Harvard University Press, 1995), 85, 94, 102, 107.

3. Jal Mehta and Sarah Fine, *In Search of Deeper Learning: The Quest to Remake the American High School* (Harvard University Press, 2019), 35.

4. From a statement published with the poem in *Rattle*. See Reyes, "Systemic Functional Linguistics."

5. Email from José Edmundo Ocampo Reyes to the author, December 17, 2024.

6. Email from José Edmundo Reyes to the author, June 19, 2023.

7. There is a general consensus about this narrative. In Chyrsi Rapanta, Luca Botturi, Peter Goodyear, Lourdes Guàrdia, and Marguerite Koole, "Online University Teaching During and After Covid-19 Crisis: Refocusing Teacher Presence and Learning Activity," *Postdigital Science and Education* 2 (July 7, 2020): 923–45. Here is a summary: "The emergency remote teaching required by Covid-19 has often been improvised rapidly, without guaranteed or appropriate infrastructural support. Given this lack of infrastructure, much of the early advice and support for non-expert online teachers has focused on the technological tools available in each institution and considered adequate to support the switch. However, this 'tools-based' approach . . . does not give many *pedagogical* hints on how, when, and why to use each of the tools" (927).

8. Documents and links pertaining to DESE policies over this period are listed and linked here: Massachusetts Department of Elementary and Secondary Education, "Guidance on Amendments to Student Learning Time Regulations," 2020, https://www.doe.mass.edu/bese/docs/fy2021/2020-12, 1, 5.

9. José Edmundo Reyes, email to the author, June 19, 2023; "Guidance on Amendments," 5.

10. Massachusetts Department of Elementary and Secondary Education, "Guidance on Amendments to Student Learning Time Regulations: Summary," December 18, 2020, https://www.doe.mass.edu /commissioner/spec-advisories/slt-regulations-guide.docx, 5; emphasis mine.

11. Janna Quitney Anderson, Jane Lauren Boyles, and Lee Rainie, "The Future of Higher Education," Pew Research Center, July 27, 2012, https://www.pewresearch.org/internet/2012/07/27/the -future-of-higher-education/.

12. "MA BESE Meeting 12.15.20," Livestream, December 15, 2020, https://livestream.com/madesestreaming /events/9446826. A transcript of Piwowar's presentation was prepared for me by Enne Kim. Emphasis added.

13. Melissa Castillo Planas and Debra A. Castillo, *Scholars in Covid Times* (Cornell University Press, 2023), 121, 3, 145, 147.

14. Tara Woods, "Cripping Time in the College Composition Classroom," *College Composition and Communication* 69, no. 2 (December 2017): 264, 275.

15. Alison Kafer, quoted in Ellen Samuels, "Six Ways of Looking at Crip Time," *Disability Studies Quarterly* 37, no. 3 (Summer 2017): https://dsq-sds.org/index.php/dsq/article/view/5824/4684.

16. Emails to the author, March 22, 29, 31, 2024.

17. Quoted in "Social Barometer: Faculty Perspectives," *EdTech*, Spring 2021, 7.

18. Nic Helms, Cait Kirby, and Asia Merrill, "Designing for Fatigue," *Hybrid Pedagogy*, January 27, 2022, https://hybridpedagogy.org/designing-for-fatigue/ [emphasis added].

19. Email from WareforCoin to the author, December 13, 2024.

20. WareforCoin, "It's taken me 4 years to finish this course," Coursera, November 27, 2024, https:// www.coursera.org/learn/modpo/discussions/forums/NzMRHW4ZEea1yQpXzAOzow/threads /eUUYoqoTEe-kTAr_2TdqLQ?utm_medium. Note: although I provide the URLs for the comments here, comments in the Coursera ModPo platform are visible only to those with Coursera accounts who have enrolled in a ModPo course.

21. Jacques Rancière, *The Ignorant Schoolmaster: Five Lessons in Intellectual Emancipation*, trans. Kristin Ross (Stanford University Press, 1991 [1987]), xx.

22. Jal Mehta and Sarah Fine, *In Search of Deeper Meaning: The Quest to Remake the American High School* (Harvard University Press, 2019), 16.

23. Travis Chi Wing Lau, "The Crip Poetics of Pain," *AModern* 10, accessed May 4, 2025, https://amodern .net/article/the-crip-poetics-of-pain/.

24. "Pandemic Pedagogy," April–June 2020, ModPo forum thread, Coursera, https://www.coursera.org /learn/modpo/discussions/forums/ZBsHxygmEeaZ8Apto8QB_w/threads/XI3LPYxjQO -Nyz2MY3DvAQ.

25. Montaigne, Tolstoy, George Eliot, Samuel Johnson, Stendhal, St. Augustine, Thucydides, Trollope, Plutarch are examples—each mentioned variously in Brooks's columns published in *The Atlantic* and the *New York Times* and in his book *The Road to Character* (2015).

26. Allan Bloom, *The Closing of the American Mind* (Simon & Schuster, 1987), 58, 62.

27. For an assessment of Hari's book as sensationalist and alarmist, see Terri Apter, "Scan and Shift: Making a Claim for a Crisis of Attention," *TLS*, January 14, 2022, https://www.the-tls.co.uk/regular -features/in-brief/stolen-focus-johann-hari-book-review-terri-apter. In a podcast interview with Vox, Hari acknowledges that there is a lack of studies tracking loss of ability to focus over time (Sean Illig, "Why you [probably] won't finish reading this story," *Vox*, February 8, 2022, https://www .vox.com/vox-conversations-podcast/2022/2/8/22910773/vox-conversations-johann-hari-stolen-focus). Stuart Richie in *UnHerd* argues that Hari's critique of social media catastrophizes, identifying social applications as agents of isolation while selectively omitting the many ways they unite people in practice ("Johann Hari's stolen ideas," *UnHerd*, January 7, 2022, https://unherd.com/2022/01/johann -haris-stolen-ideas).

28. Christina Lupton, *Reading and the Making of Time in the Eighteenth Century* (Johns Hopkins University Press, 2018), 3, 6, 8.

29. Johann Hari, *Stolen Focus: Why You Can't Pay Attention—And How to Think Deeply Again* (Crown/ Penguin Random House, 2022), 81–82.

30. Sara Hendren, *What Can a Body Do? How We Meet the Built World* (Riverhead Books, 2020), 32.

31. Jennifer Bartlett, *Sustaining Air: The Life of Larry Eigner* (University of Alabama Press, 2023), 26.

32. Unpublished letter from Larry Eigner to Cid Corman, December 25, 1961, box 42, "Eigner letters" folder 1 of 2, Cid Corman Papers, Harry Ransom Research Center, University of Texas, Austin.

33. See Bartlett, *Sustaining Air* (passim) for an analysis of Eigner's timely alignment with the Independent Living movement.

34. Petra Kuppers, "Performing Determinism: Disability Culture Poetry," *Text and Performance Quarterly* 27, no. 2 (2007): 89–106.

35. Patrick Durgin, "Post-Language Poetries and Post-Ableist Poetics," *Journal of Modern Literature* 32, no. 2 (Winter 2009): 159.

36. Robert Duncan, untitled notebook entry mailed to Cid Corman, October 17, 1954, box 46, folder titled "Other Notes from a Notebook," Cid Corman Papers, Harry Ransom Research Center, University of Texas. The notebook contained, in part, an early draft version of Duncan's essay "The Truth & Life of Myth." Emphasis added.

37. Lyn Hejinian, *The Language of Inquiry* (University of California Press, 2000), 44.

38. Aiden Hunt, "Repetition as Composition," ModPo forum thread, Coursera, https://www.coursera .org/learn/modpo/discussions/forums/ZBsHxygmEeaZ8Apto8QB_w/threads /o2hRNlorEe6UrgoL8pTFKQ.

39. Aiden Hunt, "Loving Repetition as Anti-Sisyphean Boulder Rolling & Existentialism," 2023, ModPo forum thread, Coursera, https://www.coursera.org/learn/modpo/discussions/forums /ZBsHxygmEeaZ8Apto8QB_w/threads/6Pgpw1ypEe66bBLEH6-jOQ.

40. Hendron, *What Can a Body Do?*, 14–15, 32.

41. Stephen L. Carter, "College Is All About Curiosity. And That Requires Free Speech," *New York Times*, January 24, 2024.

42. Rosmarie Waldrop, *Dissonance (If You Are Interested)* (University of Alabama Press, 2005), 263.

43. Gary B. MacDonald, ed., *Five Experimental Colleges*, ed. (Harper Collins, 1973), 69.

44. Email from Laura De Bernardi to the author, August 12, 2023.

45. "Detaining you in ModPo," 2022, ModPo forum thread, Coursera, https://www.coursera.org/learn /modpo/discussions/forums/ZBsHxygmEeaZ8Apto8QB_w/threads/3uEQXRc1Eeyjqgp Tf9CqWw /replies/JYNusRdHEeyTaApv3tYj6w.

46. Email from Raymond M. to the author, June 22, 2018.

47. Email from Laura De Bernardi to the author, August 12, 2023.

48. Francisco Ferrer Guardia, *The Origin and Ideals of the Modern School*, trans. Joseph McCabe (G. P. Putnam's Sons, 1913), 66.

49. Many others have taken an approach similar to De Bernardi's. Here is just one example, one of many variations on the theme of focusing on learner-led encounters with new poems: Emily Downey reports that she reads, annotates, and discusses the poems before watching the close reading videos moderated by me. Her process is "to draw out my own understandings before having them either fortified by that which you and your TAs said, or altered when hearing something." (Email to the author, May 8, 2024.)

50. Email from Laura De Bernardi to the author, August 23, 2023.

51. Unpublished reports attached to email from Mark Liberman to the author, December 4, 2013.

52. Hilary B., email to the author, November 10, 2024.

53. Hilary B., "FINAL WORDS, November 2024," Coursera, November 10, 2024, https://www.coursera .org/learn/modpo/discussions/forums/NzMRHW4ZEea1yQpXzAOzow/threads/5lw8E5xHEe -cGw63b0mW7Q/replies/vNW4qJ9pEe-sWwr_xtlj9Q/comments/HozyPJ9uEe -cGw63b0mW7Q?utm_medium=email&utm_source=other&utm_campaign=opencourse .discourse.modpo~opencourse.discourse.yeli1ehUEeSBtCIAC3lLIA.5lw8E5xHEe-cGw63b0mW7Q ~HozyPJ9uEe-cGw63b0mW7Q.

54. Email from Meredith Lederer to the author, June 22, 2018.

55. Carl Bereiter and Marlene Scardamalia, *Surpassing Ourselves: An Inquiry into the Nature and Implications of Expertise* (Open Court Publishing, 1993), 98–99.

56. "The Fuck-You Bow," *PoemTalk* episode #90, *Jacket2*, 2015, https://jacket2.org/podcasts/fuck-you -bow-poemtalk-90.

57. Matt Seybold, "The Medium Is Not the Method," *Modern Language Quarterly* 86, no. 1 (March 2025): 103.

58. "Begin to Awaken," *PoemTalk* episode #147, *Jacket2*, April 24, 2020, https://jacket2.org/podcasts /begin-awaken-poemtalk-147.

59. Terrence Des Pres, *The Survivor: An Anatomy of Life in the Death Camps* (Oxford University Press, 1976), 89.

60. Ken X., "On 'Spring and all (by the road to the contagious hospital')," ModPoPlus forum, 2020, Coursera, https://www.coursera.org/learn/modpo/discussions/forums/ZBsHxygmEeaZ8Apto8QB_w /threads/8NiEiw6GEeuoKgpcLmLqdw.

61. Interview with Laura Lippman, January 10, 2025.

62. Email from Meredith Lederer to the author, June 22, 2018. *The Difference Is Spreading*, ed. Al Filreis and Anna Strong Safford (University of Pennsylvania Press, 2022), 140. (The poem was first published in 1982.)

63. Email from Miranda Jubb to the author, February 15, 2024.

64. George P. Landow, *Hypertext: The Convergence of Contemporary Critical Theory and Technology* (Johns Hopkins University Press, 1991), 132–33.

65. "Letting Go," 2016, ModPo forum thread, https://www.coursera.org/learn/modpo/discussions /forums/ZBsHxygmEeaZ8Apto8QB_w/threads/sjIjU4HbEeaAtg4Z5X_Hsw.

66.   Email from Matt Lutwen to the author, April 7, 2024.

67.   Box 45, folder entitled "Misc. notes," Cid Corman Papers, Harry Ransom Research Center, University of Texas at Austin.

68.   Harry C. Boyte, *Awakening Democracy Through Public Work: Pedagogies of Empowerment* (Vanderbilt University Press, 2018), 5–6, 143.

69.   "Detaining you in ModPo," 2020, ModPo forum thread, Coursera, https://www.coursera.org/learn/modpo/discussions/forums/ZBsHxygmEeaZ8Apto8QB_w/threads/3uEQXRc1EeyjqgpTf9CqWw/replies/JYNusRdHEeyTaApv3tYj6w.

70.   Anne Jongleux, "My (Not) Final Thoughts," ModPo forum thread, Coursera, November 9, 2024, https://www.coursera.org/learn/modpo/discussions/forums/NzMRHW4ZEea1yQpXzAOzow/threads/5lw8E5xHEe-cGw63bomW7Q. "For reasons I no longer remember": "Introduce Yourselves Here," Coursera, September 1, 2024, https://www.coursera.org/learn/modpo/discussions/all/threads/qGeA-mQZEe-EAgr_yNs2xQ/replies/M4X2_mjIEe-ZuQr_7teSSw; email to the author, November 11, 2024.

71.   Maureen Bailey, "Mother Mayer," ModPo forum thread, Coursera, October 21, 2018, https://www.coursera.org/learn/modpo/discussions/all/threads/BU1C6dVmEeipeQ5Pff9Jig.

72.   Maureen Bailey, "Introduce yourself here," ModPo forum thread, Coursera, September 4, 2021, https://www.coursera.org/learn/modpo/discussions/all/threads/qqt7iQpMEeyZGA7huEeeZw/replies/8rvd9w2REeyzTxKP_hNrxQ.

73.   Earlier, I covered Bloom and Hari on this topic. Now Brooks: he extends his commentaries on the baleful effects poor contemporary reading habits to the hastened quality of personal and professional situations, concerned on behalf of young people who are "compelled to bounce around more, popping up here and there, quantumlike, with different jobs, living arrangements and partners while hoping that all these diverse experiences magically add up to something" ("Mis-Educating the Young," *New York Times*, June 23, 2017). See Dana Gioia, "Meanwhile: When Reading Wanes, It's Time to Worry," *New York Times*, April 13, 2005. See Sherry Turkle, *Reclaiming Conversation: The Power of Talk in a Digital Age* (Penguin, 2015), 69, 110, 157, 219, 237, 241.

74.   Maureen Bailey, "Final Words," ModPo forum thread, Coursera, November 2019, https://www.coursera.org/learn/modpo/discussions/forums/ZBsHxygmEeaZ8Apto8QB_w/threads/doOPmwPHEeqkTw5y9mTAbw/replies/U_G6JhMiTBSxuiYTItwULg?page=3.

75.   Sean Cavanaugh, "Student Persistence Low in MOOCs with Higher Workloads," *Education Week*, December 6, 2013, https://www.edweek.org/teaching-learning/student-persistence-low-in-moocs-with-higher-workloads-study-finds/2013/12. Laura Perna et al., "Moving Through MOOCs: Understanding the Progression of Users in Massive Open Online Courses," *Educational Researcher* 43, no. 9 (2014): 421–32.

76.   Lorine Niedecker, *Collected Works*, ed. Jenny Penberthy (University of California Press, 2002), 194.

77.   Email from Jeremy Dixon to the author, June 24, 2018.

78.   Stephen Kosselyn, *Active Learning Online: Five Principles That Make Online Courses Come Alive* (Alinea Learning, 2021), 64–65.

79.   "Japanese Renga ModPo Style," 2018, Coursera, https://www.coursera.org/learn/modpo/discussions/forums/NzMRHW4ZEea1yQpXzAOzow/threads/Gi9QJL_JEeihBBLh0Hz6wA.

80.   A note on forum archives: the ModPo "instance" was rebooted in September 2016. At that time, the thread-separated logs of previous posts and replies became unavailable. I had retained copies of selected forum discussions between September 1, 2012, and September 1, 2016, and have consulted them variously.

81.   See Rachele Gusella and Ann Peeters, "Poetry Bombing: From the Streets to Social Media," *Audioliterary Poetry Between Performance and Mediatization*, ed. Marc Matter, Henrik Wehmeier, and Clara Cosima Wolff (De Gruyter, 2024),

82.   Nic Helms, Cait Kirby, and Asia Merrill, "Designing for Fatigue," *Hybrid Pedagogy*, January 27, 2022, https://hybridpedagogy.org/designing-for-fatigue/.

83. "ModPo in the Age of the Pandemic," 2020, Coursera, https://www.coursera.org/learn/modpo/discussions/forums/ZBsHxygmEeaZ8Apto8QB_w/threads/FX6xo_nbEeqxrQ5g281r2Q.

84. "Japanese Renga – ModPo Style, 2021," Coursera, https://www.coursera.org/learn/modpo/discussions/forums/ZBsHxygmEeaZ8Apto8QB_w/threads/TnAKNHS1EeuySRJUCd2SPQ/replies/ht3wfnncEeuDUBJt31lHdQ/comments/43RQD3TCEeuySRJUCd2SPQ

85. Courtney Naum Scuro, "Timesoup, Missed Meaning, and Making a Pandemic History," in Castillo Planas and Castillo, *Scholars in Covid Times*, 41.

86. José Edmundo Ocampo Reyes, "Two Poems by José Edmundo Ocampo Reyes," *Scoundrel Time*, May 5, 2025, https://scoundreltime.com/two-poems-by-jose-edmundo-ocampo-reyes.

87. Jonathan Zimmerman, "Coronavirus and the Great Online-Learning Experiment," *Chronicle of Higher Education*, March 10, 2020: https://www.chronicle.com/article/coronavirus-and-the-great-online-learning-experiment.

88. Rhian Morgan and Lisa Moody, "Promoting Equity and Inclusion through Critical Resilience Pedagogy," in Castillo Planas and Castillo, *Scholars in Covid Times*.

89. Morgan and Moody, 136.

90. Sophia Naz, "One Thing Happens," *Rattle*, fall 2021, https://www.rattle.com/one-thing-happens-by-sophia-naz. The poem has also been published in Sophia Naz, *Bark Archipelago* (Weavers Press, 2023).

91. Thomas H. Johnson, ed., *The Collected Poems of Emily Dickinson* (Little, Brown, 1960 [1951]), 642, 691.

92. Joseph Aversano, "Possibility in the time of Covid 19," 2020, Coursera, https://www.coursera.org/learn/modpo/discussions/forums/ZBsHxygmEeaZ8Apto8QB_w/threads/ZuPl-gReRzCj5foEXtcwQg.

93. Johnson, *Collected Poems of Emily Dickinson*, 324.

94. Judith Butler, *What World Is This?: A Pandemic Phenomenology* (Columbia University Press, 2022), 62.

95. Georgio Agamben published "Requiem for the Students" on May 23, 2020, on the blog *Diario della crisi* at the website of the Istituto Italiano per gli Studi Filosofici. Here is an English translation: https://compart.uni-bremen.de/content/4-teaching/o-sommer-20/2-think-the-image-generative-art/3-material/paper-2020-agamben_requiem.pdf.

96. "Fall Scenario #6: Structured Gap Year," *Inside Higher Education*, April 29, 2020, https://www.insidehighered.com/blogs/learning-innovation/fall-scenario-6-structured-gap-year.

97. Jonathan Zimmerman, "Coronavirus and the Great Online-Learning Experiment," *Chronicle of Higher Education*, March 10, 2020.

98. Jeffrey R. Young, "Will COVID-19 Lead to Another MOOC Moment?" March 25, 2020, *EdSurge*, https://www.edsurge.com/news/2020-03-25-will-covid-19-lead-to-another-mooc-moment.

99. S. Kato, V. Galán-Muros, T. Weko, "The Emergences of Alternative Credentials," OECD Education Working Papers, no. 116, March 10, 2020. Cited by Ulrich Hommel and Kai Peters, "Shared Learning in Higher Education," in *Digital Transformation and Disruption in Higher Education*, ed. Andreas Kaplan, 239–254 (Cambridge University Press, 2022), 243.

100. Jason Pearl (@jasoninmia), "College administrators used to love online learning despite lots of evidence that it's less effective," Twitter (now X), July 27, 2020. I am grateful to Professor Pearl for engaging with me in an email exchange on this topic, July 28–30, 2020.

101. Lavinia Marin, *On the Possibility of a Digital University: Thinking and Mediatic Displacement at the University* (Springer, 2021), 59. For more on the "arm's race" see R. Godwin-Jones, "Global Reach and Local Practice: The Promise of MOOCs," *Language Learning and Technology* 18, no. 3 (2014): 5–15; Marin, *On the Possibility of a Digital University*, 59. See M. Bali, "MOOC Pedagogy: Gleaning Good Practice from Existing MOOCs," *Journal of Online Learning and Teaching*, 10, no. 1 (2014): 44; Marin, *On the Possibility of a Digital University*, 2,70.

102. Marin, *On the Possibility of a Digital University*, 67.

103. Lavinia Marin, "Abstract: On the Possibility of a Digital University: Thinking and Mediatic Displacement at the University," *ResearchGate.net*, January 2021, https://www.researchgate.net /publication/348467790_On_the_Possibility_of_a_Digital_University_Thinking_and_Mediatic _Displacement_at_the_University.

3. THE DIFFERENCE-MAKING MACHINE

1. I want to be clear that I was not an enrolled student in Hirsch's classes at the University of Virginia during my time there between 1978 and 1985. I audited class sessions and discussions on Romantic poetry he led and worked with him as a part-time assistant for two academic years during his time as chair of the department. I ran the departmental lecture series on his behalf and I also—is there irony here?—taught him how to use a word-processing computer.

2. See Michael Roth, "My Modern Experience Teaching a MOOC," *Chronicle of Higher Education*, April 29, 2013, https://www.chronicle.com/article/my-modern-experience-teaching-a-mooc. Roth, the president of Wesleyan University, had reservations hosting his xMOOC, but one positive outcome was gaining a wide readership for classic texts in modern and postmodern intellectual history.

3. By a number of learners in the ModPo forums—for example, the Shetlander poet Christie Williamson who first joined ModPo to learn the modern U.S. poetry canon: Magnus Christie Williamson, "I heard it," Coursera, 2017, https://www.coursera.org/learn/modpo/discussions/forums /ZBsHxygmEeaZ8Apto8QB_w/threads/rGqTxbloEeefTgp1JdtHeA. Williamson's ModPo story returns in chapter 8 of this book. Note: although I provide the URLs for the comments here, comments in the Coursera ModPo platform are visible only to those with Coursera accounts who have enrolled in a ModPo course.

4. Terrence O. Moore, "The Making of an Educational Conservative," *Claremont Review of Books* 10, no. 2 (Spring 2010): https://claremontreviewofbooks.com/the-making-of-an-educational-conservative.

5. E. D. Hirsch, *The Making of Americans: Democracy and Our Schools* (Yale University Press, 2009).

6. A connectivist concept promoted especially by Valerie Irvine and colleagues. See, e.g., "Realigning Higher Education for the 21st-Century Learner Through Multi-Access Learning," *MERLOT: Journal of Online Learning and Teaching* 9, no. 2 (June 2013).

7. "Disorienting the student": Lavinia Marin, "Abstract: On the Possibility of a Digital University: Thinking and Mediatic Displacement at the University," ResearchGate.net, January 2021, https:// www.researchgate.net/publication/348467790_On_the_Possibility_of_a_Digital_University _Thinking_and_Mediatic_Displacement_at_the_University. "Lack of topic control": Kimberly McGee, transcribed interview conducted by Amaris Cuchanski, 2013.

8. Hirsch, *The Making of Americans*, 64.

9. Edward Kranz, "Writing framed by context," subforum thread on Hejinian's *My Life* 2022, https:// www.coursera.org/learn/modpo/discussions/forums/ZBsHxygmEeaZ8Apto8QB_w/threads /e2aRCkUhEe2GWw5xCmtijQ/replies/LQwAMVMAEe2gJQoSBJDjPw.

10. Hirsch, *The Making of Americans*, 64, 210.

11. E. D. Hirsch Jr., "Culture and Literacy," *Journal of Basic Writing* 3, no. 1 (Fall/Winter, 1980).

12. E. D. Hirsch, Jr., *The Philosophy of Composition* (University of Chicago Press, 1977), 85.

13. Hirsch, Jr., *The Philosophy of Composition*, 75.

14. Hirsch, *The Making of Americans*, 56, 75, 42, 26.

15. Hirsch, *The Making of Americans*, 175.

16. Hirsch, *The Making of Americans*, 39.

17. Hirsch, *The Making of Americans*, 67, 80.

18. Hirsch, *The Making of Americans*, 175

19. Hirsch, *The Making of Americans*, 6. There's been some disagreement among conservative critics about the accuracy of Hirsch's historical claims. Neal McCluskey, writing for the Austro-libertarian *Cato Journal*, casts doubt on the use of *Federalist* No. 55 in which James Madison expresses what Hirsch describes as a "need [for] a special new brand of citizens who . . . would subordinate their local interests to the common good" for the sake of education. It's an "egregious misreading" of Madison who "says nothing of needing a new brand of citizens." Neal McCluskey, *Cato Journal* 30, no. 1 (2010): 248.

20. Hirsch, *The Making of Americans*, 65.

21. Wai Chee Dimock, "Education Populism," *PMLA* 132, no. 5 (2017), 1095.

22. "It is a task for the historian of culture to explain why there has been in the past four decades a heavy and largely victorious assault on the sensible belief that a text means what its author meant. In the earliest and most decisive wave of the attack (launched by Eliot, Pound, and their associates) the battleground was literary: the proposition that textual meaning is independent of the author's control was associated with the literary doctrine that the best poetry is impersonal, objective, and autonomous." E. D. Hirsch Jr., *Validity in Interpretation* (Yale University Press, 1967), 1.

23. Fred Moten, "It's Not That I Want to Say," in *Poets on Teaching: A Sourcebook*, ed. Joshua Marie Wilkinson (University of Iowa Press, 2010), 58.

24. Hirsch, *The Making of Americans*, 12. Emphasis added.

25. Ulla Dydo, ed., *A Stein Reader* (Northwestern University Press, 1993), 3.

26. Dydo, *A Stein Reader*, 17.

27. Stein receives two brief mentions in *The New Dictionary of Cultural Literacy*, rev. ed. (Houghton Mifflin, 2002). Under "Stein, Gertrude," she is the apparent inventor of the phrase "lost generation" and her line, "Rose is a rose is a rose is a rose" is quoted (140). No mention of how she writes. A second short entry is alphabetized under "Rose" for a reprise of the famous phrase (138).

28. Such views abound even in critical accounts. On "continued and even amplified presence": Catherine R. Simpson is typical in "Gertrude Stein: Humanism and Its Freaks," *boundary 2* 12, no. 3 (1984), 301–19: "Decades after her death, she is a freakish ghost that terrifies and frees us. Some trails of our terror must ooze out from our apprehension of that freedom." For an overview of assessments around the time Hirsch was forming his views on cultural literacy, see Marjorie Perloff, "The Difference Is Spreading: On Gertrude Stein," in *The Poetics of Indeterminacy: Rimbaud to Cage* (Princeton University Press, 1981), 67–99.

29. E. L. McCallum, *Unmaking the Making of Americans* (State University of New York Press, 2018), xvii.

30. The phrase "patriotic education" was used in a presidential Executive Order published a few days before the 2020 U.S. election. "Executive Order on Establishing the President's Advisory 1776 Commission," November 2, 2020, Trump White House archives, https://trumpwhitehouse.archives .gov/presidential-actions/executive-order-establishing-presidents-advisory-1776-commission. The order to renew the project is called, "Ending Radical Indoctrination in K–12 schooling, White House, January 29, 2025, https://www.whitehouse.gov/presidential-actions/2025/01/ending-radical -indoctrination-in-k-12-schooling.

31. Gertrude Stein, *The Making of Americans: Being a History of a Family's Progress* (Albert & Charles Boni), 293.

32. E. L. McCallum, *Unmaking the Making of Americans* (State University of New York Press, 2018), xiv.

33. Stein, *The Making of Americans*, 3.

34. "Prolonged present": Gertrude Stein, "Composition as Explanation," in *Selected Writings of Gertrude Stein* (Knopf Doubleday, 1990), 517–18.

35. Stein, *The Making of Americans*, 648.

36. As quoted from memory by her former student, the novelist and essayist Alexander Chee, *How to Write an Autobiographical Novel* (Mariner Books, 2018), 50.

37. McCallum, *Unmaking the Making of Americans*, xvii.

38. McCallum, *Unmaking The Making of Americans*, 27.

39. Gertrude Stein, "A Transatlantic Interview 1946," in *The Gender of Modernism: A Critical Anthology*, ed. Bonnie Klime Scott (Indiana University Press, 1990), 503.

40. McCallum, *Unmaking the Making of Americans*, xv.

41. Janet Malcolm, "Someone Says Yes to It," *New Yorker*, June 5, 2005.

42. Stein, *The Making of Americans*, 33–34.

43. Ferdi Çetin, " 'Continuous Present' in Gertrude Stein's Plays" (PhD diss., Istanbul University, 2013), 59, https://nek.istanbul.edu.tr/ekos/TEZ/50560.pdf.

44. Julian Murphet, "Gertrude Stein's Machinery of Perception," *Literature and Visual Technologies: Writing After the Cinema* (Palgrave, 2004), 77.

45. Stein, *The Making of Americans*, 625.

46. George B. Moore, *Gertrude Stein's The Making of Americans: Repetition and the Emergence of Modernism* (Peter Lang, 1998), 2.

47. Pierre Lévy, *Collective Intelligence: Mankind's Emerging World in Cyberspace* (Basic Books, 1999), 18–19.

48. Stein, *The Making of Americans*, 772.

49. Dydo, *A Stein Reader*, 18.

50. Stein, *The Making of Americans*, 291.

51. McCallum, *Unmaking the Making of Americans*, xxvi, 1.

52. Martha Nussbaum, *Not for Profit: Why Democracy Needs the Humanities* (Princeton University Press, 2010), 85.

53. The video is primarily available inside the ModPo Coursera site. It is also linked at modpo.org—and a third copy is available at ModPo, "On Stein's 'A Long Dress' (Kehillah Jewish High School)," class discussion, October 28, 2016, YouTube, 44 min., 8 sec., https://www.youtube.com/watch?v=lToWzGtkRJA.

54. ModPo subforum on Stein's "A Long Dress," thread titled "This poem is about poetry itself," 2023, Coursera, https://www.coursera.org/learn/modpo/discussions/forums/ZBsHxygmEeaZ8Apto8QB_w/threads/8jO9p16REe6KTQ6VeaO8xQ/replies/-wljKGCpEe66bBLEH6-jOQ.

55. ModPo, "Bob Perelman on the idea of a poem as a machine made of words," panel discussion, October 2, 2013, posted February 5, 2015, YouTube, 1 min., 19 sec., https://www.youtube.com/watch?v=ht1PugAEkNs.

56. Joan Retallack, *The Poethical Wager* (University of California Press, 2004), 159.

57. McCallum, *Unmaking the Making of Americans*, xix.

58. Stein, *The Making of Americans*, 454.

59. Interview with erica kaufman, February 17, 2024.

60. Michelle Y. Burke, "Writing from the Senses," Poetry Foundation, August 29, 2013, https://www.poetryfoundation.org/articles/70049/writing-from-the-senses.

61. Sally O'Brien, "Poets Imagining the City," Teachers Institute of Philadelphia, 2019, https://theteachersinstitute.org/curriculum_unit/poets-imagining-the-city.

62. Troy Dean Phillips, emails of January 28, January 30, and February 1, 2025. Zoom session, March 19, 2025.

63. Interview with Julia Carey Arendell, March 4, 2024.

64. Gertrude Stein, *Tender Buttons: Objects, Food, Rooms* (Broadview Press, 2017), 126.

65. The CLASP Fellows program, Bard College, https://iwtclasp.bard.edu/fellows. See also, https://opensocietyuniversitynetwork.org/.

66. Hirsch, *The Making of Americans*, 156.

67. Hirsch, *The Making of Americans*, 104–5.

68. Interview with erica kaufman, February 17, 2024.

69. Hirsch, *The Making of Americans*, 121.

70. Quoted in erica kaufman, "Portraits & Grammar: Gertrude Stein, a lesson play," *Jacket2*, May 23, 2012, https://jacket2.org/commentary/portraits-grammar.

71. E. D. Hirsch Jr., *Innocence and Experience: An Introduction to Blake* (Yale University Press, 1964); E. D. Hirsch Jr., "The Two Blakes," *Review of English Studies* 12, no. 48 (November 1961), 373–90.

72. William Blake, *All Religions are One* (Catherine Blake, 1795), Object 3.

73. Lyn Hejinian, "The Rejection of Closure," in *The Language of Inquiry* (University of California Press, 2000), 48.

4. I HEAR/YOU HEAR

1. Paolo Freire, "Education & Community Involvement," *Critical Education in the New Information Age* (Rowman & Littlefield, 1999), 86, 87, 88.

2. Charles Bernstein, ed., *Close Listening: Poetry and the Performed Word* (Oxford University Press, 1998), 73.

3. Robin DeRosa and Scott Robison, "Pedagogy, Technology, and the Example of Open Educational Resources," *Educause Review*, November 9, 2015, https://er.educause.edu/articles/2015/11/pedagogy-technology-and-the-example-of-open-educational-resources.

4. Yoko Tawada, "The Art of Being Synchronous," quoted by Marjorie Perloff and Craig Dworkin in their introduction to *The Sound of Poetry/The Poetry of Sound* (University of Chicago Press, 2009), [1].

5. See Marjorie Perloff, *Unoriginal Genius: Poetry by Other Means in the New Century* (University of Chicago Press, 2010), 136–44.

6. Jerome Rothenberg, *Pre-Faces and Other Writings* (New Directions, 1981), 36. Emphasis added.

7. Bernstein, *Close Listening*, 4.

8. Quoted in Steve McCaffery and bpNichol, *Sound Poetry: A Catalogue* (Underwich Editions, 1978), http://www.ubu.com/papers/cobbing.html.

9. "Dance, gesture & event," etc.: in his preface to *Shaking the Pumpkin* (1972), reprinted in *Pre-Faces*, 94–95. "Blaze of reality": e.g., Jerome Rothenberg, "Total Translation: An Experiment in the Presentation of American Indian Poetry," in *Pre-Faces and Other Writings*, 77.

10. Bernstein, *Close Listening*, 7–8.

11. McCaffery and Nichol, *Sound Poetry*.

12. "Poems are not made of thoughts": quoted in *Voices & Visions* at Annenberg Learner. Transcript: https://test-learnermedia.pantheonsite.io/wp-content/uploads/2019/02/william-carlos-williams.pdf, 6. "No ideas but in things": "A Sort of Song," in *The Collected Poems of William Carlos Williams*, vol. 2, *1939–1962*, ed. Christopher MacGowan (New Directions, 1988), 40.

13. Stephanie Strickland and Cynthia Lawson, "Vniverse," in *New Media Poetics: Contexts, Technotexts, and Theories*, ed. Adalaide Morris and Thomas Swiss (MIT Press, 2006), 177.

14. Strickland and Lawson, "Vniverse," 177.

15. Bernstein, *Close Listening*, 178, 13.

16. Peter Quartermain, "Sound Reading," in Bernstein, *Close Listening*, 227.

17. Marjorie Perloff, *Poetic License: Essays on Modernist and Postmodernist Lyric* (Northwestern University Press, 1990), 220.

18. Peter Middleton, *Distant Reading: Performance, Readership, and Consumption in Contemporary Poetry* (University of Alabama Press, 2005).

19. Peter Middleton, "The Contemporary Poetry Reading," in Bernstein, *Close Listening*, 270.

20. Middleton, "The Contemporary Poetry Reading," 270.

21. Edwin Torres, "[I spk lyric sht]," in *quanundrum: [I will be your many angled thing]* (Roof Books, 2021), 38. The square-bracketed words and phrases appear in the original.

22. Deanna Fong, "'The fact of my mouth': An interview with Jordan Scott," in *Resistant Practices in Communities of Sound*, ed. Deanna Fong and Cole Mash (McGill-Queens University Press, 2024), 79–88.

23. Edwin Torres, "The Impossible Sentence," *The Poetry Project Newsletter*, #198, February-March 2004, https://www.poetryproject.org/publications/newsletter/198-february-march-2004, 19.

24. Fong and Mash, *Resistant Practices in Communities of Sounds*, 4.

25. Albert Edmund Trombly, *Vachel Lindsay, Adventurer* (Lucas Brothers, 1929), 119–20.

26. See PennSound's Vachel Lindsay page: http://writing.upenn.edu/pennsound/x/Lindsay.html.

27. An LP put out by Smithsonian Folkways Recordings in 1957 might have been available to teachers who could play it on a record player in a classroom, as was the earlier Caedmon record (1953), although these were not available at my college.

28. Harold Bloom, ed., *The Complete Poetry and Prose of William Blake* (University of California Press, 2008), 18.

29. See Charles Bernstein, "Richard Hyland on Vachel Lindsay's 'The Congo,'" *Jacket2*, October 5, 2013, https://jacket2.org/commentary/richard-hyland-vachel-lindsays-congo; and episode #26 of *PoemTalk*, "Noncanonical Congo: A Discussion of Vachel Lindsay's 'The Congo,'" November 30, 2009, https://www.poetryfoundation.org/podcasts/75438/noncanonical-congo-a-discussion-of -vachel-lindsays-the-congo.

30. Ivan Illich, "Text and University—On the Idea and History of a Unique Institution," trans. Lee Hoinacki (keynote address delivered at the Bremen Rathaus, September 23, 1991, on the occasion of the twentieth anniversary of the founding of the University of Bremen). My copy of the English translation is a typescript provided by Silja Samerski.

31. William Clark, *Academic Charisma and the Origins of the Research University* (University of Chicago Press, 2005), 86–87.

32. Kant's phrase is quoted by Sean Franzel, "A 'Popular,' 'Private' Lecturer? Kant's Theory and Practice of University Instruction," *Eighteenth-Century Studies* 47 (2013): 1–18.

33. Email from Edwin Torres to the author, February 28, 2024.

34. Tanya E. Clement, *Dissonant Records: Close Listening to Literary Archives* (MIT Press, 2024), xi.

35. Charles Bernstein has performed this poem and recorded it: http://writing.upenn.edu/ezurl/5/.

36. Interview with Jack Foley on WKPFA, Berkeley, March 9, 1994, archived at PennSound: https://writing.upenn.edu/pennsound/x/Eigner.php.

37. Faith Ryan, "Listening as Access: Toward Relational Listening for Nonnormative Speech and Communication," in Fong and Mash, *Resistant Practices in Communities of Sound*, 95–96.

38. Anne Waldman, "Notes for a Rally (Speech)," Poets Path, accessed May 9, 2025, http://www .poetspath.com/waldmanimages/notes_for_rally.html.

39. Audio recording here: https://media.sas.upenn.edu/pennsound/authors/Waldman/KWH4-15-03 /Waldman-Anne_Rogue-State_UPenn_4-15-03.mp3.

40. See Tonya Foster, "On Claude McKay's 'If We Must Die,'" Poetry Foundation, April 30, 2020, https://www.poetryfoundation.org/harriet-books/2020/04/on-claude-mckays-if-we-must-die.

41. A few instances: Anthony Reed, *Soundworks: Race, Sound, and Poetry in Production* (Duke University Press, 2021); Tobias Wilke, *Sound Writing: Experimental Modernism and the Poetics of Articulation* (University of Chicago Press, 2022); Lytle Shaw, *Narrowcast: Poetry and Audio Research* (Stanford University Press, 2018). See also Jason Camlot, "Sound Pedagogy—Teaching the Audible Dimensions of Poetry: A Conversation (plus clips and sample syllabus) with Chris Mustazza," *SpokenWeb*, September 25, 2020, https://spokenweb.ca/sound-pedagogy-teaching -the-audible-dimensions-of-poetry-a-conversation-plus-clips-and-sample-syllabus-with-chris -mustazza/.

42. See, for example, Jessica C. E. Gienow-Hecht, "Shame on US?: Academics, Cultural Transfer, and the Cold War—A Critical Review," *Diplomatic History* 24, no. 3 (Summer 2000): 465–94; and Miranda B. Hickman and John D. McIntyre, *Rereading the New Criticism*, (Ohio State University Press, 2012).

43. David Antin, *tuning* (New Directions, 1984), 268. Quoted by Louis Cabri, "Discursive Events in the Electronic Archive of Postmodern and Contemporary Poetry," *ESC* 30, no. 1 (March 2004), 51.

44. Camlot, "Sound Pedagogy."

45. Marit McArthur, "Teaching Slow Listening: A Theory, a Tool, and Methods," panel presentation, Computational Methods of Audiotextual Analysis, SpokenWeb Futures conference, Calgary, Alberta, December 9, 2024.

46. Georges Duhamel, *Defense of Letters* (Graystone Press, 1939), 30.

47. Sven Birkerts, *The Gutenberg Elegies: The Fate of Reading in an Electronic Age* (Faber and Faber, 1994), 84.

48. Barry Sanders, *A Is for Ox: Violence, Electronic Media, and the Silencing of the Written Word* (Pantheon, 1994), 67, 11.

49. Sanders, *A Is for Ox*, 146–47 (italics mine).

50. The recording has been made available by the web site *Vox Populi*: "Audio: Allen Ginsberg reads 'America' " (2016), https://voxpopulisphere.com/2016/04/03/10631.

51. David Antin, *Tuning*, 218.

52. Craig Dworkin and Marjorie Perloff, introduction to *The Sound of Poetry/The Poetry of Sound* (University of Chicago Press, 2009), 1.

53. "Radio Free Poetry: PennSound @ 14," *Omnia*, November 28, 2017, https://omnia.sas.upenn.edu /story/radio-free-poetry-pennsound-14-video.

54. Daniel Scott Snelson, *The Little Database: A Poetics of Media Formats* (University of Minnesota Press, 2025), 183. The PennSound chapter: 97–131, esp. 113–16; Danny Snelson, "Reissues: Inventory of Digitized Magazines," *Jacket2*, February 28, 2021, https://jacket2.org/reissues; Danny Snelson, "Incredible Machines: Following People Like Us Into the Database." *Avant Magazine*, June 4, 2012, http://vvvnt.com/media/incredible-machines; on the Edit series, see https://dss-edit.com/series. "Constructing Primary Dispersion" was the title given to one of the events.

55. My response is included in Alan Filreis, "Kinetic Is as Kinetic Does: On the Institutionalization of Digital Poetry," in Morris and Swiss, *New Media Poetics*, 123–40.

56. Andreas Kaplan, "Nothing Is Constant Except Change: Academia's Digital Transformation," *Digital Transformation and Disruption in Higher Education* (Cambridge University Press, 2022), 2.

57. Brian Kim Stefans, *Fashionable Noise: On Digital Poetics* (Atelos Press, 2003), 48, 45. Emphasis added.

58. Loss Pequeño Glazier, *Digital Poetics: The Making of E-Poetries* (University of Alabama Press, 2008), 37.

59. Katherine Parrish, untitled statement in "New Media Literature: A Roundtable Discussion on Aesthetics, Audiences, and Histories," *NC1*, Spring/Summer 2002, 94.

60. Adelaide Morris, ed., *Sound States: Innovative Poetics and Acoustical Technologies* (University of North Carolina Press, 1998), 4.

61. Michael Joyce, *Of Two Minds: Hypertext Pedagogy and Poetics* (University of Michigan Press, 1995), 199.

62. John Dewey, *Democracy in Education* (Myers Education Press, 2018), 169.

63. Michael Joyce, *Of Two Minds: Hypertext, Pedagogy and Poetics* (University of Michigan Press, 1995), 199, 121.

64. Kenneth Goldsmith, *Duchamp Is My Lawyer: The Polemics, Pragmatics, and Poetics of UbuWeb* (Columbia University Press, 2020).

65. Snelson, *The Little Database*, 179–83.

66.   The Machine series: https://writing.upenn.edu/wh/involved/series/machine.

67.   Trope Tank at MIT: https://tropetank.com/.

68.   Lawrence Lessig, *Free Culture: The Nature and Future of Creativity* (Penguin, 2004), see especially 53–79.

69.   Goldsmith, *Duchamp Is My Lawyer*, 134.

70.   Shaw, *Narrowcast*, 3.

71.   Dorothea Lasky, *Thunderbird* (Wave Books, 2012), 47.

72.   Henry A. Giroux, "Liberal Arts Education and the Struggle for Public Life: Dreaming About Democracy," *South Atlantic Quarterly* 89, no. 1 (Winter 1990): 121.

73.   Paulo Freire, *Pedagogy of the Oppressed*, trans. Myra Bergman Ramos (Continuum, 1984), 59.

5. HTML WAS MY FLEMISH

1.   John Dewey, *Democracy and Education* (Myers Education Press, 2018), 169–70.

2.   Dorothea Lasky, Dominic Luxford, and Jesse Nathan, eds., *Open the Door: How to Excite Young People About Poetry* (Poetry Foundation, 2013), 181, 182.

3.   E.g., Lawrence Buermeyer, *The Aesthetic Experience* (Barnes Foundation, 1924).

4.   Dorothea Lasky, "A Word Is a Thing: Teaching Poetry Through Object-Based Learning and Felt Experience," in *Poets on Teaching: A Sourcebook*, ed. Joshua Marie Wilkinson (University of Iowa Press), 166–67. Emphasis added.

5.   Lawrence Ladd Buermeyer, *The Aesthetic Experience* (Barnes Foundation, 1929), 78. See also 26, 27, 33.

6.   Interview with Dorothea Lasky, January 11, 2025.

7.   Dorothea Lasky, "What Poets Should Do," in *Thunderbird* (Wave Books, 2012), 47–48

8.   Dorothea Lasky, "Why Poetry Can Be Hard for Most People," in *Rome* (Liveright, 2014), 15–16.

9.   Dorothea Lasky, "Genius" in *Thunderbird*, 95–97.

10. Dewey, *Democracy and Education*, 203.

11. Lasky, "A Word Is a Thing," 166–69.

12. John Dewey, *Art as Experience* (Penguin, 1980 [first published, 1934]), 247, 248.

13. Lasky, Lexford, and Nathan, *Open the Door*, 134.

14. Dewey, *Art as Experience*, 246.

15. Interview with Dorothea Lasky, January 11, 2025.

16. Dewey, *Art as Experience*, 246.

17. John Darling, *Child-Centered Learning and Its Critics* (Paul Chapman Publishing, 1994), 25.

18. Dewey, *Art as Experience*, 247.

19. Dewey, *Art as Experience*, 248.

20. Dewey, *Art as Experience*, 246.

21. John Dewey, "Review: Philosophy and Political Economy in Some of Their Historical Relations by Jame Bonar," *Political Science Quarterly* 9, no. 4 (December 1894): 743.

22. John Dewey, *The Later Works 1925–1953*, vol. 17 (Southern Illinois University Press, 1991), 298.

23. Quoted in Darling, *Child-Centered Learning*, 47, 43.

24. Mehdi El Hajoui and Anna O'Meara, eds., *On the Poverty of Student Life Considered In Its Economic, Political, Psychological, Sexual and Particularly Intellectual Aspects, with a Modest Proposal for Its Remedy*, Members of the Situationist International and Students from Strasbourg (Common Notions, 2022), 90; facsimile of the first English translation by Donald Nicholson-Smith and T.J. Clark (1967), 6.

25. Hajoui and O'Meara, *On the Poverty of Student Life*, 107; facsimile of the English translation, 23. Emphasis mine.

26. Greil Marcus, *Lipstick Traces: A Secret History of the Twentieth Century* (Harvard University Press, 1990), 179.

27. Jacques Rancière, *The Ignorant Schoolmaster: Five Lessons in Intellectual Emancipation*, trans. Kristin Ross (Stanford University Press, 1991), 4.

28. Hajoui and O'Meara, *On the Poverty of Student Life*, 108; facsimile of the English translation, 24.

29. According to Kristin Ross in Rancière, *The Ignorant Schoolmaster*, vii.

30. Rancière, *The Ignorant Schoolmaster*, 4, 68, 68.

31. Mark Nowak, *Social Poetics* (Minneapolis: Coffee House Press, 2020), 174; he is quoting Deleuze and Guttari.

32. Rancière, *The Ignorant Schoolmaster*, 71.

33. Nowak, *Social Poetics*, 143, 142. Jacques Rancière, *Proletarian Nights: The Workers' Dream in Nineteenth-Century France* (Verso Books, 2012).

34. William Carlos Williams, *The Collected Poems of William Carlos Williams*, vol. 2, *1939–1962*, ed. Christopher MacGowan (New Directions, 1991), 54.

35. See Alan Filreis, *Modernism from Right to Left: Wallace Stevens, the Thirties & Literary Radicalism* (Cambridge University Press, 1994), 190–93, 281. See also Alan Filreis, *Counter-Revolution of the Word: The Conservative Attack on Modern Poetry* (University of North Carolina Press, 2008), 150, 133.

36. "Social Poets Number," *Poetry* 48, no. 2 (May 1936), including an editorial statement by Gregory and poems by Edwin Rolfe, Alfred Hayes, Kenneth Fearing, Muriel Rukeyser and others.

37. Nowak, *Social Poetics*, 9.

38. Quoted from a review of Sandburg by Stephen Vincent Benet, "Carl Sandburg—Poet of the Prairie People: His Tall Tales and Folk Stories Have the Flavor of Whitman," *New York Herald Tribune*, August 23, 1936, 11.

39. See Filreis, *Counter-Revolution of the Word*.

40. Quoted in Nowak, *Social Poetics*, 11.

41. See Cary Nelson, *Repression and Recovery: Modern American Poetry and the Politics of Cultural Memory, 1910–1945* (University of Wisconsin Press, 1989).

42. Paul Stephens, *The Poetics of Information Overload: From Gertrude Stein to Conceptual Writing* (University of Minnesota Press, 20150), 70.

43. Stephens, *The Poetics of Information Overload*, 9. He is disagreeing with Jean Baudrillard's *Simulacra and Simulation*: "We live in a world where there is more and more information, and less and less meaning."

44. Caroline Harris, "Censorship in Brown's Gems," October 2016, Coursera, https://www.coursera .org/learn/modpo/discussions/forums/ZBsHxygmEeaZ8Apto8QB_w/threads/K9Sk-LWrEeaP2goq4S490A/replies/bLssI7XmEeavShIAFgB4-A; emphasis added. Note: although I provide the URLs for the comments here, comments in the Coursera ModPo platform are visible only to those with Coursera accounts who have enrolled in the ModPo course.

45. Bob Brown, quoted in Jed Rasula and Steve McCaffrey, *Imagining Language: An Anthology* (MIT Press, 1998), 287.

46. Bob Brown, *Gems: A Censored Anthology*, ed. Craig Saper (Roving Eye Press, 2014 [1930]), 59–60.

47. Michelle Pereira, "Censorship in Brown's Gems," October 2016, Coursera, https://www.coursera .org/learn/modpo/discussions/forums/ZBsHxygmEeaZ8Apto8QB_w/threads/K9Sk -LWrEeaP2goq4S490A/replies/UZ8Jg7ZDEeaVegrLvStXDg

48. Orchid Tierney, "The Politics and History of Digital Poetics," in *The Cambridge Companion to American Poetry and Politics Since 1900*, ed. D. Morris (Cambridge University Press, 2023), 296.

49. Craig Saper, *The Amazing Adventures of Bob Brown: A Real-Life Zelig Who Wrote His Way Through the 20th Century* (Fordham University Press, 2016), 167.

50. Bob Brown as quoted by Augusto de Campos in "Bob Brown: Optical Poems" (1965), in Saper, *Amazing Adventures of Bob Brown*, 153.

51. Saper, *Amazing Adventures*, 9.
52. Bob Brown, *Words*, ed. Craig Saper (Rice University Press, 2009), 27.
53. Brown, *Words*, 1.
54. Saper, *Amazing Adventures*, 3.
55. Katherine Parrish, "How We Became Automatic Poetry Generators: It Was the Best of Times, It Was the Blurst of Times," UbuWeb Papers, 2001, https://www.ubu.com/papers/object/07_parrish.pdf, 46. N. Katherine Hayles, *How We Became Posthuman: Virtual Bodies in Cybernetics* (University of Chicago Press, 1999), 290.
56. Tierney, "The Politics and History of Digital Poetics," 299.
57. Tierney, "The Politics and History of Digital Poetics," 298.
58. Julian Dibbel, quoted by C. T. Funkhouser, *Prehistoric Digital Poetry, An Archeology of Forms, 1959–1995* (University of Alabama Press, 2007), 195.
59. Funkhouser, *Prehistoric Digital Poetry*, 203.
60. Parrish, "How We Became Automatic Poetry Generators," 46.
61. On "finding negotiating the niceties of online identity-maintenance tiresome" and other related aspects of "Day-to-Day MOO Administration," see Shawn P. Wilbur's essay in *High Wired: On the Design, Use, and Theory of Educational MOOs*, ed. Cynthia A. Haynes and Jan Rune Holmevik (University of Michigan Press, 1998), 149–58.
62. Haynes and Holmevik, *High Wired*, e.g., 157–58.
63. See Sherry Turkle, *Alone Together: Why We Expect More from Technology and Less from Each Other* (Basic Books, 2011); and *Life on the Screen: Identity in the Age of the Internet* (Simon & Schuster, 1995).
64. Al Filreis, "Concepts for PennMOO," University of Pennsylvania, January 1996, https://writing.upenn.edu/~afilreis/moo-principles-jan96.html
65. The best account of preparing students to learn in an educational MOO is Cynthia Haynes, "Help! There's a MOO in This Class!" in Haynes and Holmevik, *High Wired*, 161–76.
66. Landow, *Hypertext: The Convergence of Contemporary Critical Theory and Technology*, 123.
67. Charles Bernstein, "Wreading, Writing, Wresponding," in *Teaching Modernist Poetry*, ed. Peter Middleton and Nicky Marsh (Palgrave Macmillan, 2010), 170.
68. Yochai Benkler, *The Wealth of Networks: How Social Production Transforms Markets and Freedom* (Yale University Press, 2006), 10, 169, 171–74, 465–66. "Collaborative reception": I am quoting Paul Stephens's cogent summary in *The Poetics of Information Overload*, 15.
69. Bernstein, "Wreading, Writing, Wresponding," 178.
70. Bernstein borrowed the term *wreading* from Jed Rasula. See Jed Rasula, *Wreading: A Poetics of Awareness, or How Do We Know What We Know?* (University of Alabama Press, 2022).
71. Bernstein, "Wreading, Writing, Wresponding," 172–73.
72. Parrish, "How We Became Automatic Poetry Generators," 44. Calvino quoted in Michael Wood, introduction to Italo Calvino, *Letters, 1941–1985*, updated edition, trans. Martin McLaughlin (Princeton University Press, 2013), vii.
73. Joyelle McSweeney and Johannes Göransson, "The Anxious Classroom," in Wilkinson, *Poets on Teaching*, 189.
74. Diana Laurillard, *Rethinking University Teaching: A Framework for the Effective Use of Educational Technology* (Routledge, 1993), 108–09.
75. Lavinia Marin, *On the Possibility of a Digital University: Thinking and Mediatic Displacement at the University* (Springer 2021), 18.
76. The SEI Center for Advanced Studies in Management at the Wharton School, University of Pennsylvania, hosted a pivotal conference titled "The Virtual University," on January 11–12, 1995. The conference took place at Penn, in Steinberg-Dietrich Hall. Meyerson gave a talk (I don't have the title) but the comment I quote here was made during a discussion; Meyerson's remarks were part of a Q&A.

everybody, Dan told me, "It's right if you want to enjoy words and their sounds, and associations. It's wrong if you want to be told what to think or see." But again, at first, in the "darkness"—darkness is Dan's metaphor for all that in his childhood seemed "fragmented, confusing, and therefore meaningless"—Stein's writing joined "everything else [that] was a soup." After his mention of soup in connection with his evolving encounter with Steinian writing, we talked about reading Gertrude Stein during the pandemic and about Courtney Naum Scuro's idea of timesoup. Dan reminded me that such a sense of time, in relation to literary understanding, is a basic aspect of his own experience, plague or not. "It took me all week to do each week [of the course]. But I was able to do it in my own way and time. I still prefer that to other ways of learning."[60]

Reinforced by asynchronicity, Stein was the turning point for Dan in his sense of poetics and temporality taken together, and having made this turn, he doesn't hesitate to offer his impractical, dramatic claims for Steinian pedagogy: "I think [Stein] should be required of every autistic person and maybe everyone else"! Why? Because then *everyone* is better off. When a group is augmented by cognitive heterogeneity in its work on (according to Page) "complex, high-dimensional," "non-routine" tasks—understanding Stein's approach to language being an excellent example, as Julia Arendell in New Orleans, Troy Phillips in Saigon, and Sally O'Brien in West Philadelphia have discovered in their classrooms—then the close relationship between diversity and complexity is affirmed, and people realize, as Dan put it, "it's not the subject matter that's important. It's the human contact around the subject matter." Crowd-powered effort provides the human contact, but its Deweyite social value depends on thinking together in no particular sequence—what the Minerva University people call "*fully* active learning."[61] Dan knows there is no bonus in that because rigid sequencing of ideas about what things mean only supports the painful intellectual discrimination with which he is all too familiar. Here is how Page sees the problem: "If cognitive tools must be accumulated in a particular order, like the stations on a train trip, then the best team consists of the highest-ability person and no diversity bonus exist[s]. If cognitive tools can be accumulated along multiple paths, that is, if the field . . . is complex, then diversity bonuses can exist because different people master different relevant tools."[62]

Page might as well be describing the differences between narrative and non-narrative, with a preference for the latter—recommending something like the disjunctive and nonrealist adventure of reading Steinian or Dickinsonian sentences to achieve a new *kind* of common understanding. I notice how Dan's remarkable description of his own encounters with Stein emphasize this quality of thought and experience accumulating along multiple paths. It's "like making

77. See Taylor Walsh, *Unlocking the Gates: How and Why Leading Universities are Opening Up Access to their Courses* (Princeton University Press, 2011), xviii.

78. John Seely Brown and Duguid, "The University in the Digital Age," *Times Higher Education Supplement*, May 10, 1996, 1–4.

79. Leon Sachs, "The Ignorant Schoolmaster: Intellectual Emancipation in Circular Form," in *Understanding Rancière, Understanding Modernism*, ed. Patrick M. Bray (Bloomsbury, 2017), 59.

80. Judith Borreson Caruso and Gail Salaway, "The ECAR Study of Undergraduate Students and Information Technology, 2007," Educause, September 12, 2007, https://www.educause.edu/ir/library/pdf/ers0706/ekf0706.pdf?snoball_referral=9z4s.

81. Stephen M. Kosslyn and Ben Nelson, eds. *Building the Intentional University: Minerva and the Future of Higher Education* (MIT Press, 2017), 46.

82. Ben Nelson, quoted by Sam Chaltain, "In Seven Cities Around the World, A New Kind of College Takes Flight," Letters from the Future (of Learning) (substack), March 11, 2024, https://samchaltain.substack.com/p/in-seven-cities-around-the-world.

83. Quoted in Chaltain, "Seven Cities."

84. Magee's speech marking the reopening of the Writers House after the 1997 renovation has been archived here: https://media.sas.upenn.edu/writershouse/97C/celebration/Magee-Mike_KWH-Marathon-ReadingIII-Ceremony_KWH_12-11-97.mp3.

85. Kenneth Goldsmith, response to Al Filreis, "Notes Toward a Modernist Pedagogy," *Jacket2*, October 12, 2007, https://jacket2.org/commentary/notes-toward-modernist-pedagogy.

86. See Kenneth Goldsmith, *Wasting Time on the Internet* (HarperCollins, 2016), 43–47.

87. Here is more Goldsmith: "The web itself is a non-fixed space. Much of what is there on Wednesday afternoon is gone or unavailable on Thursday morning. So, I must, within reason, somehow fix that space for lecture purposes. I PDF like mad and archive; I always bring an external hard drive crammed with hundreds of gigabytes should the thing I'm looking for not be available. Also, much of the stuff I teach is so non-fixed that it never appeared in any sort of stable form, rather its nature is ephemeral. So, the teacher becomes an archivist (but haven't we always?). The secret, though, is making the materials available in a sharable form that can be passed around. Xeroxes can only go so far. So in that way, the pedagogical materials need to be truly non-fixed, even at the risk of breaking arcane and outdated notions of copyright law. The students need things to take away with them, to listen to on their iPods, to share, to love . . . to possess" (quoted in Filreis, "Notes Toward a Modernist Pedagogy").

88. C. T. Funkhouser, *Prehistoric Digital Poetry, An Archeology of Forms, 1959–1995* (University of Alabama Press, 2007), 195. Kenneth Goldsmith, in a blog exchange with the author: http://afilreis.blogspot.com/2007/10/new-thoughts-on-modernist-pedagogy.html.

89. Goldsmith, *Wasting Time on the Internet*, 29–49.

90. Charles Bernstein, "Pounding Fascism," in *A Poetics* (Harvard University Press, 1992), 122–23.

91. Goldsmith, *Wasting Time on the Internet*, 30.

92. The project was first produced during Mencia's work as a Promising Researcher Fellow in 2005, a collaboration of Kingston University and the Media Research Lab, New York University, September 2005 to March 2006. https://www.mariamencia.com/pages/autocalligraphy.html.

93. See https://writing.upenn.edu/bernstein/wreading-experiments.html.

94. See Karis Shearer and Erín Moure, " 'It Was an Extension of the Moment: Five Poets in Conversation on Analog Audio Recording and Creative Practice," in *Resistant Practices in Communities of Sound*, eds. Deanna Fong and Cole Mash (McGill-Queen's University Press, 2024), 286–323.

95. Kenneth Goldsmith, *Duchamp Is My Lawyer: The Polemics, Pragmatics, and Poetics of UbuWeb* (Columbia University Press, 2020), 25.

96. Donna J. Haraway, "A Cyborg Manifesto: Science, Technology, and Socialist-Feminism in the Late Twentieth-Century," in *Simians, Cyborgs, and Women: The Reinvention of Nature* (Free Association Books, 1991), 176.

97.   See http://afilreis.blogspot.com/2007/11/patchen-cant-type-turns-to-picture.html.

98.   Susanne S. Choo, "Expanding the Imagination: Mediating the Aesthetic-Political Divide Through the Third Space of Ethics in Literature Education," *British Journal of Educational Studies* 69, no. 1 (2021): 65–82. Choo was citing Harold Bloom, *The Western Canon: The Books and School of the Ages* (Penguin, 1994), 16–17.

99.   Such as the poetry walk created in Lancaster, Pennsylvania, by the first director of the Kelly Writers House, Kerry Sherin Wright. She founded and has led the Philadelphia Alumni Writers House at Franklin & Marshall College (established in 2000).

100. Numerous ModPo meet-ups have taken place in such spaces.

101. Susan Grigsby, quoted in Dorothea Lasky, Dominic Luxford, and Jesse Nathan, ed., *Open the Door: How to Excite Young People about Poetry* (Poetry Foundation, 2013), 12. Teaching in these spaces "opens up possibilities that we don't have in the classroom for students to observe, discover, and respond."

102. E.g., the Basement Workshop, the Asian American arts and literary collective (founded 1969).

103. Ray Oldenberg, "Every Community Deserves a Third Space," *New York Times*, April 13, 2014, https://www.nytimes.com/roomfordebate/2014/04/13/the-pros-and-cons-of-gentrification/every-community-deserves-a-third-place.

104. Martha C. Nussbaum, *Not for Profit: Why Democracy Needs the Humanities* (Princeton University Press, 2016), 116.

105. Many examples of urban lofts in which art performances and happenings open to the public have been fully documented. One is Yoko Ono's Manhattan loft at 112 Chambers Street during her years affiliated with Fluxus.

106. Nowak, *Social Poetics*, 144.

107. Patti Smith, *M Train* (Vintage, 2016), 8.

108. "Speakeasy: Poetry Prose & Anything Goes" is the longest-running ongoing series at the Kelly Writers House, founded by students in 1997.

109. Jerome Rothenberg, "Harold Bloom: The Critic as Exterminating Angel," *Sulfur* 2 (1981): 4–26.

110. Stuart M. Butler and Carmen Diaz, " 'Third Places' as Community Builders," Brookings Institution, September 14, 2016, https://www.brookings.edu/articles/third-places-as-community-builders/.

111. June Thomas, *A Place of Our Own: Six Spaces That Shaped Queer Women's Culture* (Seal Press, 2024), 68–69.

112. Thomas, *A Place of Our Own*, 4.

113. E. W. Soja, "Thirdspace: Toward a New Consciousness of Space and Spatiality," *Communicating in the Third Space*, ed. K. Ikas and G. Wagner (Routledge, 2009), 50.

114. David Rothenberg, *Nightingales in Berlin: Searching for the Perfect Sound* (University of Chicago Press, 2019), 50.

115. Rothenberg, *Nightingales in Berlin*, 68.

116. Kris Gutiérrez, "Developing a Sociocritical Literacy in the Third Space," *Reading Research Quarterly* 43, no. 2 (April–June 2008): 152.

6. THE READING

1.   Aaron Levy and Louis Cabri, "On the Event, the Real-Time Image, the Archive, and Other Philly-Talks Matters," *Slought*, March 31, 2002.

2.   Louis Cabri, talk given at the Event of the Archive panel organized for Archiving Modernism conference, University of Alberta, Edmonton, Canada, July 22–26, 2003, 5; published at Slought as "Notes on Recording and Performance."

3. Levy and Cabri, "On the Event." See also: "Extensions: Matt Hart on The Subject of PhillyTalks," a paper presented by Matthew Hart at the Oxford Brookes University, Research Centre for Modern & Contemporary Poetry, 3rd Research Colloquium, The Politics of Presence: Re-Reading the Writing Subject in 'Live' and Electronic Performance, Theatre and Film Poetry, April 2, 2001.

4. Peter Middleton, "The Contemporary Poetry Reading," in *Close Listening: Poetry and the Performed Word*, ed. Charles Bernstein (Oxford University Press, 1998), 270.

5. Charles Bernstein, "Making Audio Visible: The Lessons of Visual Language for the Textualization of Sound," *Textual Practice* 23, no. 6 (2009): 963.

6. David Rothenberg, *Nightingales in Berlin: Searching for the Perfect Sound* (University of Chicago Press, 2019), 31.

7. Ted Berrigan, author page, PennSound, https://writing.upenn.edu/pennsound/x/Berrigan.php.

8. Steve Evans, "The Phonotextual Braid: First Reflections & Preliminary Definitions," *Jacket2*, March 25, 2012, https://jacket2.org/commentary/phonotextual-braid.

9. See Steve Evans and Al Filreis, "Recordings of Poetry: Technologies, Pedagogies, Institutional Politics," *Jacket2*, July 11, 2013.

10. Tanya E. Clement, *Dissonant Records: Close Listening to Literary Archives* (MIT Press, 2024), xiii.

11. Evans, "The Phonotextual Braid."

12. E.g., PennSound's media server uses a strict filename protocol so that automated alphabetization of segmented readings are numbered according to the order the poems were performed, such that the list of files in the media server for a single reading—its subdirectory—will retain that order despite the various alphabetic titling of the poems.

13. See https://media.sas.upenn.edu/pennsound/authors/Mayer/Ear-Inn/Mayer-Bernadette_06_The-Tragic-Condition_Ear-Inn-A_10-15-88.mp3.

14. In Andrei Codrescu, ed., *Up Late: American Poetry Since 1970* (Four Walls Eight Windows, 1987), 70–71.

15. Bernadette Mayer Papers, MSS 420, "Uncollected" series, box 29, folder 48, Mandeville Special Collections Library, University of California at San Diego.

16. Bernadette Mayer, "Do You Have Sex in the Bed of the Floor?", PennSound, https://media.sas.upenn.edu/pennsound/authors/Mayer/Ear-Inn/Mayer-Bernadette_05_Do-You-Have-Sex_Ear-Inn_10-15-88.mp3.

17. On SpokenWeb, see Annie Murray and Jared Wiercinski, "Looking at Archival Sound: Enhancing the Listening Experience in a Spoken Word Archive," *FirstMonday* 17, no. 4 (April 2, 2012), http://firstmonday.org/ojs/index.php/fm/article/view/3808/3197. Others include critics following Bernstein's *Close Listening* (1999), scholars and archivists organized through the High Performance Sound Technologies for Access and Scholarship project in association with PennSound, etc.

18. Lytle Shaw, *Narrowcast: Poetry and Audio Research* (Stanford University Press, 2018), 11.

19. "I now make two assertions: (1) poetry readings are narcissistic exhibitions devastating to poets, audience, and American poetry; (2) poetry readings are the best thing that ever happened to poet, audience, and American poetry." Donald Hall, "The Poetry Reading: Public Performance/Private Art," *The American Scholar* 54, no. 1 (Winter 1985): 71.

20. Hall, "The Poetry Reading," 71.

21. Quoted by Hall, "The Poetry Reading," 71.

22. Hall, "The Poetry Reading," 71.

23. See also Frederick C. Stern, "The Formal Poetry Reading," *TDR* 35, no. 3 (Autumn 1991): 67–84.

24. See Al Filreis, "Anti-Ordination in the Visualization of the Poem's Sound," *Jacket2*, February 27, 2014, https://jacket2.org/commentary/anti-finality-visualization-poems-sound.

25. Chris Mustazza, "Machine-Aided Close Listening: Prosthetic Synaesthesia and the 3D Phonotext," *Digital Humanities Quarterly* 12, no. 3 (2018): https://www.digitalhumanities.org/dhq/vol/12/3/000397/000397.html.

26. See Tanya Clement, "Distant Listening: On Data Visualisations and Noise in the Digital Humanities," *Text Tools for the Arts*, special issue of *Digital Studies / Le champ numérique* 3, no. 2 (2012).

27. Bernstein, *Close Listening*, 10.

28. John Ashbery, *Selected Poems* (Viking Penguin, 1985), 236. Copyright (c) 1977, 1985, 1986, 2008 by John Ashbery. All rights reserved. Used by arrangement with Georges Borchardt Inc. for the author's estate.

29. Here is the PennSound copy of the BBC taping: https://media.sas.upenn.edu/pennsound/authors /Ashbery/BBC-radio-3/Ashbery-John_03_What-is-Poetry_Contemporary-American-Poetry _BBC-Radio-3_7-24-99.mp3.

30. Here is my own copy of one reading of the poem: https://media.sas.upenn.edu/afilreis/Stafford -William_Traveling-Through-the-Dark.mp3.

31. William Stafford, "Traveling Through the Dark," in *The Way It Is: New and Selected Poems* (Graywolf Press, 1998), 77.

32. See https://media.sas.upenn.edu/pennsound/authors/Armantrout/segue-84/Armantrout-Rae_05 _Traveling-Through-the-Yard_Segue-Series_Ear_4-7-84.mp3.

33. See https://media.sas.upenn.edu/pennsound/authors/Armantrout/segue-84/Armantrout-Rae _Complete-Reading_Segue-Series_Ear-Inn_4-7-84.mp3.

34. Rae Armantrout, *Precedence* (Burning Deck Press, 1985), 18.

35. Ron Silliman asked Armantrout a question about Stafford's sentimentality: https://media.sas.upenn .edu/pennsound/authors/Armantrout/KWH-4-29-14/Armantrout-Rae_09_on-the-sentimentality -and-overwriting-of-Staffords-poem_Fellows-Brunch_KWH-UPenn_4-29-2014.mp3.

36. Tanya E. Clement and Stephen McLaughlin, "Visualizing Applause in the PennSound Archive," *Jacket2*, October 18, 2015, https://jacket2.org/commentary/clement-mclaughlin-pennsound-applause.

37. Gaston Bachelard, *The Poetics of Space* (Beacon Press, 1994 [first published, 1958]), 5, 47.

38. See e.g. Frederick C. Stern, "The Formal Poetry Reading," *TDR* 35, no. 3 (Autumn 1991): 80.

39. Lorenzo Thomas, "Neon Griot," *Extraordinary Measures: Afrocentric Modernism and Twentieth -Century American Poetry* (Alabama University Press, 2000), 196.

40. Although the essay doesn't refer to Morris, see a relevant essay about performance: Magali Nachtergael, "Prosthetic Poetry: Sound and Media Extensions of the Body in Performance," in *Audioliterary Poetry Between Performance and Mediatization*, ed. Marc Matter et al. (De Gruyter, 2024), 159–75.

41. Nicole Brittingham Furlonge, " 'It's Resistance but It's Also Embrace': Tracie Morris's Collaborative Ear, An Open Letter," in *Resistant Practices in Communities of Sound*, ed. Deanna Fong and Cole Mash, 155–62 (McGill-Queens University Press, 2024).

42. Tracie Morris, PennSound author page: https://media.sas.upenn.edu/pennsound/authors/Morris /11-14-13/Morris-Tracie_18_The-Mrs-Gets-Her-Ass-Kicked_KWH-UPenn_11-14-13.mp3.

43. Tracie Morris, Caroline Rothstein Oral Poetry series performance, Kelly Writers House, October 28, 2008, https://media.sas.upenn.edu/pennsound/authors/Morris/10-28-08/Morris-Tracie_05 _Africa%28n%29_Rothstein-Oral-Poetry_KWH_UPenn_10-28-08.mp3.

44. Tracie Morris, "Conceptual Poesis of Silence: Stop and Glottal (Notes on Practice)," in *I'll Drown My Book: Conceptual Writing by Women*, ed. Caroline Bergvall et al. (Les Figues Press, 2012), 389.

45. Morris, "Conceptual Poesis of Silence," 391. Morris is quoting Fred Moten, "Tonality of Totality," in *In the Break: The Aesthetics of the Black Radical Tradition* (University of Minnesota Press, 2003).

46. Rothenberg, *Nightingales in Berlin*, 31. See also David Rothenberg, *Sudden Music: Improvisation, Sound, and Nature* (University of Georgia Press, 2002).

47. "Tracie Morrison" [sic], ModPo forum thread November 2021, https://www.coursera.org/learn /modpo/discussions/forums/ZBsHxygmEeaZ8Apto8QB_w/threads/OhoIsoT6Eeyj8g6I-69uow.

48. Joan Retallack, *The Poethical Wager* (University of California Press, 2004), 97.

49. "Africa(n)," ModPo forum thread, November 2021, https://www.coursera.org/learn/modpo /discussions/forums/ZBsHxygmEeaZ8Apto8QB_w/threads/Pu7lVoHxEeywAgrLjvwVNQ.

50. "An astounding sound poem," ModPo forum thread, November 2022, https://www.coursera.org/learn/modpo/discussions/forums/ZBsHxygmEeaZ8Apto8QB_w/threads/e4TTeWA8Ee23tgra952CRw.

51. Daniel Scott Snelson, *The Little Database: A Poetics of Media Formats* (University of Minnesota Press, 2025), 99.

52. Erín Moure and Karis Shearer, "The Public Reading: Call for a New Paradigm," *Public Poetics: Critical Issues in Canadian Poetry and Poetics* (2015): 280.

53. Caroline Bergvall, *Drift* (Nightboat Books, 2014), 42.

54. Here is a six-minute video excerpt from an interactive reading-performance in 2016: https://www.youtube.com/watch?v=_B8DElVIT6s.

55. Bernadette Mayer, "Chocolate Poetry Sonnet," in *Poetry State Forest* (New Directions, 2008), 3.

56. Robert Majzels, Clair Huot, and Lianne Moyes, "'The Public Reading Is a Matter of the Public Reading': The 85 Project," *Open Letter* 13, no. 7 (Fall 2008): [1], https://www.robertmajzels.com/RobertMajzels/Assets/Documents/Articles/RM_Moyes_Majzels_Huot_The_Public_Reading.pdf.

57. See https://jacket2.org/commentary/michael-hennessey-charles-bernsteins-1976-tapework-class.

58. See Michael S. Hennessey, "From Text to Tongue to Tape: Notes on Charles Bernstein's '1–100,'" *English Studies in Canada* 33, no. 4 (December 2007): 67–72.

59. Charles Bernstein, "1–100," 1969, PennSound, https://www.writing.upenn.edu/pennsound/x/Bernstein-Class.php.

60. Cid Corman, unpublished notebook, Box 45, folder titled "Misc. notes, 3 pp." Cid Corman Papers, Harry Ransom Research Center, University of Texas.

61. Such letters can be found in the correspondence files among the fifty boxes of manuscripts housed in the Cid Corman Papers at the Harry Ransom Research Center, University of Texas.

62. Jennifer Bartlett, *Sustaining Air: The Life of Larry Eigner* (University of Alabama Press, 2023), 29–30. "Non-declamatory": Quoted in Eigner's biographical note in Donald Allen, ed., *The New American Poetry* (University of California, 1999), 436.

63. Cid Corman, "Cid Corman on Poetry Over the Radio, October 1952," UPenn, last updated July 18, 2007, https://writing.upenn.edu/~afilreis/88/corman-on-radio.html.

64. See https://writing.upenn.edu/wh/archival/events/2001/corman.php.

65. This practice also has gotten a name: "writing lines." Writing as punishment for "talking in class" has been discussed widely over the years. See Michal Hogan, "Writing as Punishment," *English Journal* 74, no. 5 (1985): 40–42. As late as 1984, the National Council of Teachers of English passed and published a resolution titled "Resolution on Condemning the Use of Writing as Punishment," NCTE, November 30, 1984, https://ncte.org/statement/writingaspunishment.

66. Larry Ferlazzo, "Should Students Be Allowed to Eat in Class? Here's What Teachers Have to Say," *Education Week*, January 23, 2023; Claire McCarthy, "Snacks & Sugary Foods in School: AAP Policy Explained," American Academy of Pediatrics, republished by Healthychildren.org, February 23, 2105; Aziz Mrioued, "The Real Reason Food Isn't Allowed In Class," *The Blackshirt* [a student newspaper], January 29, 2018; "Charles Basch: School Breakfasts Affect Learning" Teachers College, Columbia University, April 22, 2015, http://www.tc.columbia.edu/articles/2015/april/charles-basch-school-breakfasts-affect-learning.

67. Mayer, "Chocolate Poetry Sonnet," 3.

68. Interview with Max Warsh, February 2, 2024, New York City. Subsequent uncited quotations and paraphrases are from this interview.

69. One of many studies: D. W. Massaro, "Reading Aloud to Children: Benefits and Implications for Acquiring Literacy before Schooling Begins," *American Journal of Psychology* 130, no. 1 (2017): 63–72.

70. Poetry Project Papers, Rare Book and Special Collections Division, Library of Congress: https://www.loc.gov/item/2014659017.

71. Bernadette Mayer, "Max Carries the One," in *A Bernadette Mayer Reader* (New Directions, 1992), 119.

72. Bernadette Mayer, "The Incorporation of Sophia's Cereal," in *A Bernadette Mayer Reader*, 118.

73. Max Warsh, "Artist's Statement," Rema Hort Mann Foundation, accessed June 15, 2024, www.remahortmann.org/project/max-warsh.

74. Lewis Warsh, "100 Poetry Readings," in *Out of the Question: Selected Poems (1963–2003)* (AmazonUs/INDPB, 2017), 90.

75. "Max Warsh, Artist of the Week," *LVL3*, December 10, 2012, lvl3official.com/artist-of-the-week-max-warsh.

76. Susan Gingell and Wendy Roy, "Opening the Door to Transdisciplinary, Multimodal Communication," in *Listening Up, Writing Down, and Looking Beyond, Interfaces of the Oral, Written and Visual* (Wilfrid Laurier University Press, 2012), 4.

77. Shaw, *Narrowcast*, 1–3.

78. Louis Cabri, "On Discreteness: Event and Sound in Poetry," *English Studies in Canada* 33, no. 4 (December 2007): 2.

79. Howard Gardner, *The Disciplined Mind: What All Students Should Understand* (Simon & Schuster, 1999), 131.

80. Quoted in Matthew Hart, "Extensions: Matt Hart on The Subject of PhillyTalks," paper presented at the Oxford Brookes University, Research Centre for Modern & Contemporary Poetry, 3rd research colloquium, *The Politics of Presence: Re-Reading the Writing Subject in 'Live' and Electronic Performance, Theatre and Film Poetry*, April 2, 2001.

81. Moure and Shearer, "The Public Reading," 271, 279. "Poetic exploration and inquiry" is quoted from Hank Lazer, "Poetry Readings and the Contemporary Canon," in *Opposing Poetries*, vol. 1 (Northwestern University Press, 1996), 54.

82. Moure and Shearer, "The Public Reading," 283; emphasis added.

7. NOTES TOWARD A CITIZEN POETICS

1.   Post by Epistolaris [pseud. Edel Grace Altares], Coursera, September 16, 2024, https://www.coursera.org/learn/modpo/discussions/forums/ZBsHxygmEeaZ8Apto8QB_w/threads/YmRQVXFIEe-b7BI7vMDEkw/replies/aETzoHHFEe-RBQ7SFl3aqw/comments/zJ9zeXSMEe-Nbgr_2G_v1Q. Note that although I provide the URLs for the comments here, comments in the Coursera ModPo platform are visible only to those with Coursera accounts who have enrolled in the ModPo course.

2.   Interview with Laura Lippman, January 10, 2025.

3.   Raymond M., email to the author, January 11, 2025.

4.   "How we say what we say," Coursera, June 2024, https://www.coursera.org/learn/modpo/discussions/forums/ZBsHxygmEeaZ8Apto8QB_w/threads/GYqpMPZ4Ee6ihBJ8rUtPoQ?page=1

5.   Jim Lynch, email to the author, December 21, 2024.

6.   Sanjeev Naik and Vijaya M., emails to the author, January 12, 2025. I received two dozen responses to my request. Several dozen more comments can be found in the thread cited above.

7.   ModPo, discussion forums, week 1, "I dwell in Possibility" subforum, Coursera, September 2023, https://www.coursera.org/learn/modpo/discussions/forums/FOANTGisEeagGRLDSl9OXw/threads/9lSQ6ommEe6KTQ6VeaO8xQ.

8.   Carl Sandburg, *The People, Yes* (Harcourt Brace, 2006 [1936]), 215.

9.   Jon Pareles, "2006, Brought to You by You," *New York Times*, December 10, 2006.

10. Tim Wu, *The Attention Merchants: The Epic Scramble to Get Inside Our Heads* (Alfred A. Knopf, 2016), 273. This phrase comes in his chapter about the "wave of noncommercial content creation" that "spread across formats and media" (271).

11. Sara Hendren, *What Can a Body Do? How We Meet in the Built World* (Riverhead, 2020), 111.

12. Anthony Kolasny, transcribed interview conducted by Amaris Cuchanski, 2013.

13. Interview with Pang Wei Koh, April 17, 2024.

14. "Pang Wei Koh" (personal web page), accessed May 15, 2025, https://koh.pw.

15. Zhiyuan Hu et al., "Uncertainty of Thoughts: Uncertainty-Aware Planning Enhances Information Seeking in Large Language Models," *Arxiv*, February 5, 2024, https://arxiv.org/abs/2402.03271.

16. Email from Mark Marziale to the author, May 10, 2024.

17. Timothy B. Lee, "Ars Book Review: 'Here Comes Everybody' by Clay Shirky," *ArsTechnica*, April 3, 2008, https://arstechnica.com/features/2008/04/book-review-2008-04-1/4.

18. Kris D. Gutiérrez, "Developing a Sociocritical Literacy in the Third Space," *Reading Research Quarterly* 43, no. 2 (April–June 2008): 152.

19. See Isabella Peters, *Folksonomies, Indexing, and Retrieval in Web 2.0* (de Gruyter, 2009).

20. Daren C. Brabham, *Crowdsourcing* (MIT Press, 2013), xv, xxi, 4, 6–7, 9, 14, 44.

21. See Lior Zoref, *Mindsharing: The Art of Crowdsourcing Everything* (Portfolio Penguin, 2015), 177–92.

22. See, e.g., Mia Ridge, ed., *Crowdsourcing Our Cultural Heritage* (Ashgate, 2014). See also Jean-Fabrice Lebraty and Katia Lobre-Lebraty, *Crowdsourcing: One Step Beyond* (Wiley, 2013), 88–92.

23. See, e.g., Julia Bryan-Wilson, *Art in the Making: Artists and the Materials from the Studio to Crowdsourcing* (Thames & Hudson, 2016), 199–220.

24. Stuart Dunn and Mark Hedges, "How the Crowd Can Surprise Us: Humanities Crowdsourcing and the Creation of Knowledge," in Ridge, *Crowdsourcing Our Cultural Heritage*, 231–32.

25. David Blaine, transcribed interview conducted by Amaris Cuchanski, 2013.

26. Gustavo Le Bon, *The Crowd: A Study of the Popular Mind* (Floating Press, 2009).

27. See Jaap van Ginnken, *Crowds, Psychology, and Politics, 1871–1899* (Cambridge University Press, 1992), 130 ff.

28. Horace Gregory, "Chorus for Survival No. 5," in *Chorus for Survival* (Covici-Friede, 1935), 43.

29. For an account of Riesman's shifting relationship with the Left, see Daniel Geary, "Children of The Lonely Crowd: David Riesman, the Young Radicals, and the Splitting of Liberalism in the 1960s," *Modern Intellectual History* 10, no. 3 (2013), 603–33.

30. Riesman, *The Lonely Crowd*, 53.

31. Riesman, *The Lonely Crowd*, 54.

32. Riesman, *The Lonely Crowd*, 54, 55.

33. See Daniel Thomières, "Emily Dickinson: What Is Called Thinking at the Edge of Chaos," *Journal of Philosophy* 8, no. 20 (2015), 17–33.

34. Thomas H. Johnson, ed., *The Collected Poems of Emily Dickinson* (Little, Brown, 1960 [1951]), 270–71.

35. The archive of the ModPo forums is complete dating back to September 1, 2016. Prior to that, the time of a reboot to a new platform version, I rely partly on my own records and screenshots, and/or must approximate based on averages and various notes from the period 2012–2016. Moreover, Coursera has discontinued showing the number of views of any one thread. So the numbers I give could be partial and are, in any case, probably undercounts.

36. Zoref, *Mindsharing*, 21–36, 73–84.

37. Clay Shirky, *Here Comes Everybody: The Power of Organizing Without Organization* (Penguin, 2009), 49.

38. Email from Mark Marziale to the author, May 10, 2024.

39. See https://allpoetry.com/Robert_Boucher.

40. See "How an Online Class in Poetry Changed a Student's Life," *PennToday*, December 20, 2012, https://penntoday.upenn.edu/2012-12-20/latest-news/how-online-class-poetry-changed-student%E2%80%99s-life.

41. Sonya Arnold, "General Introductions #1," ModPo forum thread, September 2016, Coursera, https://www.coursera.org/learn/modpo/discussions/all/threads/Ite_1ndcEeaAlg6zA9zuZQ /replies/BTs4wXhREeaX3g4cIbI3IQ?page=4.

42. John Dewey, *How We Think* (D. C. Heath, 1910), 34

43. "When you edit this video don't cut out all my pauses," Dan told me. "It would be better to get an artist to draw animations during them."

44. Interview with Dan Bergmann, March 9, 2024.

45. James Surowiecki, *The Wisdom of Crowds: Why the Many Are Smarter than the Few and How Collective Wisdom Shapes Business, Economies, Societies, and Nations* (Random House, 2004), 40–65.

46. Jonathan B. Spira, *Overload! How Too Much Information Is Hazardous to Your Organization* (Wiley, 2011).

47. Katherine Price, "Millwheel Metaphor, Hinted at in the Video," Coursera, 2018, https://www .coursera.org/learn/modpo/discussions/forums/ZBsHxygmEeaZ8Apto8QB_w/threads /_fJeCMNBEeiALwrKWTa7ig.

48. "Maybe ED is arguing AGAINST diversion," ModPo forum thread, September 2017, Coursera, https://www.coursera.org/learn/modpo/discussions/all/threads/bkF4KpczEee7-BLdMTdK8A.

49. The main syllabus "Brain" videos are in two parts: https://www.coursera.org/learn/modpo/lecture /TSPrR/watch-video-on-emily-dickinsons-the-brain-within-its-groove-part-1 and https://www .coursera.org/learn/modpo/lecture/sw0zc/watch-video-on-emily-dickinsons-the-brain-within-its -groove-part-2.

50. Clark Kerr, "The Uses of the University," in Simon Marginson, *The Dream Is Over: The Crisis of Clark Kerr's California Idea of Higher Education* (University of California Press, 2016), 21–27.

8. PLANNING TO STAY

1. Tom Leonard, *Outside the Narrative: Poems 1965–2009* (Word Power Books, 2011), 38.

2. ModPo Edinburgh, "ModPo Edinburgh November 2012," discussion, YouTube video, posted November 2, 2012, 19 min., 24 sec., https://www.youtube.com/watch?v=sfgBeoi5BYs.

3. ModPo Edinburgh, "ModPo Edinburgh November 2012," transcription made by Jesse Schwartz.

4. The rejoinder can be understood in the context of Hugh MacDiarmid's modernist-nationalist long poem in Scots, "A Drunk Man Looks at The Thistle." That modern Scottish epic was a response to the predominance of Anglo-American "international" modernism.

5. Jeremy Knox, *Posthumanism and the Massive Open Online Course* (Routledge, 2016), 157, 152. Emphasis added.

6. Christie Williamson, "Cry Me a Makar: On Translating Lorca into Shaetlan," *Jacket2*, December 5, 2024, https://jacket2.org/article/cry-me-makar.

7. Quoted in Al Filreis, "New Book by Shetland Poet Rewrites Williams's 'Nantucket,'" *Jacket2*, May 7, 2020, https://jacket2.org/commentary/new-book-shetland-poet-rewrites-williamss-nantucket.

8. William Carlos Williams, "Nantucket," in *The Collected Poems of William Carlos Williams*, vol. 1 (1909–1939), ed. A. Walton Litz and Christopher MacGowan (New Directions, 1986), 372.

9. "Nantucket Style Chic Design Inspiration," accessed June 2024, https://www.pinterest.com /pin/767793436456156082/; and "Nantucket Style Chic Design Inspiration & House Exteriors!" accessed June 2024, https://www.hellolovelystudio.com/2018/07/nantucket-style-chic-design -inspiration-summer-vibes.html.

10. Christie Williamson, "St Catherine's," in *Doors tae Naewye* (Luath Press, 2020), 66.

11. ModPoPLUS video on "Nantucket" and "St Catherines" with Christie Williamson, Lee Ann Brown, Laynie Browne, Sophia DuRose, Glasgow, October 2023, https://www.youtube.com/watch?v =aVj2QktXIGo.

12. Daren C. Brabham, *Crowdsourcing* (MIT Press, 2013), xxi.

13. Brabham, *Crowdsourcing*, 68.

14. Mary Hannahan, transcribed interview with Amaris Cuchanski, 2013.

15. Ann Sayas, transcribed interview conducted by Amaris Cuchanski, 2013.

16. Al Filreis and Anna Strong Safford discuss John Keene's "Persons and Places," Cambridge, Massachusetts, October 11, 2019, https://www.youtube.com/watch?v=OjbfZbVZboU (YouTube).

17. "Rochelle," transcribed interview conducted by Amaris Cuchanski, 2013.

18. William R. Morrish and Catherine R. Brown, *Planning to Stay: Learning to See the Physical Features of Your Neighborhood* (Milkweed Editions, 2000), 1.

19. Brabham, *Crowdsourcing*, 1.

20. Wai Chee Dimock, "Education Populism," *PMLA* 132, no. 5 (2017): 1095.

21. Kathleen Fitzpatrick, *Generous Thinking: A Radical Approach to Saving the University* (Johns Hopkins University Press, 2019), 36, 116. See also Jocelyn Wills, "Generous Thinking: A Radical Approach to Saving the University," *Radical Teacher* (blog) 116 (Winter 2020): 102: "Fitzpatrick insists that listening, deep, generous listening is the foundation for generous thinking, but we need to do more. Drawing on her career in literary studies and research into 'connected communities of readers' (including Oprah Winfrey's Book Club)," Fitzpatrick argues that faculty also need to hear, pay attention, and "open ourselves to the same questioning we ask of others." That begins with attempting to understand "why students read what they read, including the connections they seek, so that faculty can lead them from more to less accessible texts over time."

22. Louis Menand, *The Marketplace of Ideas: Reform and Resistance in the American University* (W. W. Norton, 2010), 104.

23. Fitzpatrick, *Generous Thinking*, 36, 39, 35.

24. Lisa Ruddick, "When Nothing Is Cool," *Point Magazine*, December 7, 2015, https://thepointmag .com/criticism/when-nothing-is-cool. "For our profession, alienated in various ways from the American mainstream, needs members who will band together. One way to get members to commit to the group and its ideology is to make them feel ashamed of the varied, private intuitions and desires that might diversify their interests."

25. Anthony Watkins, chapter 20 of *The Minister*, an unpublished memoir.

26. Paulo Freire, *The Pedagogy of the Oppressed* (Continuum, 2000), 59.

27. Menand, *The Marketplace of Ideas*, 104.

28. Interview with Elisa New, January 8, 2025.

29. "Creative Destruction," *The Economist*, June 28, 2014, https://www.economist.com/leaders /2014/06/28/creative-destruction. See also: Stephen Gudeman, "Creative Destruction: Efficiency, Equity or Collapse?" *Anthropology Today* 26, no. 1 (2010): 3–7.

30. John Potter and Julian McDougall, *Digital Media, Culture, and Education: Theorizing Third Space Literacies* (Palgrave Macmillan, 2017), 11.

31. Clay Shirky, *Here Comes Everybody: The Power of Organizing without Organizations* (Penguin, 2008), 70.

32. Shirky, *Here Comes Everybody*, 99.

33. Carl Bereiter and Marlene Scardamalia, *Surpassing Ourselves: An Inquiry into the Nature and Implications of Expertise* (Open Court, 1993), 98–99.

34. Interview with Elisa New, January 8, 2025.

35. Brabham, *Crowdsourcing*, xxi.

36. John Fadely, emails to the author, May 29 and 30, 2024.

37. Shirky, *Here Comes Everybody*, 42, 47.

38. Mark S. Granovetter, "The Strength of Weak Ties," *American Journal of Sociology* 78, no. 6 (May 1973): 1360–1380.

39. Lior Zoref, *Mindsharing: The Art of Crowdsourcing Everything* (Penguin Random House, 2015), 8.

40. James Surowiecki, *The Wisdom of Crowds: Why the Many Are Smarter Than the Few and How Collective Wisdom Shapes Business, Economics, Societies and Nations* (Doubleday, 2004), xix, 10, 28–32.

41. Among Scott Page's presentations of his studies: *The Difference: How the Power of Diversity Creates Better Groups, Firms, Schools, and Societies* (Princeton University Press, 2008) and *The Diversity Bonus: How Great Teams Pay Off in the Knowledge Economy* (Princeton University Press, 2017). Page also hosted a MOOC through Coursera on the topic.

42. Surowiecki, *The Wisdom of Crowds*, 28, 29, 31.

43. Danielle Allen, "Toward a Connected Society," in *Our Compelling Interests: The Value of Diversity for Democracy and a Prosperous Society*, ed. Earl Lewis and Nancy Cantor (Princeton University Press, 2016), 87.

44. Allen, "Toward a Connected Society," 100–101.

45. At the Ash Center for Democratic Governance (Harvard University), Danielle Allen directs the Allen Lab for Democracy Renovation. One of the lab's main research projects in the early 2020s has been "power-sharing liberalism." The concept is outlined in Allen's book *Justice by Means of Democracy* (2024).

46. "We learn that often, diversity merits equal standing with ability and that sometimes, although not every time, it even trumps ability" (Page, *The Difference*, 5).

47. Page, *The Difference*, xvii.

48. Page, *The Diversity Bonus*, 2.

49. At the University of Pennsylvania, out of a pool of 65,235 applicants, 3,508 students were admitted in 2024 into the class of 2028.

50. Cathy Davidson, *The New Education: How to Revolutionize the University to Prepare Students for a World in Flux*, (Basic Books, 2017), 95.

51. Davidson, *The New Education*, 75–100.

52. Al Filreis, Anna Strong Safford, and Davy Knittle, "Collaborative Close Reading and Global Conversation in the Co-Constitutive Online Classroom," in *Teaching Literature in the Online Classroom*, ed. John Miller and Julia Wilhelm (Modern Language Association, 2022), 54.

53. Filreis et al., "Collaborative Close Reading," 55.

54. Valerie Irvine, "Personalizing Modality Through Multi-Access Learning: What You Need to Know," Zoom seminar sponsored by TESL Saskatchewan, January 27, 2022.

55. Page, *The Difference*, 13.

56. Laura C. [name abbreviated], transcribed interview conducted by Amaris Cuchanski, 2013.

57. Laura Lee, transcribed interview conducted by Amaris Cuchanski, 2013.

58. Therese Pope, transcribed interview conducted by Amaris Cuchanski, 2013.

59. Laura C., transcribed interview conducted by Amaris Cuchanski, 2013.

60. Interview with Dan Bergman, March 9, 2024.

61. Stephen M. Kosslyn and Ben Nelson, eds., *Building the Intentional University: Minerva and the Future of Higher Education* (MIT Press, 2017), 11.

62. Page, *The Diversity Bonus*, 98.

63. Page, *The Difference*, xv.

64. Simon Hill and Alpheus Bingham, *One Smart Crowd: How Crowdsourcing is Changing the World One Idea at a Time* (Hill Bingham, 2021), 87, 93.

65. Allan Keaton, email interview with the author, June 21, 2018.

66. Aiden Hunt, emails to the author, March 28 and 31, 2024.

67. Jennifer Bartlett, *Sustaining Air: The Life of Larry Eigner* (University of Alabama Press, 2023), 58.

68. Interview with Dan Bergmann, March 9, 2024. All subsequent quotations from Bergmann in this section are from this interview.

69. Erica Hunt, "Reader we were meant to meet," *Jump the Clock: New & Selected Poems* (Nightboat Books, 2020), 109.

70. Interview with Christopher Forman, April 24, 2024.

71. Juliana Spahr, *Everybody's Autonomy: Connective Reading and Collective Identity* (University of Alabama Press, 2001), 10.

72. Stephen Downes, *Connectivism and Connective Knowledge* (Stephen Downes, 2012), 97.

73. Downes, *Connectivism and Connective Knowledge*, 95–109.

74. Spahr, Everybody's Autonomy, 5, 6, 7, 9, 10, 11.

75. David Rothenberg, *Nightingales in Berlin: Searching for the Perfect Sound* (University of Chicago Press, 2019), 5, 31.

76. Steven Sloman and Phillip Fernbach, *The Knowledge Illusion: Why We Never Think Alone* (Riverhead Books, 2017), 15.

INDEX

Page numbers in *italics* refer to illustrations.

GPSR Authorized Representative: Easy Access System Europe, Mustamäe tee
50, 10621 Tallinn, Estonia, gpsr.requests@easproject.com